OPTIMUM

Collection dirigée par Fabien Fichaux

SMART

Strategic, Measurable, Ambitious, Relevant, Timely

Réussir en anglais en classes préparatoires aux grandes écoles : une fiche/une semaine

2e édition

Guillaume Delaby

Professeur agrégé d'anglais au lycée Buffon (Paris)

ellipses

ISBN 9782340-039674

32, rue Bargue 75740 Paris cedex 15

www.editions-ellipses.fr

Pour Laure

Sommaire

Avant-propos

Ce manuel d'anglais est le résultat de neuf ans d'expériences et d'expérimentations en CPGE (classes préparatoires aux grandes écoles). Plus qu'un simple manuel de vocabulaire, il aborde en neuf thématiques et trente-six chapitres un grand nombre de sujets d'actualité dans un monde en mouvement, dans lequel l'anglais est devenu une langue fondamentale de communication à l'échelle globale.

Destiné aux apprenants français dans les cycles post-baccalauréat (BTS, IUT), aux étudiants de CPGE sections économiques et scientifiques, mais aussi à des étudiants de classe de Terminale souhaitant déjà se préparer aux études supérieures (cycles Sciences Politiques) et aux étudiants de Licence, il a pour principal objectif d'encourager tous les élèves, quel que soit leur niveau de départ. C'est la raison pour laquelle il a été élaboré dans un souci constant de progression, allant des notions simples aux concepts plus complexes, des connaissances générales à des notions plus élaborées, non seulement au sein d'un chapitre, mais aussi dans l'articulation générale de l'ouvrage.

L'acronyme SMART, autrefois destiné aux étudiants en marketing, a pu facilement être adapté pour l'enseignement (car l'apprentissage en cycle court post-baccalauréat doit nécessairement être **Stratégique**, **Mesurable**, **Ambitieux**, en **Rapport** et dans les **Temps**).

SMART: Strategic, Measurable, Ambitious, Relevant and Timely.

Strategic: goals have to be precisely defined, since ambiguity would result in unconvincing results. Learning the appropriate vocabulary in two years, without wandering about. You have to be organised so that learning will be optimised.
Measurable: ten thousand words in one or two years depending on your strategy, that is to say 200 words in a week, or 1000 words each of the ten working periods of 6-7 weeks over two years, that is a measurable and attainable goal for a student. Given that you might already know some of them, you might even be in for a good surprise.
Ambitious: it would be detrimental to set goals that are not attainable, therefore your goals have to be defined and never discouraging. The best is the enemy of good, in other words less is often more, particularly in the conditions of a competitive exam.
Relevant: make your goal a reality, focus on what is really important to you: embrace your future success, and make your preparation coherent with the current circumstances.
Timely: the timeframe of your work is essential. To meet with the requirements, consider adapting your timetable on a regular basis. Always meet the deadlines, as you cannot afford to lag behind. Make your preparation worth it.

C'est la raison pour laquelle ce manuel est divisé en 9 thématiques de 4 chapitres. Ces 36 projets pédagogiques sont parfaitement adaptés à une ou deux années de préparation. En effet, une année scolaire contient 36 semaines au minimum, un cycle court post-bac de deux ans comme la prépa contient 9 périodes (5 en première année, puis 4 en deuxième). L'étudiant a donc le choix : soit une préparation plus intensive en un an, soit une préparation plus approfondie en deux ans, jusqu'aux examens écrits. L'objectif final est de réussir non seulement les écrits, mais aussi de se préparer aux oraux de type synthèse / commentaire et/ou entretien.

L'articulation générale du manuel va du simple au complexe : de la découverte à l'approfondissement, du concret vers l'abstrait, de l'évident au surprenant, de l'explicite vers l'implicite, et des causes vers les conséquences. C'est le cas pour l'organisation d'ensemble sur les neuf grandes thématiques (autour des trois grands axes *Mankind, Our world, Our time*) mais aussi au sein de chaque thématique, et de chaque chapitre.

Ainsi, chacun des 36 chapitres proposés dans SMART comporte :

- une image d'illustration Word cloud, résumant l'objectif lexical du chapitre, pour rassurer et motiver : vous constatez dès le début que vous disposez déjà de quelques acquis. Cette première approche est **stratégique** ;
- une liste de 200 à 250 mots-clés et expressions classées en quatre à huit sections (dont une section *bonus*, pour le plaisir des expressions idiomatiques) : un objectif **mesurable** ;
- des exercices de traduction corrigés (des phrases simples de l'anglais vers le français, puis des extraits d'articles de presse de l'anglais vers le français, et enfin des extraits de presse ou de littérature du français vers l'anglais). Cette progression permet d'encourager l'ensemble des apprenants sur cet exercice difficile mais **ambitieux** qu'est la traduction pour une expression plus authentique en anglais : observation, acquisition puis réutilisation de structures lexicales et syntaxiques ;
- quatre extraits de la presse anglophone (plus de cent sources au total), adaptés afin de rebrasser le vocabulaire et de présenter des structures idiomatiques en **rapport** avec le sujet. Ces lectures peuvent être approfondies en consultant les articles correspondants, disponibles sur Internet ;
- trois à cinq points culturels (*food for thought*) rédigés en anglais, de 100 à 150 mots chacun, pour élargir votre champ de connaissances culturelles tout en suggérant des pistes de commentaires, de travaux d'expression, etc. Concluant ainsi le chapitre, vous savez comment vous organiser pour parachever votre formation dans les **temps**.

À la fin du manuel, une série de fiches complémentaires aborde la préparation aux concours de façon plus linguistique, sur ce que l'on peut appeler les bases : sélection de verbes irréguliers, fautes les plus fréquentes, mots et structures de liaison, faux-amis et barbarismes, différences entre l'anglais britannique et américain et quelques autres remarques concernant la qualité de l'expression. Cette série de fiches doit être travaillée régulièrement pour être plus facilement assimilée.

Pour les professeurs comme pour les étudiants, ce manuel est une aide stratégique pour un travail en autonomie. Le professeur peut ainsi organiser son dispositif de formation sur un ou deux ans, et faire travailler les élèves en amont, avec une visibilité sur l'ensemble du programme de façon rassurante. Ainsi, l'apprentissage se fait sereinement, et donc efficacement. C'est l'objectif principal de cet ouvrage : enseigner ou apprendre l'anglais de façon **Stratégique**, **Mesurable**, **Ambitieuse**, en **Rapport** et dans les **Temps**.

Je tiens à remercier chaleureusement Laure BOURDET, Denis LAGAE-DEVOLDERE, Johanna NEPOTE-CIT et Éléonore OBIS pour leur relecture rigoureuse de cet ouvrage, leurs conseils avisés et leurs encouragements. Un grand merci à mes élèves présents et passés et à Jules S. en particulier, pour leurs remarques et questions qui m'ont permis de mener à bien ce projet.

Liste des abréviations et conventions de notation

- sth / sb something / somebody
- qqch / qqn quelque chose / quelqu'un
- / séparation entre deux mots au sens ou à la catégorie syntaxique différents
- , séparation entre deux mots au sens identique
- GB British English
- US American English
- Terminaisons des verbes et composés en –ise (GB) et –ize (US)

Topic one

Mankind

Section 1
The human being

Chapter A

Mankind and family

Vocabulary list

BODY PARTS	**LES PARTIES DU CORPS**
the head	la tête
the face	le visage
the skin	la peau
a hair / hair	un poil / les cheveux (chevelure)
the forehead	le front
the ear	l'oreille
the eye	l'œil
eyebrow / eyelash / eyelid	sourcil / cil / paupière
the nose	le nez
the mouth	la bouche
the lips	les lèvres
the cheek / cheekbone	la joue / pommettes
the jaw	la mâchoire
the chin	le menton
the nape (of the neck)	la nuque
the neck	le cou
the throat	la gorge
the shoulder	l'épaule
the trunk	le tronc
the chest	la poitrine, la cage thoracique
the back	le dos
a rib	une côte
the elbow	le coude
the belly / the tummy	le ventre
the navel / the belly button	le nombril
the buttocks	les fesses
the breasts / a breast	les seins / un sein
the arm	le bras
the forearm	l'avant-bras
the armpit	l'aisselle
the hand	la main
to be left-handed	être gaucher
the wrist	le poignet
the fist	le poing
a finger	un doigt
the knuckles	les articulations
a nail	un ongle
the palm	la paume
the hip	la hanche
the leg	la jambe
the thigh	la cuisse
the knee	le genou
the calf	le mollet

the ankle	la cheville
the foot / the feet	le pied / les pieds
the heel	le talon
the toe	l'orteil

INTERNAL ORGANS	**LES ORGANES INTERNES**
the skeleton	le squelette
a bone	un os
the skull	le crâne
the backbone, the spine	la colonne vertébrale
a joint	une articulation
a muscle	un muscle
a nerve	un nerf
flesh	la chair
a vein, an artery	une veine, une artère
blood	le sang
to bleed	saigner
a cell	une cellule
the brain	le cerveau
the tongue	la langue
a tooth / teeth	une dent / les dents
the heart	le cœur
a lung	un poumon
the stomach	l'estomac
the guts / the bowels	les tripes / les intestins
the liver / kidney / bladder	le foie / le rein / la vessie
the genitals	les organes génitaux

PHYSICAL APPEARANCE	**L'APPARENCE PHYSIQUE**
the features	les traits
handsome	beau (homme)
ugly	laid(e), repoussant(e)
pretty	beau / belle, joli(e)
beautiful	beau, belle
attractive	séduisant(e)
good-looking	beau, belle, élégant(e)
plain	sans charme, quelconque
the figure	la silhouette
to be brawny	être musclé
to have a strong constitution	être solide
fleshy / plumpy	charnu
skinny	malingre, maigre
thin	mince
to be naked	être (tout) nu
the complexion	le teint
dark / tanned / light skin	la peau noire / le teint mat / pâle

a wrinkle	une ride
freckles	tâches de rousseur
short / long / medium-length hair	les cheveux courts / longs / mi-longs
a lock / a curl	une mèche / une boucle
wavy / curly / frizzy	ondulé / bouclé / crépu
fair / dark / auburn / red	blond / brun / châtain / roux
to be bald	être chauve
a wig	une perruque
a moustache / a beard	une moustache / une barbe
beardless	imberbe
hairy	poilu

AGE, AGEING (AGING)	**L'ÂGE, LE VIEILLISSEMENT**
an infant	un nourrisson, nouveau-né
a toddler	un tout-petit, un bambin
boyhood, girlhood	l'enfance
childhood	l'enfance
a child / children (pl.)	un enfant / les enfants
to look after children	(s'occuper de) garder des enfants
childcare	la garde des enfants
adolescent, teenager	un adolescent (de 13 à 19 ans)
puberty	la puberté
a young / youngster / a youth	un jeune
to be in one's teens	être un ado / à l'adolescence
to come of age	atteindre la majorité
an adult, a grown-up	un adulte
middle-aged, in one's prime	d'âge moyen, dans la force de l'âge
early / mid / late thirties	début / milieu / fin de la trentaine
an underage, a minor	mineur
to look (older than) one's age	paraître son âge (plus vieux que son âge)
to act one's age	agir avec la maturité propre à son âge
aged, old	vieux
to grow old	vieillir
old age	la vieillesse
overage	trop âgé
the elderly / a third-ager	les vieux, les personnes âgées / une personne âgée
an old-age pensioner	un retraité
to retire	prendre sa retraite
life expectancy	l'espérance de vie

FAMILY	**LA FAMILLE**
the nuclear family / the extended family	le noyau familial / la famille étendue
a relative	un parent, un proche
a home, a household	un foyer
to be born	naître

the husband, the wife	le mari, la femme
a partner / a spouse	un compagnon / un conjoint
marriage / wedding	le mariage (institution / événement)
the parents / father / mother	les parents / le père / la mère
the brother / the sister / the siblings	le frère / la sœur / les frères et sœurs
brotherhood, sisterhood	la fraternité
a twin brother	un frère jumeau
the son / the daughter	le fils / la fille
an only child	un enfant unique
a brat	un marmot (colloq.), un rejeton
an urchin	un garnement
a kid / a lad	un gamin / gosse, un gars, un jeune garçon
the grandfather	le grand-père
the great-grandmother	l'arrière-grand-mère
the stepfather	le beau-père (suite à remariage)
the stepsister	la demi-sœur (suite à remariage)
the mother-in-law	la belle-mère
the brother-in-law	le beau-frère
the godfather / the godchild	le parrain / le filleul
a guardian	un tuteur
a ward	un pupille
the uncle / the aunt	l'oncle / la tante
the nephew / the niece	le neveu / la nièce
a spinster, an old maid	une vieille fille
a bachelor	un célibataire
the foster parents	les parents adoptifs
an adopted child	un enfant adoptif
an orphan / orphanage	un orphelin / l'orphelinat
a widower / a widow	un veuf / une veuve
a name / a surname / a nickname	un nom / nom de famille / un surnom
a maiden name	un nom de jeune fille
to look like somebody	ressembler à qqn
the offspring	la progéniture
a descendant	un descendant
a distant cousin	un cousin éloigné
a single mother	une mère célibataire / parent isolé
to separate, to split up	se séparer
a family tree	un arbre généalogique
to support the family	entretenir la famille / subvenir aux besoins...
to gain custody of the children	obtenir la garde des enfants
to be part of the family	faire partie de la famille
a family man	un bon père de famille
family ties	les liens familiaux

BONUS	**BONUS**
*to make s.o.'s **flesh** creep*	donner la chair de poule
*to make s.o's **hair** stand on end*	faire dresser les cheveux sur la tête
*to gasp for **breath***	haleter
*to shrug one's **shoulders***	hausser les épaules
*cold-**blood**ed*	sans pitié, de sang froid
barefoot	nu-pieds, pieds nus
*to be frozen to the **bone***	être glacé jusqu'aux os
*to be soaked to the **skin***	être trempé jusqu'aux os
*to be **head** over **heels***	avoir un coup de foudre
*to be all **thumbs***	être très maladroit
*to fight **tooth** and **nail***	se battre avec acharnement
*by word of **mouth***	le bouche à oreille
*to keep an **eye** on s.b*	garder l'œil sur qq'un / surveiller
*to pull a **face***	faire la grimace
*to rub **shoulders** with s.b*	fréquenter qqn
*to raise / to lower one's **hand***	lever / baisser la main
*to put one's **feet** down*	faire preuve de fermeté
*to see **eye** to **eye** with s.o.*	être totalement d'accord
*to set **foot** somewhere*	mettre les pieds quelque part
*as **old** as the hills*	aussi vieux que le monde
*the awkward **age***	l'âge ingrat
*for **ages***	depuis des lustres
the generation gap	le fossé des générations
*a **child** could do it*	c'est un jeu d'enfant
Boys** will be **boys	Il faut bien que jeunesse se passe
*mid-**life** crisis*	la crise de la quarantaine
*to be getting on in **years***	prendre de l'âge
*to be past one's **prime***	ne plus être tout jeune
*out of **wedlock***	en dehors du mariage
*to bear the **name** of...*	porter le nom de
to be a chip of the old block	être bien le fils de son père
*it runs in the **family***	c'est (un trait) de famille
*Spare the rod and spoil the **child***	Qui aime bien châtie bien
*the **child** is **father** to the man*	L'enfant est le père de l'homme.

Translation: English-to-French exercise

- Your brain is your most powerful organ, yet weighs only about three pounds.
- In second grade the principal was a bulky man, about two hundred and thirty pounds and six feet two inches tall.
- Parents and the family play a big part in providing children with knowledge and practical assistance with regards to human rights issues: more than half of pupils receive information about human rights from their parents, and they also turn to their parents when their rights are infringed.
- She had her mother's light complexion and blue eyes but her Italian father's black hair.
- The age of 65 is typically used as the criterion for defining the "elderly" population, because this is the age at which persons become eligible for certain age-related pension and income security benefits, and because of its association with mandatory retirement.

Adapted press excerpts (about 400 words)

Excerpt 1 – The evolution of family life (adapted from *The Telegraph*)

Your experience of family changes as you travel through life, from relying on your **parents** to looking after your own **children.** The word "**family**" is defined as "a group of people consisting of two **parents** and their **children**, or who are related by **blood** or **marriage**". Of course, there are many variants of that **nuclear** definition. Family is such an emotive word that a dictionary definition will always **struggle to pin it down**. It is a **core** element of personal economy, and it gives us **a sense of place in the world**. The **bonds** between **life partners** can feel more **tightly wound** than those between **siblings** or even **parent and child.**

Excerpt 2 – A Statisical Portrait of the "Typical" American (adapted from *The New York Times*)

The **typical** American is a white woman who is 32.7 years old. In 2010, whites were 80.3% of the population, blacks were 12.1%, others were 7.7%. Hispanic people, who can be of any race, were 9.0%. Females were 51.2%. **Age figure** was a median. The **average** American male is 5 feet 9.1 inches **tall** and **weighs** 172 pounds. The average female is 5 feet 3.7 inches tall and weighs 144 pounds. They think this current **weight is just about right.** The **typical** American is a Democrat, and considers herself a moderate. She considers herself an environmentalist.

Excerpt 3 – The look of a leader (adapted from *The Economist*)

In gorilla society, power belongs to silverback **males**. These splendid **creatures** have numerous status markers besides their back **hair**: they are **bigger**, strike space-filling **postures**, produce deeper **sounds**, thump their **chests** lustily and exude an air of **physical fitness**.

Things are not that different in the **corporate world**. The typical chief executive is more than **six feet tall**, has a **deep voice**, a good **posture**, **a touch of grey in his thick, lustrous hair** and, for his age, a **fit body**. Bosses **stand tall** when talking to subordinates. Their conversation is laden with **prestige pauses and declarative statements**.

Excerpt 4 – Thank viruses for your skin and bone (adapted from *The New Scientist*)

Next time you have a cold, rather than cursing, maybe you should thank the virus for making your **skin**. **Genes** borrowed from viruses seem to give cells the ability to grow into **tissues** and **organs**, and even reproduce sexually. Without these genes, animals could not have evolved beyond simple **blobs of cells**. Our cells often need to fuse with other cells, making big cells with multiple nuclei. This mixing is essential for the production of **most organs** – such as **muscles**, **skin** and **bone** – and even for **reproduction**, when **eggs and sperm fuse**. For instance, internal tubes like **blood vessels** are made of fused cells.

Food for Thought and Quotations (about 500 words)

The spread of Mankind

The spread of humans represents an evolutionary success due to a larger brain, which brings about high levels of abstract reasoning, language, problem solving mainly through social learning. Humans use tools to a much higher degree than any other animal (fire, cooking, construction...) and are the only species to clothe themselves and create and use numerous other technologies and arts. Anatomically modern humans first appeared in Africa about 200,000 years ago.

Darwin, Evolution of Species

The theory of linking humans with apes by descent was stated in 1859 with the publication of British researcher Charles Darwin's *On the Origin of Species*, in which he promoted the idea of the evolution of new species from earlier species. Darwin's book did not address the question of human evolution. In 1863, the debates about the nature of human evolution came to a climax: human evolution was explained by illustrating many of the similarities and differences between humans and apes. Later, the origin of the mental capacities and the moral sensibilities of humans could be explained by the theory of evolution and sexual selection to humans.

Biological adaptation

There is biological variation in the human species (blood type, skull features, eye colour, hair colour and type, height and build, and skin colour) varying across the globe. Human body types vary substantially. The typical height of an adult human is between 1.4 metre (4 ft 7 in) and 1.9 metre (6 ft 3 in), although this varies significantly depending, among other things, on sex and ethnic origin. Body size is partly determined by genes and is also significantly influenced by environmental factors such as geography, diet, exercise, sleep patterns, occupation and so on.

Kinship, marriage

Marriage is the legally or formally recognized union of two people as partners in a personal relationship (historically and in some jurisdictions specifically a union between a man and a woman). All human societies organize social relationships on relations between parents and children, and relations through marriage. Such relationships are generally called kinship relations. Marriage (matrimony or wedlock), is a union between spouses that defines rights and duties between them, with their children, and their in-laws, as well as society in general. In very general terms, marriage is considered a cultural universal. The **wedding** is the actual ceremony, **marriage** refers to the institution.

Family

A family is a group of affiliated people: a social group united by blood or the descendants of a common ancestor. Members of the **immediate** family include spouses, parents, brothers, sisters, sons and / or daughters. Members of the **extended** family include grandparents, aunts, uncles, cousins, nephews, nieces, and / or siblings-in-law. Sometimes these are also considered members of the immediate family, depending on an individual's specific relationship. In most societies, the family is the principal institution for the socialization of children. Sexual relations among the members are regulated by rules concerning incest such as the incest taboo. The word "family" can also be used to refer to inclusive categories such as a community.

Old age

Old age is the later part of life, and defines the state of being old. For various reasons (morphological and physiological), women live on average about four years older than men. There are significant geographical variations in human life expectancy, mostly correlated with economic development. The developed world is generally ageing, with the median age around 40 years. In the developing world the median age is between 15 and 20 years. In 2016, the number of centenarians (humans 100 years of age or older) in the world was estimated by the United Nations at 300,000. At least one person, Jeanne Calment, a French woman, is known to have reached 122 years of age. However, recent studies tend to show that 117 years is the physiological limit to human life expectancy.

"One general law, leading to the advancement of all organic beings, namely, multiply, vary, let the strongest live and the weakest die." Charles Darwin, *The Origin of Species*

Chapter B

Health and Medicine

Vocabulary list

PREVENTION	**LA PRÉVENTION**
health	la santé
healthy (unhealthy)	en bonne (mauvaise) santé
a GP (general practitioner)	un médecin généraliste
fit / fitness	en forme / la forme physique
unfit	souffrant
well / unwell	bien portant / souffrant
to exercise	faire de l'exercice
healthy lifestyle	une bonne hygiène de vie
a condition	un état de santé
the figure	la silhouette
nutrition	la nutrition
a nutritionist	un nutritionniste
a diet	un régime
a dietician	un diététicien
to cut down on fat / on sugar	réduire la consommation de graisses / de sucres
overweight / underweight	en surpoids / trop maigre
obese / obesity	obèse / l'obésité
anorexic / anorexia	anorexique / l'anorexie
to slim down (to lose weight)	maigrir
to put on weight	grossir
wellness	le bien-être
herbal medicine	la phytothérapie
effective	efficace
effectiveness / efficiency	l'efficacité
traceability	traçabilité
public health	la santé publique
health care	la santé publique / les soins médicaux
a check-up	un bilan de santé
a vaccine	un vaccin
mandatory screening	le dépistage obligatoire
booster	un rappel
a prevention programme	un programme de prévention
to be on the pill	prendre la pilule
a condom, a sheath	un préservatif

INJURIES	**LES BLESSURES**
an accident	un accident
an injury, a wound	une blessure, une blessure provoquée
a cut	une coupure
a scratch	une éraflure, une égratignure
a scar	une cicatrice
a fracture, a sprain	une fracture, une foulure
to twist one's ankle	se tordre la cheville

a bruise	une ecchymose, un bleu
a first-degree burn	une brûlure au premier degré
a trauma	un traumatisme
to be wounded	se blesser grièvement
to injure oneself	se blesser accidentellement
a bandage, a cast	un bandage, un plâtre
crutches	des béquilles
a walking stick (Br.) / cane (US)	une canne
a wheelchair	un fauteuil roulant
to limp	boiter

DISEASES	**LES MALADIES**
an ailment	un mal
a disease	une maladie
to detect	dépister, détecter
a diagnosis / to diagnose	un diagnostic / diagnostiquer
to catch a disease	attraper une maladie
to contract a virus	contracter un virus
contagious / infectious	contagieux / infectieux
to pass on a virus	transmettre un virus
bacteria / germ	bactéries / microbes
to harbor (harbour) / carry a virus	être porteur d'un virus
to suffer from...	souffrir d'une maladie
to go down with...	attraper...
to feel sick	avoir mal au cœur
ache, pain	la douleur
to itch	démanger
discomfort	le malaise, la gêne
to have a temperature	avoir de la fièvre
to sweat	transpirer
to feel dizzy	avoir des vertiges
to go into a coma	tomber dans le coma
to cough	tousser
a sore throat	un mal de gorge
a cold	un rhume
a toothache / a stomachache	un mal (une rage) de dents / de ventre
an allergy	une allergie
to sneeze	éternuer
to blow one's nose	se moucher
asthma	l'asthme
to be out of breath	être essoufflé
a heart attack	une crise cardiaque
a coronary disease	une maladie cardiaque
to die of / from...	mourir d'une maladie
AIDS / HIV positive	sida / séropositif

a STD (sexually-transmitted disease)	une MST (maladie sexuellement transmissible)
the flu (influenza)	la grippe
the plague / cholera	la peste / le choléra
malaria	paludisme
smallpox	variole
lung / breast / skin cancer	cancer du poumon / du sein / de la peau
a tumour	une tumeur
the liver cirrhosis	la cirrhose du foie
hepatitis	l'hépatite
TB (tuberculosis)	la tuberculose
to infect / to contaminate	infecter / contaminer
epidemic / pandemic	une épidémie / une pandémie
to break out	se déclarer
to spread	se propager
blood poisoning	la septicémie
terminal, lethal, fatal	mortel(le)
terminally ill	en phase terminale

HANDICAPS	**LE HANDICAP**
mental / physical handicap	handicaps mentaux / physiques
mentally / physically impaired	handicapé mental / physique
handicapped / a handicapped	infirme / personne à mobilité réduite / (un) handicapé moteur
disabled	handicapé physique
cripple / lame	estropié / boiteux
a phobia	une phobie
paranoia / paranoid	paranoïa / un paranoïaque
anxiety	anxiété, angoisse
neurosis / neurotic	névrose / névrosé
psychosis / psychotic	psychose / psychotique
schizophrenia	la schizophrénie
bipolar disorder	trouble bipolaire
PTSD (post-traumatic stress disorder)	le SSPT (syndrome de stress post-traumatique)
insanity / insane	démence / aliéné
senility / senile	sénilité / sénile
a sex maniac	un obsédé sexuel
a nervous breakdown	une dépression nerveuse
depressed / depressive	déprimé / dépressif
autism / autistic	autisme / autiste
a genetic disease	une maladie génétique
mentally retarded / retardation	attardé / retard mental
innate	inné
hereditary	héréditaire
to run in the family	être héréditaire

to inherit a defect	hériter d'une déficience
an abnormality	une anomalie
a birth defect	une malformation congénitale
Down's syndrome / mongolism	la trisomie 21 / le mongolisme
a malformation	une malformation
a disability	un handicap
blindness / blind	la cécité / un non-voyant
deafness / deaf	la surdité / sourd, malentendant
short- / long-sightedness, far-sightedness	myopie / presbytie
colour-blind	daltonien
a speech impairment	un défaut d'élocution
mutism, dumbness / mute	le mutisme / muet
to stutter	bégayer

REMEDIES AND CURES	**REMÈDES ET GUÉRISON**
medicine / prescription drugs	médicaments
antibiotics	des antibiotiques
a shot / an injection	une piqûre
a tablet	un comprimé
a cure	un remède, une guérison
(a) treatment	un traitement
to treat	traiter
side-effects	les effets secondaires
to undergo	subir
chemotherapy	chimiothérapie
to take effect	faire de l'effet
to boost the immune system	renforcer le système immunitaire
over-the-counter	en vente libre
delivered on prescription	uniquement sur ordonnance
to prescribe	prescrire
to be on prescription drugs	prendre des médicaments
detoxication / rehab	la désintoxication / une cure de désintoxication
overmedication	la surmédication
acupuncture	l'acupuncture
homeopathy	l'homéopathie
sophrology	la sophrologie
to meditate / meditation	méditer / la méditation
a painkiller	un antalgique / analgésique
to quarantine	mettre en quarantaine
to recover	se rétablir, guérir
a recovery	rétablissement, guérison
to relapse	rechuter
to soothe the pain	soulager la douleur
surgery / a surgeon	la chirurgie / un chirurgien
to operate on a patient	opérer un patient

to be operated on	subir une intervention chirurgicale
to anaesthetise (-ize US)	anesthésier
life-saving	vital
a tranquillizer	un tranquillisant
organ transplant	greffe d'organe
an organ donation	un don d'organe
a donor	un donneur
a recipient	un receveur
a faith healer	un guérisseur
the placebo effect	l'effet placebo

BONUS	**BONUS**
*as **fit** as a fiddle*	qui respire la santé
*a **health** scare*	un péril sanitaire
Prevention** is better than **cure	Mieux vaut prévenir que guérir
*a **blind** spot*	un point faible
*a **pain** in the neck*	un casse-pieds
*as **deaf** as a doorpost*	sourd comme un pot
*to **bleed** somebody dry*	saigner à blanc
*a bitter **pill** to swallow*	c'est dur à avaler
No pain no gain	Qui ne risque rien n'a rien
*to **nurse** hopes / grievances*	nourrir des espoirs / une rancune
in bad shape	en mauvaise forme
*back on one's **feet***	être remis / en bonne santé
*a clean bill of **health***	un excellent bilan de santé
"dogs are barking"	avoir mal aux pieds
to be on the mend	se remettre
*to look the picture of **health***	être en parfaite santé
*to have pins and **needles** in the leg*	avoir des fourmis (dans les jambes...)
to pull through	se remettre d'une maladie
to be run down	être en très mauvaise santé
to be under the weather	ne pas se sentir bien
*to be full of vim and **vigour***	être plein de vigueur et d'énergie
black and blue	être couvert de bleus
***pale** around the gills*	être pâle comme un linge
*to rub salt in sb's **wound***	remuer le couteau dans la plaie
*to be on **sick** leave*	être en arrêt maladie
to be up and about	être en parfaite santé
to be out of sorts	ne pas être dans son assiette
*to be out **cold***	tomber dans les pommes

Translation: English-to-French exercise

- Drinking alcohol, even in small amounts, before a surgical operation, may delay recovery and weaken the immune system.
- A handicap may exist even without proof of physical limitations or the presence of an ailment.
- Always tell your doctor, nurse or pharmacist if you are taking any other medicines, either prescription or over-the-counter, herbal medicines or natural health products.
- Medical treatment can often significantly increase life expectancy without, however, ensuring a cure.
- In some cases, these services primarily help a person adjust to living with a disability on a day-to-day basis.

Adapted press excerpts (about 400 words)

Excerpt 1 – The problem of pain (adapted from *The Economist*)

Opioids kill by slowing the **respiratory system**. A person who has taken too many – or who combines a standard dose with **depressants** such as alcohol, anti-**anxiety pills** or **sleeping aids** – may lose **consciousness** and stop breathing. The difference between an **effective** and a **lethal** dose is small and unpredictable. Data are patchy, but state statistics suggest that many victims of opioid **poisoning** have legitimate **prescriptions** for **chronic pain**. Britain has largely avoided creating opioid addicts. Its publicly funded national **health-care system** means **doctors** have no **incentive** to **over-prescribe**.

Excerpt 2 – Researchers develop genetic test that can predict your risk of Alzheimer's disease (adapted from *The Los Angeles Times*)

New **research** into the **genetic** underpinnings of **Alzheimer's disease** offers fresh evidence that the devastating **brain disorder** may gain a foothold years before **dementia** sets in, and takes a key step toward earlier **detection** of the **disease**. In a study that scoured the **genes** of **healthy** people for the presence of variants linked to Alzheimer's disease, researchers have found that older study participants without dementia underwent the same broad **genetic** query, the test was able to distinguish those with poorer **memory** and **cognitive** function from those whose **mental faculties** were still strong.

Excerpt 3 – Children and coronavirus: what we know and don't know (adapted from *The Guardian*)

As the number of Covid-19 cases rises worldwide, parents trying to protect their children from the disease can take solace in one thing: the disease has generally been milder in children.

However, there are many unknowns about coronavirus, and research is ongoing. It is generally believed to cause milder symptoms in children, but the specific impacts by age are becoming clearer as the outbreak goes on.

Much of what we know today is based on reports out of China, where the outbreak began. There 2.4% of all identified cases were in children under 19 years old. An even smaller number within this group of children had severe symptoms, 2.5%, or what the World Health Organization (WHO) described as "a very small proportion". But more research is being done and a clearer picture is still emerging. Authorities recommended parents homeschool their children in an effort to expand social distancing. Here is more information on how to practice social distancing. Of course, social distancing has caused its own kind of upheaval. Efforts are being made to ease the burden on parents with bored children at home.

Excerpt 4 – Patient's self-rating of health (adapted from PsychCentral.com)

A couple of years ago there was a boom of work in **psychology** and **medicine** about what we call **patient-reported** outcomes, the idea that what **patients** actually feel like and say they feel like seems to be more **prognostic** of **morbidity** and **mortality** than all the cholesterol ratings and **blood tests** we get from **doctors**' offices. The researchers set out to find evidence that would connect the dots between **feelings** and **fate**. They found it in existing data that established links between **self-rated health** and rising levels of **virus** activity, a marker of poor cellular **immunity** that promotes high levels of **inflammation.**

Food for Thought and Quotations (about 500 words)

Hippocratic Oath

The Hippocratic Oath is a promise historically made by physicians (medical doctors). It is one of the most widespread Greek medical texts. Its original form requires a new physician to swear to uphold specific ethical standards as regards his or her profession. Of historic and traditional value, this oath is considered as a rite of passage for practitioners of medicine in many countries, although it has today adapted to modernity.

I swear to fulfill, to the best of my ability and judgment, this covenant: [...]

I will respect the privacy of my patients, for their problems are not disclosed to me that the world may know. [...] I will prevent disease whenever I can, for prevention is preferable to cure.

If I do not violate this oath, may I enjoy life and art, respected while I live and remembered with affection thereafter. May I always act so as to preserve the finest traditions of my calling and may I long experience the joy of healing those who seek my help.

Preventive healthcare

Preventive healthcare consists of various measures taken for the prevention of diseases, as opposed to disease treatment. Health, disease, and disability begin before individuals realize they are affected (see Disease, Sickness and Illness below).

Each year, millions of people die of preventable deaths. Leading causes are (among many others) cardiovascular disease, chronic respiratory disease, diabetes, infectious diseases and involuntary injuries. Preventive healthcare is particularly important if one considers the global rise in development of chronic diseases and deaths from these diseases, and the induced costs for the public systems of healthcare. For a better prevention of disease, adults and children are recommended to visit their physician for check-ups on a regular basis even if they feel healthy, to perform disease screening, to get to know risk factors for disease, discuss tips for a healthy and balanced lifestyle and stay up to date with immunizations and boosters. However, the cost of preventive healthcare is sometimes problematic.

Disability and Handicap

Disability is the consequence of an impairment that may be physical, cognitive, mental, sensory, emotional, or developmental. A disability may be innate, or occur during a person's lifetime.

A handicap is an inability to accomplish something one might want to do, that most others are able to accomplish, it is any physical or mental defect, congenital or acquired.

It is generally acknowledged that it is politically correct to say that a person has a disability while it is considered impolite to call someone handicapped.

Organ transplant

Organ transplantation (the surgical removal of a healthy organ from one person and its transplantation into another person whose organ has failed or was injured) is a life-saving medical procedure for the recipient. Organ transplants include kidney, pancreas, liver, heart, lung and intestine. In 2015, over 25,000 people received organs in the U.S. On average, recipients are aged 50 to 65. Most transplanted organs have come from deceased donors.

Disease, Sickness and Illness

In 1973, Susser, a South-African epidemiologist, suggested some definitions that remain useful. He used **illness** to refer to the subjective sense of feeling unwell; illness does not define a specific pathology, but refers to a person's subjective experience of it, such as discomfort, tiredness or general malaise. The term **sickness** refers to socially and culturally held conceptions of health conditions, which in turn influence how the patient reacts. **Disease** implies a focus on pathological processes that may or may not produce symptoms and that result in a patient's illness. For example, a patient complains of tiredness and malaise (his illness as he experiences it). He consults a doctor about it because he believes that he might have a sickness. The doctor might attribute the patient's symptoms to a thyroid conditioned disease.

"*The first wealth is health*" Ralph W. Emerson

"*Be not sick too late, nor well too soon*" Benjamin Franklin

Chapter C

Personality and Relations

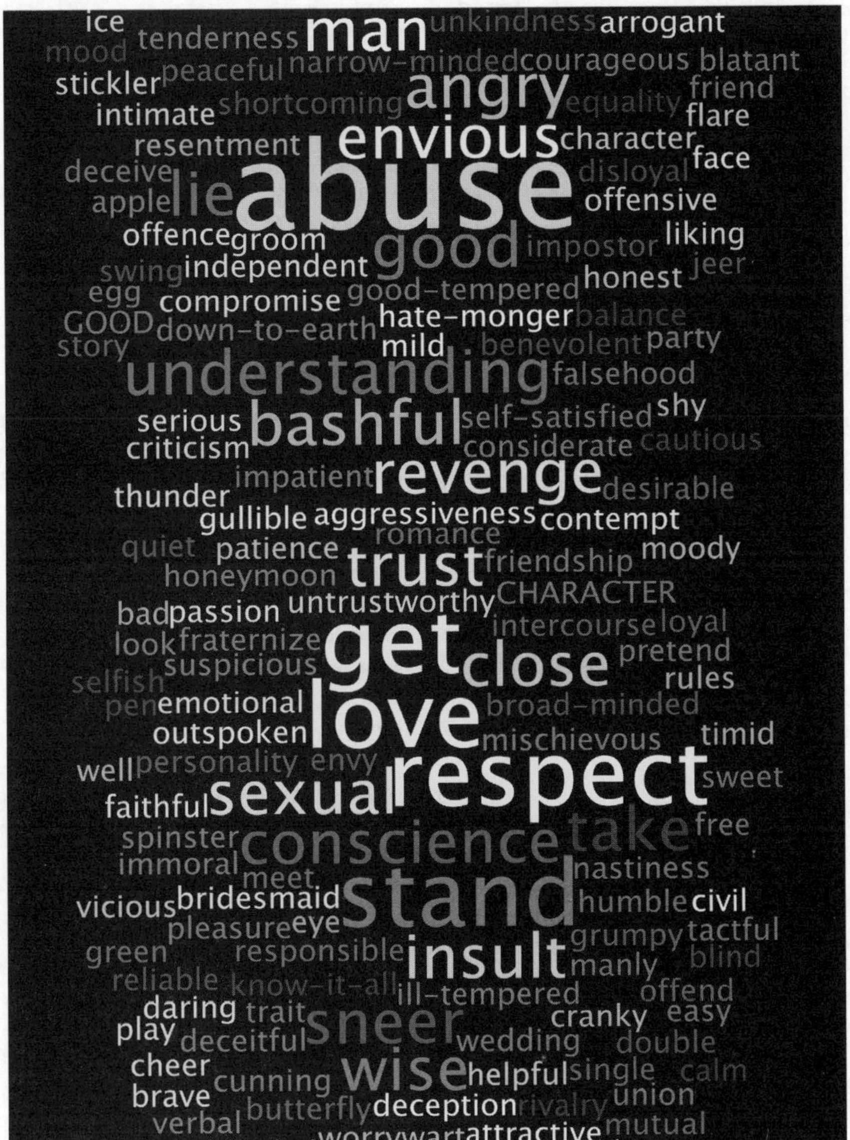

Section 1 • The human being

Vocabulary list

CHARACTER FEATURES	**LES TRAITS DE CARACTÈRE**
character, personality	le caractère, la personnalité
a trait	un trait de caractère
a failing / a shortcoming	un défaut, un travers
brave, courageous	courageux
loyal	loyal
faithful	fidèle, loyal, fiable
respectful	respectueux
cautious	prudent, regardant
mild	doux, douce
quiet, calm	calme, posé
wise	sage
mature	mature, adulte
good-tempered	modéré
humble	humble
generous	généreux
helpful	utile, obligeant, serviable
considerate	attentionné, courtois
honest	honnête
serious	sérieux
hardworking	industrieux, travailleur
demanding	exigeant
responsible	responsable
ambitious	ambitieux
self-confident	sûr de soi, plein d'assurance
trustworthy, reliable	digne de confiance, fiable
independent	autonome, indépendant
smart, cunning / intelligent	malin, futé / intelligent
daring	audacieux
broad-minded / narrow-minded	tolérant / intolérant
mischievous	espiègle / malicieux / malveillant
timid / shy	craintif, timide / timide
moody	lunatique, d'humeur changeante
ill-tempered	désagréable, déplaisant
grumpy / cranky	grognon / grincheux
weak	faible, médiocre
lazy	paresseux
gullible	crédule
stubborn	obstiné, têtu
selfish	égoïste
jealous / envious	jaloux / envieux
arrogant	arrogant
touchy	susceptible

IN GOOD TERMS	**EN BONS TERMES**
friendship	l'amitié
to trust someone	avoir confiance en qqn
trust, confidence	la confiance
respect	le respect
brotherhood	la fraternité
equality	l'égalité
close, intimate	proches, intimes
to be close to	être intime avec
to have a liking for	avoir un penchant pour
to be keen on someone	apprécier beaucoup qqn
emotional balance	l'équilibre émotionnel
to be in a good mood	être de bonne humeur
pleasant	agréable, aimable
politeness	la politesse
tactful	délicat
benevolent	bienveillant
hospitality	l'hospitalité
well-meaning	bien intentionné
decent	convenable, présentable
understanding	l'entente
mutual understanding	la complicité
to take pleasure in doing sth	prendre plaisir à faire qqch
to fraternize with	fraterniser avec
a pen friend	un correspondant
devotion	l'attachement, le dévouement
selflessness	l'altruisme
tolerance	la tolérance
a compromise	un compromis
peaceful	pacifique, paisible
non-violent	contre la violence

LOVE	**L'AMOUR**
to fall in love with	tomber amoureux de
to be crazy about	être fou de
tenderness	la tendresse
passion / passionate	la passion / passionné
attractive	attirant
handsome	beau
alluring	attirant
adorable	adorable
a proposition	une avance
a date	un rendez-vous galant
a romance	une idylle
to stand someone up	poser un lapin à qqn
to chat up	draguer

an affair	une liaison
marriage	le mariage (institution)
a wedding	un mariage (cérémonie)
a honeymoon	une lune de miel
a commitment	un engagement
a civil / free union	une union civile / libre
the groom	le marié
the bride	la mariée
the best man / the bridesmaid	le témoin / la témoin
a spinster	une vieille fille
a bachelor	un célibataire
to be single	être célibataire
sexual intercourse	les rapports sexuels
to desire, to lust for	désirer
to make love (with) / to have sex with	faire l'amour (avec)
manly	viril
desirable	désirable
a swing party	une soirée échangiste
a one-night stand	une aventure sans lendemain

CONFLICT	**LE CONFLIT**
manners	le savoir-vivre
nastiness	la méchanceté
unkindness	la méchanceté
perversity	la perversité
hostility	l'hostilité
rivalry	la rivalité
aggressiveness	l'agressivité
evil	mauvais
nasty	méchant, vilain
wicked	méchant, pervers
vicious	brutal, méchant, vicieux
stern	sévère
to insult	insulter
discontent, displeasure	mécontentement, déplaisir
a nuisance, an inconvenience	un désagrément
to offend	offenser
an offence	une offense, une infraction
offensive	insultant
to abuse	insulter, maltraiter
racist abuse	injures racistes
verbal abuse	violence verbale
sexual abuse	violences sexuelles
an insult	une insulte
to deceive	tromper
deceit / deceitful	la fourberie / fourbe

disloyalty / disloyal	la déloyauté / déloyal
deception	la tromperie
a fraud, an impostor	un imposteur
suspicious	soupçonneux
a lie, a falsehood	un mensonge
to pretend	faire semblant
sly	rusé, sournois
malevolent	mal intentionné
hypocrisy / a hypocrite	hypocrisie / un hypocrite
a hoax	un canular
immoral	immoral
untrustworthy	indigne de confiance
to criticize	critiquer
criticism	une critique
indignant	indigné
misunderstanding	l'incompréhension
to upset	affecter, perturber
impatient	impatient
an argument	une dispute
a jeer	une raillerie, un quolibet
jealousy	la jalousie
envious	envieux
resentment	la rancune, le ressentiment
to look down on	mépriser
contempt	le mépris
to sneer at	railler, regarder avec dédain
a sneer	un sarcasme
a boaster	un vantard
self-satisfied	suffisant, arrogant
to be angry at / with	être en colère contre...
to get angry about	se mettre en colère à propos de...
to flare up	s'enflammer

BONUS	**BONUS**
to be on good terms	entretenir de bonnes **relations**
to get on well with someone	bien **s'entendre** avec qqn
*to **cheer** somebody up*	réconforter qqn
to break the ice	briser la glace
*to meet **demands***	satisfaire des exigences
*to **stand by** someone*	être solidaire de qqn
*with all due **respect***	avec tout le respect que je vous dois
*to owe somebody **respect***	devoir le respect à qqn
*a pang of **guilt***	une pointe de culpabilité
*a clear **conscience***	bonne conscience
*to have an easy **conscience***	avoir la conscience tranquille
*to be **outspoken***	avoir son franc-parler

*in all **fairness** to somebody*	à la décharge de qqn
*a blatant **lie***	un mensonge éhonté
a con man	un escroc
a cock-and-bull story	une histoire à dormir debout
*to get on sb's **nerves***	porter sur les nerfs de qqn
*to try sb's **patience***	éprouver la patience de qqn
*to take **revenge** on sb for sth*	se venger sur qqn de qqch
*to be **bashful** about sth*	être embarrassé par qqch
*a **bashful** smile*	un sourire embarrassé
to trick someone (into doing sth)	piéger qqn
to play a double game	jouer double jeu
a hate-monger	un propagateur de haine
to be blinded by rage	être aveuglé par la colère
to be green with envy	être vert de jalousie
revenge is sweet	la vengeance est un plat qui se mange froid
love is blind	l'amour est aveugle
head over heels	être fou amoureux
down-to-earth	pratique, pragmatique
a go-getter	un fonceur, un ambitieux
wise guy, know-it-all	un monsieur-je-sais-tout
a social butterfly	une personne très sociable
a stickler for the rules	très à cheval sur les principes
a worrywart	un éternel inquiet
a bad egg	une personne non fiable
the apple of my eye	la prunelle de mes yeux
a face like thunder	très en colère

Translation: English-to-French exercise

- We will carve out our future with our strength of character.
- She has a friendly sociable personality, and has proved able to work as part of the team and to establish excellent relationships with work colleagues and students.
- Her vivacious personality dulled, and her head remained bowed in shame.
- Most couples spend a year planning their wedding but no time planning their marriage.
- They are honest, trustworthy and guided by a sense of propriety.

Adapted press excerpts (about 400 words)

Excerpt 1 – The Screening Room – "People are becoming clouds" (adapted from *The New Yorker*)

In a flashback scene in "Clouds," John and Eleanor, who are moving in together for the first time, **effortfully** lug a mattress up a flight of stairs, **bickering**. Upstairs, John brightly decides to unpack all the boxes. Eleanor doesn't want to. He insists. She watches in **annoyance**. He begins to unpack, improvising a zippy unpacking song. In real life, Eleanor's **feeling** in that moment, a flat, **fatigued disappointment** at not being seen or heard, could lack levity; here, we get the gift of her becoming a puffy cloud, escaping him. Or, from his perspective, we see the **maddening frustration** of a partner shutting down, retreating. Either way, it's a lovely cloud.

Excerpt 2 – Obituary – Muhammad Ali (adapted from *The Economist*)

How then did Ali **deservedly** end up a worldwide hero? His **humour** helped. His first big breakthrough into **popularity** came via the radical young after he famously said "Man, I ain't got no **quarrel** with them Vietcong" and refused to be conscripted into military service during the Vietnam war. When, in consequence, he was stripped of his title he was immediately in demand as a **pacifist** speaker. His **witty** doggerel, like the lyrics of Bob Dylan and John Lennon, came to symbolise the **rebellious** 1960s. Nonetheless, Ali achieved extraordinary **serenity** in his old age, where he spent much of his time in **quiet** contemplation as a man who never **looked down on** those who **looked up to** him.

Excerpt 3 – The Psychology of Barack Obama, a former US president (adapted from *National Interest*)

Barber assessed presidents based on two indices: first, whether they were "**positive**" or "**negative**"; and, second, whether they were **"active" or "passive."** The first index – the positive / negative one – assesses how presidents regarded themselves in relation to the challenges of the office; so, for example, did they embrace the job with a **joyful optimism** or regard it as a **necessary martyrdom** they must sustain in order to prove their **own self-worth**? The second index – active vs. passive – measures their degree of wanting to accomplish big things or retreat into a **reactive** governing mode.

Excerpt 4 – The Psychology of Barack Obama, a former US president (adapted from *National Interest*)

Active-Positive: They have big national **ambitions** and are **self-confident, flexible, optimistic, joyful** in the exercise of power, possessing a certain **philosophical detachment**.

Active-Negative: These are **compulsive** people with low **self-esteem** but high **rigidity** and **pessimism.** But they harbor accomplishments of large historical dimension.

Passive-Positive: These are **compliant** presidents who can be easily **manipulated.** They are "superficially **optimistic**" but **healthy** in both **ego and self-esteem.**

Passive-Negative: These are **withdrawn** people who avoid conflict and take no joy in the uses of power. They tend to get themselves **boxed up** through a preoccupation with principles, rules and procedures.

Food for Thought and Quotations (about 500 words)

Defining personality

Personality is the combination of characteristics or qualities that form an individual's distinctive character. It refers to individual differences in characteristic patterns of behaving, thinking and feelings. The study of personality focuses on two main areas: individual differences (in particular personality characteristics, such as sociability or irritability for instance), and the organisation of the various parts of a person. The individual differences of personality are affected by the socio-cultural development of an individual: values, attitudes, personal memories, social relationships, habits and skills. Personality is split into components called the *Big Five*, which are openness to experience, conscientiousness, extraversion, agreeableness and emotionality.

FoMO (fear of missing out)

Fear of missing out or FoMO is affecting someone who believes that others might be having rewarding experiences from which he or she is absent. This social angst is characterized by a desire to stay continually connected with what others are doing. It begins with envy. Next comes anxiety, self-doubt, a gnawing sense of inadequacy, before irritation. In other words, FoMO perpetuates the fear of having made the wrong decision on how to spend your time, as you can imagine how things could be different. With the development of technology, people's social and communicative experiences have been expanded from face-to-face to online. A psychological dependence to being online could result in anxiety when one feels disconnected, thereby leading to a fear of missing out or even pathological

Internet use. As a consequence, FoMO is perceived to have negative influences on people's psychological health and well-being, because it could contribute to people's negative mood and depressed feelings.

Networking

Networking is a newly formed word that refers to the exchange of information or services among individuals, groups or institutions. It is the cultivation of productive relationships for employment or business in particular. On the surface, networking and making friends may look rather similar: meeting new people, finding common interests and hoping that the relationship will go on. But it is important to distinguish between the two. Indeed, networking is about building a relationship, having conversations and finding common features in a professional environment or in a social environment one has to fit in. It is an opportunity to connect with others – but it's more about advancing one's professional goals or boosting one's social scene. This notion of professional opportunity is essential in the definition of the word.

Effective criticism: how to criticize productively

Giving criticism can be as hard as receiving it. Holding on to negative feelings will not help, as teachers and students already know. The most basic "rule-of-thumb" of effective criticism is: *Respect the individual, focus the criticism on the behavior that needs changing – on what people actually do or actually say.* Therefore, effective criticism should always be positively intended and appropriately motivated by relevant remarks. Acknowledging the person's good as well as bad points is essential: it balances what is acquired and what needs to be reinforced. It ought to be specific and clearly illustrated by facts. Also, if the criticism is objective, it is much harder not to take it into account. Finally, avoiding evaluative language – such as "you are wrong" or "that idea was stupid" – reduces the need for the receiver to respond defensively.

"Criticism may not be agreeable, but it is necessary. It fulfills the same function as pain in the human body. It calls attention to an unhealthy state of things." Winston Churchill

"I have faults enough, but they are not, I hope, of understanding. My temper I dare not vouch for. It is, I believe, too little yielding – certainly too little for the convenience of the world. I cannot forget the follies and vices of others so soon as I ought, nor their offenses against myself. My feelings are not puffed about with every attempt to move them. My temper would perhaps be called resentful. My good opinion once lost, is lost forever." Jane Austen, *Pride and Prejudice*

Chapter D

Successes and Failures

Vocabulary list

PROBLEM SOLVING	**RÉSOUDRE DES PROBLÈMES**
an analysis	une analyse
an argument	un argument
an issue	un problème, une question
a problem statement, a line of argument	une problématique
a hypothesis	une hypothèse
a brainstorming	un remue-méninges
the focus	le centre, l'accent, la mise au point, l'objet
the form, the manner	la forme
the content, the matter	le contenu, le fond, la matière
a goal, an objective, a purpose	un but, un objectif
an idea	une idée
an investigation	une enquête, une étude, une vérification
mental toughness	la rigueur
persistence	la persévérance
a cause	une cause
productivity	la productivité
research	des recherches
a solution	une solution
a hitch, a snag	un problème inattendu
intricate	complexe, confus
a hazard	un danger, un risque
to hamper someone from, to prevent someone from doing	empêcher qqn de faire qqch
to hinder	faire obstacle
a hindrance	un obstacle
adverse	défavorable
inability	inaptitude, incapacité
an endeavour	un effort soutenu
a target	une cible
to target	cibler
to aim at doing, to aim to do	viser

ATTEMPTS	**TENTATIVES**
a strategy	une stratégie
a policy	une politique (publique)
to start, to begin	commencer
to undertake sth	entreprendre qqch
a successful attempt	une tentative réussie
to initiate	initier, commencer
the onset, the outset	le début, le commencement
to look for	chercher
to try, to attempt	essayer, tenter
to contrive sth	trouver le moyen de faire qqch
to strive to do, to struggle to do	s'efforcer, lutter pour faire qqch

a request	une requête
an effort	un effort
willingness	la volonté
a strain	une tension
to thwart	contrarier, contrecarrer
to empower sb to do sth	habiliter qqn à faire qqch
support	le soutien, l'aide
to support	soutenir
proper	adéquat
suitable, appropriate	approprié, qui convient
to see to sth	s'occuper de qqch
to take something up	se mettre à...

ACTION	**AGIR**
to initiate	lancer (projet...)
to do	faire (abstrait)
to make	faire / fabriquer (concret)
to act / to perform	agir / accomplir
to carry sth out	accomplir qqch
to take measures	prendre des mesures
method / methodical	méthode / méthodique
to resort to sth	recourir à qqch
to improve	s'améliorer, progresser
an achievement / to achieve	une réussite, un succès / réussir
an accomplishment	une grande réussite
a feat	un exploit
to overcome sth	surmonter qqch
smooth / smoothly	sans difficultés
to opt for	choisir, opter pour
to face a dilemma	faire face à un dilemme
to hesitate, to waver about sth	hésiter sur qqch
to make a decision	prendre une décision
to consider doing sth	envisager de faire qqch
to make up one's mind	se décider
to stick to sth	s'en tenir à qqch
to settle sth	arranger qqch
out of necessity	par nécessité
to design	concevoir
to concentrate on	se concentrer sur
to size sth up	jauger, évaluer qqch
to conceive	concevoir
to build, to construct	construire
to conclude	conclure
to complete	réaliser, compléter, terminer
to arouse	susciter
to succeed	réussir

QUALITIES	**LES QUALITÊS**
accurate	précis
adventurous	aventurier
ambitious	ambitieux
appreciative	reconnaissant
caring	affectueux, chaleureux
considerate	attentionné, courtois
creative	créatif
dedicated	dévoué, zélé
determined	décidé, résolu
disciplined	discipliné
enthusiastic	enthousiaste
flexible	adaptable, flexible
forceful	énergique, vigoureux
friendly	amical
generous	généreux
honest	honnête, droit
humorous	drôle, plein d'humour
idealistic	idéaliste
independent	indépendant
inspiring	enthousiasmant, exaltant
intelligent, smart, bright	intelligent
lively, bright	plein d'entrain, vif
logical	logique
observant	observateur / respectueux
open-minded	ouvert d'esprit
optimistic	optimiste
orderly	ordonné
patient	patient
convincing, persuasive	convaincant, persuasif
practical	pratique, adroit
respectful	respectueux
self-assured	plein d'assurance
serious	sérieux
spontaneous	spontané
straightforward	direct, franc, honnête
tactful	plein de tact, délicat
tolerant	tolérant
trustworthy	digne de confiance, fiable
versatile	versatile, taciturne
warm	chaleureux
witty, spirited	spirituel

WEAKNESSES	**LES POINTS FAIBLES**
aggressive	agressif
arrogant	arrogant
blunt	abrupt, catégorique, tranché
bossy	dirigiste
chaotic	chaotique
complaining	qui se plaint
contemptuous	méprisant
cynical	cynique
distrustful of sb / sth	méfiant à l'égard de qqn / qqch
dull	ennuyeux
fanatical	fanatique
fearful	craintif
greedy	gourmand, avide
hard	dur
impatient	impatient
indifferent	indifférent
inflexible	inflexible, rigide
inhibited	inhibé, refoulé
intolerant	intolérant
lazy	paresseux
loose-tongued	qui ne tient pas sa langue
mistrustful	méfiant
moody	taciturne
naive	naïf
obstructive	récalcitrant
passive	passif
plain	simple, quelconque
prejudiced	plein de préjugés, partial
pushy	arriviste, autoritaire
reckless	téméraire, imprudent
rude	impoli, mal élevé
selfish	égoïste
shallow	superficiel, creux
short-sighted	peu clairvoyant, peu perspicace
shy	timide
sloppy	débraillé, peu soigné
stand-offish	distant
strict	strict
stubborn	obtus, obstiné, borné, entêté
undisciplined	indiscipliné
vague	évasif, distrait
wasteful	dépensier, gaspilleur

BONUS	**BONUS**
*to **seek** to do sth*	rechercher
*to **do** one's utmost*	faire de son **mieux**
*to **set** about doing sth*	entreprendre de faire qqch
*a fruitless **attempt***	une tentative infructueuse
*at the first **attempt***	du premier coup
*to **make** the best of sth*	se contenter de qqch
to sleep on it	y **réfléchir** / la nuit porte conseil
*for **argument's** sake*	à titre d'exemple
selling point	**argument** de vente
*to be **relevant** to*	avoir rapport à
*to be full of **ideas***	avoir plein d'idées
*to have no **idea** of / about*	n'avoir aucune idée de
*now I get the **idea***	maintenant je vois !
*the very **idea!***	quelle idée !
*to be at the **sharp** end*	être en première ligne
*to look **sharp***	se dépêcher / être bien habillé
*to miss the **point***	ne pas comprendre
to misunderstand	ne pas comprendre
*to **mistake** sth for sth*	confondre qqch avec qqch
*to do **good** / to do **well***	faire le bien / faire bien
*for the **good** of...*	pour le bien de...
*a **good** deed*	une bonne action
*to be very **good** about*	se montrer compréhensif au sujet de
*to look **good** on a CV*	faire de l'effet sur un CV
*as **good** as new*	quasiment, comme neuf
*for **good***	pour toujours
*to be caught with the **goods***	être pris en flagrant délit
*to go to the **bad***	mal tourner
*that's **bad!***	c'est une honte
*to be in **bad** (US)*	avoir des ennuis
*he is **bad** news*	il faut se méfier de lui
*he is having a **bad** hair day*	ce n'est pas son jour
*to take **action***	prendre des mesures
*to drive sb into **action***	pousser qqn à agir
*Lights, camera, **action!***	Moteur, ça tourne, action !
*to be of two **minds***	être partagé, être indécis
*to look **forward** to doing sth*	avoir hâte de faire qqch
*to come to a **decision***	prendre une décision
*to think **fit** to do sth*	juger bon de faire qqch
*to have **will**power*	avoir de la volonté
*an iron**will***	une volonté de fer
*when there's a **will** there's a way*	quand on veut on peut
*at **will***	à volonté
*to come up **against***	se heurter à

*never put off till tomorrow what **can** be **done** today*	ne remettez jamais à demain ce qui peut être fait le jour même
*to **do** business*	faire des affaires
*to **do** a favour*	rendre service
*to **do** without*	se débrouiller sans
*to **make** arrangements (for / with)*	prendre les dispositions pour
*to **make** a fool of oneself*	se ridiculiser
*to **make** time for / to*	prendre le temps de
*to **make** up for lost time*	rattraper le temps perdu / gagner du temps
*to **make** sure that*	s'assurer que
*a recipe for **failure***	voué(e) à l'échec
*to enjoy the sweet smell of **success***	savourer son succès

Translation: English-to-French exercise

- It is a question of people's rights to communicate with one another, share ideas and to do business.
- Over the next years he made up for lost time, by completing two years of schooling in one.
- He said he would not commit to any deadlines and described rushing into things as a recipe for failure.
- Get immersed in the enthralling success story of a young hopeful in the music milieu evolving into the greatest pop star in the world!
- After secondary school, young people become more inclined to view cultural diversity as an asset for a person or a country.

Adapted press excerpts (about 400 words)

Excerpt 1 – Sweet smell of success (adapted from *The Economist*)

Getting the **upside** of **down** often means letting go of your **instincts**, ignoring conventional **wisdom** and leaping for something no one has done before. America has a long history of doing this. As Ms McArdle explains, "We're the descendants of **failures** who fled to these shores from their creditors, their failed farms, their disastrous love affairs." Embracing **risk** and forgiving **failure** in others, they built the richest nation on earth. One may identify three traits that characterise racial, religious and ethnic groups that excel in business: a sense of **superiority**, but **insecurity** and **capacity** for impulse **control**, especially the **ability** to **resist**.

Excerpt 2 – Microsoft has zoomed back to relevance after hitting bottom (adapted from Wired.com)

Four years ago to the day, Microsoft **hit bottom**. That's when the company posted its first-ever quarterly **loss**. From that low point, Microsoft tried to **regain its footing** on the long path back to **prominence**. It was sometimes **rough** going. Google passed Microsoft in market cap. The company bought Nokia for billions only to take another big loss after the acquisition floundered. Finally, Ballmer stepped down. But **doubts lingered**. "Microsoft has lost its **ability** to **inspire** – not only in terms of inspiring people to do great **development work**, but even to inspire them with **confidence**," we wrote back then.

Excerpt 3 – The secrets of success (adapted from *Forbes*)

Of all the **goals** people **set** in life, two **stand out**: **success** in our personal and professional lives. It turns out, these two are interdependent. Personal success **supports** and **reinforces** professional success. Professional success reinforces personal success. And together, they reinforce life's most important **pursuit** – happiness. Put **good** things in your mind, and they'll happen. While **positive thought** may be a **necessary condition** for bringing out **strengths** and **capabilities**, it isn't **sufficient**. You must find your own "element," your passion. Besides, luck often makes a big difference – which is why you should be **willing** to **try** and try again, learning how to **endure failure**.

Excerpt 4 – Faster, better, cheaper: the successes and failures of NASA (adapted from BBC)

The **ups and downs** of NASA's Jet Propulsion Laboratory illustrate the boundaries between the medical profession and other industries for **valuable** lessons that might **be of use** to us all. The story begins in the early 1990s when NASA's budget was significantly **cut back**. They were forced to adopt a very different and **riskier approach** to space exploration. It was dubbed: Faster, Better, Cheaper. This approach came at a price and would lead to nearly a decade of **failures** as the cost-cutting **took its toll**, but in the end to the most **ambitious** and **successful** planetary mission which landed the Curiosity rover on the surface of the red planet in 2012. How did they **overcome** repeated **failures** to **achieve** this remarkable **success**?

Food for Thought and Quotations (about 500 words)

Personal development: the SMART approach in English learning

The acronym SMART in language learning means Strategic, Measurable, Ambitious, Relevant and Timely.

Strategic: goals have to be precisely defined, since ambiguity might result in unconvincing results. Learning the appropriate vocabulary in two years, without wandering about. You have to be organised so that learning will be optimised.

Measurable: ten thousand words in one or two years depending on your strategy, that is to say 200 words in a week, or 1000 words each of the ten working periods of 6-7 weeks over two years, that is a measurable and attainable goal for a student. Given that you might already know some of them, you might even be in for a good surprise.

Ambitious: it would be detrimental to set goals that are not attainable, therefore your goals have to be defined and never discouraging. The best is the enemy of good, in other words less is often more, particularly in the conditions of a competitive exam.

Relevant: make your goal a reality, focus on what is really important to you: embrace your future success, and make your preparation coherent with the current circumstances.

Timely: the timeframe of your work is essential. To meet with the requirements, consider adapting your timetable on a regular basis. Always meet the deadlines, as you cannot afford to lag behind. Make your preparation worth it.

"Yes we can!" Barack Obama's victory speech in 2008

"[...] The road ahead **will** be long. Our climb **will** be steep. We may not get there in one year or even in one term, but America – I have never been more **hopeful** than I am tonight that we will get there. I promise you – we as a people will get there.

There will be **setbacks** and **false starts**. There are many who won't agree with every **decision** or **policy I make** as president, and we know that government **can't solve** every **problem**. But I will always be **honest** with you about the **challenges** we **face**. I will listen to you, especially when we disagree.

And above all, I will ask you to **join** in the work of **remaking** this nation the only way it's been done in America for 221 years – block by block, brick by brick, calloused hand by calloused hand."

Do or Make

DO is used when talking about work, jobs, activities in general (do something, to do one's homework). It can also replace any other verb when the meaning is simple or obvious (to do one's hair). DO is generally not used for physical creations. Remember that DO is also an auxiliary verb, due to its very general meaning.

MAKE is used for the construction, the production or the creation of something new: a product, an action or a reaction (Made in France, don't make me sad). Used with nouns, MAKE is compatible with speech and sounds (to make a noise, a speech, a fuss), with foods and drinks, with decision plans (make a decision).

A success story: J.K. Rowling

"Failure is so important. We speak about success all the time. It is the ability to resist failure or use failure that often leads to greater success. I've met people who don't want to try for fear of failing."

J.K. Rowling, the author of the *Harry Potter* novels, was on public benefits and could not make ends meet when she started writing what would become one of the best selling series in fiction history. The book was initially rejected by a dozen publishers. Once released, it became a huge worldwide success. It has been translated into 75 languages. Legend has it that the only reason it got published at all was because the CEO's eight-year-old daughter begged him to publish it.

"Success consists of going from failure to failure without loss of enthusiasm." Winston Churchill

"Success does not consist in never making mistakes but in never making the same one a second time." George Bernard Shaw

Section 2

Basic needs

Chapter A

Eating and Drinking

Vocabulary list

AGRICULTURE	L'AGRICULTURE
the countryside	la campagne
farmland	la terre cultivée
the soil	la terre cultivable
fallow land	la jachère
a field	un champ
a meadow	une prairie
fertile, fruitful	fertile
barren	stérile
farming	l'agriculture
fish farming	la pisciculture
dairy farming	l'industrie laitière
animal farming	l'élevage
natural	naturel
industrial	industriel
organic	biologique
to yield / the yield	donner, produire / le rendement
a crop	une récolte
extensive / intensive farming	l'agriculture extensive / intensive
a landowner	un propriétaire terrien
a countryman / country people	un paysan / les campagnards
a farmer	un fermier, un agriculteur
a ploughman	un laboureur
a wine-grower	un vigneron
to run a farm	diriger une exploitation agricole
to cultivate	cultiver
to harvest / to mow	moissonner, récolter / faucher
to gather the grapes	vendanger
cereal, grain	les céréales
corn	le blé (GB) / le maïs (US)
sweet corn	le maïs
wheat	le blé, le froment
barley	l'orge
rye	le seigle
oats	l'avoine
rice	le riz
fruit	les fruits
vegetables	les légumes
poultry	la volaille
a cattle breeder	un éleveur
to breed	élever
cattle	le bétail
a herd	un troupeau
a horse / a mare	un cheval / une jument
a cow / an ox	une vache / un taureau

a pig / a sow	un porc / une truie
a sheep / an ewe	un mouton / une brebis
a lamb	un agneau
a goat	une chèvre
a calf	un veau
a fowl / a hen / a cock / a chicken	une volaille / poule / coq / poulet
a duck	un canard
a turkey	une dinde
a goose	une oie
to lay an egg	pondre un œuf
fish	les poissons
a fishpond	un vivier
milk / cream / butter / cheese	lait / crème / beurre / fromage
to skim	écrémer
to milk	traire
frost / hail / frostbitten	le gel / la grêle / gelé
flood / to flood / rotten	l'inondation / inonder / pourri
drought / parched	la sécheresse / desséché
to fertilise / fertilizer	fertiliser / l'engrais

COOKING	**CUISINER**
cooking	la cuisine, la cuisson
a utensil	un ustensile
cutlery: fork / knife / spoon	les couverts : fourchette / couteau / cuillère
a cook, a chef	un cuisinier, un chef cuisinier
a cooker	une cuisinière (objet)
a (microwave) oven	un four (à micro-ondes)
a pan / a frying pan	une casserole / une poêle
a dish	un plat
a plate / a glass / a cup / a saucer	une assiette / un verre / une tasse / une soucoupe
salt / pepper	le sel / le poivre
spices	les épices
peppers	les poivrons
mustard	la moutarde
olive oil / vinegar	huile d'olive / vinaigre
to fry / to grill / to roast / to bake / to boil	(faire) frire / griller / rôtir / cuire / bouillir
to freeze / to defrost	congeler / décongeler
raw / cooked	cru / cuit
breakfast	petit déjeuner
lunch	déjeuner
dinner	dîner
salty	salé
sweet	sucré, doux
bitter / sour	amer / aigre

sweet and sour	aigre-doux
hot, spicy	épicé
tasty / tasteless	savoureux / insipide
delicious	délicieux
disgusting	dégoûtant
a fast-food restaurant	un fast-food
appetizers	les apéritifs, les amuse-gueule
a starter / a main dish, an entrée	un hors d'œuvre, une entrée / un plat principal
traditional	à l'ancienne
genuine	authentique
trendy	tendance, à la mode
typical	typique
takeaway	à emporter
ready-to-eat / processed food	plat cuisiné / nourriture transformée
tinned food	en conserve

FOOD BASICS	**LES ALIMENTS DE BASE**
apple / pear	pomme / poire
banana	banane
grapes	raisin
orange / lemon / lime / grapefruit	orange / citron / citron vert / pamplemousse
pineapple / coconut	ananas / noix de coco
berries / cherry	baies / cerise
apricot / fig / peach	abricot / figue / pêche
melon / watermelon	melon / pastèque
strawberry / raspberry / blueberry	fraise / framboise / myrtille
beetroot	betterave
mushroom	champignon
peas / green beans / beans	petits pois / haricots verts / haricots rouges
eggplant	aubergine
radish	radis
zucchini	courgette
asparagus / artichoke	asperge / artichaut
avocado	avocat
carrot	carotte
cabbage / Brussels sprouts	chou blanc / choux de Bruxelles
lettuce / salad	laitue / salade
onion / garlic / shallot	oignon / ail / échalote
potato(es)	pomme(s) de terre
tomato(es)	tomate(s)
cucumber	concombre
cauliflower	chou-fleur
greens	les légumes verts
spinach	les épinards

meat	la viande
beef / pork / lamb / veal	du bœuf / du porc / de l'agneau / du veau
mince meat	de la viande hachée
a sausage	une saucisse
venison	du gibier
liver / kidneys / offal	le foie / les rognons / les abats
fish	du poisson
salmon / tuna / cod	du saumon / du thon / de la morue
lobster / scallops / shrimps / prawns	homard / langouste / crevettes (roses ou grises)
seafood	des fruits de mer
chips, French fries	des frites
crisps	des chips
pasta	des pâtes
rice	du riz
a hamburger / a sandwich	un hamburger / un sandwich
fish and chips	du poisson frit avec des frites
a stew / a curry	un ragoût / un curry
nuggets	des beignets de poulet
a pizza slice	une part de pizza
junk food	de la nourriture peu équilibrée
desserts	les desserts
flour	la farine
a pie / a pudding / a tart / a cake	une tourte / un pudding / une tarte / un gâteau
custard	de la crème anglaise
chocolate spread	de la pâte à tartiner au chocolat
whipped cream	crème chantilly
a yoghurt	un yaourt
bread / toast / slices of toast	le pain / du pain grillé / des tranches de pain grillé
walnuts / peanuts / hazelnuts / almond	noix / cacahuètes / noisette / amande
cracker / biscuit	biscuit salé / sucré
butter / jam	le beurre / la confiture
to nibble	grignoter

DRINKS	**LES BOISSONS**
water	eau
spring / natural water	eau de source / naturelle
sparkling water	eau pétillante
a jug of water	une carafe d'eau
juice	jus
tea	thé
iced tea	thé glacé
tea with milk	thé au lait
coffee	café
cocoa / hot chocolate	chocolat / chocolat chaud

soft drinks / sodas	boisson sans alcool / gazeuses / sodas
coke, cola	coca-cola
milk-shake	milk-shake
beer	la bière
brown / light / pale ale	bière brune / légère / blonde
a half pint of lager	un demi pression (blonde)
a stout	une bière brune épaisse
cider	du cidre
port wine	du porto
red / white / rosé wine	du vin rouge / blanc / rosé
spirits, liquor	les spiritueux, les alcools forts
whisky (Bourbon, Scotch, Rye, Irish)	whisky (États-Unis, Écosse, Canada, Irlande)
brandy	eau-de-vie
a glass, a flute	un verre, une flûte
a mug	grande tasse, chope
a wine glass	un verre à vin

BONUS	**BONUS**
*to live off the **land***	vivre de la terre
*to **have** a **drink***	prendre un verre
*mouth-**watering***	qui met l'eau à la bouche
the leftovers	les restes
*to be **hungry** / **thirsty***	avoir faim / avoir soif
*to **lunch** off something*	déjeuner de qqch
*to **eat** on the run / on the go*	manger sur le pouce
*he cannot hold his **liquor***	il ne tient pas l'alcool
*to have a bun in the **oven***	être enceinte
*a big **cheese***	une personne très importante
*a bad **egg***	un trouble-fête
*to have **egg** on one's face*	avoir l'air fin
*to **egg** sb on to do sth*	forcer qqn à faire qqch
bread** and **butter	l'essentiel
*to have one's **cake** and eat it too*	avoir le beurre et l'argent du beurre
*it's no good crying over spilled **milk***	Il est trop tard pour pleurer
*a hard **nut** to crack*	une personne difficile à comprendre
*to be **nuts** / **crackers** about someone*	être fou de qqn
*to spill the **beans***	dire la vérité / dévoiler
*a pinch of **salt***	avec légèreté
*easy-**peasy***	facile, fantoche
*piece of **cake**, easy as **pie***	simple comme bonjour
cream** of the **crop	le meilleur du meilleur
*cool as a **cucumber***	qui a du sang-froid
*one smart **cookie***	une personne très intelligente
*dead in the **water***	paralysé, à l'arrêt
*other **fish** to **fry***	d'autres chats à fouetter
***pie** in the sky*	une chimère, une illusion

Translation: English-to-French exercise

- You can enjoy a simple bar meal or else choose from our extensive restaurant menu which includes a wide-ranging variety of meals.
- The employees often make coffee or tea in the small kitchen and bring their lunch to work.
- The Vegetable Seeds activity concerns about thirty different crops from among those most consumed in the world such as: tomato, cucumber, onion, sweet and hot peppers, melon, carrot, watermelon, lettuce, cabbage, bean and cauliflower.
- The professional cookery course – at the end of which a masterly 4-course meal from ragout of venison to mousse was presented – found not only enthusiastic participants but also sophisticated experts of their trade among the journalists.
- Fruit and vegetable production (above all, bananas, oranges and passion-fruit) is severely affected, and the vineyards have been all wiped out.

Adapted press excerpts (about 400 words)

Excerpt 1 – Robochef gets cooking (adapted from *The Economist*)

Some people relish putting on an **apron** and cooking **dinner**. Others, though, find **cookery** a black art best delegated to a domestic helpmeet, a **microwave oven** or the local **home-delivery** service. Specialised **cooking** devices do already exist. These, though, are essentially **food-processors** with bells and whistles. A better machine resembles a mini-**kitchen**, complete with conventional **appliances** and **utensils**. This can, in principle, be used to cook more or less anything. A pair of dexterous robotic hands assemble the **ingredients**, **mix** them and **cook** them in **pots** and **pans** as required, on a **hob** or in an **oven**. When the **dish** is ready, they then serve it with the **flourish** of a professional.

Excerpt 2 – Jamie Oliver Cookery Courses Praised For Improving People's Eating Habits By Scientists (adapted from *Huffington Post*)

An independent report found that those who took part in the **chef's** Ministry of Food courses ended up eating more **fruit** and **vegetables**. They also reduced their intake of snacks and became more confident about cooking. [...] Participants reported significant gains in their levels of **cooking** confidence, with men reporting a greater growth in confidence than the women who took part. "Our study shows that if you help people improve their cooking **skills**, using **basic ingredients**, and their confidence in these skills, then they might make **healthier food** choices."

Excerpt 3 – Organic Valley Traces Milk Back From Table to Farm (adapted from *The New York Times*)

Jana McMelland is a third-generation **dairy farmer** in Petaluma, Calif. This October, she expects 600 to 1,200 people to visit her family's **farm**. She plans to take them to the **nursery**, the **milking parlor** and the **pastures**. "We know people care where their food comes from," she said. It is all part of an outreach strategy from **Organic** Valley, which bills itself as the largest **cooperative** of **organic farmers** in the United States. Call it **table-to-farm** marketing. These initiatives are meant to cater to people's increasing interest in "transparency in the **supply chain** and to know where food comes from."

Excerpt 4 – I don't drink. Don't hold it against me (adapted from *Slate*)

I don't drink **alcohol** the way other people don't eat **oysters**, or don't start the day with a **cup** of **coffee**. I don't drink because I don't like it, I never have. Alcohol isn't just a **drink**, it's a rite of passage. The irony being that alcohol is essentially childhood in a **bottle**. For a few bucks, you get a trip back to the carefree days of slurred speech, impaired balance and nonexistent inhibitions. Who'd turn down a bargain like that? I am the midnight **milkshake** drinker. According to my boyfriend, I regularly replace alcohol with **food**. Apparently I ask to see the **dessert menu** every time I accompany him to the **bar**. Presumably, the **drunker** he gets, the **fatter** I get.

Food for Thought and Quotations (about 500 words)

Recent developments in the agricultural sector: several "green" revolutions

Research and development in agronomy has aimed to increase the yield of agricultural production, through the use of synthetic fertilizers and pesticides, during the 20th century. These have greatly increased crop yields, and this technology was later exported to the developing world, to guarantee food for more people, thus keeping them from starvation. Although it is termed green, this revolution mainly aims to develop the productivity of crops, but not the quality of the products themselves. A new Green revolution has more recently raised concerns about the food and soil poisoning due to the systematic abuse of fertilizers, and tries to encourage the development of organic farming through a more sensible use of natural resources.

Slaughterhouses or abattoirs

A slaughterhouse is a facility where animals are slaughtered and processed for consumption as food for humans. Some other slaughterhouses process meat not intended for human consumption. Slaughtering animals on a large scale poses significant logistical problems, animal welfare problems and public health requirements. Recently, scandals (horse meat scandal, conditions of slaughter, traceability) have caused public outrage. Animal rights groups frequently raise concerns about the methods of transport, preparation and killing of the animals through awareness campaigns based on hidden cameras filming the conditions in slaughterhouses.

Vegetarian v. Vegan

Vegetarians exclude meat, poultry, and seafood from their diets. Some vegetarians also exclude dairy, some don't, and some may consume eggs. Vegans take it a step further by eliminating all animal products from their diets. This includes any type of animal milk and eggs. Vegans therefore avoid foods produced using animals or animal products in any way, including honey. Many vegans also avoid household products, clothing or other items made from animal products or tested on animals. They have to guarantee that their diet is properly balanced in terms of nutritional needs, without any deficiency.

Food for Thought (adapted from the BBC, Good Food Podcast by Jo Levin)

Wholegrains, because the brain cannot work without energy. Opt for "brown" wholegrain cereals, granary bread, rice and pasta.

Oily fish that contain omega-3 fats, such as salmon, trout, mackerel, herring, sardines, pilchards and kippers.It is thought to help us manage stress and helps make the good mood brain chemical, serotonin.

Blueberries are effective in improving or delaying short term memory loss.

Tomatoes with a little olive oil optimise absorption and efficacy.

Pumpkin seeds are vital for enhancing memory and thinking skills.

Broccoli is a great source of vitamin K, which is known to enhance cognitive function and improve brainpower.

Sage has long had a reputation for improving memory and concentration.

Eat more nuts to prevent cognitive decline.

"One cannot think well, love well, sleep well, if one has not dined well." Virginia Woolf

"An idealist is one who, on noticing that a rose smells better than a cabbage, concludes that it makes a better soup." H.L. Mencken

Chapter B

In the household

Vocabulary list

DWELLING	**LE LOGEMENT**
a dwelling	un logement
a detached house	une maison individuelle, un pavillon
a semi-detached house	une maison jumelée
a terraced house	une maison mitoyenne
a flat (GB) / an apartment (US)	un appartement
ground floor (GB) / first storey (US)	le rez-de-chaussée
first floor (GB) / second floor (US)	le premier étage
a block of flats / an apartment building	un immeuble
a tower block	une tour
a hovel / a cottage	une masure / un cottage
a palace / a manor house	un manoir
to dwell in	loger dans
to move house / to move in	déménager / emménager
a tenant	un locataire
a landlord / landlady	un(e) propriétaire
the rent	le loyer
to own / an owner	posséder / le propriétaire
a loan	un emprunt
a mortgage	un emprunt immobilier, une hypothèque
a lift (GB) / an elevator (US)	un ascenseur
a studio flat / a one-bedroom flat	un studio / un T2 (appartement deux pièces)
convenient, well-planned	pratique, bien agencé
roomy, spacious	spacieux, vaste
cosy, snug	douillet, confortable

ROOMS	**LES PIÈCES**
a bathroom	une salle de bains
toilet (GB) / bathroom (US) / restroom	les toilettes
a bedroom	une chambre (à coucher)
a dining-room	une salle à manger
a dressing-room	un dressing
a living-room	un salon
a terrace / a balcony	une terrasse / un balcon
a spare room / guest room	une chambre d'amis
the doorstep / the threshold	le perron / le seuil
a basement / a cellar	un sous-sol / une cave
a garden / a backyard	un jardin / une cour
a kitchen(ette)	une cuisine / une cuisine américaine
a garage	un garage
an attic / a loft	un grenier

PARTS	**L'ÉQUIPEMENT**
a window	une fenêtre
a door / a door handle	une porte / une poignée

a lock / a bolt	une serrure / un verrou
a (partition) wall	un mur / une cloison
a French window	une porte-fenêtre
stairs / the stairway / the steps	un escalier / les marches
a banister	une rampe d'escalier
the ceiling	le plafond
the roof	le toit
the floor / parquet floor	le sol, plancher / un parquet
a shower / a bath	une douche / baignoire
a washbasin / a handbasin	un lave-mains / un lavabo
a tap / a pipe	un robinet / un tuyau
a lamp	une lampe
a bulb	une ampoule
a switch	un interrupteur
air conditioning	la climatisation
heating / a radiator / a boiler	le chauffage / un radiateur / une chaudière
the fireplace	une cheminée
a socket	une prise (femelle)
to plug in / out	brancher / débrancher

FURNITURE	**MOBILIER**
furniture	le mobilier
a piece of furniture	un meuble
a chair / a stool / an armchair	une chaise / un tabouret / un fauteuil
a table / a dining table / bedside table	une table / une table de salle à manger / table de nuit, un chevet
a desk	un bureau
a couch / a sofa / a settee	un divan / un canapé
a sideboard	un buffet
bookshelves / a bookcase	étagères de bibliothèque / une bibliothèque
a wardrobe	une armoire
a chest of drawers / a drawer	une commode / un tiroir
a single / double bed	un lit simple / double
a king-size bed	un très grand lit / un lit grande taille
a rug / fitted carpet	un tapis / la moquette
a cushion / a pillow	un coussin / un oreiller
bedclothes / a sheet	draps et couvertures / un drap
a curtain	un rideau
a looking-glass, a mirror	un miroir
a trunk	une malle
a welcome mat	un paillasson
a storage cabinet	un meuble de rangement
a kitchen cabinet	un meuble de cuisine
a filing cabinet	un classeur à tiroirs
a coffee table	une table basse
a TV stand / a media stand	un meuble TV / multimédia

EQUIPMENT AND APPLIANCES	**ÉQUIPEMENTS ET APPAREILS**
electric / gas cooker (stove US)	une cuisinière électrique / à gaz
a hotplate	une plaque de cuisson
a refrigerator / a fridge	un réfrigérateur
a freezer	un congélateur
a dishwasher	un lave-vaisselle
a washing machine	une machine à laver
a tumble dryer	un sèche-linge
a sink	un évier (de cuisine)
a kettle	une bouilloire
a toaster	un grille-pain
a blender	un mixeur
a vacuum-cleaner, a hoover	un aspirateur
a TV set / a Blu-ray player	un poste de télévision / un lecteur Blu-ray
a wireless router	une box / un routeur
a laptop	un ordinateur portable
a hi-fi stereo	une chaîne Hi-Fi
a telephone	un téléphone
a mobile (GB) / a cellphone (US) / a smartphone	un téléphone portable / un smartphone
remote control	une télécommande
an iron / an ironing board	un fer à repasser / une planche à repasser
a hair-dryer	un sèche-cheveux
a towel	une serviette
a napkin / a tablecloth	une serviette de table / une nappe
a can opener / a tin opener	un ouvre-boîtes
a coffee-maker	une cafetière

HOUSEHOLD CHORES	**LES CORVÉES MÉNAGÈRES**
to load / empty a dishwasher	remplir / vider le...
to do the washing-up	faire la vaisselle
to do the housework	faire le ménage
to make one's bed	faire son lit
to do one's bedroom	faire / ranger sa chambre
to iron / to do the ironing	repasser / faire le repassage
to hoover	passer l'aspirateur
to sweep the floor	balayer
to dust	faire la poussière
to wipe something clean	essuyer
to set / clear the table	mettre / débarrasser la table
to sweep / to mop the floor	balayer le sol / passer la serpillière
to fold and put away clothes	plier et ranger le linge
to water plants	arroser les plantes
to take out the rubbish bin (GB) / the garbage can (US)	sortir les poubelles
to walk the dog	promener le chien

DIY	**LE BRICOLAGE**
DIY (Do-it-yourself)	le bricolage
a handyman / a handywoman	un bricoleur / une bricoleuse
paint	de la peinture
a paintbrush	un pinceau
a roller	un rouleau à peinture
wallpaper	papier peint
decoration	la décoration
to spray-paint	peindre au pistolet
a coat / an undercoat	une couche / une sous-couche
a ladder	une échelle
an extension cord	une rallonge électrique
a hammer	un marteau
a screwdriver	un tournevis
a spanner	une clé à molette
pliers	des pinces
a screw / a nail	une vis / un clou
a nut / a bolt	un écrou / un boulon
a soldering iron	un fer à souder
a drill	une perceuse
a sander	une ponceuse
an electric saw	une scie électrique
to be out of order	être hors d'usage
to break down	tomber en panne
to mend / to repair sth	réparer
a repairman	un réparateur
to refurbish / to renovate	rénover
plumbing	la plomberie
to plug a leak	boucher / réparer une fuite
a toolbox	une boîte à outils
a tape measure	un mètre
a spirit level	un niveau à bulle
a plumb line	un fil à plomb
a box cutter	un cutter

BONUS	**BONUS**
***home** sweet home*	on n'est nulle part aussi bien que chez soi
*to be a bit too close to **home***	être blessant
*to be **home** and dry, to be safe and sound*	être sain et sauf
*to push one's point **home***	enfoncer le **clou**
*to get on like a **house** on fire*	s'entendre à merveille
*to set one's **house** in order*	mettre de l'ordre dans ses affaires
*to make **room***	faire de la place
*to take up **room***	prendre de la place
***room** for improvement*	marge de manœuvre pour des progrès
*there is always **room** at the top*	quand on veut on peut

*to get out of **bed** on the wrong side*	se lever du pied gauche
*her life is a **bed** of nails*	sa vie est un calvaire
*life is not a **bed** of roses*	tout n'est pas rose dans la vie
*every cloud has a silver **lining***	à quelque chose malheur est bon
to be in a bad way	avoir du **plomb** dans l'aile
*to be at the top of the **table***	être en haut du classement
*to **table** something for discussion*	soumettre à débat (GB)
*I can drink you under the **table***	je tiens mieux l'alcool que toi
*to do sth under the **table***	faire qqch sous le manteau
to let others wait on you	mettre les pieds sous la **table**
to reach seventh heaven	grimper aux **rideaux**
*to fall between two **stools***	être ni chair ni poisson / avoir le c** entre deux chaises (familier)
*to **stool***	moucharder
*to lead sb on / to lead sb up (GB) / down (US) the **garden** path*	mener qqn en bateau
*everything in the **garden**'s rosy (ironic)*	tout va pour le mieux / tout baigne
*to go through the **ceiling***	crever le plafond
*to hit the **ceiling** (US) / to raise the **roof***	sortir de ses gonds (aussi : faire un boucan de tous les diables)
*to have one's head **screwed** on*	avoir la tête sur les épaules
*to put the **screws** on sb*	forcer la main à qqn
*to be as tough as **nails***	être sans cœur
*to fight tooth and **nail** (against)*	se battre avec acharnement contre, se battre corps et âme
*cash on the **nail***	argent comptant
*to hit the **nail** on the head*	mettre le doigt dessus
*you really **nailed** it! / to nail it*	bravo, tu as réussi ! / taper dans le mille

Translation: English-to-French exercise

- Energy efficiency, use of recyclables and low-toxicity materials are all a step in the right direction but an important addition is the elimination of planned obsolescence.
- Planned obsolescence is the deliberate creating of products that will not last and that are not repairable.
- However, we need to look at the facts: DIY is a leisure time activity that is not just socially useful but also economically beneficial for families and should therefore be encouraged.
- The first and second floors have exactly the same plan with a flat comprising a hallway, a living room, a bedroom, a study and a shower room; at the other end, two large adjoining rooms used as a living room and a bedroom.
- Mechanization is making household chores easier but it is also multiplying them!

Adapted press excerpts (about 400 words)

Excerpt 1 – No place like home (adapted from *The Guardian*)

Renting in London "costs twice as much as elsewhere". Private rents in London are almost double those in the rest of the UK, but the supply of **properties** means that the scrabble for newly available **homes** is greater in other cities around the country. It said the current asking price for **homes** in London was £1,516, with landlords typically asking £1,211 a month for **one-bedroom flats** and £1,605 for **two-bedders.** Across the rest of the UK the overall average was £665. Rents for new **tenancies** have soared in recent years as would-be **first-time buyers** have been unable to raise the required **deposits** to buy, and have been forced to remain in **rented accommodation.**

Excerpt 2 – The home of the future (adapted from *The Economist*)

Houses resemble electronic control **rooms** with all sorts of **gadgets, computers, routers, antennae, screens** and **remote controls.** Everything is connected to a **central computer** through **wireless** links. Among the things automated are the opening and closing of **garage doors**, the re-ordering of **groceries** in the **refrigerator**, the **locking** and **unlocking** of doors, and so on. The Sears catalogue in those days was full of what would today be called "converged" **devices** – a **food processor** doubling as a pleasure vibrator for women; a **vacuum cleaner** that also dried hair, **heated** rooms and **spray-painted walls**; a **washing machine** that also beat eggs and minced meat. Few of these **devices** ever made it into homes.

Excerpt 3 – How to build your own home (adapted from CNN)

Dale, who has no training as a **builder**, built his **eco-home**. His ecologically-friendly house uses water from a nearby stream, and is heated by a wood burning **stove** with wood gathered from the surrounding forests. The property has a **compost toilet**, and is **powered** by **solar panels** on the **roof.** The tiny house has two distinct **spaces** – one half with a **sofa bed, table, chairs** and **storage** and the other split into a **kitchen** and **bathroom.** Simon Dale built his own "Hobbit House" for less than $5,000, with just a **hammer**, a one-inch **chisel** and a **chainsaw**, and was made largely of **scavenged materials.** "Anything you could possibly want is in a rubbish pile somewhere – **windows, burner, plumbing, wiring.**"

Excerpt 4 – We are makers (adapted from TED Talks)

All of us are **makers**. We're born makers. We have this ability to **make** things, to **grasp** things with our hands. We use words like "grasp" **metaphorically** to also think about understanding things. We don't just live, but we **make**. We **create** things. [...] Makers today, to some degree, are out on the edge. They're not mainstream. They're a little bit radical. They're a bit subversive in what they **do**. But at one time, it was fairly commonplace to think of yourself as a maker. It was not something you'd even remark upon. And we've got to get this into communities – the ability to **tinker**, to **shape** and **reshape** the world around us.

Food for Thought and Quotations (about 500 words)

The punk culture of DIY

When the punk movement emerged in the 70s, opportunities were found by musical bands to create their own labels, their own production means, their own gig management in order to perform low-cost DIY touring. This enabled many bands to reach success and get wider recognition, since it was considered politically and ethically coherent with the anti-consumerism spirit of the movement. The burgeoning zine movement covered and promoted the underground punk scenes. These self-made magazines were also more personal; they quickly became one of the youth culture's gateways to DIY culture. This led to tutorial zines showing others how to make their own shirts, posters, zines, books, food, etc. Hence, a punk culture of DIY.

3D printing at home

Domestic 3D printing was originally mainly used by enthusiasts and geeks. However, little was used for practical household applications. Today, home 3D printing tends to include backscratchers, coat hooks, door knobs, etc., through the assistance of some open-source projects that help design spare parts and small objects, in order to repair appliances at home. The printer can print with anything that can be dispensed from a syringe as liquid or paste, a door knob and even more complex parts in the home environment. 3D printing is now working its way into households. It enhances not only creativity, but also fights against the excesses of consumerism, by limiting the consequences of planned obsolescence. The different types of programmed obsolescence can be related to the deterioration of some components or spare parts, the style and design, or a prevention of repairs (the infamous practise of Apple, for instance).

Planned / built-in obsolescence

In economics and in design, built-in obsolescence is a deliberate policy of planning the limitation of the lifespan of a product, so that it will become either obsolete or dysfunctional after a programmed period of time. This enables the company to plan long-term sales for repeated purchases of a similar product, since it will allegedly limit the cost of research and development and therefore improve the profitability. In reality, the consumers who become aware of such a strategy will turn to competitors instead of purchasing a similar product from the same business. If the company is in position of monopoly, built-in obsolescence can be profitable in economic terms. But competition tends to reduce the advantage of such a strategy, since consumers are more likely to encourage better quality products, hence a longer lifespan for products. Political institutions around the world are beginning to address this question, on grounds of economic and environmental coherence, but no significant action has been taken so far to compel businesses not to invest in built-in obsolescence.

Small and Tiny house movement

This movement advocates living in a simple fashion in a small home. Defining a small home is difficult, but below 1000 square feet (93 square meters) could define a small house, and below 500 square feet (46 square meters) could define a tiny house. The movement is most active in the USA, but tends to expand to other countries (Germany, Britain, Spain and Japan). Both amateur and professional builders have contributed to the increased popularity of such projects, and concerns over security have recently led to define principles in order to promote ethical business practices and offer guidelines for construction of tiny houses. The pros concern the low prices, the limited repair costs and heating and maintenance costs. Tiny houses encourage a simpler lifestyle with a reduced ecological impact, also with the technological improvements that miniaturization of appliances offer today. Space optimization is indeed a fundamental criterion in the organization of space. It also offers opportunities for the poor, since the house construction process is simplified and therefore less costly and easier. Self-sufficiency can be guaranteed to many families in need, this is how the Tiny house movement gathered momentum after the financial crisis in 2008.

*"Choose Life. Choose a job. Choose a career. Choose a family. Choose a f*** big television, choose washing machines, cars, compact disc players and electrical tin openers. Choose good health, low cholesterol, and dental insurance. Choose fixed interest mortgage repayments. Choose a starter home. Choose your friends. Choose leisurewear and matching luggage. Choose a three-piece suit on hire purchase in a range of f*** fabrics. Choose DIY and wondering who the f*** you are on Sunday morning. Choose sitting on that couch watching mind-numbing, spirit-crushing game shows, stuffing f*** junk food into your mouth."* Irvine Welsh, *Trainspotting*

"Have nothing in your house that you do not know to be useful, or believe to be beautiful." William Morris

Chapter C
City and Country

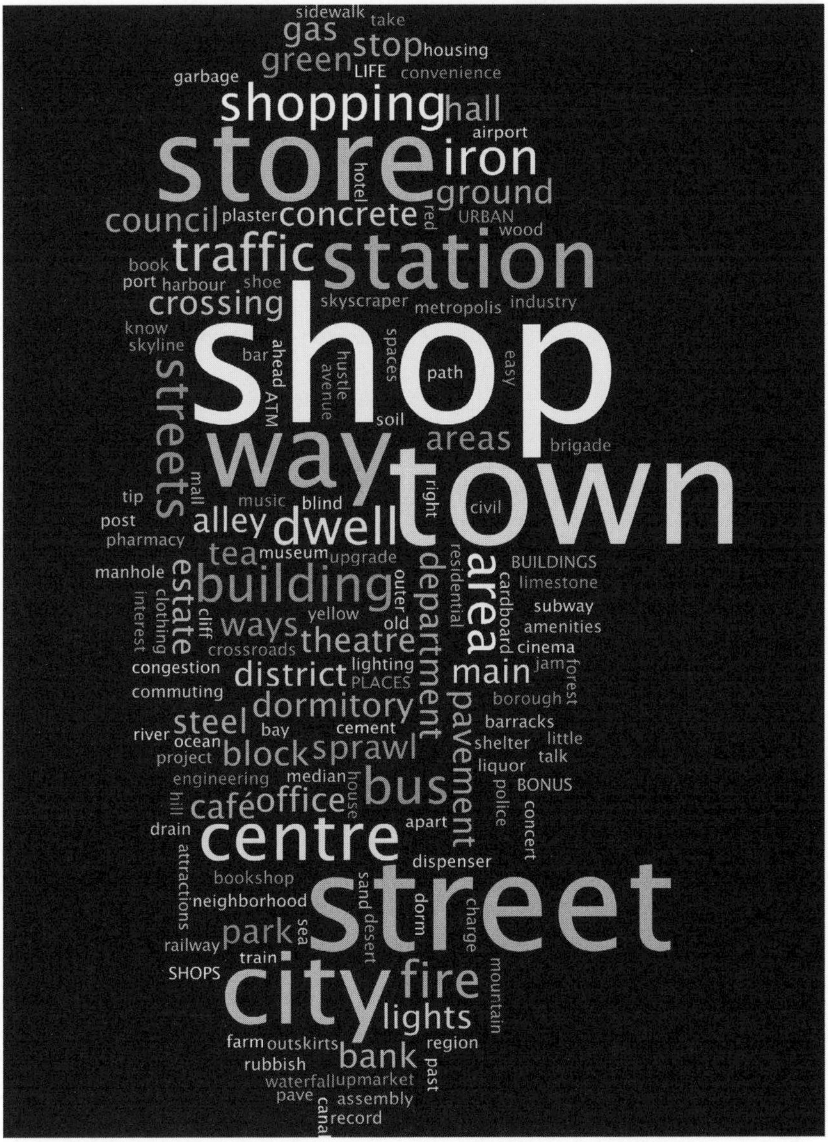

Vocabulary list

LANDSCAPES	**LES PAYSAGES**
the area	la région, le lieu, la zone
the ocean	l'océan
the sea	la mer
the seaside	le bord de mer
the bay	la baie
the harbour, the port	le port
the beach	la plage
the cliff	la falaise
the island	l'île
the quay, the bank	le quai, le quai aménagé
the lake	le lac
the river	le fleuve
a stream	un ruisseau, cours d'eau, courant, flot
a canal	un canal
the desert	le désert
the earth	la terre
a farm	une ferme
a field	un terrain, un champ, un domaine
a forest	une forêt
a hill	une colline
the land	les terres, le terrain
a mountain	une montagne
a path / a track	un sentier, un chemin / une piste
railway	voie de chemin de fer, ligne (de train)
a rainforest	une forêt (tropicale ou tempérée) humide
a region	une région
rock	roche, rocher, pierre
sand	sable
the scenery	les paysages
the sky	le ciel
the soil	le sol
a valley	une vallée
a village	un village
a waterfall	une chute d'eau
a wood	un bois

CITIES	**LES VILLES**
a capital city	une capitale
a metropolis	une métropole, un grand centre urbain
an urban area, an agglomeration	une zone urbaine, une agglomération
a town	une ville
a city / the City	une grande ville / le quartier financier de la ville de Londres
a district	un quartier

a borough	un arrondissement
the city council / the town hall	la municipalité / la mairie
a citizen	un citoyen
to dwell / a dweller	habiter, résider / un résidant (-ent)
a street	une rue
a thoroughfare	une artère
an alley, a lane	une ruelle, un passage, une allée
an avenue	une avenue
a blind alley, a dead end	une voie sans issue, une impasse
a road	une route
a maze	un dédale / un labyrinthe
the main street	la grand-rue
a side street	une rue secondaire
the pavement (GB) / sidewalk (US)	le trottoir
a housing estate / a project (US)	un lotissement, une cité / cité HLM
suburban area / suburb	banlieue, faubourg
the outskirts, the outer suburbs	la grande banlieue
the city / town centre	le centre-ville
a dormitory town	une ville dortoir
council house / flat	équivalent d'un HLM
a square	une place
a park / a garden	un parc / un jardin
green spaces / areas	les espaces verts
a wasteland, a waste ground	un terrain vague

BUILDINGS AND PLACES	**BÂTIMENTS ET LIEUX**
an apartment building	un immeuble d'habitation
a block of flats	une résidence
a skyscraper	un gratte-ciel
an airport	un aéroport
an assembly hall	un hall de réunion
barracks	une caserne
dormitory / dorm	une résidence universitaire
a train station	une gare
a library	une bibliothèque
a bus stop	un arrêt de bus
a church / a mosque	une église / une mosquée
a department store	un grand magasin
the fire department (US) / a fire brigade (GB)	pompiers
service station / gas station (US)	station-service
a hospital	hôpital
a cinema / a movie theatre / a theatre	un cinéma / un théâtre
a museum	musée
an office block (GB) / building (US)	immeuble de bureaux
a shopping centre (GB) / mall (US)	un centre commercial
a police station	un poste de police

a rubbish tip / a garbage dump	une décharge
a concert hall	une salle de concert
a fun fair	une foire (une fête foraine)

SHOPS / STORES	**LES MAGASINS**
a hotel	un hôtel
a café / a bar / a pub	un café-restaurant / un bar, un café / un pub
a tea shop, a tea room	un salon de thé
a restaurant	un restaurant
a drugstore (pharmacy) / a chemist's	une pharmacie / droguerie
a barber shop	le coiffeur
a clothing shop	un magasin de vêtements
a shoe shop / a cobbler	un magasin de chaussures
a jewellery shop	une bijouterie
a record shop, a music store	un disquaire
a bookshop / bookstore (US)	une librairie
a newsagent's	un marchand de journaux
a bank	une banque
a post office	un bureau de poste
a butcher's shop	une boucherie
a supermarket	un supermarché
a fishmonger's (shop)	une poissonnerie
a convenience store	une épicerie
a greengrocer's (shop)	un magasin de fruits et légumes
a delicatessen, a deli	une épicerie fine / un traiteur
an off licence, a liquor store	magasin de vins et spiritueux
a florist's (shop)	un fleuriste

EQUIPMENT	**LA VOIRIE**
a pedestrian crossing (a zebra crossing GB, a crosswalk US)	un passage piétons
a roadsign	un panneau de signalisation
a crossroads	un carrefour
traffic lights (green / yellow / red)	les feux de signalisation
a roundabout	un rond-point
a vehicle	un véhicule
public transport	les transports publics
a subway station	une station de métro
a bus shelter / a bus stop	un abribus / un arrêt de bus
street lights / lighting	les réverbères, l'éclairage public
a drain / a sewer	un égout
gas / water main	canalisation de gaz / d'eau
the median strip	le terre-plein central
a fire hydrant	une bouche d'incendie
a barrier	une barrière / une entrave

a manhole	une bouche d'égout
a car park / a parking lot (US)	un parking

URBAN DEVELOPMENT	**LE DÉVELOPPEMENT URBAIN**
sprawl / to sprawl	l'étendue urbaine / s'étendre
the skyline	l'horizon urbaine
an architect	un architecte
a town planner	un urbaniste
architecture	l'architecture
the building industry	l'industrie du bâtiment
civil engineering	les travaux publics
a developer	un promoteur immobilier
real estate	l'immobilier
to design, to plan	concevoir, élaborer les plans de
to build	construire
to rise from the ground	sortir de terre
to upgrade	moderniser
to demolish	démolir
the district, the neighbourhood	le quartier, le voisinage
the financial district	le quartier financier
a shopping precinct	un quartier commerçant
residential / deserted areas	quartiers résidentiels / désertés
stone / brick / limestone /	pierre / brique / calcaire
concrete / reinforced concrete	béton / béton armé
cement / plaster	ciment / plâtre
slate / brick	ardoise / brique
steel / stainless steel	acier / acier inoxydable (inox)
iron / cast iron / wrought iron	le fer / la fonte / le fer forgé
basic amenities	les équipements socio-culturels
commuting	les transports (entre le lieu de travail et le domicile), le trajet
to commute	faire la navette

CITY LIFE	**LA VIE URBAINE**
pedestrians / passers-by	les piétons, les passants
rush hour	l'heure de pointe
traffic jam / traffic	les embouteillages / la circulation
a busy / congested street	une rue passante / embouteillée
the hustle and bustle / bustling	l'agitation urbaine / grouillant
to queue	faire la queue
the congestion charge	la taxe embouteillage
polluted / unbreathable	pollué / irrespirable
to flock into	affluer
to loiter	traîner
hectic	trépidant, mouvementé, agité
chain store / shop	magasin faisant partie d'une chaîne

an upmarket store	un magasin de produits haut de gamme
tourist attractions	attractions touristiques
a visitor centre	centre d'accueil et d'information des visiteurs
place of interest	point d'intérêt / site intéressant
lively bars / cafés	bars animés
a cash dispenser / an ATM	un distributeur automatique de billets
pavement café	café avec terrasse donnant sur la rue
out of town shopping centre	grand centre commercial (de banlieue)
gentrification	l'embourgeoisement

BONUS	**BONUS**
*a **city** slicker*	un citadin branché
a yuppie	un jeune cadre branché dynamique
the gilded youth / the happy few	la jeunesse dorée / les privilégiés
*a cardboard **city***	zone urbaine où les sans abri dorment sur des cartons
*he is the talk of the **town***	on ne parle que de lui en ville
***town** and gown*	les citadins et les universitaires
*to be to **town** on*	ne pas lésiner sur, mettre le paquet sur
*to come from out of **town***	ne pas être d'ici
*to be on easy **street***	se la couler douce
*to take to the **streets***	manifester, descendre dans la rue
*the man on the **street***	monsieur-tout-le-monde
*it is right up my **street***	c'est exactement ce qu'il me faut
*they are **streets** apart*	un abîme les sépare
*to be **streets** ahead of*	être bien meilleur que
*to pave the **way** for*	ouvrir la voie à
*have it your own **way***	comme tu voudras / comme bon te semble
*if I had my **way***	si cela ne tenait qu'à moi
*he likes to have his own **way***	il n'en fait qu'à sa tête
*the old **ways***	les coutumes d'autrefois, le bon vieux temps
*I know all her little **ways***	je connais toutes ses petites habitudes
*no **way**!*	pas question
*to make **way** for*	s'écarter, faire place à
*he's from the **hood***	il vient des quartiers / de la banlieue
*to **dwell** on sth*	s'étendre sur qqch
*to **dwell** on the past*	ruminer le passé

Translation: English-to-French exercise

- The company also offers established skills and expertise in developing new districts that pave the way for the city of the future.
- These large shopping centres have wrecked the livelihoods of small traders and service providers in the immediate area, many of whom have been forced to close down.
- Window shopping is not all lost time, because in a stroll down Main Street we soak up impressions about what is on the market.
- While urban sprawl is one of the main reasons for this huge increase of private motorised transport, the driving force behind increases in urban goods transport is economic growth and prosperity.
- This variety of urban flight can sometimes be attributed to the attractiveness of modern lifestyles and the social prestige linked to living in a new, modern building.

Adapted press excerpts (about 400 words)

Excerpt 1 – Redesigning cities – Los Angeles (adapted from *The Economist*)

Los Angeles has long epitomised car-oriented **sprawl,** a collection of **suburbs** in search of a **city**. Rare are **neighbourhoods** where basic needs can be met without hopping into a car or bus. **Urban planners** elsewhere routinely invoke L.A. as an example of what to avoid. The original **metropolitan** miscreant is now trying to reform itself. Last summer the city council changed zoning rules to allow tiny **apartments** to be built in and around **downtown** Los Angeles. From next month **developers** will be allowed to build **blocks of flats** up to 35% bigger than previously, so long as they include some cheap **housing**.

Excerpt 2 – San Francisco is ground zero for an AirBnB freakout (adapted from *Wired*)

Airbnb is a seven-year-old tech company valued at $25 billion. During this decade's tech boom, San Francisco **neighborhoods** have **gentrified** rapidly. **Home** prices have surged, as have **rents**, putting the **city** in the grip of a **housing** crisis. Much of that **built-up** tension will come flooding out tomorrow when San Franciscans head to the polls to vote on Proposition F – known to many as the Airbnb initiative – which would more severely restrict Airbnb-style **short-term rentals**. The measure pits San Franciscans who say Airbnb is chasing long-term **renters** out of the city against **residents** who say Airbnb gives them a bump in income that allows them to stay.

Excerpt 3 – Gentrification in Harlem (adapted from *BBC News*)

Harlem is transforming. Harlem is finally **gentrifying**: the **brownstone apartment** houses that line Marcus Garvey **Park** are being **gutted**, re-**fitted** and sold for upwards of $3 million – even during the Credit Crunch; 125th Street, which used to be a **no-go area** for whites, now holds the **offices** of Bill Clinton. But what of the Harlem's **long-term residents**? For years they had to put up with violent crime, burnt-out **buildings**, and very limited services – with rising rents can they afford to live in the new Harlem? **"Fusion" restaurants, delicatessens, wine bars** and **smart coffee shops** have moved onto 125th Street – along with the white and black professionals who like use them. Starbucks café tables now line the street corner where Malcolm X used to preach.

Excerpt 4 – Is London's High-Rise Boom Destroying the City's Skyline? (adapted from *Slate*)

In 2019, London has more than 300 mostly **residential high-rises** of more than 20 **stories** and up to 70 stories high in the works, most of which are "poorly **conceived**, inadequately **designed**, and badly **built**," de Botton argues, "erratically **scattered**, like needles, across the **landscape**" and "destroying vistas and **sightlines** at every turn." What's more, he says, these 21st-century **buildings** are mostly alien to the character of London. The integration of **skyscrapers** in older cities – such as Paris, which is building its tallest skyscraper in 40 years and has other high-rises on the horizon is always controversial.

Food for Thought and Quotations (about 500 words)

Sprawl

Urban sprawl or suburban sprawl refers to the expansion of human populations away from central urban areas into low-density and car-dependent communities, in a process called suburbanization or horizontal growth. By extension of its meaning it also relates to the social and environmental consequences it implies. In continental Europe the terms "peri-urbanisation", or "banlieue" (etymologically meaning "banned afar from the centre") describe similar dynamics. The term urban sprawl is highly politicized, and almost always has negative connotations. It is criticized for causing environmental degradation, intensifying segregation and undermining the vitality of existing urban areas and also attacked on aesthetic grounds and concerns for city planning.

Inner cities and gentrification

The inner city is the central area of a major city. Inner city areas tend to have higher population densities than outer suburbs, with more of the population living inside multi-floored townhouses and old apartment buildings. But the understanding of the expression may differ in the US and in Europe. For example, the inner parts of Paris and other continental capital cities are today the richest and most expensive areas of the "agglomerations", while the suburbs may sometimes be derelict, with a high rate of crime. The phenomenon of gentrification has also gathered momentum in these cities, and the main consequence has been an exodus of poorer populations to the outskirts. In the USA and in London, the term used to have a negative connotation, and referred to impoverished neighbourhoods. Today, it tends to change, since the gentrification process has also reached the US and central areas of major cities have been renovated.

Pubs and bars

Various sorts of drinking establishment can be defined in English. Pub is short for Public House. Bars emerged in the US. Café refers to a place where one can drink coffee (from the French "café"). The ambience of a British or Irish pub is more relaxed and calm with no loud music, but occasional musical bands. It is a place patronised by both young and old clientele. They specialize in beer, cider and wine. Bars, on the contrary, tend to have a younger clientele with loud music, dance floors or DJs, and sell liquors and spirits, or selections of cocktails. As for food, bars only propose snacks, while pubs offer more elaborate food (fish and chips, shepherd's pie and so on). Patrons can also "bar hop" (move from one bar to another). Bars are generally frequented late in the evening and patrons bar hop from one place to another, whereas pubs generally close about midnight.

The changes in shopping attitudes over the last fifty years

Over the last half-century the shopping attitudes of consumers have followed those in technology. Most of the shopping used to be done in traditional shops (local Butchers, Bakers, Grocers and Newsagents...). As supermarkets and hypermarkets appeared (Tesco in the UK, Walmart in the US), some of those traditional corner shops closed down. Today, hypermarkets have grown even larger and have expanded their areas of shopping to clothing, hardware, petrol and even banking. The initial gain for consumers was a drop in prices, but in the end the cities have lost a part of their local economy and tradition (milk delivery in the UK, old fashioned bakery shops...). The Internet has also revolutionized shopping over the last twenty years and today threatens some other shops (clothes, DIY, furniture, electronics and even food). Services tend to fare better than goods in the city centres, and lately a form of resistance in major European cities shows that even among the youths local shopping is irreplaceable.

"*City life – millions of people being lonesome together.*" Henry David Thoreau

"*What is the city but the people?*" William Shakespeare

Chapter D

Sports and leisure activities

Vocabulary list

ABCs OF SPORTS	**LISTE ALPHABÉTIQUE SPORTS**
acrobatics	acrobatie
aikido	aïkido
archery	tir à l'arc
(horse-, car-bike-...) racing	course (sport hippique, auto), cyclisme
badminton	badminton
baseball	baseball
basketball	basket-ball
biathlon	biathlon
(bi)cycling	course à bicyclette
bowling	bowling / jeu de boules
boxing	la boxe
cricket	cricket
croquet	croquet
cross-country skiing	ski de fond
curling	curling
cycling	cyclisme
decathlon	décathlon
dancing, ballet	danse, ballet
discus	lancer de disque
diving	plongeon / plongée sous-marine
equestrian	cavalier / cavalière / sport hippique
fencing	escrime
fishing	pêche
football	football (Br) / football américain (US)
go-carting	kart / karting
golf	golf
gymnastics	gymnastique
hammer throw	lancer de marteau
(ice-)hockey	hockey (sur glace)
horseback riding	équitation
hunting	chasse
hurling	hockey irlandais / lancer de projectile
ice dancing	danse sur glace
jacks	osselets
javelin throw	lancer de javelot
judo	judo
karate (expert)	karaté (karatéka)
kayaking	kayak
luge	luge / toboggan
marathon	marathon
moto-cross	moto-cross
poker	poker
race walk	marche

racing	course
racquetball	squash avec raquette à manche court
road race	course sur route
rugby	rugby
running	course à pied
sailing	la voile
shuffleboard	jeu de palets
scooter	une trottinette
skateboarding	planche à roulette / skateboard
skiing	ski
slalom	slalom
sledding	luge / traîneau
snowboarding	surf des neiges / snowboard
soccer	football
spinning	pêche à la cuillère
squash	squash
stock-car racing	course de stock-cars
sumo wrestling	lutte de sumo
surfing	surf
swimming	natation
table tennis	tennis de table / ping-pong
tae kwon do	taekwondo
tennis	tennis
tobogganing	toboggan
(athletics / speedway) track	piste (d'athlétisme / de vitesse)
triathlon	triathlon
trekking, hiking	randonnée pédestre, marche
vaulting	saut / voltige
volleyball	volley-ball
waterpolo	water-polo
weightlifting	haltérophilie
wrestling	lutte / catch
Xtreme sports	sports extrêmes
yoga	yoga

PRACTICE	**LA PRATIQUE**
indoor sport	les sports en salle
outdoor sport	les sports en plein air
intellectual game	sport cérébral
team sport	sport d'équipe
a player	un joueur / une joueuse
to exercise / training	faire de l'exercice / l'entraînement
cardio-training	cardio-training, entraînement cardio
sportsmanship	l'esprit sportif
an athlete	un athlète
to practise a sport	pratiquer un sport

a coach	un entraîneur
a workout, a drill	une séance d'entraînement
stretching	les étirements
a routine	un enchaînement
warming-up	l'échauffement
push-ups / press-ups	des pompes / des tractions
effort	l'effort
fitness	la forme physique
strength	la force
grit, guts	le cran
balance	l'équilibre
stamina, endurance	l'endurance
team spirit	l'esprit d'équipe
suppleness	la souplesse
to keep fit	se maintenir en bonne forme
muscular	musclé
resilient	résistant
fast	rapide
light	léger
gifted	doué
CONTESTS	**LES RENCONTRES SPORTIVES**
contest	une rencontre
competition	la compétition
a meeting	une rencontre
the Olympic Games	les Jeux olympiques
a championship	un championnat
an event / a heat	une épreuve / éliminatoire
a match, a game	un match, une partie
to qualify	se qualifier
to challenge sb	défier / lancer un défi à qqn
to compete in / with	participer à / être en compétition avec
a team	une équipe
a contestant, a competitor	un adversaire, un concurrent
a challenger	un prétendant au titre
to confront	faire face à, affronter
a winner / to win	un vainqueur, gagnant / gagner
a loser / to lose	un perdant / perdre
a reigning champion	un champion en titre
elimination	l'élimination
to withdraw	déclarer forfait
the outcome	l'issue
a gold / silver / bronze medal	une médaille d'or / d'argent / de bronze
a prize	un prix
a reward	une récompense
to have the edge over	avoir l'avantage sur

to beat, to defeat	battre, vaincre
to set / break / smash a record	établir / battre / pulvériser un record
to overpower	dominer

LEISURE ACTIVITIES	**ACTIVITÉS DE LOISIRS**
leisure time / spare time	le temps libre
a holiday / a vacation (US)	des vacances
a pastime / a hobby	un passe-temps / une passion
crafts	activités manuelles
to play video games	jouer à des jeux vidéo
a game of skill	un jeu d'adresse
mah-jong	mah-jong
chess	les échecs
gardening	le jardinage
to mow the lawn	tondre la pelouse
fertilizer	l'engrais
to water	arroser
boating	la navigation de plaisance
to row / a rowing boat	ramer / une barque
a sailing boat	un voilier
angling, fishing	la pêche à la ligne
the bait	l'appât
a fishing rod	une canne à pêche
the line / the hook	la ligne / l'hameçon
to stroll	se promener, flâner
a hiker	un randonneur
a mountaineer	un alpiniste
a backpack	un sac à dos
a backpacker	un routard
card games	les jeux de cartes
hearts / diamonds / spades / clubs	cœurs / carreaux / piques / trèfles
to cut / to shuffle	couper / mélanger, battre
a trump	un atout

BONUS	**BONUS**
*to **run** a race*	faire la course
*to come fifth in a **race***	arriver cinquième dans une course
*a **race** against time*	une course contre la montre
*to **race** sb with sth*	faire la course avec qqn jusqu'à qqch
*to **race** through*	faire qqch rapidement
*my mind started to **race***	je me suis mis à imaginer toutes sortes de choses
*to do sth for **sport** / for the fun of it*	faire qqch pour s'amuser / pour l'amour du **sport**
this is no picnic	ça c'est du **sport** / pas de la tarte !
*to be a good / bad **sport***	être beau / mauvais joueur

*to **match** up*	aller ensemble
*to **match** up to*	être à la hauteur
draw (Br.) / tie (US)	**match** nul
first / second leg	**match** aller / retour
***win** some, **lose** some*	on ne peut pas gagner à tous les coups
*to **win** back*	récupérer, regagner, reprendre
*to **win** through to*	se qualifier
*to **lose** it totally*	péter les plombs
*to **lose** out to sb*	se faire dépasser par qqn
*to **lose** oneself in*	se plonger dans / se perdre dans
*a package **holiday***	des vacances organisées
*off the beaten **track***	hors des sentiers battus
*to call a spade a **spade***	appeler un chat un chat
*to take a **break** / a nap*	faire une pause / la sieste
*to be one **jump** ahead of sb*	avoir une longueur d'avance sur qqn
*to **jump** to conclusions*	tirer des conclusions hâtives
***jump** to it!*	et que ça saute !
*to **jump** the lights*	passer au feu rouge
*the **ball** is in / out*	la balle est bonne / faute
*to **play** ball*	coopérer avec / jouer franc jeu
*to keep the **ball** rolling*	entretenir la conversation
*to have a **ball***	s'amuser comme un fou
*it is no **contest***	c'est couru d'avance
the drawback / the other side of the coin / the downside	le revers de la **médaille**
*to do everything in one's **power***	faire tout son possible
*to be at the height of one's **powers***	être au sommet de son art
*to switch on the **power***	mettre le courant, allumer
*to be running out of **power***	perdre de la puissance
*to be **fit** for purpose*	être adapté aux besoins
to be fit for duty	être apte au service
*to be only **fit** for the bin*	être juste bon à jeter à la poubelle
*his story does not **fit***	son histoire ne tient pas debout
*the **leisure** society*	la civilisation des loisirs
*gentleman / lady of **leisure***	rentier / rentière
to do sth at one's leisure	faire qqch à tête reposée

Translation: English-to-French exercise

- Road racing is a team sport and it's important that you learn early on how to race within a team and know the rules of the road.
- Why would one want observer status in an organization that cannot even rely on its own membership to play ball?
- In the final, India defeated England by a single point, with some help from the local heckling crowd denounced by an English archer in the press conference as "not the kind of sportsmanship we are used to in archery".
- In addition, the community has extensive programs now so that municipalities can move from the traditional practices to more sustainable forms of gardening and lawn care.
- Greece is famous for having created the Olympic Games, which have today become a genuine worldwide sports festival.

Adapted press excerpts (about 400 words)

Excerpt 1 – Rio 2016: IOC announce first ever refugee team to compete under the Olympic flag (adapted from *The Independent*)

The International **Olympic** Committee (IOC) unveiled its first ever **team** of refugees which had 10 **members** and 12 **officials** and **competed** at the 2016 Rio de Janeiro Games under the Olympic flag. On a historic day, the team included five **athletes** from South Sudan, two from Syria, two from DRC and one from Ethiopia. These refugee **athletes** had no home, no **team**, no flag, no national anthem. The invention of this refugee team was to give them a home in the Olympic village together with all the athletes around the world. The athletes, six men and four women, competed in the **sports** of **swimming**, **judo** and **athletics**.

Excerpt 2 – Here's why watching sport makes you cry (adapted from TheConversation.com)

When London **hosted** the Olympic games in 2012, the combination of patriotic pride and **sporting** success created an irresistible opportunity for crying – one that was taken not only by **medal-winning** athletes and audiences at home, but also even by the **broadcasters** interviewing **athletes** on television.

People have been crying at **sports** for years, particularly at the Olympics, where national pride further ramps up the **emotion levels**, for stars and spectators alike. Our tears are orators, announcing sometimes admiration, sometimes pity, for the

achievements and sufferings of **sporting performers**. It is easy enough to see that crying is a social, and sociable activity, arising from an identification and empathy with the life stories of others.

Excerpt 3 – Extreme athletes take major risks. Should we pay for them? (adapted from *Washington Post*)

Every **adventurer** sets out with the hope that all will go according to plan and that they will return from their endeavors to adulation and praise. [...] When things go wrong, should we pull all the stops to rescue **extreme athletes** and thrill seekers? Taking an occasional **risk** is good **fun**. Few things make one feel more alive than running a **marathon** for the first time, or trying a **double** black diamond on the **ski** slope.Then there are those who choose to **row** an unpowered boat **unaided** across the Atlantic ocean or **skydive** into a Siberian lake ice hole. For these people, ordinary risks are not enough, and in seeking their thrills they go **outside** normal **parameters**.

Excerpt 4 – Gardening is the best medicine for the mind (adapted from *The Guardian*)

While I was **off work**, I threw myself into my **garden**. I felt like the world around me was a dangerous sea and my garden was a **green life raft**. I cut a new, long bed out of the **grass**. I worked the **soil** until I couldn't find a sliver of **weed root**. I barrelled tons of **compost** and poured it all over the garden to improve the structure of the heavy clay. I **sowed seeds**, bought more herbaceous **perennials** than I could afford, and scarified the **grass** like a man possessed. As I worked on the garden the garden worked on me. I could feel myself start to **relax**.

Food for Thought and Quotations (about 500 words)

The Olympic Games / The Olympics

The Olympic Games are a major international sporting event, in summer and winter every four years (alternatively two years apart), in which athletes from all around the world participate in a great many competitions. They are considered to be the world's most important sports competition. It originated in the Ancient Greek Olympic Games, some 2800 years ago. The French Pierre de Coubertin founded the new games in 1894. The Olympic intertwined rings represent the five inhabited continents, and the motto is "Faster, Higher, Stronger". The ideals expressed in the Olympic creed can be summarized as follows: "The most important thing in the Olympic Games is not to win but to take part, just as the most important thing in life is not the triumph but the struggle. The essential thing is not to have conquered but to have fought well." After the 2020 Tokyo Games, Paris will host the 2024 Olympics.

Hooliganism in Europe

The word has come to be associated with violence in sports, and more particularly with football in Europe (Belgium, England, Russia). Sports crowd violence is a global concerning phenomenon explained by individual, social and environmental factors that interact and influence one another. Sociological factors suggest that poverty and lack of education can imply huge levels of violence and territoriality, which is a common feature of football hooliganism. Social cleavage facilitates group identification and affect the appreciation of fan violence. In 1985, a disaster occurred in the Heysel stadium in Belgium, where 39 people died and hundreds were badly injured, because of the hostility of two English teams' supporters. It was described as the darkest hour in the history of European competitions.

The passion for community gardening

In the United Kingdom, community gardens are plots of land rented to individuals for their cultivation by local authorities or other public bodies, or community-managed allotments. They are designed to provide fresh products and plants within a built-up urban area, participate in the construction of the community spirit and the connection to the environment and gradual awareness of health concerns. Many gardens are built on patches of derelict land, waste ground or land that is not being used for any purpose.

Trail running

Trail running (mountain running) consists in running and hiking over trails over long routes, while cross-country running which generally takes place on hiking trails is a more governed discipline. The ranks of trail runners are increasing annually, because of this rather loose definition. Runners often prefer trail running for its lesser impact stress compared to road running, as well as for the natural and scenic landscape and non-urban environment. A growing number of people from all around the world have taken to participating in solo backcountry trail running trips, today considered as an ultralight form of backpacking. According to them, such challenges are extremely rewarding and also have a limited impact on the natural environment.

Doping in sport

In competitive sports, doping refers to the use of banned athletic performance-enhancing drugs by athletic competitors. The use of drugs to enhance performance is considered unethical, and therefore prohibited, by most international sports organizations, including the International Olympic Committee.

Now a widespread practise, doping has become a scourge for competitions. The strict regulation of the use of drugs in sport is justified by the necessary exemplarity of sport athletes for the public, the health risks and the unequal opportunity for athletes during a competition. Anti-doping authorities therefore state that using performance-enhancing drugs goes against the spirit of sports.

"It isn't the mountains ahead to climb that wear you out; it's the pebble in your shoe." Muhammad Ali

"You can't put a limit on anything. The more you dream, the farther you get." Michael Phelps

Section 3
Discovering and learning

Chapter A

Transport and Tourism

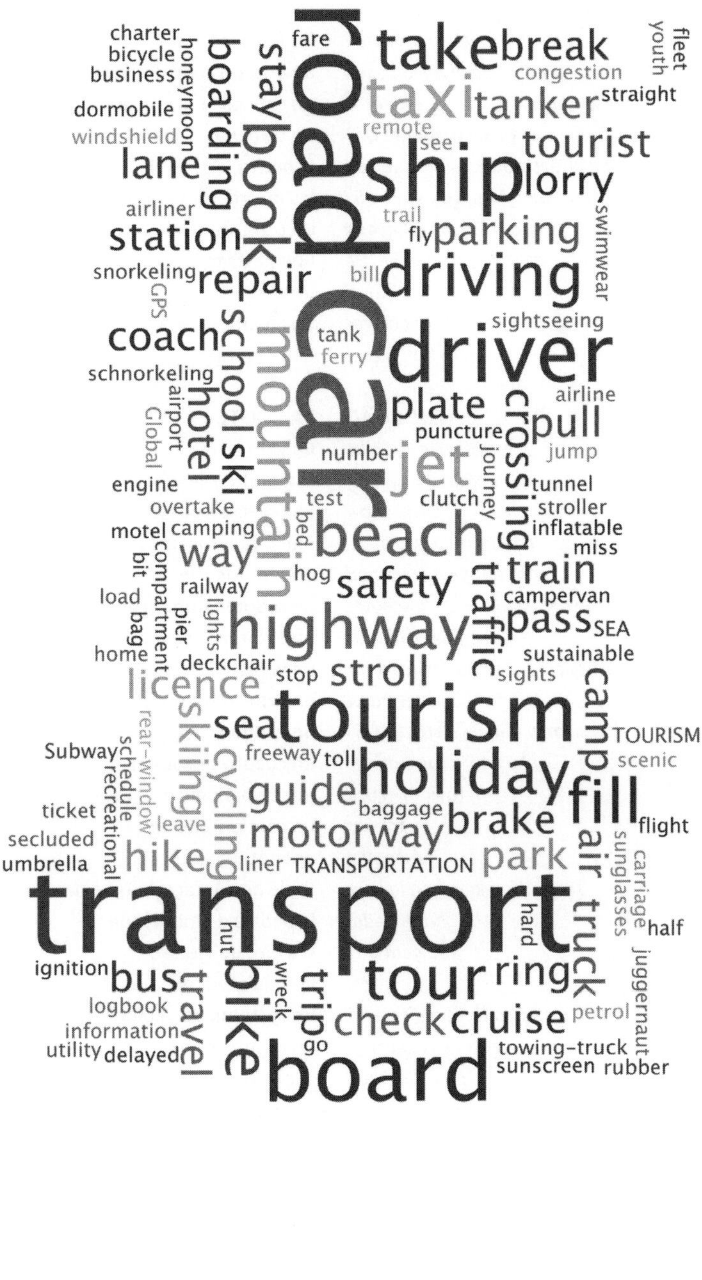

Vocabulary list

PUBLIC TRANSPORTATION	**LES TRANSPORTS PUBLICS**
to transport / to convey	transporter / acheminer
a means of transport / of transportation	un moyen de transport
public transport	les transports en commun
a passenger	un passager
departure / arrival	le départ / l'arrivée
to leave / to arrive	quitter / arriver
a ticket / the fare	un billet / le prix du trajet
to book / to reserve	réserver
a timetable / a schedule	les horaires
a bus / a coach	un bus, un autobus / un car, un autocar
a school bus / a double-decker	un car scolaire / un autobus à impériale
a tram / a streetcar (US)	un tramway
the underground / the subway	le métro
the Tube (GB) / the Subway (US)	les métros de Londres et de New York
a train, a trolleybus	un train, un trolley
a shuttle	une navette
a cab / a taxi	un taxi
a taxi driver	un chauffeur de taxi
to hail a taxi	héler un taxi

THE ROAD	**LA ROUTE**
a bicycle / a bike	un vélo
walking / cycling	la marche / le vélo
a rickshaw	un pousse-pousse
a motorbike / a biker	une moto / un motard
a motorcycle, a moped	une motocyclette
a scooter	un scooter / une trottinette
a convertible car	une voiture décapotable, un cabriolet
a SUV (sports utility car), a cross-country car	un véhicule tout-terrain, un 4x4
a juggernaut	un semi-remorque
a lorry (GB) / a truck (US)	un camion
a lorry- / truck-driver	un chauffeur routier
a towing-truck	une dépanneuse
a tanker	un camion-citerne
an engine	un moteur
an ignition key / an igniter	la clé de contact / un démarreur
the clutch pedal	la pédale d'embrayage
the gear box	la boîte de vitesse
cruise control	le régulateur de vitesse
a GPS (Global Positioning System)	un système de géolocalisation
a brake / to brake	un frein / freiner
the safety belt	la ceinture de sécurité
air-conditioning	la climatisation
the windscreen / windshield (US)	le pare-brise

a rear-window	un rétroviseur
a tyre	un pneu
a licence plate, a number plate	une plaque d'immatriculation
headlights	les phares
petrol (GB) / gas (US)	l'essence
a petrol / gas station	une station-service
leaded / unleaded	au plomb / sans plomb
diesel oil	le diesel
to fill in the tank, to fill up	faire le plein
fill her up please!	faites le plein, s'il vous plaît !
the boot (GB) / trunk (US)	le coffre
a puncture	une crevaison
a repair / to repair	une réparation / réparer
to break down	tomber en panne
a vintage car	une voiture de collection
a second-hand car	une voiture d'occasion
a road / highway	une route nationale
a motorway / a freeway (US)	une autoroute
a crossroads, a junction	un carrefour, un croisement, une intersection
a roadsign / roadsigns	un panneau de signalisation / la signalisation routière
a bridge / a tunnel	un pont / un tunnel
roadworks	des travaux
a speedbump, a road hump	un ralentisseur
a detour	une déviation
traffic lights	les feux de croisement
a bike lane, a cycling lane	une piste cyclable
a toll motorway	une autoroute à péage
a hard shoulder	une bande d'arrêt d'urgence
a ring road	un périphérique, une ceinture
the highway code	le code de la route
a driving license (US) / driver's licence (GB)	un permis de conduire
to take one's driving test	passer son permis de conduire
a driving school	une auto-école
to speed up / to slow down	accélérer / ralentir
to overtake, to pass	dépasser
to do a U-turn	faire demi-tour
to give way, to yield	céder le passage
road safety	la sécurité routière
a reckless driver, a road hog (US)	un chauffard
a pedestrian precinct / a zebra crossing	une zone piétonne / un passage piétons
traffic jam, congestion	les embouteillages
to park / a car park, a parking lot (US)	se garer / un parking
a parking space	une place de stationnement
carpooling	le covoiturage
a car rental	une location de voiture

AIR, SEA, RAIL	**TRANSPORT AÉRIEN, MARITIME ET FERROVIAIRE**
air transport	le transport aérien
an airport	un aéroport
an airline / an airliner	une compagnie aérienne / un avion de ligne
an aircraft / a jetliner	un appareil / un avion à réaction
a jumbo jet	un gros porteur
to fly / a flight	voler / un vol
to stop over / a stopover	faire escale / une escale
to charter	affréter
the check-in / to check in	l'enregistrement / s'enregistrer
to board / the boarding	embarquer / l'embarquement
a boarding pass	une carte d'embarquement
to take off / to land	décoller / atterrir
a runway	une piste de décollage / atterrissage
jet lag	le décalage horaire
the crew	l'équipage
a steward / an air hostess	un steward / une hôtesse
sea transport	le transport maritime
a ship / to ship	un bateau, un navire / expédier par bateau
a tanker	un pétrolier
a liner	un paquebot
a ferry	un ferry
to board a ship / to disembark	embarquer / débarquer
to load / to unload	charger / décharger
a crossing, a passage	une traversée
the anchor	l'ancre
a quay, a wharf	un quai
a pier	une jetée, une digue, un embarcadère
a gangway	une passerelle d'embarquement
a fleet	une flotte
a logbook	un journal de bord
to steer	gouverner
a (ship)wreck / a wreckage	une épave / les débris, une épave
a lifeboat, a lifejacket	un canot de sauvetage, un gilet de sauvetage
rail transport	le transport ferroviaire
a railway (GB) / a railroad (US)	un chemin de fer
a line, a track	une ligne, une voie ferrée
a high-speed train	un TGV (train à grande vitesse)
a carriage, a coach, a car (US)	un wagon, une voiture
a station	une gare
a connection	une correspondance
to be delayed	avoir du retard
a platform	un quai de gare
a compartment / a rack	un compartiment / un porte-bagages
to pull in / to pull out	entrer en gare / partir

TOURISM	**LE TOURISME**
tourism	le tourisme
mass tourism	le tourisme de masse
sustainable tourism	le tourisme durable
volunteer tourism	le tourisme bénévole
the hotel industry	l'industrie hôtelière
the tourist information office	l'office de tourisme
a tour operator	un voyagiste
a travel agency	une agence de voyages
a business trip	un voyage d'affaires
to book / a booking	réserver / une réservation
luggage (GB) / baggage (US)	les bagages
a suitcase / a travelling bag	une valise / un sac de voyage
a rucksack, a backpack	un sac à dos
sunglasses, shades	les lunettes de soleil
to pack	faire ses bagages
a guide book / a tour guide	un guide (livre / personne)
a trip / a journey	un voyage / un trajet
a holiday / a vacation (US)	les vacances
holiday makers	les vacanciers
accommodation	l'hébergement
a guesthouse	une pension de famille
a youth hostel	une auberge de jeunesse
a motel (motor hotel)	un hôtel de bord de route / un motel
a single / double en-suite bedroom	une chambre avec salle de bains simple / double
full board / half board	pension complète / demi-pension
all inclusive	tout compris
the bill (GB) / the check (US)	l'addition
to travel	voyager
to see the sights	visiter les monuments
to go sightseeing	faire du tourisme
to explore / an explorer	explorer / un explorateur
remote, distant, secluded	lointain, à l'écart
picturesque, scenic / unspoiled	pittoresque / préservé
scenery	les paysages
a trek / a safari / a cruise	un trek / safari / une croisière
an outing, an excursion	une excursion
to stay / a stay	rester, séjourner / un séjour
a world traveller	un globe-trotter
a honeymoon	une lune de miel
to be homebound	être sur le chemin du retour
to be homesick	avoir le mal du pays

HOLIDAYS	LES VACANCES
mountain and countryside	la montagne et la campagne
a holiday camp (GB) / a summer camp (US)	une colonie de vacances
a camping ground, a campsite	un terrain de camping
a mountain hut	un refuge de montagne
a tent / a caravan	une tente / une caravane
a dormobile, a campervan	un camping-car
a RV (recreational vehicle)	un véhicule de loisirs
wildlife	la faune sauvage
a footpath, a trail	un sentier de randonnée
to stroll / a stroller / a stroll	se promener / un promeneur / une promenade
to hike / a hike	randonner / une randonnée
to climb / rock climbing, mountaineering	grimper / l'escalade, l'alpinisme
a mountain bike	un VTT (vélo tout-terrain)
to ski / skiing / a skier	skier / le ski / un skieur
a sandy beach	une plage de sable
the seaside	le bord de mer
to bathe / a bather	se baigner / un baigneur
a swimsuit	un maillot
boxers	un caleçon de bain
swimwear / a bikini	une tenue de bain / un bikini
to sunbathe	prendre un bain de soleil
tan / to be tanned	le bronzage / être bronzé
a sunburn / a sunstroke	un coup de soleil / une insolation
a sun lotion, sunscreen	une crème solaire
a beach towel	une serviette de bain
a rubber ring	une bouée
an inflatable bed, a lilo	un matelas pneumatique
a beach umbrella / a deckchair	un parasol / une chaise longue
goggles / a mask / a snorkel	des lunettes de plongée / un masque / un tuba
snorkeling / schnorkeling (US)	plongée en palmes, masque, tuba
to dive / diving	plonger / la plongée
a jet ski	un scooter des mers
water skiing	le ski nautique
a windsurf / a surfboard	une planche à voile / une planche de surf
a coral reef	un récif de corail
the depths of the sea	les fonds marins

BONUS	BONUS
to show sb round a place	faire visiter qqch à qqn
a tourist attraction	une attraction touristique
the museum that attracts the most visitors	le musée le plus visité
folklore, razzmatazz (fam.)	le folklore
to tour around a bit	faire du tourisme

to take a break in the country	se mettre au vert
to jump on the bandwagon	prendre le train en marche
to miss the boat	ne pas se saisir d'une opportunité
a backseat driver	un inspecteur des travaux finis
my way or the highway	à prendre ou à laisser
to hit the road	commencer un voyage, prendre la route
home straight	la dernière ligne droite

Translation: English-to-French exercise

- There is certainly a link with regional development and tourism.
- The importance of tourism is shown in the higher percentage of jobs in accommodation and catering sectors.
- International bus lines are competing through low fares with international railway services and low-cost airlines.
- Young people must be informed of the risks they and other road users face once they have obtained their driving licence.
- When it is about fighting fires in subway, railroad and road tunnels, one thing is for sure: in the event of a fire very particular demands are placed on the fire department.

Adapted press excerpts (about 400 words)

Excerpt 1 – Hybrid cars – At last, the 48 show (adapted from *The Economist*)

Voltage is to **electricity** what **pressure** is to **water**: the more you have of it the more oomph you get. That is why electrical power lines work at high voltage. In the 1950s carmakers needed extra oomph to start the powerful high-compression engines, so they increased the voltage of their vehicles' **electrical** systems from 6 to 12. Now **voltages** are going up again – to 48. One reason is that cars are packed with more **components**, demanding more **electrical power**. Extra voltage lets engineers design cars in novel ways that **boost engine output** and **efficiency**. This can be used to make **hybrids**, with **electric motors** and **combustion engines** to cut both **fuel consumption** and **polluting emissions**, as required by the COP 25 agreement in Madrid in 2019.

Excerpt 2 – Spread of Zika, and cloud of fear, threatens Florida's tourism way of life (adapted from *Washington Post*)

The **threat** has heated up at the end of Florida's **summer**, when the state's **vacation business** is at a lull. But it also comes in the thick of mosquito **season**, raising alarm about how quickly the virus could spread. More than 1.2 million Floridians work in the state's **tourism industry**. But **tourism** stands at the peak of Florida's economy: those dollars filter down into virtually every industry, including **hotels, restaurants, health care and housing**. The state has released no data on Zika's effects on **tourism**, including trip **cancellations** or **postponements**. Businesses say they're worried that even the appearance of a dangerous outbreak could shake confidence in the state's **tourism backbone** – young families.

Excerpt 3 – Endless highway: How to drive the ultimate American road trip (adapted from CNN)

Route! How much time? **Desert** or **forest**? Big **cities, country routes** or a bit of both? **Guides** abound for **trips** along the classic U.S. **routes**. If you want a unique **itinerary**, there are plenty of resources to help design a **journey** that leaves room for unexpected **adventure** while taking in **sights**. With no fixed **schedule** for their **road trip**, a couple found themselves drawn to the coast in the evenings, where they'd pull into a **beach parking lot** and watch the **sunset** together. "It was wonderful," McKirdy says. "We had no **itinerary** starting out, we had only two **spots** planned. Their 13,699-mile route is the shortest way to take in a **national park, monument, historic site** or **natural landmark** in each of the lower 48 states."

Excerpt 4 – Could this be the first nuclear-powered airliner? (adapted from BBC)

A **supersonic airliner** that flies at three times the **speed of sound** – and runs on nuclear fusion. Stephen Dowling investigates the challenges of making **airliners** run on atomic power. It would take you in no small comfort – luxuriously so, if you're in **first class** – at **speeds** approaching 2,300 mph (3,680 km/h), the Atlantic Ocean racing below your feet. The Flash Falcon is a futuristic **spacecraft** that fills the hole left by the retirement of the Supersonic Concorde in 2003. No **prototypes** have been built though – apart from the design of a "whale-shaped" giant **airliner** BBC Future profiled back in 2014. The giant **aircraft** would carry up to 250 **passengers** at three times the speed of sound.

Food for Thought and Quotations (about 500 words)

Advantages of public transportation

Public transport (also known as public transportation, public transit, or mass transit) is a shared passenger-transport service available for use by the general public, as distinct from individual modes such as taxicab, carpooling, or hired buses, which are not shared by strangers without a private arrangement. Public transportation is a crucial part of the solution to a nation's economic, energy, and environmental challenges – helping to bring a better quality of life. In increasing numbers, people are using public transportation and local communities are expanding public transit services. Every segment of a western society – individuals, families, communities, and businesses – benefits from public transportation. It provides personal mobility and freedom for people from every walk of life but also economic opportunities. Public transportation has a proven record of reducing congestion. It also saves money, reduces the consumption of fossil fuels and therefore the carbon footprint.

Carpooling and hitch-hiking

Carpooling and hitch-hiking are two unconventional ways of travelling, both have advantages and disadvantages. **Hitchhiking** is mostly preferred by backpacker students, but also ideal for everyone who would like to travel completely free. Hitchhiking is much more spontaneous, it can be attractive for some people, but it is recommended to remain alert: there is no denying that if you don't use your common sense you might get yourself in trouble. However, not everyone would feel comfortable getting into a stranger's car and being driven into the unknown. For those of us who are ready to pay a bit more for the peace of mind, **carpooling** is becoming increasingly popular. It is not completely free, but good for those who would like to save money and have new experiences. Carpooling is similar to hitchhiking in many respects, but is much safer, and conditions of the travelling are more calculable. Carpooling is also environmentally friendly as it reduces carbon emissions and road congestion. The disadvantage is the fact that not always will you be able to find people who would travel the same distance, exactly the same day you're planning your trip for.

Eco-tourism

Ecotourism, also known as ecological tourism, means responsible travel to fragile and protected areas that strive to be low-impact and generally small-scale. It helps educate the traveller; provides funds for conservation; directly benefits the economic development and political empowerment of local communities; and fosters respect for different cultures and for human rights. *Take only memories and leave only footprints* is a very common and telling slogan in protected areas. Tourist destinations are shifting to low carbon emissions following the trend of visitors more focused on being environmentally responsible adopting a sustainable behavior. Ecotourism typically involves travel to destinations where flora, fauna, and cultural heritage are the primary attractions. Ecotourism is intended to offer tourists insight into the impact of human beings on the environment, and to foster a greater appreciation of our natural habitats. Unfortunately, the overall effect of ecotourism is negative, since philanthropic aspirations generally give way to hard-nosed immediate self-interest.

Travelling broadens the mind

Recent studies suggest that taking a gap year or studying abroad can positively influence your brain to make you more outgoing and open to new ideas. The benefits of travelling are well documented. First, those who have lived abroad are more creative. Travelling and living abroad can also affect the way we interact with people: those who studied abroad were generally higher in extraversion than those who chose not to travel during their university years: the travellers were likely to enjoy being around other people more than being alone. Last, but not least: challenging new experiences can boost cognitive health, as when your brain is exposed to an environment that is novel and complex, it reacts by forming new connections as it tries to categorize the new and unusual stimuli. This keeps memory active in a similar way as taking up a new hobby or learning a language.

"Travel is fatal to prejudice, bigotry, and narrow-mindedness, and many of our people need it sorely on these accounts. Broad, wholesome, charitable views of men and things cannot be acquired by vegetating in one little corner of the earth all one's lifetime."
Mark Twain

Chapter B
Education

Vocabulary list

SCHOOL	**L'ÉCOLE**
kindergarten	un jardin d'enfant
a daycare centre (GB) / center (US)	une crèche, une garderie
a nursery	une crèche
a nursery school	une école maternelle
a preschool child	un élève de maternelle
pre-school education	l'éducation pré-scolaire
a state school	une école publique
a public school	un collège privé (GB) / une école publique (US)
a preparatory school	une école primaire privée (GB)
a private school / a fee-paying school	une école privée (US)
a form / a grade	une classe / un niveau
a day school	un externat
a boarding school	un internat
a boarder	un interne
a refectory, a dining hall	un réfectoire
a vocational school	un lycée professionnel
compulsory / mandatory education	la scolarité obligatoire
a boys' school / a girls' school	une école de garçons / de filles
a charter school	une école à charte (une école sous contrat pédagogique)
a high school	un établissement secondaire (GB) / un lycée (US)
mixed / co-educational (co-ed-	mixte
a state-run school	une école gérée par l'État
denominational	religieux / confessionnel
non-denominational	laïque

HIGHER EDUCATION	**L'ENSEIGNEMENT SUPÉRIEUR**
a college	une faculté / un établissement d'enseignement supérieur
further education	la formation continue
higher education	l'enseignement supérieur
a credit / ECTS (European credit transfer system)	des crédits ECTS
a polytechnic	un IUT
a state / private university	une université publique / privée
an engineering school	une école d'ingénieur
a business school	une école de commerce
a medical school	une école de médecine
a law school	une faculté de droit
an arts college	une faculté de lettres et de sciences humaines
an art college	une école des beaux-arts

a graduate school (US)	un troisième cycle
to register / to enrol (enroll US)	s'inscrire / s'enregistrer
to read a subject	étudier une matière
to major in (US)	se spécialiser dans
the finals	les examens de fin d'année
tuition fees	les frais de scolarité
tuition	les cours / la scolarité
a lecture	un cours magistral
a seminar	un séminaire
practical work, lab work	travaux pratiques (TP)
a practical lesson	travaux dirigés (TD)
a lecture room	un amphithéâtre
to attend a lecture	assister à une conférence
a laboratory	un laboratoire
research facilities	les équipements de recherche
a university library	une bibliothèque universitaire
a grant	une bourse d'études (selon revenus)
a scholarship	une bourse d'études (selon résultats)
a fellowship	une allocation de recherche
a Master's degree	une maîtrise
a PhD (Doctor of Philosophy)	un doctorat (toutes matières)
a schoolmaster / a teacher	un instituteur, un enseignant, un professeur
a professor	un professeur d'université
a fellow / a lecturer (GB)	un chargé de cours / un maître de conférence

SUBJECTS	**LES MATIÈRES**
the curriculum	le programme scolaire
the syllabus	le programme d'une matière
a field / a subject	une discipline / une matière
the three Rs (reading, writing, arithmetics)	les trois compétences fondamentales (lecture, écriture, arithmétique)
algebra	l'algèbre
art / arts	les arts plastiques / les lettres
biology	la biologie
business studies	les études de commerce
chemistry	la chimie
coding	le code, la programmation
computer sciences, computer studies	l'informatique
economics	les sciences économiques
English studies	Études de la littérature et des civilisations anglophones
a foreign language	une langue étrangère
a classical language	une langue morte
a modern language	une langue vivante
geography / history	géographie / histoire

grammar	la grammaire
the humanities	les lettres
linguistics	la linguistique
literature	la littérature
mathematics / maths	les mathématiques
musical education	la musique
philosophy	la philosophie
P.E. (physical education)	l'EPS / l'éducation sportive
physics	les sciences physiques
psychology / sociology	psychologie / sociologie
R.E. (religious education)	l'éducation religieuse

SCHOOLWORK	**TRAVAUX SCOLAIRES**
schoolwork	le travail scolaire
homework	le travail personnel / les devoirs / des recherches
prep work	le travail en amont, le travail de préparation
a course / a lesson	un cours / une leçon
an activity	une activité
a drill / an exercise	un entraînement / un exercice
an assignment / an essay	un devoir / une rédaction
a paper	une dissertation, un devoir écrit
a dictation	une dictée
to add / subtract / multiply / divide	les quatre opérations de base

METHODS	**LES MÊTHODES**
teaching / to teach	l'enseignement / enseigner
education / to educate	l'éducation / éduquer
e-learning	l'enseignement en ligne / la formation en ligne
learning / to learn	l'apprentissage / apprendre
teaching material / tools	les documents / outils pédagogiques
group teaching	la pédagogie différenciée
student-centered approach	approche mettant l'élève au centre de l'apprentissage
MOOCs (Massive Open Online Courses	les MOOCs, cours en ligne ouverts tous et gratuits
to stream	répartir en fonction du niveau
the top / middle / bottom stream	le groupe fort / moyen / faible, le 1er, 2e, 3e tiers
cramming / to cram	le bachotage / bachoter
a remedial course	un cours de soutien
individual tuition	un cours particulier
to revise	réviser
a review card	une fiche de révisions
to concentrate	se concentrer
to motivate	motiver / encourager

to double-check	se relire, vérifier
to proofread	relire
to volunteer	se porter volontaire

SCHOOL LIFE	**LA VIE À L'ÉCOLE**
a classroom	une salle de classe
a blackboard / a smart board	un tableau noir / un tableau numérique
chalk / a marker	la craie / un marqueur
a desk	un bureau
a row	une rangée
the staffroom	la salle des professeurs
the sickroom	l'infirmerie
the cloakroom	le vestiaire
the playground	la cour de récréation
the gym	le gymnase
the dormitory	le dortoir
an exercise book	un cahier (d'exercices)
a textbook	un manuel
a pen / a fountain pen	un stylo / un stylo plume
a felt pen	un crayon feutre
a highlighter	un surligneur
a calculator	une calculatrice
the headmaster (mistress / the principal	le chef d'établissement

SUCCESS AND FAILURE	**LES SUCCÈS ET LES ÉCHECS**
to assess / assessment	évaluer / l'évaluation
to achieve (a goal) / achievement	atteindre un objectif / la réussite
to reach (a level)	atteindre un niveau
to master a subject	maîtriser un sujet
to know	savoir, connaître
know-how	le savoir-faire
knowledgeable, learned	savant, instruit
educated, well-read	cultivé
studious, industrious	studieux
a skill, a competence	une aptitude, une compétence
to concentrate on / to focus on	se concentrer sur
to be proficient at	être fort / être très doué en...
to be gifted for	avoir un don pour / en
a whizz kid	un surdoué
a bookworm	un rat de bibliothèque
bright / clever / smart / intelligent	intelligent
sharp	vif
a performance	un résultat
to hand in a paper	remettre un devoir
to mark papers	corriger des copies / des travaux
the average / on average	la moyenne / en moyenne

a requirement	une exigence / un niveau requis
to rate / a score, a mark	noter / une note
a quiz	un jeu de questions-réponses
a multiple choice questionnaire	un QCM (questionnaire à choix multiples)
to fill in the blanks	compléter l'exercice à trous
to have / take an exam	passer un examen
a test / to test	une interrogation, un contrôle / évaluer, contrôler
to pass an exam	réussir un examen
to examine / an exam(ination)	interroger / un examen
to graduate	obtenir son diplôme / sa qualification
a diploma, a degree	un diplôme
to get a degree	obtenir un diplôme
a law degree	un diplôme en droit
to succeed in doing sth	réussir à faire qqch
to succeed at a test	réussir à un examen
to sail through	réussir avec aisance / haut la main
to be a credit to	faire honneur à / être exemplaire pour
a repeater	un redoublant
a dropout / to drop out of school	un élève qui abandonne / abandonner ses études
a dunce	un cancre
dull	médiocre, terne
to fail / to get a fail / to flunk	échouer / être recalé
impairment	des troubles, des difficultés
behavioural difficulties	les troubles du comportement
monitoring / to monitor	le suivi, le contrôle / suivre
the lack of memory	mauvaise mémoire
memory skills	capacité de mémorisation

DISCIPLINE	**LA DISCIPLINE**
a disciplinary committee	un conseil de discipline
to suspend / suspension	exclure temporairement
to be expelled / expulsion	être renvoyé / le renvoi
to punish	punir
detention	la retenue, la colle
disciplined / obedient	obéissant
to cheat	tricher
to talk back	répondre avec insolence
to play truant	faire l'école buissonnière
to misbehave	mal se comporter
slapdash work	ni fait ni à faire / bâclé
talkative, chatty	bavard
boisterous	turbulent
bullying	le harcèlement
disruptive	perturbateur

unmanageable	ingérable
truancy / absenteeism	l'absentéisme

BONUS	**BONUS**
*to go to the **school** of hard knocks*	aller à l'école de la vie
*of the old **school***	de la vieille école
***school** days*	les années d'école
***mark** my words!*	Crois-moi !
*to be an easy **mark***	être une bonne poire
***mark** you + phrase*	N'empêche que…
*to **mark** one's place in a book*	marquer la page
*to be **marked** as*	être considéré comme
*to **make** the grade*	se montrer à la hauteur
*to **grade** up / **grade** down*	relever / abaisser (une note)
*in recent **memory***	de mémoire d'homme
*to have a good **memory** for faces*	être physionomiste
*from **memory***	de mémoire
*a writer of great **skill***	un écrivain de talent / talentueux
***skills** shortage*	manque de main d'œuvre qualifiée
*his past is an open **book***	il n'a rien à cacher sur son passé
*to throw the **book** at sb*	passer un savon à qqn
*to be in sb's good **books***	être dans les petits papiers de qqn
*here's one for the **book***	on s'en souviendra !
*don't judge a **book** by its cover*	l'habit ne fait pas le moine / ne pas se fier aux apparences
*in my **book***	À mon avis, selon moi
*a **dunce** cap*	un bonnet d'âne
slow on the uptake	qui ne comprend pas vite, long à la détente
*dim-**witted***	lent d'esprit

Translation: English-to-French exercise

- The subjects covered vary depending on the grade and the subject matter covered by the curriculum.
- Reference is made to French conventions for naming classes: 6e is equivalent to British Year 7, 2de corresponds to Year 11, 1re is equivalent to British lower sixth, terminale to British upper sixth.
- Our academic requirements are to educate and train undergraduates, graduates, and postgraduates in an environment that mandates a vigorous pursuit of research.

- Three "Ivy League" institutions now have women presidents. The eight private colleges and universities in the Ivy League are considered among the most prestigious of all higher education institutions in the United States.
- Within a gap year, typically between the end of high school and the beginning of post-secondary education, young people take time to travel and work.

Adapted press excerpts (about 400 words)

Excerpt 1 – English universities to raise tuition fees for first time since they trebled (adapted from *The Guardian*)

Universities in England have started telling potential **students** that their **tuition fees** will go up across the **board** from next year, the first rise since fees were nearly trebled to £10,000 in 2019. Manchester and Durham are among **universities** already listing annual **undergraduate** fees as rising to £9,250. A government spokesperson said: "The ability to maintain fees in line with inflation has been in place since 2004, and is subject to regulations." This is not part of the higher education and **research** bill. "The **teaching** excellence framework will allow universities to maintain fees in line with inflation only if they meet a quality bar, as set out in the recent higher education white paper."

Excerpt 2 – Grit: The power of passion and perseverance (adapted from Ted Talks)

I went to **teach** seventh **graders maths** in the New York City **public schools**. And like any teacher, I made **quizzes** and **tests**. I gave out **homework assignments**. When the work came back, I calculated **grades**. [...] I came to the conclusion that what we need in **education** is a much better **understanding** of **students** and **learning**. In education, the one thing we know how to measure best is **IQ**. But what if doing well in **school** and in life depends on much more than your **ability** to **learn** quickly and easily? **Grit** is passion and **perseverance** for very **long-term goals**. Grit is having **stamina**. Grit is living life like it's a marathon, not a sprint.

Excerpt 3 – Teaching the teachers (adapted from *The Economist*)

Great **teaching** has long been seen as an **innate skill**. But reformers are showing that the best teachers are made, not born. Teachers must impart **knowledge** and **critical thinking**. Those who do so embody six aspects of great teaching. The first and second concern their **motives** and how they get on with their **peers**. The third and fourth involve using time well, fostering good behaviour and high

expectations. Most important, though, are the fifth and sixth aspects, high-quality **instruction** and so-called "**pedagogical content knowledge**" – a blend of subject knowledge and teaching **craft**. "I don't teach physics; I teach my pupils how to learn physics." for example.

Excerpt 4 – Why disciplining kids can be so tricky for parents and teachers (adapted from TheConversation.com)

How does **discipline** get in the way of **learning**? If most of what children hear are teachers trying to get everyone to **sit still**, be **quiet** and **listen** to **directions**, what does this **teach** them about learning and being a **learner**. In my work on how young children use their **ability** to **make decisions** at school, I find that most describe learning as **following directions**. "Learning is quiet." Children often see **obedience** as the point of school. In fact, **teachers** and **students** both tell me that they can tell children are learning when their "eyes are on the teacher." Of course, just because a child is obedient doesn't mean they are learning.

Food for Thought and Quotations (about 500 words)

British and American school systems, in a nutshell

The British system starts out rather similar to the US System: pre-school / nursery school. Then Year 1 corresponds to 1st Grade, and so on (Primary / Elementary school). After 6 or 5 years pupils start secondary school / junior high school. It corresponds to Year 7 to Year 11 in Britain, at the end of which you take a GCSE examination (General Certificate of Secondary Education), before carrying on with the 6th Form in order to take the A-Level examination, at age 18. In the US it starts with 6th to 8th grade (age 11-14). Afterwards, from 9th to 12th grade (high school), a pupil is termed a freshman when he is a ninth grader. In the 10th grade you are a sophomore, 11th you are a junior, and 12th a senior, then aged about 18 and taking the examination termed SATs (Scholastic Aptitude Test, intended to forecast a student's ability to perform in his or her freshman year at college) or ACTs (Scholastic Assessment Test, a standardized test to determine a high school graduate's preparation for college-level work), for selection to an American university. Then students may then start the admission process to university or college, where a similar designation applies.

Top universities in the UK

The University of Oxford and the University of Cambridge take the top two spots, while some of the best universities in London complete the top five. Two of the most prestigious universities in the world, Oxford and Cambridge attract top scholars and students to their colleges and halls. Undergraduates and postgraduates belong to a college and often live in the college building or college-owned accommodation. Social life and recreational activities are also part of these universities. Getting a place at such a prestigious university as an undergraduate is extremely competitive; the acceptance rate is less than 25 per cent and more than half of rejected candidates go on to receive A grades for all their final school exams. Also, Imperial College London is consistently ranked as one of the best universities in the world for science, technology, engineering, medicine and business. University College London (UCL) was the first university in England to admit students irrespective of class, race or religion, and the first to admit women on equal terms with men, following the educational philosophy of Jeremy Bentham – the British university's "spiritual founder".

Top universities in the US

The Ivy League refers to eight universities of the East coast, most founded before the American Revolution of 1776, among which Columbia University (New York City), Harvard University (Cambridge, Massachusetts), the University of Pennsylvania (Philadelphia), Princeton University (Princeton, New Jersey), and Yale University (New Haven, Connecticut). Ivy League schools are generally viewed as some of the most prestigious, and are ranked among the best universities worldwide."Planting the ivy" was a customary class day ceremony in many colleges in the 1800s. Other prestigious universities can be found on the West coast: UCLA, the University of California (Los Angeles), the University of California (Berkeley). The California Institute of Technology (CalTech, Pasadena near Los Angeles) and Stanford University (Palo Alto, near San Francisco) both specialize in new technologies. Their main Eastern challenger is the M.I.T (Massachusetts Institute of Technology) which cultivates a strong entrepreneurial culture and an innovative educational model based on science, technology, and practical application of science.

Tuition costs in the UK and in the US

State universities – the great engine room of US higher education – have a two-tier fees system, so that students living in the state pay much less than those from outside. Many state university students live at home, so they avoid all the extra costs for accommodation. The annual cost is around $10,000 per year, compared to an average $60,000 annual fee for a private college (bed and board included in this case). In the UK, fees are, in effect, flat – with more or less all universities charging £9,000 (much less in Scotland, about £4,000). But families are often taken aback at the separate cost of accommodation and living costs. All in all, costs in the US and the UK are comparable, particularly with the fall of the £ after Brexit.

The average debt of the students is considered unsustainable, and most of the middle-class families now cannot afford paying for higher studies.

"*Where the press is free and every man is able to read, all is safe.*" Thomas Jefferson

"Again, you can't connect the dots looking forward; you can only connect them looking backward. So you have to trust that the dots will somehow connect in your future. You have to trust in something – your gut, destiny, life, karma, whatever. This approach has never let me down, and it has made all the difference in my life." Steve Jobs

Chapter C
The media

Vocabulary list

THE PRESS	**LA PRESSE**
the print media / the press	la presse
a newspaper / a paper	un journal
a daily / weekly / monthly	un quotidien / hebdomadaire / mensuel
a tabloid	un quotidien populaire / tabloïd
a broadsheet	un journal de qualité
a copy	un exemplaire
the circulation	le tirage
the quality press	la presse de qualité
the gutter press	la presse à scandale
the popular press	la presse à grand tirage
a magazine	un magazine
a journal	une revue spécialisée
a rag	une feuille de chou
a newspaper cutting / press clipping	une coupure de journal
a press tycoon	un magnat de la presse
a journalist / journalism	un journaliste / le journalisme
a commentator / news analyst	un commentateur
a freelance	un pigiste
a reporter	un reporter
a muckraker	un dénicheur de scandales
a foreign correspondent	un correspondant à l'étranger
a columnist	un chroniqueur
a press officer	un attaché de presse
a press release	un communiqué de presse
a press agency / news agency	une agence de presse
a headline	un gros titre
the editorial line / policy	la ligne éditoriale
a press article	un article de presse
a leading article / an editorial	un éditorial
a column	une colonne / une chronique
a feature article	un article de fond
to hit the headlines	faire la une / les gros titres
media coverage	la couverture médiatique
media hype	le matraquage / battage médiatique
the chief editor	le rédacteur en chef
the publisher	l'éditeur
the readership	le lectorat / les lecteurs

PRESS CONTENTS	**CONTENUS DES JOURNAUX**
a heading / a sub-heading	un titre / un sous-titre
a section	une rubrique
a box	un encadré
a graph	un graphique

a chart (bar chart / pie chart)	un diagramme (histogramme / en camembert)
a photograph	une photographie
a caption	une légende
a cartoon	un dessin (humoristique)
an insert	un encart
a topic	un sujet
an issue	une question / un numéro (parution)
a subscription	un abonnement
personal ads	les petites annonces
the business section	les pages économie
obituary	la rubrique nécrologique
to investigate	mener une enquête
to cover an event	couvrir un événement
to stalk	traquer
a leak / to reveal, to disclose	une fuite / révéler
a prejudice / biased	un préjugé / tendancieux, partial
scaremongering	l'alarmisme
to tamper / fake	falsifier / faux, truqué
to manipulate	manipuler
trustworthy / unbiased	digne de confiance / impartial, objectif
sensationalism	la quête du sensationnel
reliable / unreliable	fiable / non fiable
press freedom	la liberté de la presse
censorship	la censure
to ban / a ban	interdire / une interdiction
to scoop	publier en exclusivité
to sensitize public opinion	sensibiliser l'opinion publique

RADIO	**LA RADIO**
a radio set	un poste de radio, un transistor
an aerial	une antenne
short / long wave	les ondes (courtes / longues)
FM (frequency modulation)	la modulation de fréquence, la FM
interference	les parasites, les interférences
to emit, to broadcast	émettre
a radio announcement	une annonce
the audience	les auditeurs
a news bulletin	un bulletin d'informations
a news flash	un flash info
on the radio	à la radio
an independent local radio station	une radio libre
a pirate station	une radio pirate
state-owned radio station	une radio publique
a commercial station	une radio privée

TELEVISION	LA TÉLÉVISION
a television set, a TV set, the tube	un poste de télévision / la télé
a home cinema projector	un projecteur vidéo
a 3-D television set	un téléviseur 3D
cable TV / satellite TV	la TV par câble / satellite
the telly	la télé
a screen	un écran
a DVD player	un lecteur de DVD
to record / to video	enregistrer
to broadcast / to air	émettre / diffuser un programme
a studio	un studio
a programme (GB) / a program (US)	une émission
a live show	une émission en direct
broadcasting	la diffusion
a channel / to channel-hop, to zap	une chaîne / zapper
a network	un réseau de chaînes de TV ou radio
to present / a presenter, announcer	présenter / un présentateur
the newsman / newswoman	un présentateur de journal TV
an anchorman(woman) / a news anchor	un présentateur d'informations
a host	un animateur
to report on	faire un reportage sur
the weather forecast	les prévisions météorologiques
a sports broadcast	une retransmission d'événement sportif
reality TV	la télé réalité
a buzz, a media craze	un buzz, un déferlement médiatique
a game show	un jeu télévisé
a talkshow	un débat
a soap opera	un feuilleton
a series	une série
an episode	un épisode
the main character	le personnage principal
the cast / casting	la distribution
a commercial / an advertisement (an ad)	une publicité
an infomercial	une publicité informative
prime time	la période de forte audience
on the air / off the air	à l'antenne / hors antenne
infotainment	mélange d'information et de divertissement, info-spectacle
the ratings	l'audimat, la mesure d'audience
a couch potato	un pantouflard (devant la TV)
a sitcom	une comédie de situation / un sitcom
subtitles	les sous-titres
dubbing	le doublage son
the score	la bande-son (écrite sur papier)
the soundtrack	la bande-son (piste sonore)

TELEPHONE	**LE TÉLÉPHONE**
a telephone / a videophone	un téléphone fixe / un vidéophone
a smartphone / a cellphone (US)	un smartphone / un téléphone portable (US)
a cardphone / a phonecard / a prepaid phone card	un téléphone à carte / une télécarte (carte de téléphone) / carte prépayée
a public payphone	un téléphone public
a phonebooth	une cabine téléphonique
the directory	l'annuaire
to look up a number	rechercher un numéro
to phone / to telephone someone	téléphoner / appeler qqn
to dial a number	composer un numéro
a landline / mobile number	un numéro de téléphone fixe / de portable
a local call	un appel local
a long-distance call	un appel national
an international call	un appel international
a conference call	un appel en conférence
the area code GB / call sign (zip code) US	l'indicatif (le code postal)
the cord / cordless	le fil du téléphone / sans fil
an earpiece / earphones	une oreillette / des écouteurs
a hands-free kit	un kit mains libres
a touchscreen	un écran tactile
a battery	une batterie
to charge / discharge	charger / décharger
no service	pas de réception
an answering machine / answerphone	un répondeur
to leave a message	laisser un message
to cut off	couper
to hold the line / the call-waiting	rester en ligne / le signal d'appel
to call back	rappeler
to pick up / to lift the phone	décrocher
to hang up / to ring off / to put down	raccrocher
engaged / busy	(ligne) occupée
a text message / to text	un SMS / envoyer un message
ex-directory	sur liste rouge
to chat	discuter, chatter
an app	une appli(cation)
to connect / a connection	connecter / une connexion
a calendar / a diary	un calendrier / agenda
a timer / an alarm-clock	un chronomètre / un réveil
a fixed rate / a subscription / a (monthly) deal / package / plan	un forfait téléphonique
a two-year agreement	un engagement de deux ans
a hotline	une assistance à distance, une *hotline*

BONUS	**BONUS**
to come of the press	sortir dans les journaux
*to pass something for **press***	donner le bon à tirer à qqch
*to **press** on with*	faire avancer / passer à
*the **press** box / gallery*	la tribune de la presse
a press	une maison d'édition
*to go from **rags** to riches*	connaître une ascension spectaculaire
*to lose one's **rags***	sortir de ses gonds
*to **leak** out*	être divulgué
*to **show** off*	faire le fier / la fière / l'intéressant(e)
*to **show** sb round*	faire visiter
*to **show** up*	être visible, se manifester, ressortir
*to **show** somebody up*	faire honte à qqn
*a **show** of hands*	un vote à mains levées
*the **show** business*	l'industrie du spectacle
*to **show**case*	servir de tremplin à qqn
*no need to **broadcast** it!*	pas la peine de le crier sur les toits
*to **hang up on** someone*	**raccrocher** au nez
*(to leave the **phone**) off the hook*	(laisser le téléphone) décroché
*to be off the **hook***	être tiré d'affaire
Can you put me through to...	Pouvez-vous me **passer**... ?
*to **chat** sb up /... to obtain sth*	draguer qqn / baratiner
*to make / to pay a **call** on sb*	rendre visite à qqn
*it was a close **call***	c'était de justesse
*this **calls** for a celebration*	ça se fête
*to **call** sth forth*	susciter
*let's **call** the whole thing off*	laissons tomber
*to **call** in sth / sth in*	rappeler, demander le retour de, faire appel à
*the **call**-out charges*	les frais de déplacement
*he **phoned** in sick*	il a appelé pour dire qu'il était malade
*a **phone** pest*	un auteur d'appels anonymes malveillants
*So, what's the **buzz**?*	Alors, quoi de neuf ?

Translation: English-to-French exercise

- He bursts out laughing as he remembers his first broadcast in June 1999 at the Beeb.
- A potential audience of 25 million people received information via television, radio broadcasts and the Internet.
- Media campaigns on radio and television have spread messages allowing for a better knowledge and appreciation of the values of tolerance.

- Leading television, radio and streaming news organizations around the world frequently turn to audience ratings experts for objective, accurate analysis of consumer behaviour.
- Terms such as "information superhighway," "information revolution," and "information economy" are used routinely to illustrate the profound role of information in modern societies.

Adapted press excerpts (about 400 words)

Excerpt 1 – Regional newspapers – Stop press (adapted from *The Economist*)

When Mike Brooke started out in **journalism** in the 1960s, regional **newsrooms** were **buzzing**. The **paper** he worked on had a dozen **reporters** to track down **stories**. Now he **covers** the **news** by himself in a "**media centre**". Although his organisation **breaks local news** stories **online**, he rarely goes out to do reporting. **Local papers** used to be "the pillar of the community", he sighs, but now mostly just fill space. The past few years have been difficult for the **newspaper** industry. But the decline of **regional** papers, which relied more on now-extinct **classified advertisements**, has been particularly steep. Over the past decade just over 200 **titles** have closed (over half of them free). As well as having fewer journalists, most local papers have scaled back on **sub-editors**, **designers** and **photographers**.

Excerpt 2 – Don't Tell Me What Happens. I'm Recording It (adapted from TheRinger.com)

Both collectively and individually, the experience of **watching TV** in 2016 already feels totally **disconnected** from the experience of watching TV in 1996. People will still want cheap escapism, and something will certainly satisfy that desire. But whatever that something is won't be anything like the television of today. It might be **immersive** and **virtual** (like a Star Trekian holodeck) or it might be **mobile** and **open-sourced** (like a universal YouTube, lodged inside our retinas). But it absolutely won't be small groups of people, sitting together in the living room, staring at a two-dimensional thirty-one-inch rectangle for thirty consecutive minutes, consuming linear content **packaged** by a **cable** company.

Excerpt 3 – The future is a smarter world of dumber devices (adapted from TechCrunch.com)

Prior to the **digitization** of **media** around the end of the 20th century, **electronic devices** were very different from what they are today. Around 1995 I owned a **TV**, a **VHS player**, a **Walkman**, a **Discman**, a **cordless phone**, a **desktop computer**, a **CD player**, a **Hi-Fi** and more. Every new year would bring some new technology – in 1997 a minidisc player, in 1998 a LaserDisc and in 2000 a DVD player. This was the era of "peak device." Digitization changed all that; we moved to an age where physical media only got simpler. My iPod replaced three music devices before my **smartphone** allowed me to throw that away, along with a vast physical music collection.

Excerpt 4 – Some Writing About Writing About TV (adapted from NPR)

Covering a **TV show** can still mean running down what happens in each **episode** for people who didn't see it, but that alone is not **criticism**. It can mean traditional formal **analysis** of each episode, or of a whole **season**, or of a **show** over several seasons, that might not look all that different from **film criticism**. It can mean weekly **podcasts**, or weekly **GIF round-ups**, or video **supercuts**, or weekly content baubles of many other kinds, not all of which constitute criticism. **Coverage** varies in **tone** from serious to comedic, proudly reverent to overtly incendiary. Sometimes it touches on sociopolitical matters; sometimes it's limited to who should have been voted off; sometimes it's all about **camera angles**.

Food for Thought and Quotations (about 500 words)

Printing as the expansion of knowledge

Johannes Gutenberg's invention of the printing press at the end of the Middle-Ages is widely thought of as the origin of mass communication. It marked Western culture's first viable method of disseminating ideas and information from a single source to a large and far-ranging audience. The invention of the printing press depended on cultural and technological revolutions. Only through this could the spread of knowledge occur throughout Europe. In broad terms, print was among the causes of the social, cultural and political changes Europe went through: it was instrumental in bringing about all the major shifts in science, religion, politics, but also education, privacy and therefore individual rights and gradual awareness of a collective conscience of citizenship. Print, along with spoken language, writing and electronic media, is thought of as one of the markers of key historical shifts in communication that have attended social and intellectual transformation.

The Fourth and Fifth Estates

The expression refers to the force of the news media, especially print journalism. The term is an explicit reference to the separation of powers, for the governance of a state: the Judiciary, the Legislative and the Executive powers. In US English, the phrase "fourth estate" is used to emphasize the independence of the press, while the "fourth branch" suggests that the press is not independent from the government. The Watergate scandal is an illustration of the power of journalism. The cover-up by President Nixon of the break-in into the Democratic headquarters and the bugging of political opponents' offices in the early 1970s led to the President's resignation. More recently, cases such as Wikileaks show that the power of the print media has turned to a more diverse set of actors (bloggers, social media, non-governmental organizations and so on) that can disclose information to the public. This evolution has been termed the Fifth Estate. It is generally admitted that the goal of these forms of power is to move beyond traditional thinking, and propose a broader perspective in which civilians can contribute to the global political change and security.

Quality of the press in the UK

Even though the print media face an unprecedented crisis due to the rising costs of production and the development of the free media, newspaper publication in the UK is still a rather active sector. There are roughly two types of national newspapers: quality papers that cater for the better educated readership, and the popular papers that concentrate on "human interest" stories, often implying sex and scandal. The differences between the two types can be exaggerated, though: both types devote equal amounts of attention to sports; some other distinctions could be made between papers, and the treatment of the topics covered and the prominence of topics are also to be taken into account. Another distinction, also simplistic, refers to the format of publishing: either tabloid (Daily Mail, Express, Mirror, for a rather popular readership, broadsheet (Independent, Times) or Berliner (Guardian) for a more educated readership, emphasizing a traditional approach to news and an in-depth coverage and a sober tone in articles and editorials.

Texting as a potential language killer?

Writing was invented about six thousand years ago, whereas language probably traces back to a hundred thousand years. Writing takes time, much more time than speaking. It is today natural to wish to write in a spontaneous fashion. Back in the old days, there was no mechanism to reproduce the speed of conversation. But texting and instant messaging succeed in doing so: in its economy, spontaneity and even vulgarity, texting can be considered as a new kind of talking, with its own grammar and phonetic conventions. Language works unconsciously, and the meaning of words or the spelling rules change according to people's needs, and are uncontrollable. Nobody can today affirm that texting is a language killer, since it is a language creation in progress. The simplification it implies may be as much a scourge as an asset for spontaneity.

"What the mass media offers is not popular art, but entertainment which is intended to be consumed like food, forgotten, and replaced by a new dish." W.H. Auden, *The Dyer's Hand*

"Most people gaze neither into the past nor the future; they explore neither truth nor lies. They gaze at the television." Thom Yorke

Chapter D
The Internet

Vocabulary list

COMPUTERS	**L'INFORMATIQUE**
a laptop	un ordinateur portable
a desktop computer	un ordinateur de salon
a tablet	une tablette
a PC (personal computer)	un ordinateur personnel
a keyboard	un clavier
a key	une touche
a shortcut	un raccourci clavier
a screen	un écran
the display	l'affichage
a monitor	un moniteur
a mouse	une souris
a touch pad / keypad	un clavier numérique / un pavé tactile
the cursor	le curseur
an application	une application
to back up, to save	sauvegarder
a CD or DVD writer	un graveur
a disk drive	un lecteur de disque
a USB key / stick	une clé USB
a printer	une imprimante
a wireless router	un routeur sans fil
a power cable / a power cord	un câble d'alimentation
a cable	un câble
a hard drive	un disque dur
loudspeakers	des haut-parleurs
to plug in / to plug out, to unplug	brancher / débrancher
to switch on / off – to turn on / off	allumer / éteindre
to start up	démarrer
an operating system	un système d'exploitation
to restart / to reboot	redémarrer / réinitialiser
a directory	un répertoire
a file	un fichier
a folder	un dossier
a document	un document
to merge	fusionner
hardware	le matériel informatique
software / a software application	un logiciel
a network	un réseau
the space bar	la barre espace
to type	taper (à la machine, sur son clavier)
to drag and drop	glisser-déposer
to copy / cut / paste	copier / couper / coller
processor speed	la vitesse d'un processeur
memory	la mémoire

a word processor	un traitement de texte
a database	une base de données
a spreadsheet	un tableur
a slide show	un diaporama
lower / upper case letter	la touche minuscule / majuscule
a geek	un passionné d'informatique

MAIL	**LES COURRIERS ÉLECTRONIQUES**
an email / to email	un courriel, courrier électronique / envoyer un message électronique
an email address	une adresse électronique
@ / at	arobase
a screen name / the username	le pseudo / un nom d'utilisateur
a password	un mot de passe
to reply	répondre
to forward	transférer
an attachment	une pièce jointe
a chatroom	un salon de « chat »
a message board	un forum de discussion
a mailing list	une liste de diffusion
spam	messages indésirables / *spam* / pourriel
instant messaging	une messagerie instantanée
an avatar	un avatar
to twitter	gazouiller (oiseau)
a facebook	un trombinoscope
a snap	un instantané
what's up	ça va ?

(THE) INTERNET	**(L')INTERNET**
the internet, the web	l'internet, le web
a website	un site internet, un site web
broadband internet	l'internet haut débit
an ISP (internet service provider)	un FAI (fournisseur d'accès à Internet)
a firewall	un pare-feu
wireless internet	l'internet sans fil
to download	télécharger
to scroll up / down	faire défiler vers le haut / le bas
to log in – on / out – off	ouvrir / fermer une session / se (dé)connecter
to be online / offline	être en ligne, connecté / hors ligne, déconnecté
a blog (web log) / a wiki	un blogue / un wiki
a blogger	un blogueur / une blogueuse
to click	cliquer
a browser	un navigateur
to browse / to surf the internet	naviguer sur / consulter internet, surfer

a search engine	un moteur de recherche
the home page	la page d'accueil
a link (hyperlink)	un lien (hypertexte)
a bookmark	un signet / un favori, un marque-page
the newsfeed	le fil d'actualité
to access the internet	accéder à Internet
adware	un logiciel publicitaire
a domain name	un nom de domaine
hosting	l'hébergement
an IP address	une adresse IP
online posting	la mise en ligne
an massive multiplayer online game (MMOG)	un jeu en réseau multijoueurs
peer-to-peer network	un poste-à-poste / pair-à-pair
a platform	une plate-forme
to podcast	podcaster / balladodiffuser, mettre à disposition sur un site internet des fichiers téléchargeables audio ou vidéo
a pop-up window	une fenêtre contextuelle, fenêtre pop-up
privacy settings	les paramètres de confidentialité
a secure access	un accès sécurisé
social networking	le réseautage social, le fait de se construire un réseau social
a social network	un réseau social
to sort out	trier
a viewer / a player	un afficheur, une visionneuse / un lecteur
embedded	imbriqué, incrusté, intégré
a web conference	une cyberconférence
a webcam	une webcaméra, une webcam
FAQ: frequently asked questions	FAQ : foire aux questions

CONCERNS	**INQUIÉTUDE**
cyberbullying	l'intimidation / le harcèlement sur internet
cybercrime	le crime sur internet
cyberstalking	harcèlement moral sur internet
cyber-harassment	le harcèlement sur internet
a hacker	un pirate de l'internet
to hide	masquer
a fake ID	fausse identité
illegal downloading	le téléchargement illégal
a warning / a fine	un avertissement / une amende
internet safety	la sécurité sur Internet
an online predator	un prédateur en ligne
a virus	un virus informatique
antivirus software	un antivirus
a trojan horse	un cheval de Troie
a worm	un ver informatique

phishing	le hameçonnage (par courriel)
plagiarism	le plagiat
a patent	un brevet
copyright violation	violation du droit d'auteur
a flame, a troll	message obscène et violent
a griefer, a troll	un cyber-intimidateur, un rageur, un troll (personne)
identity theft	usurpation d'identité
a malware	un logiciel malveillant
a spyware	un logiciel espion
to crash a site	mettre un site hors d'usage
to track sb down	traquer, localiser, retrouver qqn
to crack down on	réprimer

E-POLITICS	**POLITIQUE NUMÉRIQUE**
the digital divide	la fracture numérique
e-government	le service d'information gouvernemental en ligne
e-petition	une pétition en ligne
hacktivism	le cyber-activisme / cyber-militantisme
netspionage	le net-espionnage
tracking	suivi, repérage, localisation
net neutrality	la neutralité du net
netroots	cyber-campagne politique
promoted tweets / posts	liens sponsorisés
targeted advertising	la publicité ciblée
transparency	la transparence
a virtual community	une communauté virtuelle
a cyber-cascade	un effet domino sur Internet
cyberwar	la guerre informatique
cyberdefence (US defense)	la cyber-défense

BONUS: E-SLANG	**BONUS**
a selfie	*a photograph that one has taken of oneself, typically with a smartphone or webcam and uploaded to a social media website*
to twerk	*dance to popular music in a sexually provocative manner involving thrusting hip movements and a low, squatting stance*
a phablet	*a smartphone having a screen which is intermediate in size between that of a typical smartphone and a tablet computer*
derp	*used as a substitute for speech regarded as meaningless or stupid, or to comment on a foolish or stupid action.*

to unlike	*withdraw one's liking or approval of (a web page or posting on a social media website that one has previously liked)*
srsly	*seriously*
a tweet	*a posting made on the social media website Twitter*
to photobomb	*spoil a photograph of (a person or thing) by unexpectedly appearing in the camera's field of view as the picture is taken, typically as a prank or practical joke*
w00t / woot	*(especially in electronic communication) used to express elation, enthusiasm, or triumph*
to sext	*send (someone) sexually explicit photographs or messages via mobile phone*
OMG (Oh! my God!)	*(exclamation) used to express surprise, excitement, disbelief, etc.*
a hashtag	*a word or phrase preceded by a hash sign (#), used on social media sites such as Twitter to identify messages on a specific topic*
to unfriend	*remove (someone) from a list of friends or contacts on a social networking website*
to troll	*make a deliberately offensive or provocative online posting with the aim of upsetting someone or eliciting an angry response from them*
AFK	*Away From Keyboard*
AMA	*Ask me anything*
BAE	*Before anyone else*
BBL / BBS	*Be Back Later / Be Back Soon*
BRB	*Be Right Back*
BTW	*By The Way*
DM	*Direct message*
ELI5	*Explain like I'm five*
FML	*F*** my life*
FOMO	*Fear of missing out*
FTFY	*Fixed that for you*
HAGN	*Have A Good Night*
HIFW	*How I feel when*
ICYMI	*In case you missed it*
IDK	*I don't know*
IMO / IMHO	*In my (humble) opinion*
IRL	*In real life*
JSYK	*Just so you know*
KISS	*Keep It Short and Simple*
KIT	*Keep In Touch*
LTNS	*Long Time No See*

MFW / MRW	*My face / reaction when*
NYOB	*None of Your Business*
NSFW / NSFL	*Not safe for work / for life*
PAW	*Parents are watching*
PM	*Private Message*
POS	*Parents Over Shoulder*
SMH / Facepalm	*Shaking my head (in disappointment)*
TL;DR	*Too long, didn't read!*
TTFN	*Ta Ta For Now*
TTYL	*Talk To You Later*
YMMW	*Your mileage may vary*
YOLO	*You only live once*

Translation: English-to-French exercise

- Illegal downloading of music files from the Internet seemed to be undermining the industry to such an extent that there were fears for its survival.
- There is a need for further training of teachers and trainers, in liaison with child protection associations, on using the Internet in the context of school education so as to maintain awareness of the possible risks of the Internet with particular regard to chatrooms and fora.
- Google has its own privacy policy.
- The internet has become an essential vector of communication and awareness for companies and their trademarks.
- The content of an individual user's facebook "newsfeed" consists of posts and conversations between other users and groups that have been added specifically by that user.

Adapted press excerpts (about 400 words)

Excerpt 1 – Sky-Fi (adapted from *The Economist*)

A number of companies have bold ambitions to use satellites, drones and balloons to bring the **internet** to the **unconnected**. Ever since the early 1990s, when it moved out of universities and was embraced by the general public, the internet has grown relentlessly. Four technology companies are pursuing ambitious plans that could, eventually, provide reasonably fast, **high-quality connections** to almost everyone on Earth. By providing an easy route to the **internet** at large, local telecoms firms should be able to provide **high-speed**, third- or fourth-generation mobile-phone **coverage** to areas far away from the big cities.

Excerpt 2 – Connected Toys Are Raising Complicated New Privacy Questions (adapted from *The Technology Review*)

Toys and other devices are collecting loads of **data** from children. What could go wrong? Talking toys have come a long way. Now they're **connected** to the Internet, use **speech recognition**, and are raising a host of new questions about the **online privacy** and security of children. **Hackers** have already **targeted** toys. Late last year, digital toy maker Vtech admitted that **cybercriminals** accessed the personal information of 6.4 million children. Researchers have also shown how **hackers** can gain control of **connected** dolls. But **privacy**-related challenges are novel. They are **collecting** new kinds of **data**, and what's at stake if something goes wrong is not always clear.

Excerpt 3 – Does the Snapchat generation even know what Yahoo is? (adapted from *The New Yorker*)

The $4.8-billion acquisition of Yahoo – the **brand** and its **Internet** properties – by Verizon, is a watershed moment in the history of the **Internet**. It caps off an era – **Web 1.0**, for lack of a better term – that will soon be remembered much like telegraphs and rotary phones. Tomorrow's Internet users lavish their attention on Instagram and Snapchat and Spotify. And **software** continues to move in directions far removed from the early **Web**, as new **voice-based interfaces**, on devices such as Amazon's Alexa and Google's Home, train us to think about the Internet beyond **browsers** and **smartphones**. Google's nimbleness, though, made it the preferred tool for the **Web 2.0** era. The rise of the **social Internet**, of Facebook and Twitter, accelerated the decline. I am not sure the Snapchat generation even knows what Yahoo is, and Facebook is already declining.

Excerpt 4 – The future of Online learning is massive! (adapted from *Huffington Post*)

In an ever-changing **technological** age, **acroynms** and **buzzwords** abound. It seems every day there is a new **trend** to follow and **new technology** designed to change the world we live in. Among the latest is **MOOC**, otherwise known as Massive Open Online Courses. **Google** the term and you'll see that widely reputed publications, from Forbes to *The New Yorker*, are reporting on the impact this technology will have on the education sector. MOOCs represent a new form of **online** education which basically consists of online videos of **real-life** lectures. Dubbed "massive" because thousands of students can enrol at a time, it is also deemed open as anyone with an **Internet connection** can **sign up**.

Food for Thought and Quotations (about 500 words)

Net neutrality

Network neutrality is the principle that all Internet traffic should be treated equally, and should flow through the Internet pipeline without interference or discrimination by those who own or are running the pipeline. The idea of an open Internet is the idea that the full resources of the Internet and means to operate it are easily accessible to all individuals and companies. A closed Internet may restrict access to web standards and artificially filter out content. Proponents of net neutrality argue that a neutral net will foster free speech and lead to further democratic participation on the internet, and some activists term it the "First Amendment issue of our time".

Targeted advertising

Advertising is one of the most important and expensive decisions a company has to make. Ensuring that an ad in a specific media is bought effectively and not directed toward the "wrong people" has always been a challenge for marketers. Targeted advertising is a form of advertising that focuses on certain traits of the consumer (social such as race, economic status, sex, age, level of education, income level and employment but also more psychological such as values, personality, attitudes, opinions, lifestyles and interests). In the past twenty years, advertising has gone online and more recently in the mobile setting. The gathering of data collecting includes information about the consumer's interests, location and time but also social networking sites, websites, search engines, which generates a lot of confusion concerning the protection of privacy. Behavioural advertising is today the most common form of targeting used online.

Cyber-bullying (source: stopbullying.gov)

Cyberbullying is bullying that takes place using electronic technology. Electronic technology includes devices and equipment such as cell phones, computers, and tablets as well as communication tools including social media sites, text messages, chat, and websites. Examples of cyberbullying include mean text messages or emails, rumors sent by email or posted on social networking sites, and embarrassing pictures, videos, websites, or fake profiles. Kids who are being cyberbullied are often bullied in person as well. Additionally, kids who are cyberbullied have a harder time getting away from the behavior. Cell phones and computers themselves are not to blame for cyberbullying. Social media sites can be used for positive activities, like connecting kids with friends and family, helping students with school, and for entertainment. But these tools can also be used to hurt people. Whether done in person or through technology, the effects of bullying are similar.

The semantic web – Web 3.0

Web 2.0 is characterized mainly by the ability of users to share information quickly with others, which has been developed into the phenomenon that we call social media. Web 3.0 is semantic: the data will come from the user and the web will essentially adjust to meet the needs of the user. If you search for "computers" for instance, the web will keep in mind your search queries, and if you have been looking for "design", it will adapt future results according to the two criteria. In terms of design, it will have consequences: the webpage will be made more simple and will aggregate various sources, various media on a same pattern. While on a web 2.0 site design was based around drawing attention and persuading audience, the focus on a web 3.0 page is to draw the viewers' eye to the content or other important information on the page. The consequence is that all media will be able to flow in and out of virtual worlds that will be created by the users themselves, through the semantic analysis of their tastes and interests.

"The world's entire scientific and cultural heritage, published over centuries in books and journals, is increasingly being digitized and locked up by a handful of private corporations." Aaron Swartz

"I still love books. Nothing a computer can do can compare to a book. You can't really put a book on the Internet. Three companies have offered to put books by me on the Net, and I said, 'If you can make something that has a nice jacket, nice paper with that nice smell, then we'll talk.' All the computer can give you is a manuscript. People don't want to read manuscripts. They want to read books. Books smell good. They look good. You can press it to your bosom. You can carry it in your pocket." Ray Bradbury

Topic two

Understanding our world

Section 4
Arts, culture and analysis techniques

Chapter A

Beliefs

Vocabulary list

RELIGION	**LA RELIGION**
to believe	croire
faith / faithful / the faithful	la foi / fidèle / les fidèles
a belief	une croyance
worship	le culte
a regular churchgoer	un pratiquant
a god / a goddess	un dieu / une déesse
a denomination	une confession
Buddhism / a Buddhist	le bouddhisme / un bouddhiste
a Christian	un chrétien
a Muslim	un musulman
a Roman Catholic	un catholique
the Roman Catholic Church	l'Église catholique romaine
the Church of England	l'Église anglicane
Anglicans	les Anglicans
fanaticism	le fanatisme
Christianity	le christianisme
the Jewish religion	le judaïsme
an atheist / atheism	un athée / l'athéisme
an agnostic / agnosticism	un agnostique / l'agnosticisme
the Pope	le pape
a priest / to say mass	un prêtre / dire la messe
a monk / a nun	un moine, un frère / une religieuse (nonne)
a bishop / a clergyman	un évêque / un ecclésiastique
the vicar / the curate	le vicaire / le curé
a rabbi	un rabbin
a Freemason / freemasonry	un franc-maçon / la franc-maçonnerie
a free thinker	un libre penseur

ARCHITECTURE	**L'ARCHITECTURE**
an architect / architecture	un architecte / l'architecture
the foundations	les fondations
the walls	les murs
to restore / restoration	restaurer / la restauration
a ruined building / a ruin	un bâtiment en ruines / une ruine
the remains	les vestiges
majestic / lofty	majestueux / élevé, haut
to design / a design, a plan	dessiner, créer, concevoir / un plan
a castle	un château
a fortress	une forteresse
a tower	une tour
a drawbridge	un pont-levis
the battlements	les remparts
a keep / a dungeon	un donjon / un cachot

a Greek temple	un temple grec
well-proportioned	bien proportionné
building materials	les matériaux de construction
a cathedral / a church	une cathédrale / une église
a bell / a belfry	une cloche / un beffroi
a steeple / a dome	un clocher / un dôme
the front	la façade
the portal	le portail
the cloister	le cloître
a rose window	une rosace
a stained-glass window	un vitrail
the choir / the altar	le chœur / l'autel
a monastery	un monastère
a convent	un couvent
an abbey / an abbot	une abbaye / un abbé
functional / aesthetic	fonctionnel / esthétique
a temple	un temple
a mosque	une mosquée

PHILOSOPHY	**LA PHILOSOPHIE**
a philosopher / philosophy	un philosophe / la philosophie
to subscribe to a doctrine	souscrire à une doctrine
to propound a theory	proposer une théorie
to put forward a theory	avancer une théorie
to expound a theory	exposer une théorie
to speculate on / about	spéculer sur
to rephrase a statement	reformuler une déclaration
to presume	présumer
to assume	supposer, présumer
to vindicate a theory	appuyer une théorie
to rule out a hypothesis	écarter une hypothèse
to refute a view	réfuter une position
to undermine a reasoning	saper un raisonnement
to challenge a principle	contester un principe
metaphysics	la métaphysique
dialectics	la dialectique
psychology / a psychologist	la psychologie / un psychologue
essence / matter	l'essence / la matière
a concept / to conceptualise	un concept / conceptualiser
an idea / an ideal	une idée / un idéal
a theory / theoretical	une théorie / théorique
a hypothesis / hypothetical	une hypothèse / hypothétique
Plato, Socrates, Aristotle	Platon, Socrate, Aristote
Epicureanism / an epicurean	l'épicurisme / un épicurien
stoicism / a Stoic	le stoïcisme / un stoïcien
positivism / a positivist	le positivisme / un positiviste

idealism / an idealist	l'idéalisme / un idéaliste
materialism / a materialist	le matérialisme / un matérialiste
empiricism / an empiricist	l'empirisme / un empiriste
existentialism / an existentialist	l'existentialisme / un existentialiste
hedonism / hedonistic	l'hédonisme / hédoniste
realism / rationalism / rational	le réalisme / le rationalisme / rationnel
determinism	le déterminisme
optimism / pessimism	l'optimisme / le pessimisme
deism / a deist	le déisme / un déiste
cartesianism / cartesian	le cartésianisme / cartésien
skepticism (US) / scepticism (UK)	le scepticisme
a skeptic /a sceptic	un sceptique

BELIEFS	**LES CROYANCES**
a legend, a myth	une légende, un mythe
mythical / mythological	mythique / mythologique
legendary	légendaire
the supernatural	le surnaturel
the unknown	l'inconnu
folklore	le folklore
a fairy / a fairytale	une fée / un conte de fées
folk tales	les contes populaires
a fairy godmother	une bonne fée
a magic wand	une baguette magique
black magic	la magie noire
a witch / witchcraft	une sorcière / la sorcellerie
a wizard	un sorcier
a medicine man, a witch doctor	un sorcier de village
a witch hunt	une chasse aux sorcières
a faith healer / faith healing	un guérisseur / la guérison par la foi
a spell / spellbound	un sort / ensorcelé
to cast a spell	jeter un sort
a gipsy	un gitan / une gitane
to tell sb's fortune	prédire l'avenir à qqn
esotericism / esoteric	l'ésotérisme / ésotérique
the occult / occult	les sciences occultes / occulte
voodoo	le vaudou
to curse / a curse	maudire / une malédiction
an omen	une malédiction, un mauvais présage
to exorcise / an exorcist	exorciser / un exorciste
a medium, a psychic	un médium
a clairvoyant	un voyant
palmistry, chiromancy	la chiromancie
palm reading	(faire) les lignes de la main
cartomancy	la cartomancie
soothsaying / a soothsayer	la divination / un devin

to foresee, to forecast, to foretell	prédire
a fortune teller	une diseuse de bonne aventure
the paranormal	les phénomènes paranormaux
a spook / spooky	un revenant / qui fait froid dans le dos
a ghost / ghostly	un fantôme / fantomatique, spectral
a spirit / spiritualism	un esprit / le spiritisme
a seance	une séance de spiritisme
eeriness / eerie	une atmosphère angoissante / angoissant
awe	crainte mêlée d'effroi
a birth chart	un thème astral
astrology / un astrologer	l'astrologie / un astrologue
a horoscope	un horoscope
the signs of the zodiac	les signes du zodiaque
a crystal ball	une boule de cristal
a unicorn	une licorne
a werewolf	un loup-garou
a mermaid	une sirène
a dwarf / a giant	un nain / un géant

BONUS	**BONUS**
an Achilles' heel	un talon d'Achille
a young Adonis	un beau jeune homme
an Amazon	une mégère, une virago
Beware of Greeks bearing gifts	ne faites jamais confiance à un ennemi
caught between Scylla and Charybdis, between a rock and a hard place	être pris entre l'arbre et l'écorce, tomber de Charybde en Scylla
to jump out of the frying pan into the fire	tomber de Charybde en Scylla, aller de mal en pis
Elysium Fields	les Champs-Élysées, le Paradis
the food of the Gods	un repas digne des dieux
a Titan	un titan
Gordian knots	un problème inextricable
a Gorgon, a Medusa	une femme très laide
to harp	ennuyer sévèrement
a Herculean effort, task (Hercules)	un travail d'Hercule
hot as Hades	une chaleur infernale
like a hound out of Hell	être fou de rage
leave no stone unturned	devoir tout mettre en œuvre
an Odyssey	une odyssée, un très long périple
Oedipus Complex	le complexe d'Œdipe
Pandora's box	la boîte de Pandore
a Trojan horse	un cheval de Troie
might is right	la raison du plus fort est toujours la meilleure

Translation: English-to-French exercise

One nation under God (adapted from *The L.A.Times*)

It seems odd that all this should come up now, more than half a century later. Since Kennedy's speech, the notion that any American politician could banish all but the faithless from the public square has become laughable.

If anything, piety has become a prerequisite in politics. Thomas Jefferson may have been relaxed about such matters, but no modern candidate for the presidency would dare to profess no faith, or to question the existence of the Almighty.

Barack Obama is a churchgoer. George Bush named Christ his favourite philosopher and started cabinet meetings with a prayer. Jimmy Carter prayed up to 25 times a day. Even Bill Clinton, a serial sinner, always took care to repent.

Adapted press excerpts (about 400 words)

Excerpt 1 – Why science and religion aren't as opposed as you might think (adapted from *TheConversation.com*)

The debate about science and **religion** is usually viewed as a competition between **worldviews**. Differing opinions on whether the two subjects can comfortably **co-exist** – even among scientists – are pitted against each other in a **battle** for supremacy. For some, science and religion represent two separate **areas** of enquiry. Others, such as the biologist Richard Dawkins see the two as fundamentally opposed **belief** systems. But another way to look at the subject is to consider why people **believe** what they do. The supposed **conflict** between science and religion is nowhere near as clear cut as some might assume. Our **beliefs** are subject to a range of often hidden influences. Much of the confusion around what people **believe** about science and **religion** relates to **evolution** and those who deny it.

Excerpt 2 – Islam and ecology – In almost perfect harmony (adapted from *The Economist*)

When Pope Francis issued his **encyclical** on climate change and pollution, this was rightly **hailed** as a landmark in the history of the **papacy**, and of environmentalism. Now **Islamic scholars** have added their voice to a crescendo of **spiritually**-inspired cries for action to conserve the planet. The statement was hailed by the head of the **Vatican's council** for justice and peace, and by **eco-religious** groups like the green-minded **Franciscans** who in common with the **pope** find inspiration in the nature-respecting, wealth-abjuring example set by **Francis of Assisi** 800 years ago. So what does **Islam** have to say about the environment? Like the **sacred scriptures** of other **creation**-based, **monotheistic religions**, the **Koran** presents the whole material world, and the animal kingdom in particular, as a **divine miracle** to which man must respond with **awe** and self-restraint.

Excerpt 3 – The Philosopher of Feelings (adapted from *The New Yorker*)

Nussbaum is drawn to the idea that creative urgency – and the **commitment** to be **good** – derives from the **awareness** that we harbor aggression toward the people we love. Nussbaum is monumentally **confident**, **intellectually** and physically. She is beautiful, in a taut, flinty way, and carries herself like a queen. Her voice is high-pitched and **dramatic**, and she often seems delighted by the **performance** of being herself. Her work, which draws on her training in **classics** but also on **anthropology**, **psychoanalysis**, **sociology**, and a number of other fields, searches for the conditions for ***eudaimonia***, a Greek word that describes a complete and flourishing life.

Excerpt 4 – Saving churches for their history – not religion (adapted from *The Guardian*)

If **churchgoing** is a reliable indicator of **Christian belief**, then England began losing its **religious impulse** when Victoria was still on the throne. **Attendance** at **Anglican services** began its **decline** in the 1890s. The social, constitutional and **moral** consequences of the church's shrinking importance are often debated, but perhaps the real threat is **aesthetic**. Three quarters of England's 16,000 **parish churches** are listed as buildings of **architectural** and **historic interest**. **Churches** comprise 45% of all England's Heritage **buildings** – **castles**, **mansions**, **banks**, **railway stations**, **markets**. These buildings are an important part of our landscape – even if they are not used for **worship**.

Food for Thought and Quotations (about 500 words)

How to classify religions

Making sense of a great variety of religious movements has been the main focus of theologians and scientists over the last two centuries. In the Encyclopaedia Britannica, the classification of religions involves: *(1) the effort to establish groupings among historical religious communities having certain elements in common or (2) the attempt to categorize similar religious phenomena to reveal the structure of religious experience as a whole.* The main purpose is to give a clear and systematised vision of various religions and beliefs, better to classify a huge variety of phenomena. It is impossible to catalogue the many approaches to the study of religion classification, but geographical, linguistic or ethnic systems may constitute a good start. According to Max Müller, a precursor in these studies, *"particularly in the early history of the human intellect, there exists the most intimate relationship between language, religion, and nationality"* even though he confessed that a science of religion is *"an impossibility"*.

The Evangelicals in the USA

The word "evangelical" is equivocal in the USA. This label is not accepted by all ethnic communities: while the Whites accept this term, the Black community has been said to prefer the expression "born again". Even though they have the same theological background, their political views are rather opposed. Evangelicals have traditionally been strong supporters of the Republican Party, they have long been opposed to gay marriage but remain in favour of limited governmental spending and curbing immigration. The growing evangelical ethnic minorities now support Democrats and their ethical standpoint could rapidly change, according to recent polls.

Spirituality

It has today become commonplace to oppose spirituality to religious belief, the latter being less modern than the former. The term is used to define the capacity for understanding moral, existential, or metaphysical concerns regarding the nature of the self, the meaning of life and the nature of consciousness, but usually in a context separate from organized religious institutions. For example, the very generic term New Age refers to a 1970s movement of people that define themselves as spiritual but not religious and reflect on the quest to one's own individual path to spirituality and understanding. Meditation is one of the many ways to practise spirituality.

Anglicanism

It is one of the major branches of the 16th-century Protestant Reformation, specific to Britain and initiated in England (Henry VIII's decision to break away from Rome) after the works of Luther, a German reformer, and it is today a form of Christianity that includes features of both Protestantism and Roman Catholicism. It finds its origins long before the Reformation though, in the early Middle-Ages. Protests against Rome had already started before King Henry VIII decided to separate England from the direct power of Rome, for very personal reasons (an annulment of marriage). Over the next decades, the Church of England settled a specific form of worship that incorporated Protestant features. It led to violent conflicts within the UK but Queen Elizabeth I confirmed the prevalence of this religion after 1558, with a Book of Common Prayer that revised traditional forms of worship to include the Protestant ideas.

King James Bible

This translation of the Bible was published in 1611 under the auspices of King James I of England. The text influenced English as a language and its literary style and became the standard English Bible from the mid-17th to the early 20th century. The King James Version is still the official translation of many Christian fundamentalists, and is one of the major literary accomplishments of early modern England. For centuries, it was this Bible that was the daily reading of millions of people throughout the English speaking world. William Tennyson considered reading the Bible *"an education in itself"*, and Charles Dickens defined the New Testament as *"the very best book that ever was or ever will be known in the world."* One surprising fact is the specific translation method for its elaboration, from Hebrew and Greek, performed in a very literal way. Translators chose not to change and adapt the text, so that readers simply got used to it, and that had a great influence on the English language.

"To be fair, much of the Bible is not systematically evil but just plain weird, as you would expect of a chaotically cobbled-together anthology of disjointed documents, composed, revised, translated, distorted and 'improved' by hundreds of anonymous authors, editors and copyists, unknown to us and mostly unknown to each other, spanning nine centuries" Richard Dawkins, *The God Delusion*

Chapter B

Writing and text analysis

Section 4 • Arts, culture and analysis techniques

Vocabulary list

LITERATURE WORDS	**LES MOTS DE LA LITTÉRATURE**
a genre	un genre
literature / literary	la littérature / littéraire
prose	la prose
poetry	la poésie
drama	le théâtre
fiction / fictional / fictitious	la fiction / imaginaire / fictif
imaginary	imaginaire
children literature	la littérature jeunesse
science fiction, pulp fiction	la science-fiction, la littérature de gare
an unabridged version	une version intégrale
a novel	un roman
an epistolary novel	un roman épistolaire
a historical novel	un roman historique
romantic fiction	les romans à l'eau de rose
a collection of short stories	un recueil de nouvelles
a selection of poems	une sélection de poèmes
a romance	un récit romanesque
a thriller, a whodunit, a detective novel	un roman policier
an allegory / allegorical	une allégorie / allégorique
a fable / fabulous	une fable / fabuleux
comic / comical	comique / risible
a parody / parodic	une parodie / parodique
caricature / caricatural	la caricature / caricatural
a classic / classical	un classique / classique
(post-)modern fiction	le roman moderne / post-moderne
an autobiography	une autobiographie
confessions	des confessions
memoirs	des mémoires

BOOKS	**LES LIVRES**
publishing	l'édition
a publication / a publisher	une publication / un éditeur
a hardback / a hardcover	un livre cartonné / relié
a paperback	un libre de poche
the front / back cover	la couverture, la 4e de couverture
the index	l'index
the table of contents	la table des matières
the foreword	l'avant-propos
the acknowledgements	les remerciements
the print, the characters	les caractères (d'imprimerie)
a typeface, a font	une police de caractères
small / large prints	en petits / gros caractères
a misprint	une coquille, une faute d'impression

to lay out / the layout	mettre en page / la mise en page
out of print / a reprint	épuisé / une réimpression
to illustrate / an illustration	illustrer / une illustration
in italics / bold characters	en italique / en caractères gras
to send off to press	mettre sous presse
a bookshop / a library	une librairie / une bibliothèque
a bookseller / a librarian	une libraire / un bibliothécaire
a copy	un exemplaire
to skim / scan through a volume	parcourir un tome
to leaf / browse through a bestseller	feuilleter un succès de librairie
a dictionary	un dictionnaire
an encyclopaedia	une encyclopédie
an atlas	un atlas
a bookcard	une carte de bibliothèque
a second-hand book	un livre d'occasion
to be immersed in, to be engrossed in	être plongé dans

DRAMA	**LE THÉÂTRE**
dramatic art	l'art dramatique
a tragedy / tragic	une tragédie / tragique
a playwright	un dramaturge
a melodrama	un mélodrame
a comedy / comic	une comédie / comique
a tragicomedy	une tragi-comédie
a farce / farcical	une farce / grotesque
a skit	une parodie, une satire
a musical	une comédie musicale
dancing	la danse
a choreographer	un chorégraphe
to act / an actor, an actress	jouer / un acteur, une actrice
an acting school / an acting lesson	une école / une leçon d'art dramatique, de théâtre
a part, a role	un rôle
to audition for a part	passer une audition
the leading role	le rôle principal
the stage / to stage	la scène / mettre en scène
to direct / director	diriger / la direction de la pièce, le metteur en scène
to rehearse / a rehearsal	répéter / une répétition
to perform / a performance	jouer / une représentation
to tour	être en tournée
the premiere, the opening night	la première
stage presence	la présence scénique
stage fright	le trac
a playhouse, a theatre	un théâtre
the scenery	le décor

the stage properties, the props	les accessoires de scène
the wings / the curtain	les coulisses / le rideau
to play to a full house	jouer à guichet fermé
to come on / off stage	entrer sur / sortir de scène
to clap / to boo / to hiss	applaudir / huer / siffler
the audience	le public
empty / crowded, packed / sold out	vide / plein / complet
a dressing room / a box	une loge (acteurs / spectateurs)
the plot	l'intrigue
an act / a scene / a line	un acte / une scène / une réplique
the stage directions	les indications scéniques
the opening scene	la scène d'ouverture
the unknotting	le dénouement
a protagonist	un protagoniste
a crisis / a catastrophe	une crise / une catastrophe
a tirade / a monologue / a dialogue	une tirade / un monologue / un dialogue
a cue, a rejoinder	une réplique
verisimilitude	la vraisemblance
entertaining	divertissant
thought-provoking	stimulant
hilarious	hilarant

POETRY	**POÉSIE**
poetry, verse	la poésie
a poet / poetess	un poète / une poétesse
a poem / poetical	un poème / poétique
a ballad	une ballade
an epic (tale)	une épopée
a nursery rhyme	une comptine
an ode / a sonnet	une ode / un sonnet
a stanza	une strophe
a line of verse	un vers
a foot	un pied
stress / rhythm	l'accent / le rythme
stressed / unstressed	accentué / inaccentué
the iambic pentameter	le pentamètre ïambique
a tetrameter / an alexandrine	un tétramère / un alexandrin
rhyme / to rhyme	une rime / rimer
an alliteration	une allitération
a burden / a couplet	un refrain / un couplet
a visual poem	un calligramme
a narrative poem	un poème narratif
a poetry reading	une lecture de vers
a figure of speech	une figure de style / figure de rhétorique
an image / imagery	une image / les images
a personnification	une personnification

an anaphora	une anaphore
a hyperbole	une hyperbole
a simile	une comparaison
a metonymy	une métonymie
a repetition	une répétition
an extended metaphor	une métaphore filée
an oxymoron	un oxymore
a semantic field	un champ lexical
a stylistic device	un procédé stylistique

PROSE	**LA PROSE**
the writer / the author	l'écrivain, l'auteur
a narrative / the narrator	un récit / le narrateur
a reliable narrative instance / entity	une instance / entité narrative fiable
a title / entitled	un titre / intitulé
a preface / a prologue	une préface / un prologue
the incipit / explicit	l'incipit / l'explicit
the opening chapter	le chapitre d'ouverture
a plot / a subplot	une intrigue / une intrigue secondaire
the story	l'histoire
story time	le temps de l'histoire
discourse	le discours, le récit
the focus	le point de vue, le point focal
the point of view	le point de vue
characterization	la description des personnages
the plot development	le développement de l'intrigue
a turning point	un tournant
the unfolding / unraveling of action	le déroulement / le dénouement de l'action
to trigger off an event	déclencher un événement
a climax	un point culminant
an anticlimax	une chute
a flash-back / a flash forward	une analepse / une prolepse
a twist	une péripétie, un rebondissement, un retournement de situation
a pause	une pause
to be set in	être situé dans / à
to see from within / from without	voir de l'intérieur / de l'extérieur
internal / external focalisation	la focalisation interne / externe
direct speech / (free) indirect speech	le discours direct / indirect (libre)
an internal monologue	un monologue intérieur
stream of consciousness	le courant des pensées
commitment / committed	l'engagement / engagé
to deride something / derision	tourner en dérision / la dérision
to ridicule / ridicule	ridiculiser / le ridicule
irony of fate	l'ironie du sort
wit / witty	l'esprit / spirituel

TEXT ANALYSIS	**L'ANALYSE DE TEXTE**
criticism	la critique
to sum up / a summary	résumer / un résumé
a review / a book reviewer, a book critic	un compte-rendu / un critique littéraire
the first five lines	les cinq premières lignes
the last paragraph but one	l'avant-dernier paragraphe
the before-last paragraph	l'avant-dernier paragraphe
to make a draft	faire un brouillon
to take down notes	prendre des notes
a mixed review / a praise	une critique mitigée / un éloge
well / poorly expressed	bien / mal exprimé
biased / unbiased	partial / impartial
an excerpt	un extrait
a quotation / to quote	une citation / citer
to interpret / an interpretation	interpréter / une interprétation
to assess / assessment	évaluer / une évaluation
clear / controlled	clair / maîtrisé
shallow / superficial	creux / superficiel
commonplace	banal
gripping, thrilling	captivant
rambling	décousu
laboured	laborieux
straightforward, direct	direct
sentimental / moving / tearful	sentimental / émouvant / larmoyant
far-fetched / hackneyed	tiré par les cheveux / stéréotypé

Translation: English-to-French exercise

Writers who spied (adapted from *The Economist*)

"Champagne, if you are seeking the truth, is better than a lie detector," Graham Greene wrote in "Ways of Escape" in 1980. "It encourages a man to be expansive, even reckless, while lie detectors are only a challenge to tell lies more successfully." When he wasn't writing (and sometimes when he was), Greene worked as an agent for MI6, the British intelligence service.

Greene was recruited in 1941, after he had already established his career as a writer. It was a credible cover for intelligence gathering and his penchant for traveling to certain significant regions – Liberia, Mexico, Haiti, Cuba, Vietnam – made him a valuable informant. Spying had the added perk of offering Greene intriguing material.

Adapted press excerpts (about 400 words)

Excerpt 1 – Literature and film help teach students to understand the brain (adapted from UCLA)

Course combining anatomy, history, philosophy and **humanities** provides an **interdisciplinary** approach to studying neuroscience. What can Shakespeare, Cervantes, Proust, and even **contemporary playwrights** and filmmakers contribute to the study of neuroscience? A lot, says UCLA **professor** of integrative biology and physiology Scott Chandler. "When we are talking about the brain, we are talking about our essence," Chandler said. For the last four years, Chandler has been **teaching** and coordinating the **pedagogy** for the freshman **cluster course** titled "Mind Over Matter: The History, Science and Philosophy of the Brain." He designed the course to incorporate medical history and **philosophy** alongside sections in cognitive **psychology** and **in-depth instruction** on **neuroscience**.

Excerpt 2 – Trump and Clinton: The Victorian Novel (adapted from *The New Yorker*)

Oh, that Trump. What a **character**! He is a character – I mean, in a Victorian **novel**. The anonymously **authored** and utterly forgotten **tale** "The Odd Trump," from 1875, is a ripe bit of Victorian preposterousness. Starting with the damsel saved from a train wreck, the **book** includes everything from a disputed will and a mysterious old servant to a cursed mansion. Also: **ghostly** sleepwalkers! Bloody duels! Secret sliding doors! (The latter, hidden in a **conservatory**, might be more accurately described as a secret sliding lemon tree.) But, most important: it has a **hero** named Trump. And his old friend and sometimes rival? Clinton, of course.

"You have a regular armory, Clinton," said Trump, as he glanced at the warlike array.

"Yes, I have gathered them up at odd times and places. Let us try a pass with the foils... We will not bother with the masks. I am anxious to see if I am as clumsy as I used to be. En garde!"

Excerpt 3 – War of words (adapted from *The Economist*)

Poetry has always occupied an **ambivalent** space in **society**. In the ancient world **Plato** banned **poets** from his **ideal** republic; today they have to navigate the "embarrassment or suspicion or anger" that follows when they admit to their profession in public. Ben Lerner, a **poet**, understands this hatred: he confesses that he has never heard what Sir Philip Sidney described as "the planet-like **music** of poetry", nor experienced the "trance-like **state**" widely said by **critics** to be induced by John Keats. He believes it to be central to the **art** form. Poets and non-poets alike hate

poetry, he argues, because poetry will always fail to deliver on the **transcendental** demands people have invested in it.

Excerpt 4 – Teaching with Graphic Novels (adapted from Edudemic.com)

Comic books have long been contraband in the classroom. These colorful **stories** are most often thought of as a distraction hidden behind the math book for slacking students. However, **modern graphic novels** have emerged as an effective teaching tool that can help improve **literacy**, explain **complex concepts**, and get students excited about **reading**. Many are beginning to view them as **literature**. Today, many American students are spending significantly more time consuming visual media than **books**. Graphic novels are a more visual **medium** than traditional **text** and can entice greater **readership** among high school and college students who are drawn to TV. When children **read** at home, they do better in both **reading** and math testing. **Visual storytelling** can build **non-visual reading skills**. Graphic novels contain all of the aspects of any **school-assigned book: a beginning, a middle, an end, conflict, character development, resolution,** and many other **literary characteristics**. However, graphic novels often use panels and images to also tell the story.

Food for Thought and Quotations (about 500 words)

Epistemology

It broadly refers to the study of the nature, origin, and limits of human knowledge. Along with metaphysics, logic, and ethics, it is one of the four main branches of philosophy. Epistemology has a long history, beginning with the ancient Greeks and going on to the present. Philosophy begins in puzzlement and wonder, but aims to go deeper in the understanding of processes that most humans accept not to comprehend. Supposing that they have a great amount of knowledge at first sight, epistemologists raise doubts about the reliability of what they think they know. In order to deconstruct this knowledge, they observe the abnormalities of our experience of the world. Epistemology may start, for instance, when one starts questioning not the nature of knowledge but the very definition of the word “knowledge” itself.

Text analysis

It is a close analysis of the content and the structure of an excerpt from a work of art in prose or in verse, of a press article or another written document. It allows you to understand meanings and ideas expressed through written words. This includes taking into account the purpose of the text and the intentionality of the author, the time period in which the text was written but also the audience for the text. An analysis focuses on bias and takes into account the literary, historical or cultural context. For a press article, one must first identify several important elements (headline, date, nature, political orientation of the paper) in order to be able to analyse the intentionality of the author, interpret the organisation of the document as a whole and draw exploitable conclusions that will help understand its interest.

Five Wits or Five Senses?

These notions are the result of centuries of philosophical thought, and find their origins in the works of Aristotle. It is important to define the terms, which overlapped in Early Modern English, that is to say at the time of William Shakespeare. Wit and Sense meant *perception,* although the common distinction, where it was made, was "five wits" for the inward and "five senses" for the outward. In broad terms, the outward wits correspond to the human organs (eyes, ears, nose, skin, and mouth) and the inward wits are *instinct, imagination, fantasy, estimation, and memory,* a sixth sense being linked to perception challenges any possible scientific explanation. As regards the five senses, they are referred to as *hearing, sight, smell, touch and taste.*

In faith, I do not love thee with mine eyes,
For they in thee a thousand errors note;
But 'tis my heart that loves what they despise,
Who, in despite of view, is pleas'd to dote;

Nor are mine ears with thy tongue's tune delighted;
Nor tender feeling, to base touches prone,
Nor taste, nor smell, desire to be invited
To any sensual feast with thee alone:

But my five wits nor my five senses can
Dissuade one foolish heart from serving thee,
Who leaves unsway'd the likeness of a man,
Thy proud heart's slave and vassal wretch to be:

Only my plague thus far I count my gain,
That she that makes me sin awards me pain.

William Shakespeare, Sonnet 141

Chapter C
Music and cinema

Vocabulary list

MUSIC CLASSICS	**LES CLASSIQUES DE LA MUSIQUE**
music / a musician	la musique / un musicien
to play / a player	jouer / un joueur
to compose / a composer	composer / un compositeur
to practise / practice	s'exercer / la pratique
a note / a scale	une note / une gamme
a score	une partition
A, B, C, D, E, F, G	la, si, do, ré, mi, fa, sol
a key	un ton
a major / minor chord	un accord majeur / mineur
to tune / to tune in	accorder / mettre au diapason
a conductor / to conduct	un chef d'orchestre / diriger
an orchestra	un orchestre
a band	un groupe, une formation
a solo, a duo, a trio, a quartet	un solo, un duo, un trio, un quartet
a concert, a concerto	un concert, un concerto
a symphony, a sonata	une symphonie, une sonate
a requiem	une messe des morts, un requiem
a choir	un chœur
to sing / a singer	chanter / un chanteur
a lyrical singer	un chanteur lyrique
to hum	fredonner
a melody / a song	une mélodie / une chanson
the lyrics	les paroles
the voice	la voix
unaccompanied	a capella
a chorus / a verse	un refrain / un couplet
a piano	un piano
a harpsichord	un clavecin
a keyboard	un clavier
an organ	un orgue
the strings	les cordes
the brass	les cuivres
the wind (instruments)	les (instruments à) vent
a violin / a cello / a double bass	un violon / un violoncelle / une contrebasse
a string / a bow	une corde / un archet
a flute	une flûte
a clarinet / an oboe	une clarinette / un hautbois
a saxophone / a trumpet	un saxophone / une trompette
a drum / drums	un tambour / les percussions
an electric guitar	une guitare électrique

CINEMA	**LE CINÉMA**
to direct / a director	réaliser / un réalisateur
a film, a movie	un film

a cinema, a movie theatre	un cinéma
to go to the movies	aller au cinéma
a major company	une grande société de production
to produce / production	produire / la production
to distribute / distribution	distribuer / la distribution (dans les salles)
to release / the release	faire sortir en salle / la sortie
a trailer	une bande-annonce
a documentary	un documentaire
a comedy	une comédie
a cartoon / an animated movie	un dessin animé / un film d'animation
a western movie	un western
a thriller / a detective film	un film à suspense, un thriller / un film policier
a drama	un drame
a rom-com (romantic comedy)	une comédie romantique
a biopic	un film biographique
a reboot, a sequel	une reprise / une suite
a remake	une nouvelle version, un remake
an adaptation	une adaptation
a blockbuster, a hit	un film à grand succès
a flop / to misfire	un flop / faire flop
box office takings	les recettes
an adventure movie	un film d'aventures
a sci-fi movie	un film de science-fiction
a studio / a set	un studio / le plateau de tournage
the plot line / the storyline	l'intrigue
a script / the scriptwriter	un script / le scénariste
to cast / the cast	distribuer les rôles / la distribution (acteurs)
a superhero	un superhéros
a stunt / a stuntman	une cascade / un cascadeur
a camera / cameraman	une caméra / un caméraman
a rush	un extrait, un rush
a shot, a take	une prise
a scene	une scène
to edit / editing	monter / le montage
to dub / dubbing	doubler / le doublage
to scan / to pan	balayer / faire un panoramique
to close up on	faire un gros plan sur
a movie review	une critique de film
to perform / performance	interpréter / l'interprétation (acteur)
a prize, an academy award / an Oscar	un prix / un Oscar
an award-winner	un film primé
to award	décerner

FAME	LA CÉLÉBRITÉ
a star, a celebrity	une star, une célébrité
fame and fortune	la gloire et la fortune
stardom	la célébrité
to rise to stardom	devenir une vedette, une star
a trend / trendy	une / être tendance
well-known, renowned	célèbre, connu
a media figure	une personnalité des médias
to be in the public eye	être connu du public
to get huge media coverage	être très médiatisé
world famous	mondialement célèbre
infamous	tristement célèbre
a celeb	une vedette
a socialite	un mondain
the jet-set / a jet-setter	la jet-set / un membre de la jet-set
an icon	une icône, une idole
an autograph	un autographe
a fancy restaurant	un restaurant chic
an exclusive club	un club fermé
appearance	l'apparence
to play to the gallery	poser pour la galerie
a photo opportunity	une séance photo
a posh neighbourhood	un quartier huppé
paparazzi	les paparazzi
to be in the limelight	être sous les projecteurs
a gossip column	une rubrique people
a publicity stunt, a buzz	un coup de pub
trash TV	la télé-poubelle
fashion / fashionable	la mode / à la mode
a model	un mannequin
to do modelling	faire du mannequinat
outdated, old fashioned	démodé, dépassé
a trendsetter	un lanceur de mode
appearances are deceptive	les apparences sont trompeuses
to revamp the image of	relooker
to raise one's profile	améliorer son image

LIVE PERFORMANCES	LES CONCERTS
a music concert	un concert de musique
a gig / to play a gig	un concert / jouer un concert
to attend	assister à
classical, rock, pop, electronic	classique, rock, pop, électronique
a ticket	un billet
the audience	le public
to pre-order online	préréserver en ligne
a box office	un guichet

the venue	le lieu du concert
the doorman, the bouncer	le contrôleur / le videur
a mixing board	une table de mixage son
the support band	la première partie (le groupe de...)
to warm up	préchauffer
the headline act	le groupe vedette / le groupe principal
encore	bis ! / un rappel

BONUS: FIVE SENSES and SPEECH	**LES CINQ SENS ET LA PAROLE**
eyesight	la vue
within sight	à portée de vue
long- / short-sighted	presbyte / myope
to squint	loucher
to grope one's way	se diriger à tâtons
visually-impaired	déficient visuel
smooth	doux au toucher
rough	rugueux
sensitive	sensible
to see to sth	veiller à, veiller sur
to keep a look-out	être aux aguets
to catch a glimpse of sth	apercevoir qqch
to make out sth	distinguer qqch
to gaze at sth	contempler
to frown at sth	regarder d'un air désapprobateur
to peep	regarder à la dérobée
to gape	regarder bouche bée
to wink at sb	faire un clin d'œil à qqn
to stare	regarder avec insistance, dévisager
to glare at sb	regarder avec colère qqn
hearing	l'ouïe
to hear from sb	recevoir des nouvelles de qqn
out of hearing	trop éloigné pour être entendu
within earshot	à portée de voix
hard of hearing	dur d'oreille
noisy, loud / noiseless, faint	bruyant, fort / sans aucun bruit, silencieux, faible
audible, perceptible	audible, perceptible
sharp, thrill	aigu
dull	sourd
smell	l'odorat
a scent / scentless	une senteur / inodore
to smell nasty, to stink	sentir mauvais, puer
a fragrance / fragrant	un parfum / parfumé
taste	le goût
touch	le toucher
to speak fluently	parler avec aisance

rhythmic	cadencé
to enunciate	énoncer, articuler
to be speechless	rester sans voix
to utter sounds	émettre des sons
deaf-and-dumb / mute	sourd et muet, muet (non prononcé)
a talk / talkative	une conversation / bavard
to chatter, to gossip	bavarder, papoter
a gossip / gossip	une commère / des commérages, des potins
a whisper	un murmure
to mutter	murmurer, grogner
to stammer / to stutter	bredouiller / bégayer
to cry out	s'écrier, crier
to yell	hurler de colère
to bawl out	brailler, hurler

Translation: English-to-French exercise

Radiohead move beyond its existential angst (adapté de Pitchfork.com)

Radiohead, who titled their ninth studio album A Moon Shaped Pool, have a unique grasp on how easily profundity can slip into banality. Their music is obsessed with the point where great truths transform into platitudes, where pure signal meets wretched noise. In the past, Thom Yorke has sharply peppered his lyrics with everyday clichés to suggest a mind consumed by meaningless data, but on the new album, he largely moves beyond cynicism.

He is now considering simpler truths in a heretofore-unexplored register: wonder and amazement. "This goes beyond me, beyond you," he sings on "Daydreaming." [...] Thom Yorke has flirted with surrender before, and on the latest opus, that submission feels nearly at its height. But that isn't to say that this is necessarily a "break-up album."

Adapted press excerpts (about 400 words)

Excerpt 1 – David Bowie (adapted from Pitchfork.com)

David Bowie was the ultimate **cultural** connector, envisioning **pop** not as a closed loop but rather an infinite **network** of intellectual curiosities that spanned **underground music**, **avant-garde art**, and left-field **literature**. David Bowie is not simply the prettiest **star** – he's a constellation. No matter which Bowie you first encountered – the orange-haired alien androgyne of Ziggy Stardust, the creepy clown in the "Ashes to Ashes" video, the louche lothario of the Let's Dance era, or even the guy refereeing Derek Zoolander's walk-offs – you were instantly disarmed by his style, sophistication, and presence. But Bowie was the rare **rock legend** whose mythology is defined more by his intellectual curiosities than his cocaine-fuelled debauchery. He lived his life as **theater**, so why would his death be any different? David Bowie's **greatest albums** always opened us up to new worlds; Blackstar leads to the most mysterious, frightening, and unknowable of all.

Excerpt 2 – Brian de Palma's Phantom of the Paradise (adapted from *The Guardian*)

In 1974, after a decade making **low-budget**, semi-**underground movies**, Brian De Palma thought he was about to enter the big time when 20th Century Fox paid $2m for this wild **satire** on indulgent **rock musicians** and the corrupt **industry** that exploited them. Basically it's a transposition of Gaston Leroux's **drama play** *The Phantom of the Opera* to the **modern pop** world, where an evil **impresario**, Swan (the diminutive, baby-faced composer Paul Williams, who also **wrote** the **songs**), steals a pretentious **rock cantata** from Winslow Leach, its naive **author**, and frames him on drugs charge. After he's been disfigured by a **record-pressing machine**, Winslow returns to seek revenge by haunting Swan's **theatre**, the Paradise. The **piece** also draws on Goethe's *Faust*, Wilde's *Dorian Gray* and Edgar Allan Poe, and refers to **movies** ranging from Psycho (the shower **scene** is reprised using a plunger) and Fritz Lang's*The Cabinet of Dr Caligari*.

Excerpt 3 – Nirvana baby recreates iconic album cover 25 years later (adapted from *The New York Post*)

The naked swimming baby from the **cover** of the **groundbreaking** Nirvana **album** Nevermind reenacted the **image** for the record's 25th anniversary – this time wearing clothes. Spencer Elden, 25, wanted to go *au naturel* when he made splash to honor the legendary grunge band. The **album**, **released** 25 years ago has **sold** more than 30 million **copies worldwide**. "Okay, throw the baby in the pool now." With those words, uttered by photographer Kirk Weddle, 4-month-old Spencer was on his way to **fame** (though not **fortune**) as the baby on the cover. "The anniversary means something to me. It's strange that I did this for five minutes when I was four months old and it became this really **iconic image**," he said.

Excerpt 4 – A Facebook First for New York Philharmonic (adapted from *The International New York Times*)

The New York **Philharmonic orchestra** will open its 175th anniversary **season** a little differently than its forebears in 1842: for the first time it will **stream** the **concert** on Facebook Live. The **program** will **feature** Gershwin's **Concerto** in F for **piano** and **orchestra**, John Corigliano's "STOMP" and Dvorak's **Symphony** No. 9, "From the New World." As part of this season's exploration, the **orchestra** is asking **ensembles** to play it, or **selections** from it, or **reinterpretations** of it. The Philharmonic will advertise their **performances**; invite participating ensembles to attend **open rehearsals**; and give them access to **arrangements**, marked **conducting** scores, and **sheet music** notated by Philharmonic **musicians**.

Food for Thought and Quotations (about 500 words)

The Academy Awards, or the Oscars

The Academy Awards, also known as Oscars, is a yearly awards ceremony hosted by the Academy of Motion Picture Arts and Sciences in Los Angeles, CA. It grants awards for excellence in cinematic achievements in the United States film industry as assessed by the Academy's voting membership. The various category winners are awarded a copy of a statuette which has become commonly known by its nickname "Oscar" (since Bette Davis's comment that the trophy made her think of her uncle Oscar, for the anecdote). The awards, first presented in 1929 at the Hollywood Roosevelt Hotel, became televised after 1950. Today streamed online, it is viewed all around the world and has granted about 3000 awards since it was first organised. The five thousand seven hundred voters of the honorary organisation choose a winner in about 30 categories, among which: Best Picture, Best Director, Best Leading Role, Best Supporting Role (masculine and feminine), Best Animated, Best Costume Design, Best Foreign Film, Best Documentary, Best Visual Effects, Best Writing, and many others.

Online streaming websites and apps

Streaming media is received by and presented to an end-user while being delivered by a provider, without interruption. It is an alternative to downloading media files, in which the user does not have to wait until the file is totally downloaded to be able to view it. As of 2016, streaming refers to a user watching or listening to digital video or audio content on an appliance ranging from a desktop computer to a smartphone over the Internet. A decent bandwidth is necessary to be able to guarantee an uninterrupted flow. Youtube and Netflix are two famous video content streaming providers. Obviously, the contents are protected by copyright laws, and this is a major bone of contention between some users who have access to illegally broadcast contents and the internet service providers. In the European Union, watching such contents is today legal, but downloading and keeping these contents on hardware is not.

Walk of Fame

Located in Los Angeles, the Hollywood Walk of Fame is undoubtedly one of the world's most famous sidewalks and there are more than 2,500 show-business celebrities honoured. Most of these brass stars represent famous actors, musicians, directors, producers, musical bands and theatrical groups, fictional characters, heroes or series. It started in 1956, with a caricatural design for actor John Wayne, but soon this was replaced by an embedded brass star, simpler to make. Among the first were actor Burt Lancaster and director Stanley Kramer. The nomination process is public, and living or deceased nominees are awarded during a presentation ceremony. Some fans show respect for star recipients both living and dead by laying flowers or other symbolic tributes at their stars, or by polishing the brass stars on a regular basis.

Speech

Speech has three major definitions: the human ability to communicate through spoken language, a formal address or discourse delivered to an audience, or a sequence of lines written for one character in a play. The latter two definitions require the use of a marked article (A or THE) before the noun, while the former is a general ability, and therefore uses the zero article. A figure of speech is a generally intentional deviation from a literal meaning of a word or a phrase or common usage that emphasizes, clarifies, or modifies both written and spoken language. Most common figures are formed by extending the vocabulary of what is already familiar to something that is less well-known. In art (cinema and literature), using a figure of speech has a particular impact and it creates associations of meanings that create imagery far beyond the common everyday use of simpler figures.

"Life is like a box of chocolates; you never know what you're going to get", a simile in Forrest Gump

Hollywood is a metonymy, *The White House* is a synecdoche.

"Words are flying out like endless rain into a paper cup", a hyperbole in *Across the Universe*, by the Beatles

Chapter D

Picture analysis

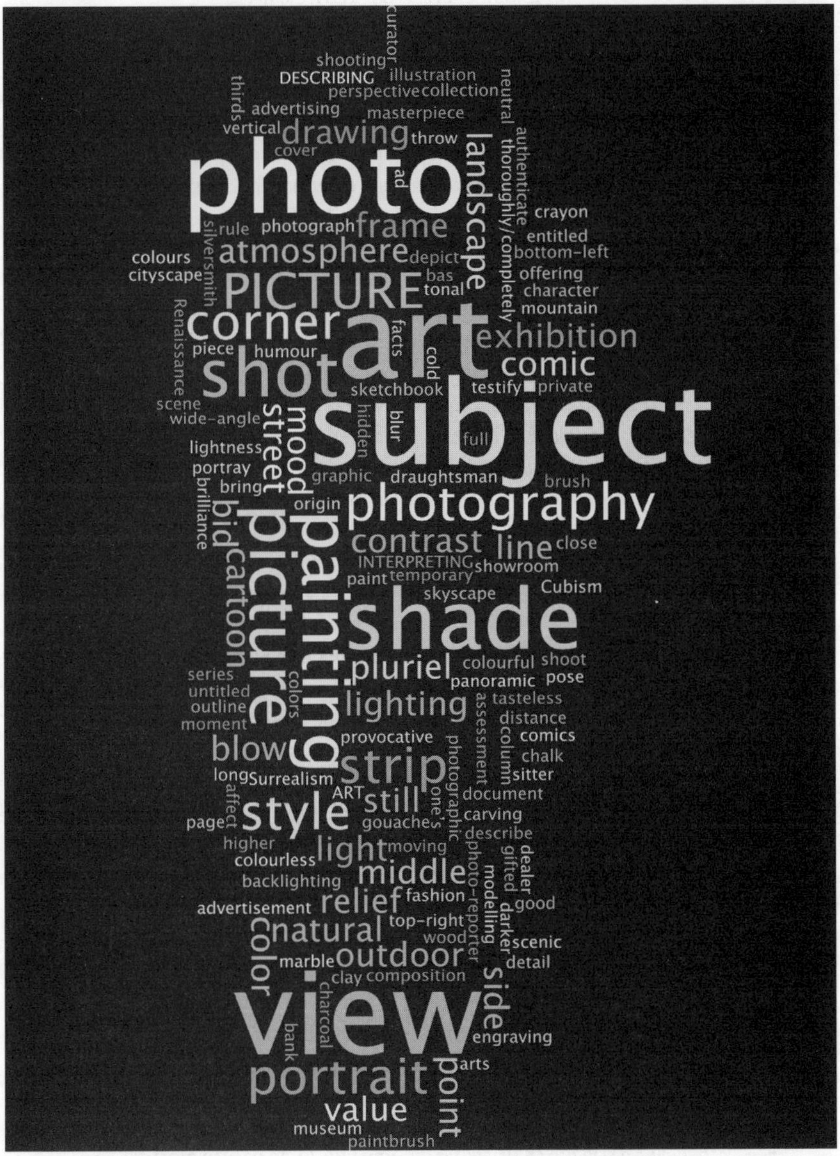

Vocabulary list

ART	**L'ART**
art / an artist	l'art / un artiste
the fine arts	les arts plastiques
drawing	le dessin
painting	la peinture
engraving	la gravure
photography	la photographie
a work of art	une œuvre d'art
a masterpiece	un chef-d'œuvre
talent / talented	le talent / talentueux
a gift / gifted	un don / doué
a style / to have style / to style	un style / avoir du style / donner du style
a museum	un musée
a picture gallery	une galerie de peinture
a showroom	une salle d'exposition
a temporary exhibition	une exposition temporaire
a curator	un conservateur
to put on an exhibition	monter une exposition
private collection	une collection privée
an auction	une vente aux enchères
to assess / an assessment	évaluer / une évaluation
to bid / an offering	enchérir / une offre
a higher bid	une enchère
an art dealer / collector	un marchand d'art / un collectionneur
authentic, genuine	authentique
to authenticate	authentifier
the value / to value	la valeur / estimer

GENERAL TERMS	**TERMES GÉNÉRAUX**
a movement	un mouvement
classical / Classicism	classique / le classicisme
Renaissance	la Renaissance
impressionist / Impressionism	impressionniste / l'impressionnisme
cubist, futurist / Cubism, Futurism	cubiste, futuriste / le cubisme, le futurisme
contemporary art / figurative art	l'art contemporain / l'art figuratif
surrealist / Surrealism	surréaliste / le surréalisme
abstract art	l'art abstrait
a picture	une image / une photo / un tableau
entitled / untitled	intitulé / sans titre
painting / a painting	la peinture / un tableau
a (self-) portrait	un autoportrait
a conversational piece	une scène de genre
a landscape / a seascape / a cityscape	un paysage / une marine / un paysage urbain
a view / a still life (pluriel lifes)	une vue / une nature morte

a mural / a fresco	une peinture murale / une fresque
a trompe l'œil	un trompe l'œil
a tag, a graffiti, street art	un tag, un graffiti, le street art
a sketch / a sketchbook	une ébauche, un croquis / un carnet à croquis
an illustration / to illustrate	une illustration / illustrer
a cartoon / a comic strip, comics	un dessin humoristique / une bande dessinée
a cartoonist	un dessinateur humoristique
a drawing / a draughtsman	un dessin / un dessinateur
a pencil / a crayon	un crayon à papier / un crayon de couleur
charcoal / chalk / India ink	le fusain / la craie / l'encre de Chine
a brush, paintbrush	un pinceau
a canvas	une toile
a photo, a photograph / a photographer	une photo(graphie) / un photographe
to shoot / a shooting	photographier / une séance photo
oil painting	la peinture à l'huile
gouache / watercolour (GB)	la gouache / l'aquarelle
to paint a atercolour (US)	peindre une aquarelle
to depict	dépeindre
to portray sb	faire le portrait de qqn
to pose / a sitter	poser / un modèle
sculpture	la sculpture
modelling	le modelage
clay	l'argile, la glaise
marble	le marbre
wax	la cire
a silversmith	un orfèvre
wood carving	la sculpture sur bois
stonecutting / to sculpt in stone	la taille de la pierre / sculpter dans la pierre
a statue / a bust / a pedestal	une statue / un buste / un piédestal
a bas relief / a column	un bas-relief / une colonne

DESCRIBING A PICTURE	**DESCRIPTION D'IMAGE**
the outline	le contour
a wide-angle / fish-eye / tele lens	un objectif grand angle / fish-eye / un téléobjectif
to center, to frame / framing	centrer, cadrer / le cadrage
the proportion / the composition	la proportion / la composition
perspective	la perspective
a line / a curve / the scale	une ligne / une courbe / l'échelle
to contrast with	contraster avec
colourful / colourless	coloré / terne
a tinge / a tint / a shade	un ton / une teinte / une nuance
the tonal range	la gamme des teintes
a contrast	un contraste

a chiaroscuro	un clair-obscur
to describe a photo (thoroughly / completely, in detail, etc.)	décrire une image (entièrement / de bout en bout, en détail, etc.)
what is depicted	ce qui est dépeint
on the photo	sur la photo
the subject matter / the photographic subject	le sujet / le sujet photographique
a black-and-white / a color print	un tirage noir et blanc / couleur
the portrait / landscape format	le format portrait / paysage
a series of pictures	une série d'images
a pic (pluriel pix)	une image / une photo de presse
a photo-reporter	un reporter photographe
a photomontage	un montage photo
a fashion / handout / archive photo	une photo de mode / de presse / d'archive
an artwork bank	une banque d'images
a view of New York / aerial / mountain / nature view	une vue de New York / aérienne / de la montagne / de la nature
a strip cartoon, a comic strip	une bande dessinée
an advertisement, an ad	une annonce publicitaire, une publicité, une pub
a snapshot	un instantané
a photo news agency	une agence de photojournalisme
the cover page of a magazine	la couverture d'une revue
a still from a movie	une photographie extraite d'un film
the origin of a document	l'origine d'un document

ANALYSING A PICTURE	**ANALYSE D'IMAGE**
outdoor / indoor photography	la photographie d'extérieur / d'intérieur
the pattern	le motif
a riverscape / a skyscape	un paysage de rivière / une photo de ciel
a scenic view / a panoramic view	un beau paysage / une vue panoramique
a portrait / an actor's headshot	un portrait de célébrité / un portrait d'acteur
a humour subject	un sujet humoristique
advertising / war photography	la photographie publicitaire / de guerre
a natural subject / a photo subject	un objet naturel / un sujet photographique
to frame a subject	cadrer le sujet
the rule of thirds	la règle des trois tiers
in the foreground	au premier plan
in the background	à l'arrière-plan
in the middle ground / middle distance	au centre / au second plan
the vanishing line / point	la ligne / le point de fuite
the edge / a side / a corner	le bord / un côté / un coin, un angle
on the top-right corner	en haut à droite
on the bottom-left corner	en bas à gauche
the point of view	le point de vue, la prise de vue subjective
close shot / full shot / long shot	plan rapproché / plan en pied / plan général

a close-up / to blow up, a blow up	un gros plan / agrandir, un agrandissement
a downward / upward shot	une prise de vue en plongée / contre-plongée
a front / side / a three-quarters view	une vue de face / de côté / de trois-quarts
the depth of field	la profondeur de champ
the subject is in good / out of focus	le sujet est net / flou
sharpness / motion blur	la netteté / le flou bougé
lightness / darkness	la clarté / l'obscurité
lighting / backlighting	la lumière, l'éclairage / le contre-jour
natural lighting	l'éclairage naturel
overexposure / underexposure	la sur- / sous-exposition
brilliance	la luminosité
a tone	un ton, une tonalité
a dark / light colour	une couleur sombre / claire
a darker shade of green	un vert plus sombre
light and shade effects	les effets d'ombre et de lumière
to shade off a color / to shade off, to soften down	estomper une couleur / s'adoucir
to throw into relief / to stand out against	mettre en relief / se détacher sur
contrasty / flat	contrasté / plat
cool / cold colours	des couleurs chaudes / froides
washed-out / saturated colors	des couleurs délavées / saturées
oblique / vertical lines	des lignes obliques / verticales
a character	un personnage
a poignant / street/outdoor scene	une scène poignante / de rue / d'extérieur
the atmosphere, the mood	l'ambiance
the action	l'action
the caption / the title	la légende / le titre

INTERPRETING A PICTURE	**INTERPRÉTATION D'IMAGE**
to capture	saisir
the decisive moment	l'instant décisif
to testify to	témoigner de
to convey a sense of	donner une impression de
to present facts	présenter les faits
to feel concerned	se sentir impliqué
neutral elements / neutrality	des éléments neutres / la neutralité
to bring out sth	faire ressortir qqch
pleasant	agréable
moving	émouvant
puzzling	intrigant
striking	saisissant
provocative	provocateur
tasteless	de mauvais goût / sans saveur
to affect one's mood	affecter un ressenti, une impression
to create an atmosphere	créer une atmosphère

an evocative picture	une photographie révélatrice, éloquente
the implicit / the explicit	l'implicite / l'explicite
clearly visible / hidden	bien visible / caché, invisible
a graphic picture	une photo explicite

Translation: English-to-French exercise

The Internet Virtual Museum (adapté de ComputerHistory.com)

First of the kind, the Big Internet Museum attracts large crowds because it is available 24/7. The web is short-lived and the temporary initiative has met with success, by telling the history of the web, for the generations to come. The three young founders see themselves as curators rather than editors of an endless catalogue.

Selecting is part of the scheme, and has sometimes been subjected to discussions, or participatory negociations through public votes with professionals and amateurs alike. The virtual museum is made out of 62 pieces placed in 7 wings devoted to history, memes, social media, and so on. Occasional curators can display temporary exhibitions. The project has been a tremendous success so far. Luckily it is not a real museum otherwise people would be packed in like sardines.

Adapted press excerpts (about 400 words)

Excerpt 1 – Polaroid photography – Instant forever, the anti-Snapchat (adapted from *The Economist*)

There is no frame for an image more familiar than the white border of a Polaroid instant **photograph**. A Polaroid imbues even the hastiest **snapshots** with a certain **artistic** flair. When Edwin Land first unveiled his **instant camera** in 1947, such thoughts were at the front of his mind. "The purpose of inventing instant photography was essentially **aesthetic**," he declared, "to make available a new **medium** of expression to numerous individuals who have an artistic interest in the world around them." A Polaroid photograph has no separate **negatives** that can be manipulated and it cannot be seamlessly **altered** like a **digital image**. This gained it a reputation for being an **authentic record** of **reality**.

Excerpt 2 – Through the lens – Capturing the Wild Power of the Sea (adapted from *National Geographic*)

What was the first ***picture*** *you made that mattered to you?*

It was a photograph of the invertebrate fauna off of Victoria, British Columbia. The **power** of this **image** to **reveal** a beautiful, unknown world to an **expert** blew me away.

If you weren't a ***photographer****, what would you be?*

I always dreamed of being a fighter pilot, just for the love of flying.

What ***fuels*** *your* ***passion*** *for* ***photography****?*

The **opportunity** to tell stories that connect people to nature in an **emotional** way.

What is the ***perfect photograph****?*

A **photo** that sucks somebody in with **awe** and **beauty** and then **inspires** action or **teaches** something – and especially one that **creates** an **emotional response**.

Excerpt 3 – How photography evolved from science to art (adapted from TheConversation.com)

Much like a **painting**, a **photograph** has the ability to move, engage and inspire **viewers. Photography** has not yet celebrated its 200th birthday, yet in the medium's first century of existence, there was a great deal of debate over its **artistic** merit. For decades, even those who appreciated the **qualities** of a **photograph** were not entirely sure whether photography was – or could be – an **art**. In its first incarnation, photography seemed to be more of a **scientific tool** than a form of **artistic expression.** Many of the earliest photographers didn't even call themselves artists: they were **scientists** and **engineers** – **chemists**, **astronomers**, **botanists** and **inventors**. While the new form attracted individuals with a **background** in **painting** or **drawing**, even early practitioners like Louis Daguerre or Nadar could be seen more as entrepreneurial **inventors** than as traditional artists.

Excerpt 4 – Here's The Story Behind One Of the Most Heartbreaking 9/11 Photos Ever (adapted from Esquire)

The old saying has always been, "**a picture is worth a thousand words.**" The Falling Man departs from this earth like an arrow. Although he has not chosen his fate, he appears to have, in his last instants of life, embraced it. If he were not falling, he might very well be flying. He appears relaxed, hurtling through the air. He appears comfortable in the grip of unimaginable **motion**. He does not appear intimidated by gravity's divine suction or by what awaits him. The **composition** of this **photograph** is relatively simple. All **lines** point down. As a **viewer**, you almost feel as if you're moving down when you look at it, and you can almost feel him moving **downwards** through the **photograph**. The **straight**, **vertical lines** of the World Trade Center **take over** the entire **background**, which makes the falling man himself, stand out a little higher than the **middle** of the background. The fact that he isn't yet to the middle of the **picture** makes it feel like he still has a long way to fall.

Food for Thought and Quotations (about 500 words)

Invention of photography

At the very origin, the forerunner of photography was invented 2000 years ago. The *camera obscura* is a dark cube with a hole in one side, through which images of objects outside the room were projected on the opposite wall. In 1827, Nicéphore Niépce was working on lithography and invented a process by which a pewter plate was exposed to the sunlight for eight hours with a camera obscura device, which produced the first modern photograph. Roughly at the same time, Louis Daguerre worked on reducing the exposure time and by 1830 he used ionized silver plates that enabled the production of a photograph in a 30-minute exposure. The exceptional quality of visible details of the daguerreotype encouraged other researchers to develop simpler processes over the following decade. By 1850, photography had already spread around the world, and there are many pictures of cities, places, peoples and subjects that account for a new realistic representation of the world. It was then that it also became a form of art and a very powerful scientific tool.

Photograph analysis

To understand photography it is necessary to develop the skills to make careful visual analysis. The first step consists in a description of the contents of the photograph: shape, size, texture, line, space, etc. It goes without saying that the historical and social context must also be taken into consideration. A closer analysis provides elements of reflection about the composition (arrangement of visual elements) as well as content (meaning). This helps understand the artist's intentions on one particular subject. Each picture offers a variety of interpretations and there is a lot of subjectivity in the way one understands a photograph. There is never a single answer when it comes to interpreting a work of art.

Magnum Photo Cooperative

Magnum is a photo agency that was created in 1947 by Robert Capa, Henri Cartier-Bresson and a collective of other photographers specialising in photoreporting. Henri Cartier-Bresson described the purpose of the agency with the following words:"*Magnum is a community of thought, a shared human quality, a curiosity about what is going on in the world, a respect for what is going on and a desire to transcribe it visually.*" By creating such a cooperative, its members guaranteed a fair redistribution of copyrights. The agency covers many topics, among which war, religion, society, poverty, social conflicts, governments, celebrities and environment. Other famous photo agencies are VII Agency, Agence VU, Oculi, Contact Press, Noor Images and Contrasto. They provide most of the photographs from quality news media covering important events.

Norman Rockwell's Triple Self-portrait: a simple interpretation

The painting shows the artist in the process of painting his self-portrait from a mirror, in an artistic strategy termed a *mise-en-abyme*, a term coined by French writer André Gide. In addition, Rockwell shows four self-portraits of major artists of the genre (Dürer, Rembrandt, Van Gogh and Picasso), visible on the actual work of art. Rockwell honours his predecessors while asserting his individuality by the presence of an eagle, emblem of the USA. Out of the three occurrences of the artist, the portrait on the canvas seems the most flattering, and it is the only one containing the signature of the author. The other two either hide his eyes, or present him in an unflattering posture. Through this work, Rockwell seems to show that all representation is ephemerous, is lying to the viewer and as a painting opposes the objective of photography. This opposition is even more surprising if one takes into account the fact that Rockwell was very much inspired by this form of art (he used photographs as a direct source for most of his paintings). Therefore the strategy of the author may simply be self-derision.

"Photography for me is not looking, it's feeling. If you can't feel what you're looking at, then you're never going to get others to feel anything when they look at your pictures." Don McCullin

"My job as a portrait photographer is to seduce, amuse and entertain." Helmut Newton

"Without thinking too much about it in specific terms, I was showing the America I knew and observed to others who might not have noticed." Norman Rockwell

"Instagram is supposed to be friendly so why is it making people so miserable?" Alex Hern

Section 5
Science and technology

Chapter A

Fundamental sciences

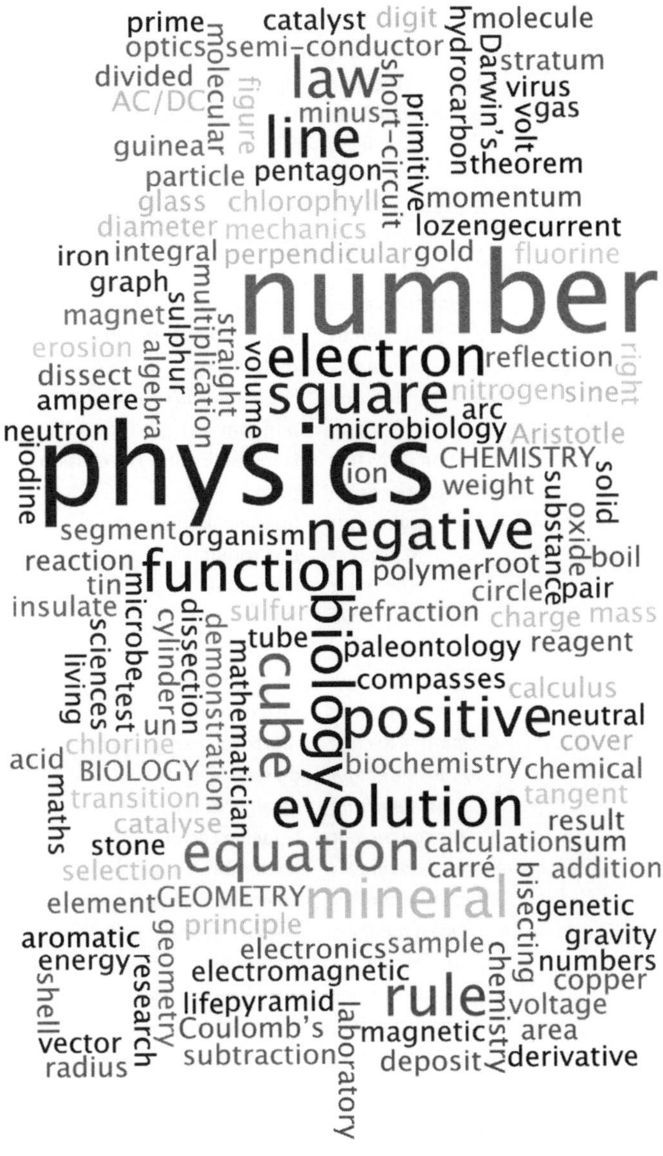

Vocabulary list

MATHEMATICS	**LES MATHÉMATIQUES**
basic research	recherche fondamentale
exact sciences	les sciences exactes
mathematics	les mathématiques
maths (UK) / math (US)	les maths
a postulate	un postulat
a rule	une règle
a proof / a demonstration	une démonstration
a principle	un principe
a reasoning	un raisonnement
a theorem	un théorème
a mathematician	un mathématicien
algebra	l'algèbre
arithmetic	l'arithmétique
a digit, a figure	un chiffre
a number	un nombre
calculus, calculation	le calcul
the four processes	les quatre opérations
plus / minus	plus / moins (opérations)
by / times / divided by	multiplié par / divisé par
addition / subtraction	l'addition / la soustraction
a sum	une somme
multiplication / division	la multiplication / la division
to put / to write down	poser
a calculator	une calculatrice
a product	un produit
the result	le résultat
to total up	totaliser
a fraction	une fraction
a graph	un graphique
an exponent	un exposant
to square / to cube	mettre au carré / au cube
to the power of 4	puissance 4
an algorithm	un algorithme
the square root	la racine carrée
a whole number / an integer	un nombre entier
a negative number	un nombre négatif
odd / even numbers	nombre impair / pair
a prime number	un nombre premier
a rule of three	une règle de trois
the logarithm	le logarithme
a function	une fonction
an equation	une équation
a derivative / primitive / an integral function	une dérivée / une primitive / une intégrale
a differential equation	une équation différentielle

GEOMETRY	**LA GÉOMÉTRIE**
geometry	la géométrie
trigonometry	la trigonométrie
sine / cosine	sinus / cosinus
tangent	une tangente
a point	un point
a straight line	une (ligne) droite
parallel to	parallèle à
perpendicular to	perpendiculaire à
a bisecting line	une ligne bissectrice
a curve	une courbe
a segment	un segment
a vector	un vecteur
an angle	un angle
acute / obtuse / right	aigu / obtus / droit
hypotenuse	une hypoténuse
a triangle	un triangle
a square	un carré
a lozenge / a trapezium	un losange / un trapèze
a rectangle / rectangular	un rectangle / rectangulaire
a pentagon / a polygon	un pentagone / un polygone
a cylinder	un cylindre
the circumference	la circonférence
a (semi-)circle	un (demi-)cercle
an arc	un arc de cercle
a pair of compasses	un compas
the diameter / the radius	le diamètre / le rayon
a sphere	une sphère
a pyramid	une pyramide
a cube	un cube
an edge	un côté
the area, the surface	l'aire, la surface
the volume	le volume

PHYSICS AND ELECTRICITY	**LA PHYSIQUE ET L'ÉLECTRICITÉ**
physics	la physique
Aristotle	Aristote
the heat	la chaleur
mechanics	la mécanique
mass / weight	la masse / le poids
the force	la force
the motion	le mouvement
the friction	la friction, les frottements
the vacuum / void	le vide (obtenu) / le vide absolu
the velocity	la vélocité, la vitesse
the momentum	l'élan / la quantité de mouvement

the energy transfer	le transfert d'énergie
the expansion	la croissance
optics	l'optique
the reflection	la réverbération
the refraction	la réfraction
gravity	la gravité / la pesanteur
an electromagnetic radiation	une radiation électromagnétique
electricity	l'électricité
electronics	l'électronique
a conductor	un conducteur
to insulate / an insulator	isoler / un isolant
the electric / magnetic field	le champ électrique / magnétique
a resistance	une résistance
a condenser	un condensateur
a magnet	un aimant
the current	le courant
a watt / an ampere / a volt	un watt / un ampère / un volt
an electron	un électron
a neutron	un neutron
the voltage	la tension
a short-circuit	un court-circuit
an electrode	une électrode
positive, negative, neutral	positif, négatif, neutre
Coulomb's law	la loi de Coulomb
DC power / AC power	le courant continu, CC / alternatif, CA
semi-conductor physics	la physique des semi-conducteurs
molecular physics	la physique moléculaire
quantum physics	la physique quantique

CHEMISTRY	**LA CHIMIE**
chemistry	la chimie
a laboratory / a lab	un laboratoire
an element	un élément
a liquid	un liquide
a solid	un solide
a gas	un gaz
an ion	un ion
a positive charge	une charge positive
a compound	un composé
the transition elements	les éléments de transition
a particle	une particule
a molecule	une molécule
an atom	un atome
a nucleus	un noyau
the electron shell	la couche électronique
an acid	un acide

a base	une base
aromatic	aromatique
a hydrocarbon	une hydrocarbure
a metal	un métal
a polymer	un polymère
silver	l'argent
nitrogen	l'azote
chlorine	le chlore
copper	le cuivre
tin	l'étain
iron	le fer
fluorine	le fluor
iodine	l'iode
gold	l'or
oxygen	l'oxygène
phosphorus	le phosphore
lead	le plomb
sulphur (GB), sulfur (US)	le soufre
a microscope	un microscope
a test tube	une éprouvette
a reagent	un réactif
a precipitate	un précipité
a reaction	une réaction
to boil	atteindre le point d'ébullition
the combustion	la combustion
to oxidise / oxide	oxyder / l'oxyde
a catalyst	un catalyseur
to catalyse	catalyser

BIOLOGY	**LA BIOLOGIE**
biology	la biologie
zoology	la zoologie
botany	la botanique
a sample	un échantillon
a chemical substance	une substance chimique
a herbarium	un herbier
chlorophyll	la chlorophylle
photosynthesis	la photosynthèse
a living organism	un organisme vivant
the structure	la structure
the growth	la croissance
a cell	une cellule
a unit of life	une unité vitale / de vie
a gene	un gène
a chromosome	un chromosome
genetics	la génétique

the theory of evolution	la théorie de l'évolution
the genetic code	le code génétique
a cross-over	un croisement
Darwin's law	la loi de Darwin
the evolution of species	l'évolution des espèces
natural selection	la sélection naturelle
heredity	l'hérédité
a bacterium (pl. bacteria)	une bactérie
a phenomenon (pl.phenomena)	un phénomène
anatomy	l'anatomie
biochemistry	la biochimie
biotechnologies	les biotechnologies
conservation biology	la biologie de la préservation des espèces
microbiology	la microbiologie
paleontology	la paléontologie
a virus / a microbe	un virus / un microbe
a cover glass	une lamelle
to dissect / dissection	disséquer / la dissection
a guinea pig	un cobaye
a tissue	un tissu
geology	la géologie
a layer / a stratum	une couche / une strate
a sediment	un sédiment
a stone / a rock	une pierre / une roche
a mineral	un minéral
a mineral deposit	un dépôt minéral
a fossil	un fossile
erosion	l'érosion

Translation: English-to-French exercise

Ideal Numbers (adapted from Douglas Hofstadter, *Gödel, Escher, Bach*)

Numbers as realities misbehave. However, there is an ancient and innate sense in people that numbers ought not to misbehave. There is something clean and pure in the abstract notion of number, removed from counting beads, dialects, or clouds; and there ought to be a way of talking about numbers without always having the silliness of reality come in and intrude. The hard-edged rules that govern "ideal" numbers constitute arithmetic, and their more advanced consequences constitute number theory.

There is only one relevant question to be asked, in making the transition from numbers as practical things to numbers as formal things. Once you have decided to capsulize all of number theory in an ideal system, is it really possible to do the job completely? Are numbers so clean and crystalline and regular that their nature can be completely captured in the rules of a formal system?

Adapted press excerpts (about 400 words)

Excerpt 1 – Why science and engineering need to remind students of forgotten lessons from history (adapted from TheConversation.com)

Lately, there has been a lot of discussion highlighting the need for incorporating **social sciences** in **STEM** (**science**, **technology**, **engineering** and **mathematics**) **disciplines** in order to foster **creativity**, increase empathy and create a better **understanding** of the human condition among **scientists**. Unfortunately, however, all this talk hasn't changed the reality on the ground. We have failed to connect students to the history of **science** through stories of **scientists**. Our students, these days, have little **knowledge** about the giants on whose shoulders we all stand. And yet there is strong **evidence** that students are more likely to develop an interest in **science** and pursue science **education** when engaged through narratives that tell a story.

Excerpt 2 – Teaching mathematics – Time for a ceasefire (adapted from *The Economist*)

Maths education has been a battlefield before: the American "math wars" of the 1980s pitted traditionalists, who emphasised fluency in **pen-and-paper calculations**, against reformers led by the country's biggest teaching lobby, who put real-world **problem-solving**, often with the help of **calculators**, at the centre of the **curriculum**. A backlash followed as parents and academics worried that the "new math" left pupils ill-prepared for university courses in **mathematics** and **sciences**. But as many countries have since found, training pupils to ace **exams** is not the same as equipping them to use their hard-won **knowledge** in work and life. Today's reformers think new technology renders this old argument redundant.

Excerpt 3 – Four More Place Settings at the Periodic Table (adapted from *Slate*)

Well, this doesn't happen terribly often: scientists recently created / discovered four new **elements**. It gets complicated quickly, and that has to do with **radioactivity**. Most of the elements you see in the **Periodic Table** are stable, so if you have a **sample** of one you can **study** it relatively easily. But after 92 (uranium) the elements are highly **unstable**, **radioactive**, and decay into lower-numbered elements sometimes in a teeny fraction of a second. It takes a **particle accelerator** to create these new elements – usually by **bombarding** lighter elements with **protons** – so not everyone can do it, or confirm someone else's work. A new element has to have a different number of protons in its **nucleus** than any element seen before. In the case of the new elements, they have 113, 115, 117, and 118 protons in their **nuclei**.

Excerpt 4 – How far can a Buddhist approach to biology take us? (adapted from *The New Scientist*)

At first glance, Buddhism and **science** seem natural bedfellows. Both seek **essential truths** about the world and the human condition and both set great store on their **empirical** approach. How far can a Buddhist approach to **biology** take us? The Buddhist approach to **understanding** is largely **subjective**: no one can meditate for you. And certain Buddhist principles, such as **reincarnation**, are blatantly **unscientific**. **Science**, on the other hand, requires **verification** and is often poor at **quantifying** personal **experience** (note the "hard problem" of consciousness). Above all, whereas **science** strives for **objective knowledge**, Buddhism offers an ethical framework in which to apply it. It is necessary to highlight the **parallels** between the two **disciplines**, which complement each other like a pair of powerful searchlights illuminating the same thing from different angles.

Food for Thought and Quotations (about 500 words)

Isaac Newton

As the British empire was expanding, universities like Oxford and Cambridge hosted and trained great scientists. Physicist, mathematician, astronomer, natural philosopher, alchemist and theologian, Isaac Newton (1643-1727) is considered to be one of the most influential men in human history. Co-inventor of calculus, a major contributor to the science of optics and a gifted mathematician, he also outlined the laws of mechanics and the principle of gravity (the apple tree anecdote). His revolutionary approach to mathematics (termed *infinitesimal calculus*) allowed scientists to analyse motion and dynamics, to explain the orbits of planets, the motion of fluids, etc. It has given birth to what is today termed differential and integral calculus in mathematics. In 1687, Newton published his "*Principia*" or "*The Mathematical Principles of Natural Philosophy*", generally considered as the greatest scientific book ever written. He is also renowned for his writings on alchemy and religion.

Pi (π)

Pi, in mathematics, corresponds to the ratio of the circumference of a circle to its diameter. The symbol π was devised by British mathematician William Jones in 1706 to represent the ratio. Pi is an irrational number (that is, not equal to the ratio of any two whole numbers), its digits do never repeat, and the approximate ratio 22/7 is used for general calculations. Four thousands years ago, the Babylonians had an approximate number for the circumference (3.12), but Archimedes (circa 250 B.C.) discovered a way to identify a very precise value (3.1418). Today, it is possible to obtain trillions of decimal places for a greater accuracy. The modern applications of Pi span mathematical problems, physics and engineering.

Alchemy and Chemistry

Alchemy can be considered the forerunner of modern chemistry. It is not exactly science, but it refers to an ancient tradition that established the use of procedures, equipment and terminology, that would ultimately form modern chemistry, which deals with matter and its transformation. The connotation is that of a magical process of transformation or creation. Chemistry, on the other hand, deals with the identification of the substances of which matter is composed. The ideal and initial goal of alchemy is to transform matter into gold. It investigates the properties, the interactions and combinations of substances the the implied changes, particularly the formation of new substances. In brief, alchemy was chemistry in its adolescence. Most alchemical concepts have been disregarded as pseudoscientific, but its developments were crucial in establishing the basis of modern chemistry.

Basic (or pure) research and applied research

Basic research is scientific study aimed at improving scientific theories to understand a phenomenon; it is the source of most new scientific ideas. It aims to explore, describe or explain phenomena in order to refute, challenge, support or validate existing theories. Applied research uses scientific theories to develop technology in order to change a phenomenon. Applied science therefore focuses on development, while basic science develops scientific knowledge in natural and empirical sciences, which are used as the scientific foundation for applied science. Applied and basic sciences can interface closely in research and development.

"There is a fundamental difference between religion, which is based on authority, and science, which is based on observation and reason. Science will win because it works."
Stephen Hawking

"The study of mathematics is apt to commence in disappointment... We are told that by its aid the stars are weighed and the billions of molecules in a drop of water are counted. Yet, like the ghost of Hamlet's father, this great science eludes the efforts of our mental weapons to grasp it." Alfred North Whitehead

Chapter B

Space exploration and movement

Vocabulary list

SPACE	**L'ESPACE**
the solar system	le système solaire
a constellation	une constellation
the Great Bear	la Grande ourse
a galaxy	une galaxie
the Milky Way	la Voie lactée
a celestial body	un corps céleste
a star	une étoile
the Sun / a sun flare	le soleil / une éruption solaire
a planet	une planète
a satellite / a moon	un satellite / une lune
an asteroid / a meteor	un astéroïde / un météore
a meteorite	une météorite
a shooting / falling star	une étoile filante
a comet	une comète
a black hole	un trou noir
a space probe	une sonde spatiale
the orbit	l'orbite
to rotate / rotation	tourner (sur soi-même) / rotation
to revolve around / revolution	tourner autour (révolution)
gravity	la gravité
an eclipse (total, partial / annular)	une éclipse (totale, partielle / annulaire)
the Moon (new / full)	la lune (nouvelle, pleine)
a crater	un cratère
Mercury, Venus, Mars	Mercure, Vénus, Mars
Jupiter, Saturn	Jupiter, Saturne
Uranus, Neptune	Uranus, Neptune
Pluto / a dwarf planet	Pluton / une planète naine
the asteroid belt	la ceinture d'astéroïdes
an inch	un pouce (2,5 cm)
a foot	un pied (30 cm)
a yard	un yard (0,9 m)
a mile	un mile (1,6 km)
an astronomical unit	une UA (150 millions de km)
a light-year	une année-lumière (9 500 milliards de km)
a centi / milli / kilo[...]meter	un (centi / milli / kilo...)mètre
one thousand miles per hour	1600 km/h
a square / cubic meter	un mètre carré / cube
1000 square feet	90 mètres carré

ASTRONOMY	**L'ASTRONOMIE**
astronomy	l'astronomie
the celestial sphere / the sky	la voûte céleste
binoculars	des jumelles

a telescope	un télescope
a lens / an eyepiece	une lentille / l'oculaire
a reflector	un miroir
a tripod	un trépied
light	la lumière
the speed of light / lightspeed	la vitesse de la lumière
an astronomer	un astronome
penumbra	la pénombre
the pitch-dark night	la nuit noire
zenith	le zénith
North star / pole star	l'étoile polaire
a radio telescope	un radio-télescope
the radio waves	les ondes radio
a parabolic reflector	un réflecteur parabolique
an observatory	un observatoire
a rotating dome	un dôme tournant
the observation post	le poste d'observation

SPACE EXPLORATION	**L'EXPLORATION SPATIALE**
astronautics	l'exploration spatiale, l'astronautique
to launch	lancer
a launcher	un lanceur
a space shuttle	une navette spatiale
a spaceship, a spacecraft	un vaisseau spatial
manned / unmanned	habité / inhabité
the International Space Station (ISS)	la station spatiale internationale
a rocket	une fusée
a booster / a retrorocket	un propulseur / une rétrofusée
a space suit	une combinaison spatiale
a spationaut	un spationaute (Fr)
a cosmonaut	un cosmonaute (Ru)
an astronaut, a spaceman(woman)	un astronaute (US)
the crew / the staff	l'équipage / le personnel
a pilot	un pilote
a flight instructor	un instructeur de vol
a flight simulator	un simulateur de vol
to explore	explorer
to orbit a satellite	placer un satellite en orbite
to retrieve	récupérer
to fly a mission	participer à une mission spatiale

GOALS	**LES OBJECTIFS**
a lift-off / a take-off	un décollage
a blast-off	une mise à feu
the countdown	le compte à rebours
we have lift-off!	Décollage !

to propel	propulser
space venture	l'aventure spatiale
weightlessness	l'apesanteur
a moon landing	un alunissage
a moon walk	une marche sur la lune
re-entry into the atmosphere	l'entrée dans l'atmosphère
the docking / to dock with	l'arrimage / s'arrimer à
a touchdown / splashdown	atterrissage / amerrissage
a breakdown	une panne
a major malfunction	un dysfonctionnement grave
to abort a launch	interrompre / abandonner un lancement
to postpone	reporter
to cancel	annuler
a space flight	un vol spatial
space-based	placé dans l'espace
a space colony	une colonie spatiale
a communications satellite	un satellite de télécommunications
a weather satellite	un satellite météorologique
a spy satellite	un satellite espion
satellite transmission	la transmission par satellite
to probe space	sonder l'espace
to sample the soil	sonder le sol / prélever des échantillons
to provide satellite images	fournir des prises de vue par satellite
to map	dresser la carte de
a stray satellite	un satellite à la dérive
a rescue attempt	une mission de sauvetage
extraterrestrial lifeform	forme de vie extraterrestre
little green men	les martiens
alien / an alien	étranger / une forme de vie inconnue
a flying saucer	une soucoupe volante
a UFO (unidentified flying object)	un OVNI (objet volant non identifié)
to colonize	coloniser
the high frontier (the final frontier)	la frontière de l'espace
space tourism	le tourisme de l'espace

MOVEMENT	**LE MOUVEMENT**
to move / a movement	bouger / un mouvement
a move	une action
motion	le mouvement
to come / to go	venir / aller (partir, quitter)
to start	commencer
to finish	finir
to continue	continuer
to turn round	faire demi-tour
to wander	errer
to pass sth / to go past sth	passer devant / dépasser qqch

to leave	quitter, partir
to approach / to draw near	approcher de
to head for	se diriger vers
to reach	atteindre
to arrive / the arrival	arriver / l'arrivée
to come again	revenir / venir à nouveau
to get back / to be back	revenir / être de retour
to cross / to come across	traverser / croiser par hasard
to drive to / to lead to	conduire à / amener à
to follow / to go after	suivre / poursuivre
to flee	fuir
to speed up / to accelerate	accélérer
to gather momentum / to quicken	s'accélérer / gagner de l'accélération
to dash / to haste	se hâter, se précipiter
to slow down	décélérer, ralentir
sluggish	très lent
to linger (on)	s'attarder, stagner
to lag behind	être à la traîne
to delay / a delay	repousser / un retard
to suspend	suspendre
to remove sth	enlever qch
to shift sth	changer qch de place
to pile up	empiler
to lean sth against sth	appuyer qch contre qch
to insert sth into sth	insérer qch dans qch
to withdraw sth from	retirer qch de
to put away sth	ranger, retirer qch

BONUS	**BONUS**
*once in a blue **moon***	rarement / de temps en temps
*to live on another **planet***	vivre sur une autre planète
*to come back down to **earth***	revenir sur terre
*everything under the **sun***	tout ce qui existe / tout ce qui est imaginable
*to be over the **moon***	être aux anges
*breathing **space***	un espace vital
*Watch this **space**!*	gardez un œil sur ce site
*out of this **world***	exceptionnel(le)
*to reach for the **stars***	vouloir décrocher la Lune
*to see **stars***	voir trente-six chandelles
*the **sky** is the limit*	le potentiel est illimité
*to fight every **inch** of the way*	lutter pied à pied
*to know every **inch** of sth*	connaître qch comme sa poche
*give her an **inch** and she'll take a **yard***	plus on lui en donne, plus elle en veut
*to **inch** across sth*	franchir qch petit à petit
*to **probe** into sth*	enquêter sur / fouiller dans

*to **boost** sb's confidence*	redonner confiance à qqn
*to take off like a **rocket***	partir en trombe
*to **rocket** to fame*	accéder rapidement à la célébrité
*to **belt** home*	rentrer chez soi à toute vitesse
*to see the **light***	commencer à comprendre
*to do sth according to one's **lights***	faire comme on l'entend
many hands make light work	à plusieurs la besogne va vite / l'union fait la force
*to go out like a **light***	s'endormir tout de suite

Translation: English-to-French exercise

One Star Over, a Planet That Might Be Another Earth (adapté de *The New York Times*)

Astronomers recently announced that they had detected a planet orbiting Proxima Centauri, the closest neighbor to our solar system. Intriguingly, the planet is in the star's "Goldilocks zone," where it may be neither too hot nor too cold. That means liquid water could exist at the surface, raising the possibility for life.

Beyond the planet's size and distance from its parent star, much about it is still mysterious. Scientists are working off computer models that offer mere hints of what's possible: conditions could be Earthlike, but they could also be hellish like Venus, or cold like Mars.

A privately funded team of scientists and technology titans are designing a project to develop and launch a fleet of iPhone-size spacecraft within two to three decades.

Adapted press excerpts (about 400 words)

Excerpt 1 – Brave New Worlds (adapted from *The Economist*)

It may turn out to be a **bare** and **barren rock**. The fact that **liquid water** could be flowing across the **surface** of the **planet** just discovered **orbiting** Proxima Centauri, the nearest **star** to the **sun**, does not mean that it has an **atmosphere**. The fact that water and air, if present, could make this new world **habitable** does not mean that it is, in fact, a **home** to **alien life**. But it might be. What is exciting about this new world is not what is known – which, so far, is almost nothing. It is what is unknown and the possibilities it may contain. In the immense **distances** of **space** that is close enough to mean that, some day, perhaps, someone might send **probes** to visit it and in so doing glimpse a totally different **form of life.**

Excerpt 2 – The hunt for Planet Nine reveals some strange, far-out objects (adapted from L.A.Times)

Astronomers hunting for **Planet** Nine have found some 50 new **objects** lying beyond the **orbit** of Neptune – including a few that may help them track down this elusive, distant world.The Kuiper **belt** lies **past** Neptune's **orbit** from 30 to 55 **astronomical units**; the Oort cloud stretches from about 5,000 to 100,000 astronomical units from the sun. Nothing significant was really thought to hang out in the thick doughnut of **space** between those two, until the 2003 discovery of a roughly 600-mile-wide **rock** called Sedna. 2012 VP113's perihelion is similar. The **scientists** noticed something else strange: 2012 VP113 and Sedna both seemed to be making their closest **approach** to the sun at similar **angles**. This could mean that something big, far out in the **darkness**, was tugging on both their **orbits** in the same way. The hunt was now on for **Planet Nine**. In 2019, the New Horizons probe reached Arrokoth, the farthest object ever visited.

Excerpt 3 – Incoming! New Warning System Tracks Potentially Dangerous Asteroids (adapted from space.com)

A new early **warning system** may help speed up **calculations** of when and where incoming **asteroids** could **strike** Earth. By monitoring **observations** of newly reported **space objects**, a computer program called Scout can quickly **identify** potentially dangerous asteroids, then automatically call for follow-ups to **calculate** a more precise path for these **bodies**. These are **objects** that **observers** have reported, and they suspect them to be asteroids. They are most likely **asteroids**, but they need to be confirmed by other observers. While **midsize** asteroids are frequently identified well before they **hit** Earth, smaller objects can be more difficult to **spot** and classify ahead of time. Correctly **classifying** these objects and determining their **orbits** takes multiple observations. And, especially for potentially **hazardous impactors**, the sooner the better.

Excerpt 4 – Reality guide: Six problems physics can't explain (adapted from *The New Scientist*)

General **relativity** and **quantum theory** are the two pillars of modern **physics**, peerlessly accurate in their respective realms of the very large and the very small. But where they meet, they produce **contradictory** answers. From the dark energy ripping the **cosmos** apart to the part consciousness plays in creating reality, **quantum physics** and **cosmology** retain many mysteries. Take dark matter. Earth whirls around the sun at a speed determined by its distance, the **sun's mass** and **gravity's strength**, which is a **universal** constant of nature. You don't need general relativity to work that out: Newton's old-school **gravitation** will do. The same law should apply to **distant galaxies** swirling around their common **centre of mass**. **Galactic clusters** contain about six parts of invisible **matter** for every one part of visible matter. This "**dark matter**" must interact **gravitationally** to produce the motion, but hardly at all through the other forces of nature. **Galaxies** rotate too quickly for their visible matter.

Food for Thought and Quotations (about 500 words)

Neil Armstrong's true words revealed

"That's one small step for a man, one giant leap for mankind," were the first words NASA astronaut Neil Armstrong uttered when he set foot on our only natural satellite on July 21, 1969. Or were they? Armstrong himself has always insisted he said "one small step for a man" not "one small step for man", without the A article that gives another meaning to the whole sentence.' This could be explained by a combination of acoustic factors including the noisy radio signal, the 250,000-mile distance, the incredibly stressful situation for the astronaut that affected his speaking pace, but unexpectedly also his particular North American Midwest accent. A study was conducted that played the two phrases including "for" or "for a" in a Midwest accent for a selection of American participants, who found the two indistinguishable and did not hear the "a" for most of them. Experts listeners expected all syllables to be lengthened proportionally, whereas the duration of the very brief "a" sound (in phonetics, this sound is termed *schwa*, and corresponds to the least phonetic effort required for the pronunciation of a vowel) became shorter in comparison to the lengthened syllables surrounding it. In phonetics, *schwa* is the pronunciation of an unstressed syllable in English in many cases.

Satellites in orbit around the Earth and elsewhere

The first artificial satellite, Sputnik 1, was placed in orbit on October 4, 1957. Since then, more than Following in these historic footsteps, many more spacecraft have been sent into Earth's orbit, around the Moon, the Sun, the other planets, and even out of the Solar System itself. In 2016, there are more than a thousand operational satellites in orbit around the Earth. Half of them are placed in low-Earth orbit (the International Space Station, the Hubble Telescope or space observation devices), and apart from a handful of medium-Earth satellites used for Global Positioning System (GPS), the rest are in geostationary orbit, at an altitude of 36,000 kilometres. Those remain above the same area in order to provide telecommunications, internet or weather forecast services. Looking farther, a few satellites are orbiting the Moon, about ten spacecrafts are revolving around Mercury, Venus, Mars, Jupiter and Saturn. Last, NASA's Voyager 1 and 2 spacecrafts that were launched in 1977, recently exited the Solar System, and have entered the interstellar zone.

Interstellar travel

Proxima Centauri is the closest star to our Solar System, 4.2 light years away. Not wishing to go into science fiction, how long will it realistically take to get there? At the speed of Voyager 1 (60,000 km per hour), it would take 76,000 years to travel that distance. But if it could attain the fastest man-made object constant speed of 240,000 km/hour, it would take only 19,000 years, which is significantly less, but still unrealistic. NASA has been exploring the potential of nuclear engines, and the best option would require several decades of travel time, followed by many more centuries of deceleration before reaching it destination. The total would amount to about 1000 years before it reaches its destination.

"*Since, in the long run, every planetary civilization will be endangered by impacts from space, every surviving civilization is obliged to become spacefaring – not because of exploratory or romantic zeal, but for the most practical reason imaginable: staying alive... If our long-term survival is at stake, we have a basic responsibility to our species to venture to other worlds.*" Carl Sagan

"*When you observe a distant star, you see it as it was in the distant past and not as it is today. In other words, looking out is looking back.*" Hubert Reeves

Chapter C
Research

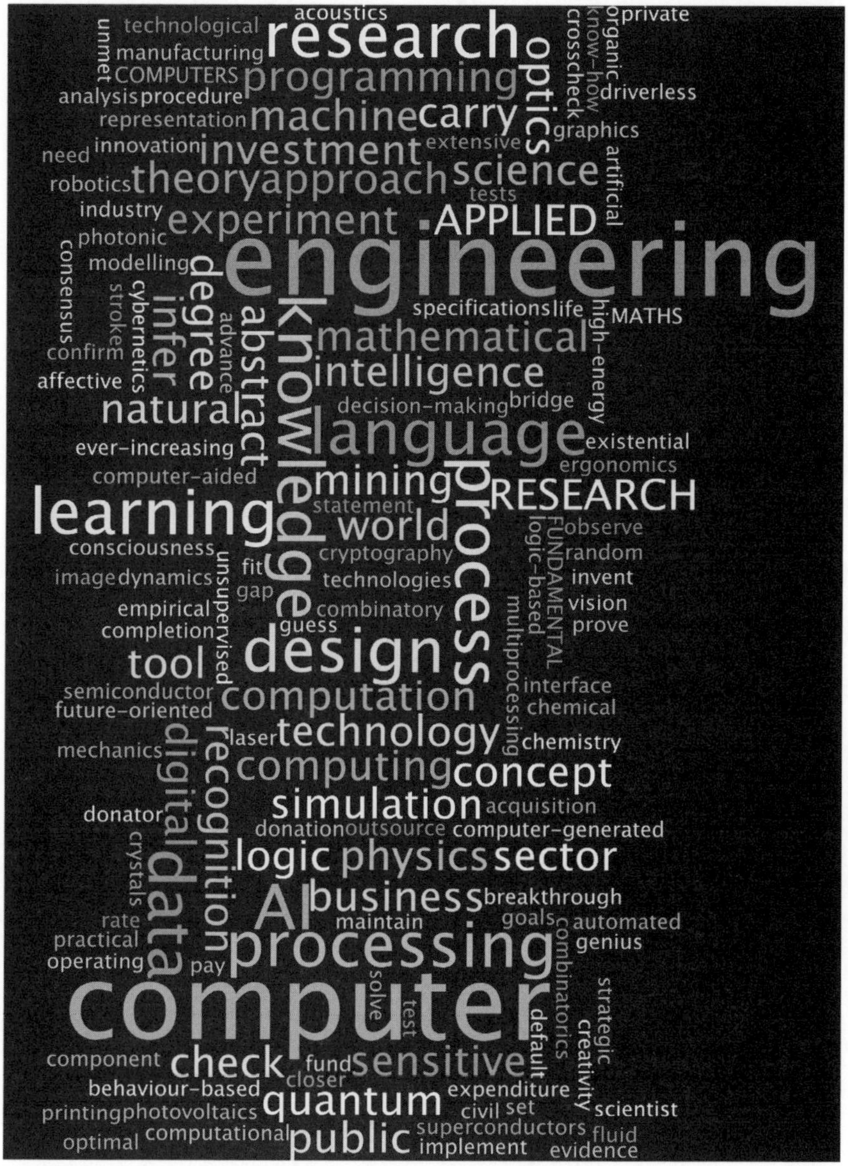

Vocabulary list

FUNDAMENTAL RESEARCH	**LA RECHERCHE FONDAMENTALE**
research	la recherche
to do research	faire des recherches
a researcher	un chercheur
a field	un domaine
to experiment with / on sth	mener des expériences sur
to carry out an experiment	mener une expérience
a hypothesis	une hypothèse
a thesis statement	une problématique
an abstract	un résumé de publication
a procedure / a protocol	une procédure / un protocole
to observe / observation	observer / l'observation
to discover / a discovery	découvrir / une découverte
to infer sth from / to infer that	inférer qch de / inférer que
to find / findings	trouver / des conclusions
to synthesise / a synthesis	synthétiser / une synthèse
to solve	résoudre
evidence	des preuves
to prove / to disprove	prouver / réfuter
to confirm / to invalidate	confirmer / infirmer
to carry out tests	réaliser / faire des tests
random	aléatoire
empirical	empirique
to check	vérifier
to double check	vérifier à nouveau
a crosscheck	un recoupement
an advance	un progrès
a major breakthrough	une avancée majeure
a milestone	une étape importante
to foster science	promouvoir la science
to revolutionise	révolutionner
a stroke of genius / of luck	un éclair de génie / un coup de chance
a patent	un brevet
funds for research	le financement de la recherche
a subsidy	une subvention
a donation / a donator	une donation / un donateur
investment	les investissements
public / private funding	le financement public / privé
cutbacks	les restrictions, les coupes budgétaires
sponsoring	le parrainage, le mécénat
to subsidise	subventionner
to fund	financer

ENGINEERING	**L'INGÉNIERIE**
engineering	l'ingénierie / le génie
to invent	inventer
to design / the design	concevoir / un projet
to maintain / the maintenance	entretenir / l'entretien
to improve / improvements	améliorer / des améliorations
a tool	un outil
a component	un composant
a process	un processus, un procédé
to process	développer / usiner
a machine tool	une machine-outil
civil engineering	le génie civil
an aircraft design process	la conception d'un projet d'avion
chemical engineering	l'ingénierie chimique
mechanical engineering	le génie mécanique
to manufacture	fabriquer
marketability	la vendabilité
serviceability	le fonctionnement, la viabilité
specifications	les caractéristiques techniques

APPLIED MATHS	**LES MATHÉMATIQUES APPLIQUÉES**
computational mathematics	les mathématiques informatiques
combinatory logic	la logique combinatoire
a practical / concrete problem	un problème concret / pratique
an abstract concept	un concept abstrait
specialised knowledge	les connaissances spécialisées
probability	les probabilités
fluid mechanics	la mécanique des fluides
the number theory	la théorie du nombre
a variational method	une méthode variationnelle
a consensus	un consensus
cryptography	la cryptographie
high-performance computing	calcul / informatique de haute performance
numerical analysis	l'analyse numérique
mathematical finance	mathématiques appliquées à la finance
mathematical modelling	la modélisation mathématique
statistics	l'étude des statistiques
combinatorics	l'analyse combinatoire

APPLIED PHYSICS	**LA PHYSIQUE APPLIQUÉE**
the technological uses	les applications technologiques
to bridge the gap between	combler une faille / rapprocher
a basic concept	un concept de base
a high-energy collider	un accélérateur de particules
a laser	un laser
quantum optics	l'optique quantique

photonic crystals	des cristaux photoniques
a semiconductor	un semi-conducteur
acoustics	l'acoustique
ballistics	la balistique
the optimal control theory	la théorie du contrôle optimal
fiber optics	les fibres optiques
organic photovoltaics	le photovoltaïque organique
quantum physics	la physique quantique
superconductors	les supraconducteurs
solid-state physics / chemistry	la physique / chimie appliquée des solides
vehicle dynamics	la dynamique des véhicules

RESEARCH AND DEVELOPMENT	**LA RECHERCHE ET LE DÉVELOPPEMENT**
the test technologies	les technologies d'essais
an innovation	une innovation
to implement	mettre en application, implémenter
to theorise	émettre une théorie
a sector of industry	un secteur industriel
a strategic alliance	une alliance stratégique
a partnership	un partenariat
a publication / to publish	une publication / publier
a Master's degree	une maîtrise
a PhD	un doctorat
the competition	la concurrence, la compétition
the degree of completion	le degré d'achèvement, d'avancement, de finition
to amortise, to pay for, to cushion	amortir (un coût)
a strategy	une stratégie
the business world	le monde des affaires
the corporate world	le monde des entreprises
a market share	une part de marché
business	les affaires
the return on investment	le retour sur investissement
public expenditure	les dépenses publiques
the technology life cycle	le cycle de vie des technologies
ergonomics / ergonomy	l'ergonomie (science) / l'ergonomie (pratique)
a closer fit	une meilleure ergonomie
a worldwide programme	un programme d'envergure mondiale
a future-oriented sector	un secteur tourné vers l'avenir
to outsource / out-sourced	sous-traiter / sous-traité
continuous	continu
an unmet need	un besoin non satisfait
a know-how	un savoir-faire
profit / profitability	le bénéfice / la rentabilité
technology transfer	le transfert de technologies

COMPUTERS	L'INFORMATIQUE
computer science	l'informatique / la science informatique
computation	le calcul (informatique)
mechanisation	la mécanisation
programming	la programmation
a computer scientist	un informaticien
computer graphics	l'infographie
ubiquitous	omniprésent
the Information age	l'ère de l'information / de l'informatisation
the digital revolution	la révolution numérique
a programming language	un langage de programmation
computer-generated imagery	l'imagerie assistée par ordinateur
computer-aided manufacturing	la PAO (production assistée par ordinateur)
3D printing	l'impression en 3D
a 3D printer	une imprimante 3D
a simulation	une simulation
to optimise / optimisation	optimiser / l'optimisation
computerisation	l'informatisation
an integrated circuit	un circuit intégré

AI	INTELLIGENCE ARTIFICIELLE
artificial intelligence (AI)	l'intelligence artificielle (IA)
software engineering	l'ingénierie informatique
machine learning	l'apprentissage automatique
computer vision	la vision par ordinateur
image processing	le traitement des images
pattern recognition	la reconnaissance des formes
data mining	l'extraction / l'exploitation des données
evolutionary computation	les algorithmes évolutifs
knowledge representation	la représentation de la connaissance
natural language processing	le traitement des langues naturelles
automated translation	la traduction automatique
robotics	la robotique
an operating system	un système d'exploitation
digital logic	la logique numérique
data processing	le traitement des données
multiprocessing	le multi-traitement
computer security	la sécurité informatique
the big data	les bases de données géantes / l'avalanche de données
a natural language interface	une interface de reconnaissance linguistique
voice recognition	la reconnaissance vocale
perception	la perception
deduction	la déduction
extensive knowledge	la parfaite connaissance

intensive learning / acquisition	l'acquisition intensive
default reasoning	le raisonnement par défaut / par élimination
commonsense	le bon sens, le sens commun
to set goals	déterminer, fixer des objectifs
unsupervised learning	l'apprentissage en autonomie
text mining	exploitation de données textuelles
intelligence	l'intelligence / les informations / le renseignement
creativity	la créativité
affective computing	la reconnaissance autonome
brain stimulation	la stimulation cérébrale
cybernetics	la cybernétique
a logic-based approach	une approche fondée sur la logique
a behaviour-based application	une application basée sur l'analyse comportementale
the best guess	la meilleure estimation / supposition
malevolent / friendly AI	l'IA malveillante / bienveillante
consciousness	la conscience
a sensitive approach	une approche sensible
sensible / sensitive	sensé / sensible
a cyborg	un cyborg
an ever-increasing rate	une vitesse en constante augmentation
existential risks	risques existentiels
moral decision-making	la prise de décision morale
a driverless car	une voiture autonome

Translation: English-to-French exercise

What happens when our computers get smarter than we are? (adapté de TED Talks)

Today, the action is really around machine learning. So rather than handcrafting knowledge representations and features, we create algorithms that learn, often from raw data. Basically the same thing that the human infant does.

The result is A.I. that is not limited to one domain – the same system can learn to translate between any pairs of languages, or learn to play any computer game on the Atari console.

Obviously, A.I. is still nowhere near having the same cross-domain ability to learn and plan as a human being has. The cortex still has some algorithmic tricks that we don't yet know how to match in machines.

Adapted press excerpts (about 400 words)

Excerpt 1 – Blind, Paraplegic, And Quite Possibly The World's Greatest Athlete: Meet The Bionic Man (adapted from *Good Magazine*)

Mark Pollock stands up – a little unsteadily at first, like a guy recovering from a long night. He exhales, centering himself, the crutch in each hand providing a modicum of support. He's in great shape – six feet tall, barrel-chested, muscles bulging through a tight shirt. He's handsome, the kind of guy who can pull it off. [...] To know Mark Pollock well, to really understand him, you have to divine something about the **relationship** between **man** and **machine**. Watching Pollock walk, it's obvious that he's achieved a certain **synchronicity** with the **mechanical**. Though he can't move his legs on his own, he stands and takes steps with the aid of an unobtrusive **bionic exoskeleton** – a **robotic suit** worn over his clothes.

Excerpt 2 – AI's Language Problem (adapted from *MIT technological review*)

Machines that truly **understand** language would be incredibly useful. But we don't know how to build them. AlphaGo's surprising success points to just how much progress has been made in **artificial intelligence** over the last few years, after decades of frustration and setbacks often described as an "**AI winter**." Deep learning means that machines can increasingly **teach themselves** how to perform **complex tasks** that only a couple of years ago were thought to require the **unique intelligence** of humans. Self-driving cars are already a **foreseeable possibility**. In the near future, systems based on deep learning will help diagnose diseases and recommend treatments. Yet despite these impressive advances, one fundamental capability remains elusive: language. Systems like Siri can't **hold a conversation** and have no real understanding of the words they use. If AI is to be truly **transformative**, this must change.

Excerpt 3 – The jobs we'll lose to machines – and the ones we won't (adapted from TED Talks)

In 2013, researchers at Oxford University did a study on the future of work. They concluded that almost one in every two jobs have a high risk of being **automated** by **machines**. **Machine learning** is the **technology** that's responsible for most of this disruption. It's the most powerful branch of **artificial intelligence**. It allows machines to **learn from data** and mimic some of the things that humans can do. Machine learning started making its way into **industry** in the early '90s. It started with relatively simple **tasks**. It started with things like assessing credit risk from loan applications, sorting the mail by reading handwritten characters from zip codes. Over the past few years, we have made dramatic **breakthroughs**. Machine learning is now capable of far, far more **complex tasks**. So complex that in 2019, Elon Musk believes it will make job pointless.

Excerpt 4 – Are we ready for quantum biology? (adapted from *New Scientist*)

For 15 years, theoretical physicist Jim Al-Khalili and molecular geneticist Johnjoe McFadden have been discussing how **quantum physics**, the science of the incredibly small, might affect **biology**. By explaining the **fundamentals** of **quantum mechanics**, and exploring recent **theories** and **findings**, they aim to convince the reader that quantum effects are more than simply the deep **substrate** on which **biology** exists – without recourse to a single **equation**. Some of quantum mechanics' apparently successful forays into biology are those focusing on how **enzymes** work and on **photosynthesis**. Even here, however, the significance of these interpretations is still debated – in particular, it remains **unclear** how decisive a part quantum **entanglement** plays in **biology**. Quantum biology is coming of age. It can equally be argued that it is still taking its first steps.

Food for Thought and Quotations (about 500 words)

Research and development (1)

As seen before, research can be either basic or applied, a distinction that was established in the first half of the 20th century. But the expression R&D at that time was unknown. Today, the concept of research and development cannot be dissociated from economic planning, by both government and by private industry. It has become a universal concept in developed countries. From the French Revolution to the end of World War Two, the priority of applied research for industrial development was for military purposes, but most of the innovations made since 1790 spread fast in the civil society: telegraph, balloon, photography and later telephone, radio, combustion engine, etc. After 1914, governments planned teamwork rather than individual research, and the corporate world also started investing huge funds in research departments, later labeled R&D departments.

Research and development (2)

Until the 1929 Great Depression, public and private laboratories spread and gave birth to cars, airplanes, television and other inventions that led to the appliances and applications of our modern 21st century society. World War Two gave the military and many businesses new opportunities to invest and create laboratories, and the R&D strategies gathered momentum, particularly in the US, and later in Europe after the post-WWII reconstruction. By then, the limit was the shortage of trained engineers and scientists. Today, the most dynamic sectors are aircraft, defense, space, electronics, and computers. Today, the role of governments has decreased in terms of financial means while independent and company laboratories have gained importance.

It refers to anything related to computing technology, such as networking, hardware, software, the internet or the people that work with these technologies.

Data mining

Data mining combines tools from statistics and artificial intelligence, in order to identify relevant patterns and relationships in large volumes of data. This knowledge discovery technique is widely used in business, scientific research, and government security. The data-mining process implies a specific organisation, in three key computational steps: the model-learning process, the model evaluation, and the use of the model. When the type of known information and the required knowledge have been clearly defined, modelling can be predictive, simply descriptive or pattern-identifying. The technical assets and limits are similar to those of statistical analysis. The privacy concerns are more worrying, since the potential breach using data mining is obvious (commercial database, medical files, banking transactions, telephone usage, geolocation, etc.).

"I believe that at the end of the century the use of words and general educated opinion will have altered so much that one will be able to speak of machines thinking without expecting to be contradicted." Alan Turing

"Geology does better in reclothing dry bones and revealing lost creations, than in tracing veins of lead and beds of iron; astronomy better in opening to us the houses of heaven than in teaching navigation; surgery better in investigating organisation than in setting limbs; only it is ordained that, for our encouragement, every step we make in science adds something to its practical applicabilities." John Ruskin

"Why does this magnificent applied science which saves work and makes life easier bring us so little happiness?... The simple answer runs: Because we have not yet learned to make sensible use of it." Albert Einstein

Chapter D

Genetics and Ethics

Vocabulary list

GENETICS	**LA GÉNÉTIQUE**
the gene / the genome	le gène / le génome
a genetic map	une carte génétique
a genetic fingerprint	une empreinte génétique
DNA fingerprinting	l'analyse d'une empreinte génétique
sequencing	le séquençage
a gene sequence	une séquence génétique
a DNA strand	un brin d'ADN
a single-celled organism	un organisme unicellulaire
a copy strand	un brin répliqué
DNA replication	la réplication de l'ADN
an allele	un allèle
the crossing-over	le croisement
a dominant trait	un trait dominant
a recessive trait	un trait récessif
the fertilisation	la fécondation
a gamete	un gamète
an egg	un œuf
a genotype / a phenotype	un génotype / un phénotype
heredity	l'hérédité
a hybrid	une forme hybride
meiosis	la méiose
pollination	la pollinisation
a DNA test	un test génétique
a DNA sample	un échantillon d'ADN
the genetic profile	le profil génétique
to be DNA-swabbed	subir un prélèvement d'ADN

ENGINEERING	**L'INGÉNIERIE**
genetic engineering	les manipulations génétiques
a genetic engineer / a gene scientist	un généticien
the genetic code	le code génétique
the gene pool / blueprint	le patrimoine génétique
a gene therapy	une thérapie génique
a stem cell	une cellule souche
an embryo	un embryon
to harvest stem cells	récolter / créer des cellules souches
human / animal cloning	le clonage humain / animal
a recipient	un receveur
a donor	un donneur
therapeutic / reproductive cloning	le clonage thérapeutique / reproductif
to repair	réparer
to extract	extraire
a replacement part	une pièce de rechange

a human organ tissue	du tissu d'un organe humain
a designer baby	un bébé sur mesure
a genetic disease	une maladie génétique
a missing gene	un gène manquant
a faulty gene	un gène défectueux
genetic counselling	le conseil génétique
the precautionary principle	le principe de précaution
a label / to label / labelling	une étiquette / étiqueter / l'étiquetage
the long-term effects	les effets à long terme
genetically engineered	produits à partir de recherches génétiques / génétiquement modifié
genetic screening	le dépistage génétique
the gene transfer	le transfert de gènes
to raise ethical issues	poser des problèmes d'éthique
immoral / unethical	immoral / contraire à l'éthique
controversial	controversé
to tamper with	manipuler
to misuse	détourner
nanotechnologies	les nanotechnologies
microsurgery	la micro-chirurgie
a manipulation	une manipulation
teleoperated	manipulé à distance
to visualize	visualiser
a microrobot	un robot miniaturisé
an scanning tunnel microscope	un microscope à effet tunnel
to magnify (by)	grossir (de)
magnification	le grossissement

ETHICS	**L'ÉTHIQUE**
abortion	l'avortement
animal rights	les droits des animaux
artificial insemination	l'insémination artificielle
assisted suicide	le suicide assisté
biopiracy	le biopiratage
bioethics	la bioéthique
body modification	les modifications corporelles
eugenics	l'eugénisme
euthanasia	l'euthanasie
genomics	la génomique
life support	un respirateur artificiel
medicalisation	la médicalisation
mitochondrial donation	un don mitochondrial
human experimentation	expérimentation sur les humains
organ donation / transplant	le don d'organe / greffe d'organe
overtreatment	la surmédication

population control	contrôle, régulation démographique des naissances
recreational drug use	usage récréatif de stupéfiants
reprogenetics	la reproduction assistée par la génétique
sex reassignment surgery	chirurgie de changement de sexe
stem cell research	la recherche sur les cellules souches
surrogacy	la maternité de substitution, la GPA, les mères porteuses
transsexuality	la transsexualité
transhumanism	le transhumanisme
vaccination controversy	la controverse sur la vaccination
xenotransplantation	la xénogreffe

CONTROVERSY	**CONTROVERSES**
the code of ethics	la déontologie
a eugenist	un eugéniste
human dignity	la dignité humaine
the sacredness of life	la caractère sacré de la vie
a taboo	un tabou
a contentious / controversial issue	une controverse
to spark a debate	provoquer un débat
to cause an uproar	provoquer une tempête de protestations
to cause public outrage	scandaliser l'opinion
a divisive issue	une question qui divise l'opinion
to decriminalize	dépénaliser
to ban / to outlaw	interdire
a dilemma	un dilemme
a heated debate	un débat enflammé
a concern	une préoccupation
questionable practices	des pratiques contestables
to tamper with nature	jouer avec la nature
humane / inhumane	humain / inhumain
to ensure	garantir
a safeguard	un garde-fou

EUTHANASIA	**L'EUTHANASIE**
the right to live / to die	le droit à la vie / à la mort
to long for death	aspirer à mourir
therapeutic fury	l'acharnement thérapeutique
the withdrawal of treatment	l'arrêt des traitements
to keep alive	maintenir en vie
mercy-killing	l'euthanasie (pratiquée)
to switch off a machine	débrancher un appareil
to ease sb's suffering	soulager les souffrances de qqn
to put an end to sb's suffering	abréger les souffrances de qqn
a vegetative state	un état végétatif

clinically dead	cliniquement mort
brain dead	en état de mort cérébrale
irreversible	irréversible
to give one's consent	donner son consentement
a terminal disease	une maladie incurable
to be terminally ill	être en phase terminale
a care unit for the terminally ill	une unité de soins palliatifs
paralysis	la paralysie
bedridden	grabataire, alité, cloué au lit
to be on life support	être sous assistance respiratoire
paraplegic / quadriplegic	paraplégique / tétraplégique
paralysed on one side	hémiplégique
to be in agony	souffrir le martyre
a painkiller	un antalgique, un analgésique
to be under sedation	être sous sédatifs
to alleviate pain	soulager la douleur
a feeding tube	un tube d'alimentation

ABORTION	**L'AVORTEMENT**
motherhood	la maternité
to conceive	concevoir
to become pregnant	attendre un enfant
pregnancy	la grossesse
a pregnancy test	un test de grossesse
an unwanted pregnancy	une grossesse non désirée
an ultrasound scan	une échographie
an abortion	un avortement
a termination of pregnancy	une IVG (interruption volontaire de grossesse)
a late-term abortion	un avortement tardif
a botched abortion	un avortement bâclé
an abortion clinic	une clinique pratiquant l'avortement
a maternity hospital	une maternité
a gynecologist	un gynécologue
an ob-gyn, obstetrician	un obstétricien
a midwife	une sage-femme
parental leave	le congé parental
maternity leave	le congé maternité
a means of contraception	un moyen de contraception
the pill	la pilule
the morning-after pill	la pilule du lendemain
a condom	un préservatif
a coil	un stérilet
a pro-lifer / a pro-life campaigner	un militant contre l'avortement / anti-IVG
a pro-choice activist	un militant pour le droit à l'avortement
to legalise abortion	légaliser l'avortement

rape / to be raped	le viol / être violée
incest	l'inceste
family planning	le planning familial
birth control	le contrôle des naissances
freedom of choice	la liberté de choisir
women's rights	les droits des femmes
to have the final say	être la personne qui décide

BONUS	**BONUS**
it runs in the ***family***	c'est héréditaire
a one-child policy	une politique de l'enfant unique
to be in the ***family*** *way*	être enceinte
to have a bun in the oven	avoir un polichinelle dans le tiroir (fam.)
to find it a bitter ***pill*** *to swallow*	trouver qqch dur à avaler
to doctor ***data***	falsifier des informations
to ***nurse*** *hopes*	nourrir des espoirs
no ***pain*** *no gain*	qui ne risque rien n'a rien
to kill sth in the ***egg***	tuer qch dans l'œuf
to have ***egg*** *on one's face*	avoir l'air fin
as sure as ***eggs*** *is* ***eggs***	aussi sûr que deux et deux font quatre
to ***egg*** *sb on to do sth*	forcer qqn à faire qqch
to stand the ***test*** *of time*	résister à l'épreuve du temps
to give sb ***tests*** */ to carry out* ***tests*** *on sb*	faire passer un test (évaluation) à qqn / faire passer des tests (médicaux)
to ***test*** *the water*	tâter le terrain
a trial week	une semaine-**test,** une semaine d'essai

Translation: English-to-French exercise

Bioethics must ban genetic manipulations (adapté de The Times)

The French Council of State has published the recommendations on assisted human reproduction. Without giving in to trends seen in other European countries which are often more liberal, the Council aims to show pragmatism and not put a brake on the evolution or the expectations of medical research.

In matters of bioethics, the purpose is to ban manipulations that can lead to the objectification and even marketing of embryos. It is in the "interest of children" that the Council of State has rejected medical aid to *in vitro* fertilisation for single and homosexual women.

Also, it has rejected the legalisation of surrogate motherhood on grounds that it can be hazardous for the surrogate mother, and that a child must not be made "the object of a transaction". Some will find the Council too fainthearted. At this stage of the sparking debate it strikes us as wise.

Adapted press excerpts (about 400 words)

Excerpt 1 – Cheating death (adapted from *The Economist*)

Imagine a world in which getting fitted with a new **heart**, **liver** or set of **kidneys**, all grown from your own **body cells**, was as commonplace as **knee** and **hip** replacements are now. Or one in which you celebrated your 94th birthday by running a marathon with your school friends. Imagine, in other words, a world in which **ageing** had been **abolished. Longevity** is known to **run in families**, which suggests that particular varieties of **genes** prolong life. Some are investigating this, with the thought that modern **gene-editing techniques** might one day be used to make crucial, life-extending tweaks to the **DNA** of those who need them. From an individual's viewpoint, this all sounds very desirable. For society as a whole, though, it will have profound effects. If longer life is expensive, who gets it first?

Excerpt 2 – This Must-See Documentary Offers a Raw, Unfiltered View of Abortion from All Sides (adapted from *Forbes*)

After the Supreme Court's much-anticipated vote in favor of **abortion rights** this summer, you might be wondering: what else is there to possibly talk about when it comes to **abortion**? The documentary highlights perspectives from all sides of the **debate** in an effort to help us find common ground and truly listen to each other. Tragos herself may be **pro-choice**, but the documentary's overall effect is eye-opening. Centered in Missouri, where she grew up – a state with only one abortion **facility** – the film follows the crisscross of **patients**, **staff**, **protestors**, and **escorts** who end up at the Hope Clinic right across the border in Illinois."I hope that this film can be a disruptor and instigator to have all kinds of conversations," says Tragos. "**Abortion** is such a loaded topic, we need to learn how to disagree more productively."

Excerpt 3 – The Search for Schizophrenia Genes (adapted from *Slate*)

Even if **genetics** is implicated in a **disease**, development of the disease is not inevitable. Given the right environment, the disease will not necessarily develop. **Post-traumatic stress disorder** is seen in veterans and abused children, for instance. Even if there is a **genetic** component to **PTSD**, it is still entirely preventable by removing the environmental stressor – not going to war or not growing up in an abusive household. With no **biological markers** that can be used to identify mental illness, even the **diagnosis** of these conditions is subject to society's vagaries of what is considered **abnormal**.

Excerpt 4 – Colorado will be the next state to vote on doctor-assisted dying (adapted from *The Economist*)

Patients with a **terminal illness** who are expected to live no longer than six months, and who are judged by doctors to be of sound mind, would be able to ask for **lethal drugs** to end their lives. A second opinion about the likely **prognosis** is required. Polls suggest that most Americans are in favour of such laws. Support is stronger from richer and better-educated people across the country; the groundswell of support for Initiative 145, and Colorado's demography, suggest that it stands a good chance of being passed. The intention is to give the **terminally** ill the right to choose from all their options. In 2020, nine states plus the District of Columbia have authorized physician-assisted suicide.

Food for Thought and Quotations (about 500 words)

DNA, cells and chromosomes

Cells are the basic building blocks of all living things. Deoxyribonucleic acid, in short DNA, is the hereditary material in humans and almost all other organisms. In a word, DNA is the recipe for life, as it stores biological information. Its smaller segments are termed genes. In general terms, DNA is a complex molecule found in the nucleus of every cell and is made up of 4 sub-units represented by the letters A, T, G, and C. An important property of DNA is that it can replicate. It is organized into long structures called chromosomes. Each chromosome consists of a DNA double helix. Their number varies from species to species: humans have 22 pairs plus the two sex chromosomes (two X chromosomes in females, one X and one Y in males). DNA is a "universal language": the genetic code means the same thing in all organisms. Nearly every cell in a person's body has the same DNA. This characteristic is critical to the success of genetic engineering.

Genetic engineering

Genetic engineering refers to the deliberate modification of the characteristics of an organism by manipulating its genetic material. The goal is to add one or more new traits that are not already found in that organism. Examples of genetically engineered organisms currently on the market include potatoes, tomatoes and rice. Historically, the first genetically modified organism to be created was a bacterium, in 1973. The following year, experiments were successfully carried out on mice, which enabled further developments in scientific research, agriculture and technology. It has led to research on Alzheimer's disease for example: gene therapy (the genetic engineering of humans) enabled to study this neurodegenerative disease by replacing defective genes with effective ones. However, there are many ethical concerns about genetic engineering, particularly concerning the human modifications of physical traits and the manipulation on the human fetus.

Stem cells

Stem cells are specific cells that are capable of giving rise to indefinitely more cells of the same type, and from which certain other kinds of cell arise. In mammals, there are two broad types of stem cells: embryonic or adult stem cells. Adult stem cells work as a repair system for damaged tissue. Embryonic stem cells maintain the normal turnover of regenerative organs, such as blood or skin. Stem cells are promising candidates for future therapies, since they help regenerate damaged or old tissue. At present, stem cell therapy treats or prevents a disease. Recent research has led to an ethical controversy about the development, use, and destruction of human embryos, sometimes used to grow stem cells artificially.

Euthanasia

Euthanasia is the voluntary termination of a sick person's life in order to relieve them of their suffering. It is the act or practice of killing or permitting the death of hopelessly sick or injured individuals in a relatively painless way. Euthanasia can be active (a person deliberately intervenes to end someone's life) or passive (a person causes death by withholding or withdrawing treatment that is necessary to maintain life). It is illegal in the USA and in the UK, even though recent stories have drawn the public attention to cases of unnecessary suffering and aggressive therapy. Active euthanasia is much more controversial, since societies are concerned by religious, moral and ethical arguments. That is the reason why the term *assisted suicide* appeared. It has allowed proponents to redefine the concept, on grounds that every individual should be given the ability to die with dignity. Opponents claim that it cannot be regulated and controled due to the belief that life is sacred.

"For, after all, how do we know that two and two make four? Or that the force of gravity works? Or that the past is unchangeable? If both the past and the external world exist only in the mind, and if the mind itself is controllable – what then?" George Orwell, *1984*

"Great scientific discoveries have been made by men seeking to verify quite erroneous theories about the nature of things." Aldous Huxley

Section 6
Our pale blue dot

Chapter A

Wildlife and resources

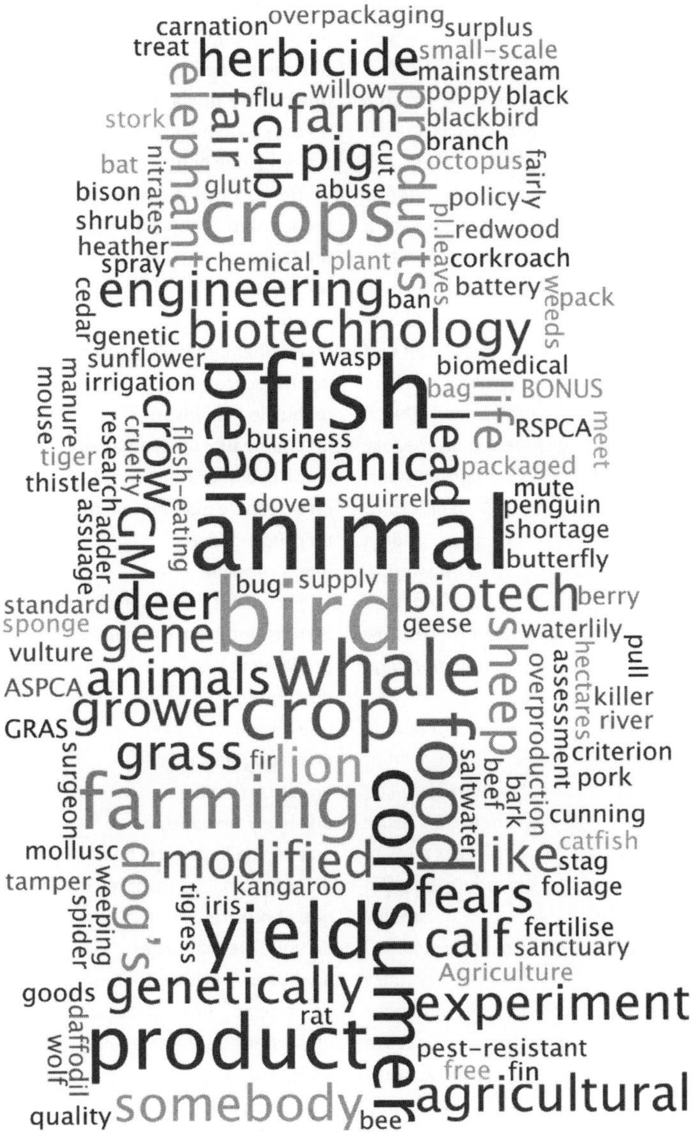

Vocabulary list

WILDLIFE	FAUNE ET FLORE
wildlife	la faune et la flore
a species	une espèce
a carnivore / a herbivore	un carnivore / un herbivore
flesh-eating	carnivore (adj.)
a mouse (pl.mice) / rat / a rodent	une souris / un rat / un rongeur
a hare	un lièvre
a squirrel	un écureuil
a wolf / a she-wolf	un loup / une louve
a pack of wolves	une meute de loups
a doe / a deer / a roe deer / a stag	une biche / un daim / un chevreuil / un cerf
a bear / a bear cub / a grizzly bear	un ours / un ourson / un grizzly
a lion / lioness / lion cub	un lion / une lionne / un lionceau
a tiger / tigress	un tigre / une tigresse
a cheetah / leopard / panther / jaguar	un guépard / léopard / panthère / jaguar
a kangaroo	un kangourou
a zebra	un zèbre
a giraffe	une girafe
an elephant / a elephant calf	un éléphant / un éléphanteau
a rhino	un rhinocéros
a buffalo / a bison	un buffle / un bison
a camel / a dromedary	un chameau / un dromadaire
a migratory bird	un oiseau migrateur
a blackbird	un oiseau de malheur, un merle
a robin	un rouge-gorge
a swallow	une hirondelle
a dove / a pigeon	une colombe / un pigeon
a nightingale / a sparrow	un rossignol / un moineau
a pink flamingo	un flamand rose
a swan	un cygne
a seagull	une mouette
a stork	une cigogne
a hawk / a falcon	un faucon
an eagle / a vulture	un aigle / un vautour
a crow / a raven	une corneille / un corbeau
a penguin, a puffin	un pingouin / un macareux moine
an owl	une chouette
a flock of wild geese (sg.goose)	un vol d'oies sauvages
a bird sanctuary	une réserve ornithologique
a snake / an adder / a grass-snake	un serpent / une vipère / une couleuvre
a rattlesnake / a cobra	un serpent à sonnettes / un cobra
a lizard	un lézard
a frog / a toad	une grenouille / un crapaud
a newt	une salamandre

a turtle	une tortue
an insect / a bug	un insecte
a cockroach / a bedbug	un cafard / une punaise de lit
a butterfly / a horsefly / a dragonfly	un papillon / taon / libellule
a caterpillar	une chenille
a bee / a beehive	une abeille / une ruche
a wasp / a hornet / a bumblebee	une guêpe / un frelon / un bourdon
a mosquito	un moustique
a spider / a cobweb	une araignée / une toile d'araignée
freshwater fish	le poisson d'eau douce
river / lake / saltwater fish	le poisson de rivière / de lac / d'eau salée
a catfish	un poisson-chat
crayfish	des écrevisses
a fin / a flipper	une nageoire
plankton	le plancton
a mollusc / an octopus / a squid	un mollusque / poulpe / calamar
a jellyfish	une méduse
a crab / a pincer	un crabe / une pince
a shark / a dolphin / a whale	un requin / un dauphin / une baleine
an orca, a killer whale	un orque
coral / a sponge	corail / une éponge
a starfish	une étoile de mer

FLORA	**LA FLORE**
vegetation / flora	la végétation / la flore
grass / moss / weeds	l'herbe / la mousse / les mauvaises herbes
seaweed(s)	les algues
heather / broom / a nettle	la bruyère / le genêt / une ortie
a fern / a thistle	une fougère / un chardon
a shrub / a bush	un arbuste / un buisson
honeysuckle / ivy	le chèvrefeuille / le lierre
a branch / a twig / the foliage	une branche / une brindille / le feuillage
a root / bark	une racine / écorce
an evergreen / a conifer	un arbre à feuilles persistantes / un conifère
the undergrowth	le sous-bois
a clearing	une clairière
an oak	un chêne
a beech	un hêtre
a poplar	un peuplier
a birch	un bouleau
a weeping willow	un saule pleureur
a redwood / a cedar / a fir, a pine	un séquoia / un cèdre / un sapin, un pin
a leaf (pl.leaves)	une feuille
a bunch / a bouquet	un bouquet
a tulip / a rose / an iris / a carnation	une tulipe / une rose / un iris / un œillet
a lily of the valley / a daffodil	le muguet / une jonquille

a sunflower / lavender	un tournesol / la lavande
a daisy / a violet / a cornflower	une pâquerette / une violette / un bleuet
a poppy	un coquelicot
a waterlily	un nénuphar

AGRICULTURE	**L'AGRICULTURE**
agronomy	l'agronomie
an agricultural engineer	un ingénieur agronome
water supply / distribution	l'approvisionnement en eau / la distribution de l'eau
irrigation / to irrigate	l'irrigation / irriguer
fertilisation / to fertilise	fertilisation / fertiliser
organic / chemical fertiliser	l'engrais organique / chimique
manure / compost	le fumier (engrais naturel) / le compost
agrochemicals	l'agrochimie
a herbicide / a weed-killer	un herbicide
a pesticide / nitrates	un pesticide / des nitrates
a crop	un produit agricole / une récolte
the yield / to yield	le rendement / produire, rapporter
crop yield	le rendement des cultures
to treat	traiter
to spray	pulvériser
to tamper with	altérer / couper (trafiquer)
to farm 500 hectares	exploiter 500 hectares
a crop failure	une très mauvaise récolte
a dairy farm	une exploitation laitière
factory farming	l'élevage industriel
avian / pig flu	la grippe aviaire / porcine
pest-resistant	qui résiste aux parasites
herbicide resistant	qui résiste aux herbicides
the surplus / glut	le surplus / la surabondance
overproduction	la surproduction
a shortage	une pénurie
farming subsidies	les subventions agricoles
the CAP (Common agricultural policy)	la PAC (politique agricole commune)
the department of Agriculture	le ministère de l'Agriculture
battery farming	l'élevage en batteries
pig / pork	un cochon / du porc
calf / veal	un veau / du veau
ox / beef	un bœuf / du bœuf
sheep / mutton	un mouton / du mouton
a feedlot	un centre d'élevage industriel
veterinary control	le contrôle vétérinaire
a veterinarian / a vet surgeon	un vétérinaire
mad cow disease	la maladie de la vache folle

BIOTECHNOLOGIES	**LES BIOTECHNOLOGIES**
genetically modified food	les aliments génétiquement modifiés / les OGM
GMOs (genetically modified organisms)	les OGM (organismes génétiquement modifiés)
genetic engineering, bioengineering / biological engineering	les manipulations génétiques
biotechnology	les biotechnologies
a biotech product	un produit transgénique
the biotechnology business	l'industrie biotechnologique
selective breeding	élevage / culture sélective
genome	le génome
modification	modification
GRAS (generally recognised as safe)	généralement considéré comme sans danger / neutre
cross-breeding / a crossbreed	le croisement (d'espèces) / un hybride
gene-splicing	insertion d'un gène / épiage génétique
gene transfer	transfert génétique
a breed	une espèce / une race
a strain	une souche
a hormone	une hormone
a gene	un gène
a mutation / transformation	une mutation / transformation
a transgenic plant	une plante transgénique
bioethics	la bioéthique
GM crops	les cultures transgéniques
conventional crops	les cultures traditionnelles
to pull up crops	arracher des cultures
cross-pollination	la pollinisation croisée
to ban biotech products	interdire les produits transgéniques
to be suspicious of	se méfier de
to enter the food chain	intégrer la chaîne alimentaire
our suspicion of biotechnologies	notre méfiance vis-à-vis de la biotechnologie
a consumer group	une association de consommateurs
consumer fears	les craintes des consommateurs
to assuage fears	apaiser les craintes
consumer resistance	la résistance des consommateurs
traceability	la traçabilité
a risk assessment test	un test de dangerosité
the pro- / anti-GM lobby	les groupes de pression pro / anti OGM (les lobbies...)

ANIMAL RIGHTS	**LES DROITS DES ANIMAUX**
animal products	les produits d'origine animale
animal testing	les expérimentations sur les animaux
to carry out an experiment	faire une expérience

to experiment on animals	faire des expériences sur les animaux
cosmetics	les cosmétiques
cruelty to animals	la cruauté envers les animaux
animal abuse	la maltraitance des animaux
RSPCA (GB) / ASPCA (US)	la SPA (société protectrice des animaux)
animal welfare	la protection des animaux
the whale cull	le massacre des baleines
biomedical research	la recherche biomédicale

FAIR TRADE	**LE COMMERCE ÉQUITABLE**
fair trade food	les denrées alimentaires issues du commerce équitable
fairly traded	issu du commerce équitable
a labelled product	un produit labellisé
fair competition	la compétition loyale
to go mainstream	se populariser, devenir grand public
a floor price	un prix plancher
a small-scale grower	un petit producteur
to certify / certification	certifier / une certification
accreditation	une accréditation
organic product	un produit issu de l'agriculture biologique, un produit bio
a standard / a criterion (pl.criteria)	un standard / un critère
to meet with requirements	satisfaire aux exigences
a coffee grower	un planteur de café
to enhance quality	améliorer la qualité
to support	soutenir
green-minded	conscient de l'écologie
to cut overpackaging / packaged goods	réduire les emballages / les produits avec emballage

BONUS	**BONUS**
to grass on somebody	dénoncer, moucharder qqn
to be as brown as a ***berry***	être très bronzé
to be as cunning as a ***fox***	être rusé comme un renard
to be as blind as a ***bat***	être myope comme une taupe
to drink like a ***fish***	boire comme un trou
to be as mute as a ***fish***	être muet comme une carpe
a ***dog****gy bag*	un sac pour emporter les restes au restaurant
to lead a ***dog's*** *life*	mener une vie de chien
to lead somebody a ***dog's*** *life*	mener une vie de chien à qqn
a black ***sheep***	une brebis galeuse
as light as a ***feather***	léger comme une plume
as the ***crow*** *flies*	à vol d'oiseau
as free as a ***bird***	libre comme l'air
to eat like a ***bird***	avoir un appétit d'oiseau

Translation: English-to-French exercise

Pale Blue Dot
(adapté de Carl Sagan, *Pale Blue Dot: A Vision of the Human Future in Space*)

Look again at that dot. That's here. That's home. That's us. On it everyone you love, everyone you know, everyone you ever heard of, every human being who ever was, lived out their lives. [...]

The Earth is a very small stage in a vast cosmic arena. Think of the rivers of blood spilled by all those generals and emperors so that, in glory and triumph, they could become the momentary masters of a fraction of a dot. [...]

Our posturings, our imagined self-importance, the delusion that we have some privileged position in the Universe, are challenged by this point of pale light. Our planet is a lonely speck in the great enveloping cosmic dark. In our obscurity, in all this vastness, there is no hint that help will come from elsewhere to save us from ourselves.

The Earth is the only world known so far to harbor life. There is nowhere else, at least in the near future, to which our species could migrate. Visit, yes. Settle, not yet. Like it or not, for the moment the Earth is where we make our stand.

Adapted press excerpts (about 400 words)

Excerpt 1 – The world has lost a tenth of all its wilderness in the past two decades (adapted from *The Washington Post*)

Wilderness areas on **Earth** have experienced alarming **losses** in the past two decades, a new study suggests. By comparing **global** maps from the present day and the early 1990s, researchers have concluded that a tenth of all the world's **wilderness** has been lost in just 20 years. The losses were more pronounced in some **areas** than in others. Big, contiguous **swaths of wilderness** – especially **forests** – often serve as **key carbon sinks**. This makes them important **buffers** in the fight against **climate change**. When these areas are **degraded**, on the other hand, they lose their carbon, and it adds to the **greenhouse gas emissions** humans are already **pouring into** the **atmosphere**.

Excerpt 2 – World Ocean Summit 2020 (adapted from *The Economist*)

The 2020 World **Ocean** Summit will bring a critical eye to the vital issue of how to finance a **sustainable** ocean **economy**, to mobilise a new discussion on how **capital** and the **private sector** can drive **scalable**, **sustainable investment** in the ocean. The **transition** from a conventional economy in the ocean to a "blue" or **sustainable economy** could be a tremendous economic and investment **opportunity**, if done right. The **risks** and **challenges** are considerable. A new and intensive **phase** of economic activity in the ocean is getting underway, but science **warns** that the seas are facing unprecedented **pressures** from **humans**, and that time to save them is quickly running out. So, the idea of the **blue economy** may be at risk before it has been properly established.

Excerpt 3 – Genetically Modified Bugs Are Great, but GMO Food Still Scares Us. Here's Why. (adapted from *Slate*)

It's all about **risk assessment**. Take **GMOs**. **Farmers** and **seed companies** reap most of the benefits. The rest of us get lower food prices – but that benefit is spread so thin that most of us haven't noticed. Therefore, the **risks** don't have to be probable, or even plausible, for us to balk. You can line up all the scientists, carrying all the authoritative **data** you want, but again, I have little incentive to read it. It's another story when you see the benefits. The outrage over the use of **genetic modification** to make **plants** for farmers doesn't extend to the use of genetic modification to make **medicines** for us. Follow the GM mosquito story and you can watch American perspectives do a 180 as we begin to see benefits for ourselves.

Excerpt 4 – Concerns about a seed-and-pesticide food monopoly (adapted from *Christian Science Monitor*)

Bayer, the **drug** and **crop** company has made a $66 billion deal to take over Monsanto. The resulting company will control a quarter of the combined global **market** for **seeds** and **pesticides**. Bayer's strength in pesticides, combined with Monsanto's capabilities in seed **genetics** and **biotechnology**, could create the world's largest **crop supply** company in terms of sales. Bayer's chief executive declared that the deal is "a fantastic combination for modern **agriculture**, to cater to the needs of society by providing the tools needed to **feed** a rapidly growing **population**." But **regulators**, **farmers**, and **consumers** are raising concerns about too much power in the hands of too few companies, which may have the power to raise **seed**, **pesticide**, and **fertilizer** prices without fear of **competition**, and leave **farmers** with fewer sources to choose from.

Food for Thought and Quotations (about 500 words)

Fair trade and development

Fair trade is an economic strategy that aims to increase standards of living as well as reduce health and economic hazards for farmers and workers. Technical solutions (minimum guaranteed price among other things) provide a safety net for farmers and producers in case of price volatility or variations in the offer and demand process. In consequence, it facilitates access to credit in order to encourage further development. Also, food security is closely linked to economic growth, stable incomes and reduced vulnerability, not to mention the social progress for each individual: better education, improved conditions of living, which in the end is a virtuous circle for the whole society. The UN Sustainable Development Goals (SDGs) define the long-term goals of such strategies: end poverty in all its forms everywhere, end hunger, achieve food security and improve the quality of nutrition by promoting sustainable agriculture. These goals will be reassessed by 2030.

Some essential species

About 20,000 species are threatened with extinction and 1,000 are already extinct. A shortlist of irreplaceable species includes (among others) bees, fungi and plankton. **Bees** serve as pollinators of our agricultural world: without bees, humans would starve. Indeed pollination is essentially plant reproduction, and without it there is no plant reproduction. **Fungi** are among the most abundant organisms on the planet. Their role is to recycle, to provide food when edible, to grow plants which are essential in the human and animal food chain. They also serve as a basis for medicines (penicillin for instance). **Plankton**, a general category that includes microscopic algae, creatures and bacteria provides food for some of the smallest and biggest animals on the planet. What is more, plankton produces half of the world's oxygen and breaks down organic material in the water and by doing so recycles dead organisms.

Water war

Wikipedia defines *water conflict* as a term describing a conflict between countries, states, or groups over their access to water resources. The United Nations recognizes that water disputes result from opposing interests of water users, public or private. Today indeed, shrinking resources of drinking water for a billion people are leading the world to potential wars. Adding to this, there are growing demands from agriculture, the increasing population, energy production and climate change. California has been drying out since 2010 and the groundwater reserves are dwindling. In the Middle-East and South-East Asia, the dramatically low level of aquifers is threatening irrigation and therefore agriculture. A 2016 US intelligence report stated that if water itself was *unlikely to bring down governments*, shortages could *threaten food production and energy supply*, suggesting that it would put *additional stress on governments struggling with poverty and social tensions.*

G.R.A.S and food safety

The Food and Drug Administration (FDA) is responsible for making sure food products or additives in food products are recognized as safe for consumption. But the problem is that thousands of food ingredients are not regulated by the FDA. A recent inquiry found that the FDA did not take into consideration an estimated 1,000 chemicals that have been added to foods and beverages since 1958. It has also neglected to state clearly what the differences are between organic and genetically-modified products. Conflictual interests, incompetence in panels of researchers and recent developments concerning food poisonings have led to throw discredit on the FDA over the last few years. No genetically engineered product can be considered substantially equal to its ordinary or organic equivalent, by any stretch of the imagination.

"If the bee disappeared off the face of the Earth, man would only have four years left to live." (Maurice Maeterlinck, but generally attributed to Albert Einstein)

"To waste, to destroy our natural resources, to skin and exhaust the land instead of using it so as to increase its usefulness, will result in undermining in the days of our children the very prosperity which we ought by right to hand down to them amplified and developed." Theodore Roosevelt

Chapter B

Energy

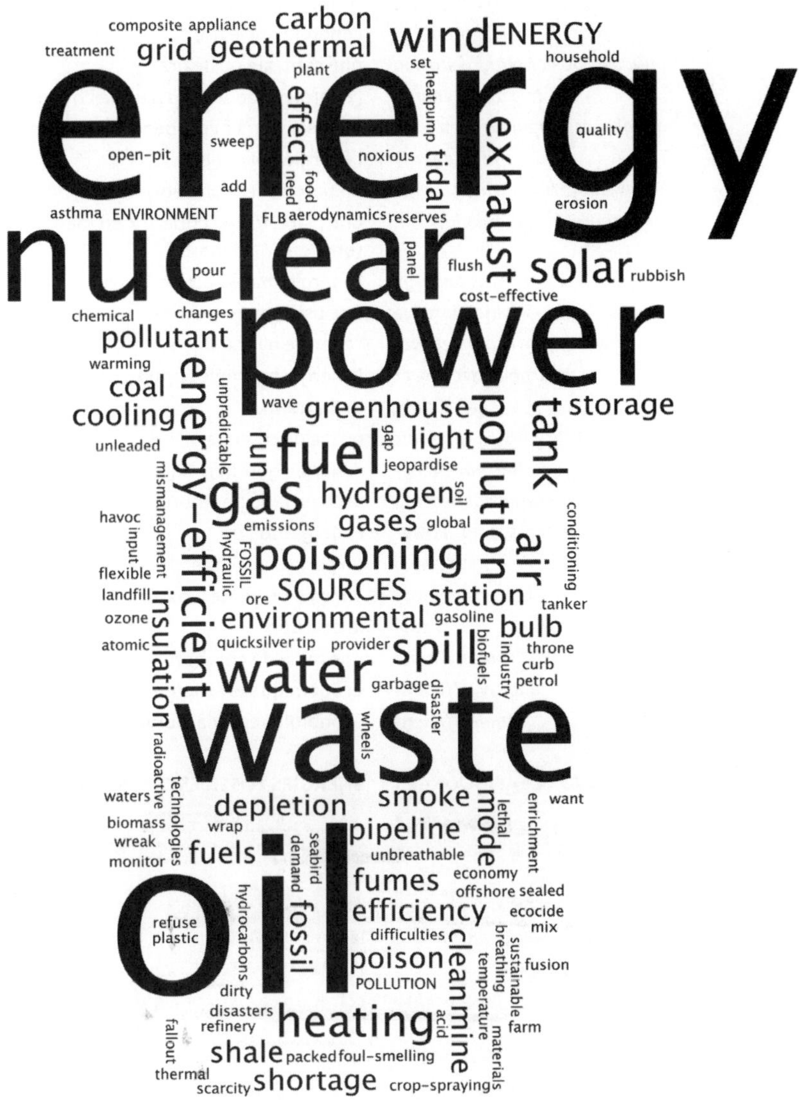

Vocabulary list

ENERGY SOURCES	LES SOURCES D'ÉNERGIE
energy / power	l'énergie
a power fuel	un combustible / un carburant
the fossil fuels	les énergies fossiles
to fuel	alimenter, ravitailler
renewable / non-renewable	renouvelable / non renouvelable
flexible fuel	les polycarburants
biofuels	les biocarburants
liquefied petroleum gas	GPL (gaz pétrole liquéfié)
atomic / nuclear energy	l'énergie nucléaire
a nuclear power plant / station	une centrale nucléaire
hydrogen energy	l'énergie produite à partir de l'hydrogène
a high-pressure hydrogen tank	un réservoir à hydrogène haute-pression
wind energy	l'énergie éolienne
a wind farm, a wind turbine	un parc éolien, une éolienne
an onshore / offshore platform	une plate-forme côtière / en mer (onshore / offshore)
tidal / wave energy	l'énergie marémotrice
a tidal barrage	une usine marémotrice
water / hydraulic power	l'énergie hydraulique
hydroelectric power	l'énergie hydroélectrique
a dam	un barrage
a reservoir	un lac de retenue
geothermal energy	l'énergie géothermique
geothermal heating	le chauffage géothermique
solar energy, solar power	l'énergie solaire
a solar panel	un panneau solaire
biomass energy	énergie produite à partir de la biomasse
coal	le charbon
a coal mine	une mine de charbon
energy-efficient	économique en énergie
fuel-efficient	économique en carburant

FOSSIL AND CLEAN SOURCES	ÉNERGIES FOSSILES OU PROPRES
oil reserves	les réserves de pétrole
the depletion of fossil fuels resources	l'épuisement des ressources en carburants fossiles
to run out of energy	être à court d'énergie
the energy gap / shortage	la pénurie d'énergie
the petrochemical industry	l'industrie pétrochimique
fracking	la fracturation hydraulique
heating oil	le fioul, le mazout
tar sands	les sables bitumineux
shale oil / shale gas	huile / gaz de schiste
crude oil	le pétrole brut

hydrocarbons	les hydrocarbures
a storage tank	un réservoir de stockage
the demand for energy	la demande en énergie
an oil refinery	une raffinerie
an oil tanker / an oil rig	un pétrolier / une plate-forme pétrolière
an oil well / an oil pipeline	un puits de pétrole / un oléoduc
a gas pipeline	un gazoduc
a barrel	un baril
an open-pit mine	une mine à ciel ouvert
ore	le minerai
a quarry	une carrière
a power station	une centrale thermique
a heatpump	une pompe à chaleur
nuclear fusion / fission	la fusion nucléaire / la fission
a nuclear reactor	un réacteur nucléaire
a cooling tower	une tour de refroidissement
nuclear facilities	les installations nucléaires
uranium enrichment	l'enrichissement de l'uranium
to bury nuclear waste	enfouir des déchets radioactifs
battery-powered	à batteries / électrique
the electric grid / the power grid	le réseau électrique
a high-voltage line	une ligne à haute tension
a provider / a subscriber	un fournisseur / un abonné
hybrid	hybride

SAVING ENERGY	**LES ÉCONOMIES D'ÉNERGIE**
to switch off	éteindre
thermal insulation	l'isolation thermique
air conditioning	la climatisation
heating / cooling costs	les coûts de chauffage / de climatisation
a ceiling fan	un ventilateur de plafond
a programmable thermostat	un thermostat programmable
an energy-efficient bulb	une ampoule à économie d'énergie
a FLB (fluorescent light bulb)	une ampoule fluocompacte
a motion-detector light	une lampe à détecteur de mouvement
to set the temperature	régler la température
energy efficiency	le rendement énergétique
an energy-efficient appliance	un appareil peu gourmand en énergie
energy input labelling	le label énergétique
the economy mode	le mode économe en énergie
an insulation wrap	une couverture isolante
a water heater	un chauffe-eau
a power strip	une rallonge multiprise
the stand-by mode	le mode veille
a double-glazing window	une fenêtre à double vitrage
high-performance	à haute performance / à haut rendement

efficiency / efficient	l'efficacité / efficace
sustainability / sustainable development	la durabilité / le développement durable
alternative means	les moyens alternatifs
energy conservation	l'économie d'énergie
energy recovery	récupération de l'énergie
cost-effective	rentable, efficace
composite materials	matériaux composites
aerodynamics	l'aérodynamique
regenerative braking	récupération par freinage
rebound effect	effet de rebond

ENVIRONMENT	**L'ENVIRONNEMENT**
environmental disasters	les désastres écologiques
the exploitation / the overexploitation	l'exploitation / la surexploitation
the depletion	l'appauvrissement
soil erosion	l'érosion des sols
acid rain	les pluies acides
the ozone layer	la couche d'ozone
global warming	le réchauffement de la planète
the greenhouse effect / greenhouse gases	l'effet de serre / les gaz à effet de serre
carbon dioxide	le dioxyde de carbone
the carbon footprint	l'empreinte carbone
exhaust fumes / industrial smoke	les gaz d'échappement / les rejets de gaz industriels
smog	le brouillard urbain polluant
poisoning	l'intoxication, la contamination
breathing difficulties / asthma	les difficultés respiratoires / l'asthme
lead-poisoning / quicksilver poisoning (mercury poisoning)	le saturnisme / l'empoisonnement au mercure
asbestos	l'amiante
to release smoke	dégager de la fumée
to inhale	respirer, inhaler
noxious / lethal	nocif / mortel
carcinogenic	cancérigène
unbreathable	irrespirable
household waste	des ordures ménagères
toxic waste	des déchets toxiques
chemical waste / radioactive waste	des déchets chimiques / nucléaires
refuse, rubbish, garbage (US)	les déchets (ménagers)
a scrap heap	une décharge de ferraille
a landfill, a tip, a dump	une décharge
waste treatment / management	le traitement / la gestion des déchets
plastic pollution	la pollution due aux plastiques
biodegradable	biodégradable
disposable / to dispose of	jetable / se débarrasser de
foul-smelling	malodorant, qui sent mauvais

to damage / to destroy	nuire à / détruire
to wreak havoc on, to devastate	ravager, dévaster
to waste	gâcher, gaspiller
shortage, scarcity	la pénurie
want, need	le manque, le besoin
mismanagement / to mismanage	la mauvaise gestion / mal gérer
to run short of sth	commencer à manquer de qqch
to be packed with	regorger de
an oil spill	une marée noire
to spill	déverser, répandre
to foul	polluer, souiller
an ecocide	un écocide
to jeopardise, to threaten	mettre en péril
the food chain	la chaîne alimentaire
extinct	éteint, disparu

POLLUTION	**LA POLLUTION**
environmental issues, concerns	les problèmes liés à l'environnement
crop-spraying	pulvérisation de pesticides sur les cultures
dirty technologies	les technologies polluantes
to emit gases / gas emissions	émettre des gaz / émission de gaz
to poison / a poison cloud	empoisonner / un nuage toxique
an exhaust pipe / exhaust fumes	un tuyau d'échappement / les gaz d'échappement
a nuclear disaster	un désastre nucléaire
nuclear fallout	les retombées radioactives
irreversible changes	des changements irréversibles
unpredictable	imprévisible
the tolerance threshold	le seuil de tolérance
to pollute	polluer
a polluter	un pollueur
a pollutant	un produit polluant
to curb pollution	réduire la pollution
wastage	les déchets
air / water pollution	la pollution de l'air / de l'eau
unleaded petrol (GB) / gasoline (US)	l'essence sans plomb
to monitor air quality	surveiller la qualité de l'air
an eco-friendly product	un produit non polluant
an oil slick / spill	une nappe de pétrole / une marée noire
to flush out one's tank	dégazer illégalement son réservoir
nuclear waste	les déchets nucléaires
a leak	une fuite
a hermetically sealed container	un conteneur hermétiquement scellé
a storage fill	un site d'enfouissement
to process waste	traiter des déchets

BONUS	**BONUS**
*to strike **oil***	découvrir du pétrole
*an **oiled** seabird*	un oiseau mazouté
***oil** and water do not mix*	on ne peut pas marier l'eau et le feu
*to **oil** the wheels*	mettre de l'huile dans les rouages
*to pour **oil** on troubled waters*	apaiser les esprits
*it is a **waste** of energy*	c'est se donner du mal pour rien
*to make a **clean** sweep of sth*	gagner haut la main
*to come **clean** about sth*	avouer qqch
*to add **fuel** to the flames*	jeter de l'huile sur le feu
*the **powers** that be*	les autorités
*the **power** behind the throne*	l'éminence grise

Translation: English-to-French exercise

Global investment in energy falls but renewables remain strong (adapté de *The Guardian*)

Global investment in energy fell by 8 percent last year, reflecting low oil and gas prices and cost falls in the sector. Nearly half of the decline was accounted for by the US, where plunging oil prices and a recent boom in shale gas, along with cost deflation in the energy sector, have played an increasing role.

China has remained the biggest investor in energy worldwide, despite a slowing in the pace of its economic growth. Despite this global fall, investment in renewable energy in 2015 remained robust. The move towards clean energy was driven by government policies, with countries fostering low-carbon growth. Renewable power takes the lion's share of available investment funds, thanks to steep falls in the cost of wind turbines and solar panels.

The investment figures show the mood before the landmark agreement on climate change reached in Paris last December. Under that accord, nearly 200 countries agreed to hold global temperature rises to no more than 2C above pre-industrial levels. Meeting these targets will require new policies to favour low-carbon energy above fossil fuels.

Adapted press excerpts (about 400 words)

Excerpt 1 – Industry and carbon limits – Claws in the dirt (adapted from *The Economist*)

What would life in America be like if the **Clean Air Act** of 1970 had never been passed? In terms of **breathing**, an activity that's easy to overlook until it becomes difficult, it would probably resemble life in many of today's developing countries, where **factories** and **cars** are multiplying unhindered by **environmental regulations**. Things are the worst in large Chinese cities, where **coal fumes**, auto **exhaust**, **smog** and **particulate matter** are so coruscating that most Americans would consider raising a family there an act of child abuse. The productive difference between a **coal-fired power plant** and a **solar** one is that the solar one does not produce **carbon dioxide**.

Excerpt 2 – Five years on: Volkswagen emissions scandal (adapted from *The Independent*)

Just a tenth of UK Volkswagen **vehicles** fitted with software to **cheat emissions tests** were fixed in the year since the scandal broke. The controversy began in September 2015 when US regulators told VW to recall 482,000 **diesel** engine cars after discovering they contained **illegal defeat devices**. The US **Environmental Protection Agency** said the **software** allowed cars to **release** fewer **smog-causing pollutants** during tests than in real-world driving conditions. Volkswagen said 1.2 million vehicles were affected by the issue in the UK, which is equivalent to nearly one in 10 of the country's diesel cars.

Excerpt 3 – California Offshore Wind Farm Will Float (adapted from *Seeker*)

Trident Winds, a Seattle-based company, plans to place 100 **floating turbines** 33 miles off the coast. The turbines would be affixed to floating **platforms**, which would be tethered to the sea floor using cables. Trident's plans are for the farm to **produce** a total capacity of 765 **megawatts**, substantially greater than the 630 MW generated by the London Array off the United Kingdom, presently the largest **offshore wind farm** in the world. In theory, by allowing installations further offshore, floating wind farms could harness stronger winds and open up the industry to a greater number of locations. Opponents are calling for a halt to the project, calling for greater investment in **solar energy**.

Excerpt 4 – U.S., Canada Aboriginal Tribes Form Alliance to Stop Oil Pipelines (adapted from *The New York Times*)

Aboriginal tribes from Canada and the northern United States have signed a treaty to jointly fight proposals to build more **pipelines** to carry **crude** from Alberta's **oil sands**, saying further development would **damage** the **environment**. The statement did not specify what actions the groups would take to stop development. The Canadian Energy Pipeline Association, whose members include the targeted companies, said in a statement that the industry would listen to aboriginal concerns. "The fact remains there is a critical need for **pipelines** in Canada," the association said, noting that they are the safest and most **environmentally friendly** way to move **oil and gas**.

Food for Thought and Quotations (about 500 words)

Energy sources, in a nutshell

There are roughly 10 main different sources of energy that are used in the world to generate power. **Solar power** harvests the energy of the sun through using collector panels. It creates conditions that can then be turned into a kind of power. **Wind power** uses large turbines to take available wind as the power to turn, the turbine can then turn a generator to produce electricity. **Geothermal energy** is the energy that is produced from beneath the earth. It is clean, sustainable and environmentally friendly. **Hydrogen** is commonplace, and once it is separated from water, it can be used as a fuel for generating electricity. **Tidal energy** uses rise and fall of tides to convert kinetic energy of incoming and outgoing tides into electrical energy. **Wave energy** is produced from the waves that are produced in the oceans. **Hydroelectric Energy** is produced from dams, from which the power of the water is used to turn generators. **Biomass energy** is produced from organic material (crops, plants, trees, yard clippings, wood chips and animal wastes). **Nuclear energy** is created through a specific nuclear reaction, which is then collected and used to power generators. Last, natural gas, coal and oil are one source of energy termed **fossil fuels**, which provide the power for most of the world, but are a polluting and limited resource.

ITER (Latin for "The way")

ITER (International Thermonuclear Experimental Reactor) is an international nuclear fusion research and engineering project to build a nuclear fusion reactor in Southern France. Fusion power has the potential to provide sufficient energy to satisfy huge demand sustainably, with a limited impact on the environment (no CO_2 emission, very limited lifespan radioactive waste). Its goals are to develop technologies required for a sustainable fusion power station in the next twenty to thirty years. About 40 countries are participating in this costly and promising project. Opponents claim that it is not much safer than a nuclear power plant in case of an accident. In 2025, initial plasma experiments will start.

The Chernobyl and Fukushima nuclear disasters

The 1986 Chernobyl and 2011 Fukushima nuclear power plant disasters both involved core meltdowns that released significant amounts of radioactivity into the environment (air, earth or sea). However, in terms of health, the two nuclear accidents had different consequences. While Fukushima involved radioactivity exposures to hundred of thousands of people, Chernobyl irradiated hundreds of millions, far beyond the imaginable. Chernobyl was by far the worst reactor accident of all time for the local populations: exposure to iodine was far higher, the meltdown was a human-caused disaster. Fukushima in contrast, was a natural disaster caused by a tsunami that flooded reactor basements.

Air quality

Since the Industrial Revolution it has become an utmost necessity to control, reduce or eliminate the emission into the atmosphere of substances that can harm the environment or human health. Pollution can come either from natural sources or human activities. Nevertheless, only pollution caused by the combustion of fuels (industry and transportation in particular) is generally controlled. The best way to protect air quality is to reduce the emission of pollutants by switching to cleaner fuels. Industrial pollutants that cannot be eliminated must be collected by air-cleaning devices or filters before they can escape into the atmosphere, further to the Kyoto Protocol of 1998. Since the 2015 C.O.P, air quality has not improved in Western countries.

"If you want to find the secrets of the universe, think in terms of energy, frequency and vibration." Nikola Tesla

"Fog everywhere. Fog up the river where it flows among green airs and meadows; fog down the river, where it rolls defiled among the tiers of shipping, and the waterside pollutions of a great (and dirty) city" Charles Dickens

"The unleashed power of the atom has changed everything except our thinking. Thus, we are drifting toward catastrophe beyond conception. We shall require a substantially new manner of thinking if mankind is to survive." Albert Einstein

Chapter C

Climate change

Vocabulary list

PLANET EARTH	**LA TERRE**
the planet / the globe	la planète / le globe
a continent / the mainland	un continent / le continent (la terre ferme)
the Northern / Southern hemisphere	l'hémisphère Nord / Sud
the compass points	les 4 points cardinaux
a territory	un territoire
a tract of land	une étendue de terre
a rolling countryside	une campagne vallonnée
an uneven land	un terrain accidenté
a time zone	un fuseau horaire
to map a country	dresser la carte d'un pays
an island / an isle	une île
a hill / the foothills	une colline / les contreforts
a slope	une pente
height / altitude	la hauteur / l'altitude
a mountain range / top	une chaîne de montagnes / un sommet
to overlook	dominer
a pass	un col
a glacier	un glacier
the sea level (above / below)	le niveau de la mer (au-dessus / en dessous du niveau de la mer)
the open sea	la pleine mer
the sea side	le bord de la mer
the (low / high) tide / the swell	la marée (basse / haute) / la houle
fresh water	l'eau douce
a river / a stream / a brook	un fleuve / un cours d'eau / un ruisseau
an estuary	un estuaire
a tributary	un affluent
to flow / to run into	se jeter dans
a waterway / a canal	une voie navigable / un canal
the watershed / the divide (US)	la ligne de partage des eaux
a lake / the lakeside	un lac / les rives du lac

THE WEATHER	**LE TEMPS, LA MÉTÉO**
a weather forecast	les prévisions météorologiques
a weather report	un bulletin météo
spring / summer / autumn, fall (US) / winter	le printemps / l'été / l'automne / l'hiver
the climate / climatology	le climat / la climatologie
tropical / temperate	tropical / tempéré
fog / foggy	le brouillard / brumeux
a patch of fog	une nappe de brouillard
mist, haze / misty, hazy	la brume / brumeux
the rain	la pluie
rainfall	les précipitations
a rainbow	un arc-en-ciel

a downpour / a shower	un déluge / une averse
April showers	les giboulées de mars
scattered showers	des averses éparses
drizzle / to drizzle	le crachin / bruiner
sunny spells	des éclaircies
cloudy / overcast	nuageux / couvert
dull	maussade
unsettled	instable
the snow / a snowflake / thaw	la neige / un flocon de neige / le dégel
snowbound	bloqué par la neige
a snowdrift	une congère
black ice	le verglas
hail / a hailstone	la grêle / un grêlon
a gust of wind	une rafale de vent
to blow	souffler
a breeze	une brise
a gale	un grand vent
a whirlwind	un tourbillon
a storm / a thunderstorm	un orage
a flash of lightning	un éclair
a clap of thunder	un coup de tonnerre
to frost / to frost over	geler / givrer
a depression / an anticyclone	une dépression / un anticyclone
damp / mild	humide / doux
the monsoon	la mousson
a scorcher	une journée de canicule
a stifling weather	un temps étouffant
at sunrise / sunset	au lever / coucher de soleil
a sultry weather	un temps lourd
a gorgeous weather	un temps splendide
a barometer / a glass	un baromètre
barometric pressure	la pression barométrique
a thermometer	un thermomètre
sub-zero / above zero temperatures	des températures en dessous de / au dessus de zéro
a lightning conductor	un paratonnerre
a weather vane / a weather cock	une girouette

CLIMATOLOGY	**LA CLIMATOLOGIE**
a field of study	un champ d'étude
the average / on average	la moyenne / en moyenne
the oscillation	l'oscillation
a projection / to project	une projection / prévoir, projeter
a dry-climate area	une zone de climat sec
a tropical wet and dry climate	une zone de mousson tropicale
arid / aridity	aride / l'aridité

the continental climate	le climat continental
Marine coast climate	le climat océanique
the polar climate (tundra, ice cap)	le climat polaire (la toundra, la calotte)
the Mediterranean climate	le climat méditerranéen
a climate shift	un changement climatique
an ice core	une carotte glaciaire
the tree rings	les cernes des arbres
a climate model	une modélisation climatique
a climate pattern	un modèle / une tendance climatique
an imbalance	un déséquilibre
the ocean circulation pattern	la circulation des flux océaniques
pattern recognition	la reconnaissance des formes
a sounding balloon / weather balloon	un ballon-sonde
weatherproof	résistant aux intempéries
the urban heat island	l'îlot de chaleur urbain
the ice age	l'ère glaciaire

DISASTERS	**LES DÉSASTRES**
to cause damage	causer des dégâts
to devastate	ravager, dévaster
a warning	un avertissement
a disaster area	une zone sinistrée
a state of emergency	un état d'urgence
an emergency operation	une opération à chaud
to evacuate / an evacuee	évacuer / un évacué
to rescue / a rescue worker	sauver / un secouriste
a rescue party	une équipe de secours
a firefighter / a fireman	un pompier
a fire engine	une voiture de pompiers
a Canadair	un avion bombardier d'eau
to wreak havoc	faire des ravages
a high-risk area	une zone à haut risque
vulnerability	la vulnérabilité
Achilles' heel	le talon d'Achille
a flood	une inondation
to be in spate	être en crue
a flash flood	une crue subite
to overflow	déborder
a mudslide	une coulée de boue
a tidal wave / a tsunami	un raz-de-marée
a cold spell	une vague de froid
a heat wave	une vague de chaleur
a drought	une sécheresse
hunger / famine	la famine / la marine
to die of thirst	mourir de soif
bush fire	des feux de broussailles

a spark	une étincelle
to blaze / blazing	flamber / en flammes
severe weather conditions	un temps violent
a typhoon / a hurricane	un typhon / un ouragan
a tornado	une tornade
a sandstorm	une tempête de sable
a blizzard	une tempête de neige
a volcano	un volcan
to erupt / an eruption	entrer en éruption / une éruption
a lava flow / a landslide	une coulée de lave / un glissement de terrain
ash	les cendres
an earthquake	un tremblement de terre
a fault line	une ligne de faille
rubble	les décombres, les ruines
an earth tremor	une secousse tellurique
an aftershock	une réplique
magnitude / the Richter scale	la magnitude / l'échelle de Richter
the epicenter	l'épicentre
safe and sound	sain et sauf
first aid	les premiers soins
a casualty	une victime
to claim lives	coûter des vies
to flee one's home	fuir son domicile
unscathed, unharmed	indemne
a snag	un problème, une difficulté
to run for shelter	courir pour se mettre à l'abri
to endanger, to imperil	mettre en danger
a looming threat	une menace qui se rapproche
unsafe	peu sûr, dangereux

PLACES	**LIEUX**
the Pacific (ocean)	l'océan Pacifique
the Atlantic / Indian Ocean	l'océan Atlantique / Indien
the Arctic / Antarctic ocean	l'océan Arctique / Antarctique
the Channel / the North Sea	la Manche / La mer du Nord
the Mediterranean Sea	la mer Méditerranée
the ice pack	la banquise
the continental drift	la dérive des continents
the South sea	les mers du Sud
the Dead Sea	la mer Morte
the Hudson Bay	la baie d'Hudson
the Persian Gulf	le golfe Persique
the Straits of Gibraltar	le détroit de Gibraltar
the Mississippi river	le (fleuve) Mississippi
the Victoria Falls	les chutes de Victoria

the River Thames	la Tamise (fleuve)
Lake Tahoe	le lac Tahoe
the Ganges	le Gange
the Great Lakes	les Grands Lacs
Mount Delani (McKinley)	le mont Delani (ex-McKinley)
Mount Blanc	le Mont Blanc
Grand Canyon National Park	la parc national du Grand Canyon
the Cape of Good Hope	le Cap de Bonne Espérance

BONUS	**BONUS**
the rumbling of ***thunder***	le grondement du tonnerre
the ***fog*** *is lifting*	le brouillard se lève
to be ***chilled*** *to the bone*	être transi de froid
a biting ***cold***	un froid pénétrant, mordant
come ***rain*** *or* ***shine***	qu'il pleuve, qu'il vente ou qu'il neige
to be up before the ***sun***	être levé aux aurores
to look on the ***sunny*** *side*	voir le bon côté des choses
sunny *side up*	(œuf) sur le plat
to be skating on thin ***ice***	s'aventurer sur un terrain glissant
to cut no ***ice***	ne faire aucun effet
it never ***rains*** *but it* ***pours***	un malheur n'arrive jamais seul
to be ***rained*** *off*	être annulé pour cause de pluie
to make heavy ***weather*** *of sth*	avoir du mal à faire qch
to keep a ***weather*** *eye on sb*	garder un œil sur qqn
whatever the ***weather***	par tous les temps
cloudy *mornings turn to clear evenings*	après la pluie le beau temps
to be ***wet*** *through*	être trempé
to be ***soaked*** *to the skin*	être trempé jusqu'aux os
every ***cloud*** *has a silver lining*	il faut voir le bon côté des choses
to feel under the ***weather***	ne pas être très en forme
to chase ***rainbows***	être en quête de l'impossible

Translation: English-to-French exercise

California's drought: Cut and dried (adapté de *The Economist*)

California is no longer taking a laid-back approach to its water crisis. This week, for the second time in its history, the Golden State imposed mandatory restrictions on water use. The measure follows five years of severe drought and its lowest ever recorded winter snowpack.

Urban water use in California has held relatively steady over the past two decades, despite massive population growth. That achievement reflects pricing incentives and water-saving technologies like low-flow toilets. Remarkably, per-capita water use in California has declined significantly, from 232 gallons per a day in 1996 to 165 in 2016.

Farmers, who receive water from other sources, will not bear much of the burden of the new rules. Unless climate conditions change dramatically, and soon, they will nevertheless have to.

Adapted press excerpts (about 400 words)

Excerpt 1 – Barack Obama shores up his environmental legacy (adapted from *The Economist*)

A new alliance between China and the US paved the way for success in Paris in 2015. Having countries sign up only to what they thought they could manage made agreement in Paris possible – but guaranteed the deal's weakness. The pledges made by countries would be expected to result in **global warming** of about 3C. Yet, the **agreement** was more robust than expected, and **mechanisms** are in place within it to encourage countries to **ramp up their efforts** every few years. Since he took office, **solar electricity** generation in America has increased 30-fold and that from **wind** has more than tripled. He became the first sitting president to visit America's **Arctic regions** and oversaw the **Environmental Protection Agency**'s attempts to introduce the **Clean Power Plan (CPP)**. This aims to work with states to **curb emissions** from **power plant.** Unfortunately in 2019, President Trump confirmed US will quit Paris global treaty.

Excerpt 2 – 10 Years After An Inconvenient Truth, Al Gore May Actually Be Winning (adapted from *Wired*)

Al Gore knows these **statistics** by heart. He has traveled the world delivering that deck to hundreds of people at a time, showing in irrefutable detail just how mind-bogglingly badly we have treated our **planet** and what we might be able to do about it. Ten years ago, ***An Inconvenient Truth***, the documentary that spread those ideas to millions was released. Gore says he still tinkers with its worldwide famous slideshow every day, because, well, the numbers keep changing. Not always for the better. Yet this year Gore and his fellow **activists** have a rare reason to celebrate. In April, 175 world leaders gathered at the United Nations to sign the Paris Agreement, a **global** pact that aims to keep global **temperatures** from rising more than 2 degrees Celsius above **preindustrial levels**. This pact has since met with several difficulties.

Excerpt 3 – The Climate Fixers – Is there a technological solution to global warming? (adapted from *The New Yorker*)

In 1991, Mt. Pinatubo, a volcano on the Philippine island of Luzon exploded with enough force to expel molten lava at the speed of six hundred miles an hour. The **heavy industrial activity** of the previous hundred years had caused the earth's **climate** to **warm** by roughly three-quarters of a degree Celsius, helping to make the twentieth century the **hottest** in at least a thousand years. The eruption of Mt. Pinatubo, however, reduced **global temperatures** by nearly that much in a single year. Most people considered the eruption a **calamity**. For geophysical scientists, though, Mt. Pinatubo provided the best model in at least a century to help us understand what might happen if humans attempted to **ameliorate** global warming by deliberately **altering** the **climate** of the earth.

Excerpt 4 – Don't waste CO_2, turn it into bottles and glue (adapted from *New Scientist*)

If **humanity** is to avoid dangerous **climate change**, we need to capture hundreds of billions of tonnes of **carbon dioxide**. But what to do with it all? There is no **shortage** of places to bury it, but we can at least put some of it to good use. A few start-up companies view **CO_2** as a **resource** rather than a **waste product**. They are using CO_2 as the **raw material** for making products including superglue and **fertiliser**. Helping **chemical** companies switch their **feedstock** to CO_2 does more than boost their **green credentials**. Almost all of their expenses are based on buying **oil** or natural **gas** or **biomass**. So **releasing** it into the air is not just **pollution**, it's actually losing value. If markets for CO_2 can be found, humanity may end up handling its **emissions** in a whole new way.

Food for Thought and Quotations (about 500 words)

Weather v. climate

The two terms are often confused with one another, presumably because the same elements (temperature, humidity, wind speed and direction, precipitation, etc.) are taken into consideration when it comes to defining the two notions, but there is more to the story. The main difference between weather and climate is duration. The weather is the observation of atmospheric conditions in a given time and space. Climate, on the other hand, describes the average atmospheric conditions observed over a long span in one specific location. Climate conditions are therefore used to describe systems or general trends in a given area, while weather conditions are simple observations at one particular time.

Natural disasters

A natural disaster is a major adverse event resulting from natural processes. Natural disasters are considered as such whenever they occur in an area where the population is vulnerable. Such disasters can be floods (China in 1931, more than 3 million casualties), hurricanes (Katrina in 2005, 2,000 fatalities), tornadoes, volcanic eruptions (Mount St Helens, 1980), earthquakes (San Francisco in 1906, 3,000 dead), tsunamis (Indian Ocean in 2004, 350,000 fatalities), and other geological processes.

The Paris Climate Agreement (2016)

The Paris deal is the world's first comprehensive climate binding agreement. As termed in The Atlantic, *the greatest triumph of the Paris climate agreement is that there is an agreement at all.* It was ratified in 2016. It sets out a global action plan to prevent the consequences of climate change (1) by limiting global warming to well below 2C above pre-industrial levels, (2) by increasing the ability to adapt to the impacts of climate change and foster low greenhouse gas emissions without endangering food production, and (3) by making finance flows consistent with sustainable development (and to do so, an annual commitment of more than $100 billion will be required). Countries furthermore aim to reach "global peaking of greenhouse gas emissions as soon as possible". In 2019, the US formally notified the UN that it would withdraw from the Paris Agreement.

Climate change deniers

Climate change deniers apply systematic reservation about any claim or statement proving the climate change origins, without recognizing skepticism as a process, but as an assumption. Whatever data, convincing evidence or irrefutable proof there may be, a denier will never be convinced that climate change is real. This is by no means skepticism, but at best a weak form of passive cynicism, based on the closed-minded pre-determined rejection of evidence, a form of unjustifiable faith-based assumption. As Jeff Schweitzer puts it, *"cynics doubt and mistrust not on the weight of evidence or lack thereof but on suspicions of underlying motivation. Cynicism can lead to the rejection of a claim but not to new discoveries, unlike skepticism which can lead to both."*.

*"Climate is what we expect, weather is what we get."*Aphorism generally attributed to Mark Twain

*"I find myself at the extremity of a long beach. How gladly does the spirit leap forth, and suddenly enlarge its sense of being to the full extent of the broad, blue, sunny deep! A greeting and a homage to the Sea! I descend over its margin, and dip my hand into the wave that meets me, and bathe my brow. That far-resounding roar is the Ocean's voice of welcome. His salt breath brings a blessing along with it."*Nathaniel Hawthorne

Chapter D
Ecology

Vocabulary list

GENERAL ABCs	**LE B.A.-BA DE L'ÉCOLOGIE**
biosphere	la biosphère
to affect	toucher, affecter
balance	l'équilibre
biodegradable	biodégradable
biodiversity	la biodiversité
to combat	combattre
to diminish	diminuer, réduire
dirt / dust	la saleté / la poussière
to disappear	disparaître
a disaster	un désastre
the disposal	élimination, évacuation, traitement
to dump	jeter, se débarrasser de
an energy source	une source d'énergie
to emit	émettre
to be exposed to	être exposé à
to harm	être nocif / nuisible, porter atteinte à
to purify	purifier
to protect	protéger
to recycle	recycler
renewable	renouvelable
reusable	réutilisable
a remedial action	une mesure corrective
the atmosphere / stratosphere	atmosphère / stratosphère
the surface	la surface
to threaten	menacer
untreated / treated	non-traité / traité
waste separation	le tri des déchets

RECYCLING	**LE RECYCLAGE**
the throw-away society	la société du gaspillage
the recycling industry	l'industrie du recyclage
the bottle / plastic bank	le conteneur de collecte du verre / du plastique
to collect (glass...)	ramasser (le verre)
to sort out	trier / faire le tri
recycled paper / cardboard	le papier / carton recyclé
a reusable bag	un sac réutilisable
the lifespan	la durée de vie
to process sewage	traiter les eaux usées
a sewage treatment plant	une station d'épuration
to decontaminate	décontaminer
to clean up	assainir
a catalytic converter	un pot catalytique
waste sorting, selective sorting	le tri sélectif

waste disposal	le traitement des déchets
pollutant-free	sans agent polluant
wholesome	sain
ozone-friendly	sans danger pour l'ozone
harmless	inoffensif

ACTIVISM AND ACTION	**L'ACTIVISME ET L'ACTION**
an ecologist, an environmentalist	un écologiste
ecology	l'écologie
an activist	un militant
a green lobby	un groupe de pression écologiste
lobbying	l'activité des groupes de pression
commitment	l'engagement
an awareness campaign	une campagne de sensibilisation
the boycott	le boycott
involvement	la participation, l'implication
to sensitize	sensibiliser
to expose, to reveal	dénoncer, révéler
to bring a lawsuit against	intenter un procès à
a green law	une loi en faveur de l'environnement
an incentive	une mesure d'encouragement
energy-saving measures	des mesures d'économie d'énergie
untapped resources	des ressources inexploitées
public transport	les transports en commun
car pooling	le covoiturage
alternate traffic	la circulation alternée
congestion charge	la taxe sur la circulation urbaine
a tax	une taxe
a fine, a penalty	une amende, une sanction
to enforce the law	faire respecter la loi
to promote	encourager, promouvoir
to control, to check	contrôler, vérifier
to abide by the law	respecter la loi
a countrycide	un acte destructeur de la nature
a seacide	un acte dangereux pour la mer
an eco-freak	un obsédé d'écologie
eco-aware	sensible à l'environnement
greenness	la conscience écologique
to be green	être naïf / ignorant
the Clean Air Act	la loi antipollution atmosphérique
to clean out / up / off	nettoyer à fond / remettre en ordre / enlever une tache
to be clean	n'avoir rien à se reprocher
eco-imperialism	l'impérialisme écologique
an ecocide	destruction méthodique de l'environnement

an eco-terrorist	un terroriste écologique
eco-	préfixe « écologique »

INDIVIDUAL MEASURES	**MESURES INDIVIDUELLES**
to get a tune-up of the car engine	entretenir le moteur d'une voiture
not to top off a gas tank	ne pas remplir un réservoir à ras bord
to conserve energy	économiser l'énergie
not to burn yard waste	ne pas brûler les déchets du jardin
to plant a tree	planter un arbre
to use mass-transit	utiliser les transports en commun
not to use fertilizer	ne pas utiliser de l'engrais
to pour nothing into a storm drain	ne rien jeter dans le réseau d'égout pluvial
to water the lawn early	arroser la pelouse tôt
to water once a week only	n'arroser qu'une fois par semaine
to use a bucket, not the hose	utiliser un seau, pas le tuyau
to do the dishes once the washer is full	n'utiliser le lave-vaisselle que lorsqu'il est plein
to wash a full load of laundry	n'utiliser la machine à laver que pleine
to repair leaky faucets	réparer les fuites d'eau du robinet
to install faucet aerators	un brise-jet à faible débit
not to put hazardous materials into the trash	ne pas jeter de produits dangereux à la poubelle
not to buy more than one needs	ne pas surconsommer
to use rechargeable batteries	utiliser des piles rechargeables
to give it away, and not to throw it away	donner, ne pas jeter

PUBLIC INITIATIVES	**INITIATIVES PUBLIQUES**
environmental rights	les droits environnementaux
greenwashing	écoblanchiment
endangered species	les espèces menacées
industrial waste	les déchets industriels
overfishing	surexploitation de la pêche, la surpêche
overgrazing	le surpâturage
the society-at-large	la société dans son ensemble
the environmental policy	la politique environnementale
to implement a policy	mettre en œuvre une politique
a policy instrument	un instrument de politique publique
an impact assessment	une étude d'impact
water scarcity	la pénurie d'eau
food scarcity	la pénurie de denrées alimentaires
climate change	le changement climatique
the peak oil	le pic de production de pétrole / le pic pétrolier
the population paradox	le paradoxe démographique
to green the economy	rendre l'économie plus compatible avec l'environnement / plus verte

a resource-efficient society	une société permettant une utilisation rationnelle des ressources
a climate-resilient economy	économie à l'épreuve du changement climatique / non préjudiciable pour le climat
an energy-performance requirement	une exigence de performance énergétique
EPI (environmental policy integration)	intégration d'objectifs environnementaux
environment science	la science environnementale
environmental law	le droit environnemental
natural resource management	gestion des ressources naturelles
shallow ecology	l'écologie peu profonde, creuse

ENVIRONMENTALISM	**SCIENCES ENVIRONNEMENTALES**
grassroots activism	l'activisme de base
environmentalism	les sciences environnementales
ecologism / green movement	l'écologisme
environmental legislation	les lois environnementales
a preservation act	une loi protégeant le patrimoine naturel
industrialisation	l'industrialisation
the back-to-nature movement	le mouvement du retour aux sources
to advocate / an advocate	soutenir, défendre / un défenseur, un partisan
an urban planning policy	une politique d'urbanisme
to live close to nature	vivre en harmonie avec la nature
a conservationist	un défenseur de l'environnement
animal welfare	la protection des animaux
public awareness	la sensibilisation du public
to curb the exploitation of	diminuer l'exploitation de...
to spray DDT on	pulvériser du DDT sur / asperger de dichloro-diphényl-trichloréthane
to release chemicals	rejeter des produits chimiques
a tree-hugger	un militant pour la protection des arbres
to be on the edge of	être au bord de
exposure to toxins	l'exposition à des toxines
free market environmentalism	la protection de l'environnement financée par l'économie libérale
a class action	une action de justice groupée
a government-run organisation	un organisme gouvernemental
the EPA (environment protection agency)	l'agence de protection de l'environnement américaine
a non-governmental organisation (NGO)	une ONG (organisation non gouvernementale)
the community development	le développement local
a volunteer organisation	un organisme bénévole
teamwork	le travail d'équipe
to disseminate information	diffuser des informations

an environmental defense fund	un fonds de défense de l'environnement
a nature conservancy	un conservatoire de la nature
a public hearing	une audience publique
to stage a demonstration	organiser une manifestation
to purchase land	acquérir des terres
to conduct research	faire des recherches
environmental wrongs	les plaies environnementales
to right a wrong	réparer une injustice
to convey a message	transmettre / faire passer un message
a coastal clean-up	le nettoyage des déchets sur la côte
a tree-planting campaign	une campagne de plantation d'arbres
a media guesting	une invitation dans les médias
an eco-fashion show	un défilé de mode écologique

BONUS	**BONUS**
a Green	un écologiste
greens / greenery	les légumes verts / la verdure
green	novice, inexpérimenté
*a recipe for **disaster***	un désastre annoncé
*no quick **fix***	pas de solution miracle
*a **race** against time*	une course contre la montre
ripple effect	effet de ricochet
to sweep it under the carpet	faire disparaître / balayer sous le tapis
*to use up **resources***	épuiser les ressources
to beat around / about the bush	tourner autour du pot
***nature's** way of doing sth*	un moyen dont dispose la nature pour faire
*debt to **nature***	la mort (euphémisme)
*heaven on **earth***	le paradis sur terre
*to go to the ends of the **earth***	faire l'impossible
waste not, want not	L'économie protège du besoin

Translation: English-to-French exercise

Time for degrowth: to save the planet, the economy must shrink (adapté de TheConversation.com)

What is so refreshing about the UN's Sustainable Development Goals report is that it recognises the inherent tension between economic development and the ecology of our planet. Or so it seems. The preamble affirms that "planet Earth and its ecosystems are our home" and underscores the necessity of achieving "harmony with nature". It calls for "sustainable patterns of production and consumption, through higher levels of economic productivity".

This language signals awareness that something about our economic system has gone terribly awry – that we cannot continue chewing through the planet without gravely endangering our security and prosperity, and indeed the future viability of our species.

But looking more closely, a glaring contradiction emerges. The report calls for both less and more at the same time. This call for more growth comes at an odd moment, just as we are learning that it is not physically possible. Scientists tell us that we are blowing past planetary boundaries at breakneck speed and witnessing the greatest mass extinction in more than 66m years.

The hard truth is that our ecological overshoot is due almost entirely to overconsumption in rich countries, particularly the West.

Adapted press excerpts (about 400 words)

Excerpt 1 – Global trade deal threatens Paris climate goals (adapted from *The Guardian*)

A far-reaching global trade deal being negotiated in secret could threaten the goals of the **Paris climate deal** by making it harder for governments to favour clean energy over fossil fuels. The controversial Trade in Services Agreement (Tisa) aims to liberalise trade between the EU and 22 countries across the global services sector, which employs tens of millions in Europe alone. But a new EU text would oblige signatories to work towards "**energy neutrality**" between **renewable energy** and **fossil fuel power**, although amendments proposed by the EU would exempt **nuclear power** from this rule. A report by the UN declared that mega-trade deals such as Tisa are becoming increasingly politicised, and fail to encourage **green energy** sources.

Excerpt 2 – New York City's Plastic Bag Fee (adapted from *The New York Times*)

The yearslong debate over whether to impose a **fee** for **plastic bags** in New York appeared to come to a **hard-fought end** last month, when the City Council voted to charge 5 cents for most plastic and paper shopping bags. The city legislation is intended to encourage shoppers to give up the plastic bags whose **omnipresence** on city sidewalks and in city trees and **landfills** have long frustrated **environmentalists**. Charge a nickel, the thinking goes, and people will start using their own **reusable bags**. In other cities, **plastic bag use** has **dropped** sharply. There are a number of exemptions built into New York's policy, including for **plastic produce bags**, and restaurant and street-vendor **carryout bags**.

Excerpt 3 – Shell in the Arctic (adapted from *Slate*)

In a pretty stunning reversal, Royal Dutch Shell announced that it would abandon its **offshore oil drilling** activities in the Alaskan Arctic "for the **foreseeable future**." Shell's Arctic **exploration** had become a favorite **target** for **environmental activists** in recent months, as controversy swirled over the Obama administration's decision to **green-light** the project. Earlier this year, hundreds of brightly colored boats briefly **blockaded** one of Shell's Arctic-bound ships in Portland, Oregon, citing **climate change** concerns. It's unclear how central these protests were in motivating Shell's turnaround, but Shell has "privately made clear it is taken aback by the **public protests** against the **drilling** which are threatening to seriously damage its reputation."

Excerpt 4 – Is the "Ecomodernist Manifesto" the Future of Environmentalism? (adapted from *The New Yorker*)

The Anthropocene, the unofficial name for our **human-influenced** geological age, has become a popular shorthand for **environmental apocalypse**. In 2016, however, a group of researchers, **activists**, and philanthropists published "An **Ecomodernist** Manifesto," that envisions a different sort of Anthropocene – not only a good one but a great one. Calling themselves **ecomodernists** and **ecopragmatists**, they argue that **technology**, supported and accelerated by government **investment**, can allow **humanity** to simultaneously **mitigate climate change**, **protect land**, and relieve poverty. They approve of **urbanization**, **intensified agriculture**, **nuclear power**, **aquaculture**, and **desalination**; they disapprove of **suburbanization**, **low-yield farming**, and forms of **renewable energy** with large acreage demands. **High-efficiency solar cells**, **advanced nuclear fission**, and **nuclear fusion** "represent the most plausible pathways toward the joint goals of **climate stabilization** and radical decoupling of humans from **nature**."

Food for Thought and Quotations (about 500 words)

Zero-waste management

It refers to the management of resources so as to encourage reusing them, in a process similar to the natural way of recycling of natural resources. It aims to encourage people to adapt their lifestyle to modernity by redesigning resources for others to reuse, and it also encourages businesses to design products that are compatible with this approach. The Cradle-to-Cradle concept (opposed to the traditional Cradle-to-Grave one where products are doomed to end in a landfill) defines a product that can be recycled into a new product at the end of its life, so that ultimately there is no waste. The economic benefits are many: it saves money and generates profit through its popularity, it fosters sustainability and improves raw material availability and it also encourages innovation. The environmental advantages are obvious!

Environmental economics

It refers to a sub-field of economics that is concerned with environmental issues and the notion that markets fail to distribute resources efficiently in order to guarantee social welfare and environmental protection. It aims to create economic sustainability that includes "*the costs and benefits of alternative environmental policies to deal with air pollution, water quality, toxic substances, solid waste, and global warming*" according to the National Bureau for Economic Research. Moreover, there are three pillars to guarantee sustainability: economic (since Westerners consume far more than their fair share), environmental (natural resources are not unlimited) and social (ethical responsibility to reduce human inequality, social injustice, and poverty). To some extent, the 2016 Paris Agreement applies this principle in order for financial interests to gradually take into account the necessity to adapt the economy to the limited resources of our planet.

Eco-activism

While the world leaders try to define the necessary political, economic, social and technological efforts in order to protect the human civilisation from the effects of climate change, citizens themselves take action by changing their daily habits and by participating in educative actions, demonstrating or standing up against industrial interests that do not hesitate to threaten them. Environmental activism requires action (strikes, protests and marches), alternatives in education, food sourcing, housing, energy or sometimes radical activism when they come to consider that this is the only means to change. What is surprising is that people have long been aware of the importance of preserving our environment and conveying this message to the greatest number. John Muir (founder of the first US National Parks), Henry D.Thoreau (a philosopher-writer-activist) and Gaylord Nelson (founder of Earth Day) are today considered as the first environmentalists in modern history.

"*A nation that destroys its soils destroys itself. Forests are the lungs of our land, purifying the air and giving fresh strength to our people.*" Franklin D. Roosevelt

"*We are being made aware that the organization of society on the principle of private profit, as well as public destruction, is leading both to the deformation of humanity by unregulated industrialism, and to the exhaustion of natural resources, and that a good deal of our material progress is a progress for which succeeding generations may have to pay dearly.*" T.S. Eliot

"*What is the use of a house if you haven't got a tolerable planet to put it on?*" Henry David Thoreau

Topic three

In our time

Section 7

Politics and society

Chapter A

Welfare, wealth and solidarity

Vocabulary list

WEALTH AND POVERTY	RICHESSE ET PAUVRETÉ
the rich, the wealthy	les riches
the poor, the destitute	les pauvres
the haves / the have-nots	les riches / les pauvres
the privileged / the underprivileged	les privilégiés / les défavorisés
the well-offs / well-off	les personnes aisées / aisé
to acquire	acquérir
to accumulate	accumuler
wealth	les richesses, la fortune
to make a fortune	faire fortune
misfortune	l'infortune, un revers de fortune
a multimillionaire / a billionaire / a zillionaire	un multi-millionnaire / un milliardaire / un multi-milliardaire
to squander money	gaspiller de l'argent
the standard of living	le niveau de vie
the way of life, lifestyle	le mode de vie
a widening gap	un fossé grandissant
penniless, broke, short for cash	sans le sou, fauché
to be in need, in want	être dans le besoin, dans la gêne
to deprive / the deprived	être privé de / les déshérités
the underdogs	les laissés-pour-compte
squalor	la misère
a plight	une situation désespérée
a tramp, a hobo	un clochard
a wretch	un misérable, une épave
a sorry plight	un état pitoyable
an outcast	un exclu, un paria
a dropout	un marginal
a beggar / to beg	un mendiant / mendier, supplier
a soup kitchen, a bread line	la soupe populaire
a slum	un taudis
shantytowns	un bidonville
down-and-out	dans la dèche
to squat / a squatter	squatter / un squatter
a homeless / homelessness	un sans domicile fixe (SDF) / la précarité des sans-abri
a freeloader	un parasite, pique-assiette
a homeless shelter	un centre d'accueil pour sans-abri
the working poor	les travailleurs pauvres
the needy	les indigents, les nécessiteux
to sink into poverty	basculer dans la pauvreté
the destitute / destitution	les plus démunis / le dénuement, la misère totale
below / above the poverty line	en dessous / au-dessus du seuil de pauvreté
a low-income household	un ménage à revenus modestes

pauperization	l'appauvrissement, la paupérisation
the bare necessities	le strict nécessaire
equality / inequality	l'égalité / l'inégalité
unequal / inegalitarian	inégal / inégalitaire
a two-tier society	une société à deux vitesses
the distribution of wealth	le partage des richesses
debt	l'endettement
a discrepancy	un écart, une différence
a balance / an imbalance	un équilibre / un déséquilibre
to redress the balance	rétablir l'équilibre
to bridge the gap	combler un fossé
to widen the gap	creuser un fossé
the gap between the haves and the have-nots	la fracture sociale

SOCIAL MOBILITY	**LA MOBILITÉ SOCIALE**
a self-made man	un self-made-man
career advancement	l'avancement social
to climb up the social ladder	monter dans l'ascenseur social / évoluer dans la société
upward mobility	l'ascension sociale
to start from scratch	partir de rien
to provide financial support	fournir une aide financière
equal opportunities	l'égalité des chances
the social status	le statut social
to bridge the social divide	réduire la fracture sociale
to struggle to get by	avoir du mal à s'en sortir
to make ends meet	joindre les deux bouts
to survive / survival	survivre / la survie
to scrape by	vivoter
marginalization	la marginalisation
to deserve / deserving	mériter / méritant
a reward / rewarding	une récompense / gratifiant
to relief / relief	venir en aide, secourir / le secours, l'aide
to assist sb / assistance	aider qqn / l'assistance

WELFARE	**LE BIEN-ÊTRE**
welfare (GB)	le bien-être, l'assistance, la prospérité
welfare (US)	les prestations sociales
the welfare state	l'État-providence
social insurance / protection	la protection sociale
social justice	la justice sociale
a social worker	une assistante sociale
welfare allowances	les allocations sociales
a benefit, an allowance	une prestation sociale, une allocation
to claim benefits	faire une demande de prestations sociales
social benefits	les acquis sociaux

the health coverage, medical coverage	la couverture santé
universal medical coverage	la CMU (couverture médicale universelle)
a social security number	un numéro de sécu
a health insurance scheme	une assurance maladie
to contribute / the social contributions	cotiser / les cotisations sociales
the nanny state	l'État protecteur / l'État nounou
the NHS (National Health Service)	la sécurité sociale britannique
a safety net	un filet de protection sociale
income support	le revenu de solidarité active
to be entitled to benefit	avoir droit aux aides sociales
publicly-funded	financé par l'État / à financements publics
a pension / the pension system	une pension de retraite / le système des retraites
the state pension scheme	le régime public d'assurance vieillesse
retirement / the retirement age	la retraite / l'age de départ à la retraite
a pensioner / a retiree	un retraité
the elderly	les vieux, les personnes âgées
a pension fund	un fonds de pension
the healthcare system	le système de santé américain
medical treatment	les soins médicaux
health spendings	les dépenses de santé
welfare dependency	la dépendance, l'assistanat
benefit fraud	la fraude aux prestations sociales
sickness benefit	les allocations maladie
an unemployment insurance	une assurance chômage
unemployment benefit	les allocations chômage
to take out an insurance	prendre / souscrire une assurance
to be covered	être couvert

SOLIDARITY	**LA SOLIDARITÉ**
a charity / charity	une association caritative, la charité
a charity shop	une boutique d'articles d'occasion tenue par une association caritative
a pawn shop	un bureau de prêteur sur gages (le mont-de-piété)
a charitable cause	une cause charitable
a volunteer worker / volunteering	un bénévole / le bénévolat
generosity	la générosité
selfishness	l'égoïsme
to give away money, to donate	faire un don
compassion / compassionate	la compassion / compatissant
to assist sb / assistance	assister, aider qqn / l'assistance
to address inequalities	s'attaquer aux inégalités
to eradicate a scourge	éradiquer un fléau
to tackle poverty	réduire la pauvreté
debt relief	l'allégement de la dette
a relief agency	une organisation humanitaire

a philanthropist	un philanthrope
philanthropy	la philanthropie
to found / to fund	fonder / financer
a foundation	une fondation
to fund a project	financer un projet
financial backing / to back	le soutien financier / soutenir
social entrepreneurship	l'entrepreneuriat social
development aid	l'aide au développement
on a voluntary basis	en tant que bénévole
a donor / a donator	un donneur / un donateur

MORAL STANDARDS	**LES CRITÈRES MORAUX**
morals / morality	la morale / les principes moraux
public morals	les mœurs publiques
good / evil	bien, le bien / mal, le mal
an evil, an ill	un mal
right / wrong	bon, juste / mauvais, injuste
to right a wrong	corriger une injustice
virtue / virtuous	la vertu / vertueux
a quality, a principle	une qualité, un principe
a defect, a failing	un défaut (de caractère), un point faible
foul / lofty	infâme / noble
to behave oneself	se comporter
behaviour, comportment	la conduite, le comportement
to set an example to sb, to be a role model	donner l'exemple à qqn
to perform one's duty	faire son devoir
to have a clear conscience	avoir la conscience tranquille
to feel guilty about sth	se sentir coupable de
shame / shameful	la honte / honteux, scandaleux
shameless	éhonté, abominable
scrupulous / unscrupulous	scrupuleux / sans scrupule, indélicat
conscientious	consciencieux
to make up for sth	rattraper, compenser qqch
to own up to sth	avouer, reconnaître qqch
to judge / a judgement	juger / un jugement (moral)
to misjudge sb	se tromper sur le compte de qqn
to be critical of sth	se montrer critique à l'égard de qch
to disapprove of sth / sb	désapprouver qqch / qqn
to agree with / to disagree with	être d'accord / ne pas être d'accord avec
to hold sb in contempt	avoir du mépris pour qqn
to approve of sth / sb	approuver qqch / qqn
to praise sb for sth	admirer qqn / marquer à qqn son admiration de qqch
to overrate / to underrate	surestimer / sous-estimer
to advocate sth	préconiser qqch
to commend sb on sth	faire l'éloge de qqn (pour qqch)

BONUS	**BONUS**
to be very down	avoir le **moral** dans les chaussettes
***share** and share alike*	il faut partager
tears welled up in my eyes	les larmes me sont montées aux yeux / mes yeux s'emplirent de larmes
*to leave **well** alone*	ne pas s'en mêler
*you may **well** ask!*	on se demande bien !
*to wish sb **well***	souhaiter bonne chance à qqn
*all's **well** that ends well*	tout est bien qui finit bien
*to be **well** up in sth*	bien s'y connaître en qqch
*to be a **poor** sailor*	ne pas avoir le pied marin
*a **poor** excuse*	une bien piètre excuse / un mauvais prétexte
*it's an **ill** wind (that blows nobody any **good**)*	à quelque chose malheur est bon
*it **ill** becomes you to criticize*	il ne vous sied guère de critiquer
*to speak **ill** of sb*	dire du mal de qqn
***ill**-suited*	inadapté, mal formé pour
*to draw a **moral** from sth*	tirer la leçon de qqch
*on **moral** grounds*	sur un terrain purement moral / pour des raisons morales

Translation: English-to-French exercise

Stop coddling the super-rich (by Warren Buffet, adapté de *The New York Times*)

Our leaders have asked for "shared sacrifice." But when they did the asking, they spared me. I checked with my mega-rich friends to learn what pain they were expecting. They, too, were left untouched. While the poor and middle class fight for us in Afghanistan, and while most Americans struggle to make ends meet, we mega-rich continue to get our extraordinary tax breaks. [...]

These and other blessings are showered upon us by legislators in Washington who feel compelled to protect us, much as if we were spotted owls or some other endangered species. It's nice to have friends in high places. If you make money with money, as some of my super-rich friends do, your percentage may be a bit lower than mine. But if you earn money from a job, your percentage will surely exceed mine – most likely by a lot.

Adapted press excerpts (about 400 words)

Excerpt 1 – The contributory myth: what you pay in isn't what you get out (adapted from *The Economist*)

Every time **pensions** or other **old age benefits** are reformed, the debate is dogged by a familar refrain. It is unfair to **cut benefits** because people are only getting back what they paid in. In Britain, Lloyd George introduced the idea of **contributory benefits** and William Beveridge, the father of the Welfare State, said in 1942 that *"**Benefit** in return for **contributions**, rather than free **allowances** from the State, is what the people of Britain desire"*. In America, when Franklin Roosevelt launched **Social Security**, he told Congress that *"First, the system adopted, except for the money necessary to initiate it, should be **self-sustaining**"*. **Benefit cuts** or **tax increases** are inevitable. When that happens, let us have a debate on how best to **distribute** the pain, not on the idea that past payments are being "stolen" from their rightful **recipients**.

Excerpt 2 – Housing is essential to ending child poverty (adapted from *Thecourier.co.uk*)

The Scottish Government's consultation on ending **child poverty** and the ambitious targets it is proposing are very welcome. However, in this week's announcement there was little focus on the crucial role of **decent housing** for every child in Scotland. A safe, secure and affordable home is a basic right for everyone and fundamental to life chances. Without this, children are less likely to have the same level of **educational attainment** as their peers. Without a warm and safe home, children are more likely to have **poorer health** outcomes over their **lifetime**. So, in considering the various paths towards ending child poverty in Scotland, it is paramount that tackling Scotland's **housing crisis** is at the heart of it.

Excerpt 3 – Is There a Link Between Mental Health and Gun Violence? (adapted from *The New Yorker*)

There is one exception, however, that runs through all of the data: violence against oneself. **Mental illness**, increases the risk of gun violence when that violence takes the form of suicide. According to the **C.D.C.**, between twenty-one and forty-four per cent of those who commit suicide had previously exhibited **mental-health problems** – as indicated by a combination of family interviews and evidence of mental-health **treatment** found at the scene, such as **psychiatric medications** – while between sixteen and thirty-three per cent had a history of psychiatric treatment. Many studies have shown an even **higher risk** of suicide among the **mentally ill (bipolar disorder, depression** and **schizophrenia disorders)**. The factors responsible for mass violence are messy, complex, and dynamic.

Excerpt 4 – Should Charity Be Logical? (adapted from *Slate*)

Suppose someone walks by a pond and notices a bit of garbage floating in it. A **devoted** environmentalist, he wades into the pond, retrieves the garbage, and throws it in a wastebasket. However, he doesn't help a small child who has fallen into the pond and subsequently drowns. We would all condemn this person, wouldn't we? This implausible-seeming story is a metaphor for a **movement** called effective **altruism**. Rich Westerners should **contribute money** to **charities** that help **poor** people in **developing countries**. Failing to **donate** one's excess **income** to **international charities** such as Oxfam is like failing to save a child from drowning when one can do so at no risk to oneself. A small amount of money can pay for malaria nets that **save** the **lives** of children in foreign countries. There is no **morally relevant** distinction between saving a child in a foreign country and saving a child one sees in a pond.

Food for Thought and Quotations (about 500 words)

Relative and absolute poverty

Absolute poverty is the lack of one or more basic needs over a period that is long enough to endanger your life or cause you harm. As opposed to relative poverty, it covers vital and biological needs such as food, water, clothing, basic housing, a decent roof over one's head, and a minimum of sanitation. Extreme poverty generally refers to a poverty line. It is defined as the amount of income one needs to satisfy the most basic needs: absolute needs (food, shelter) plus health care, education and specific needs depending on where people live. For example, urban residents of capital cities will have greater education, energy and transportation costs that are greater than anywhere else. People living in extreme poverty risk from marginalization to malnutrition and disease infections. All this causes health damages which are no doubt one of the most striking and universal effects of poverty. A universal characteristic of absolute poverty is therefore the state of health and life expectancy.

Welfare State in the UK

In 1948, the Labour Party created the National Health Service (NHS) in order to give equitable access to free and universal healthcare. Before the war, patients used to pay for their own health care, so the poorest were unable to afford the medical treatment they required. Soon it became obvious that this system would be almost impossible to maintain and to control due to financial costs. Thus, in 1951, the NHS was forced to introduce some fees in order to acquire advantages never to be lost. Throughout the 60s and until the late 80s, financial and organisational difficulties accumulated, so that in 1990, Margaret Thatcher organised a gradual privatisation of services through the NHS and Community Care Act. Competition started between newly created NHS trusts, and therefore the system was no longer providing fair and equal access to health care, and discrepancies appeared between health professionals' salaries. Since then, the National Health Service has somewhat reduced inequalities, so it can still claim to be largely successful despite its many flaws, even if the spirit of the Beveridge Report of 1942 is no longer present.

The Health Care reform in the USA

The history of the health care coverage started in 1964 when President Lyndon Johnson established the Social Security, a pension system consisting of a contribution on wages, dividends or rental property. Medicare is a public health insurance granted to seniors while Medicaid refers to a health insurance for the poor. The main problem is that healthcare expenses are rising every year because of the overconsumption of drugs and services, costing 16% of the GDP. About 70% of the Americans subscribe a private insurance policy, but the insurance companies are often criticized because of the pre-existing conditions which prevent some people from subscribing. The Patient Protection and Affordable Care Act (termed Obamacare) consists of improving the healthcare system by granting 47 million people a private insurance policy guaranteed by public funds. The Federal government and the States are of two minds regarding the financing of this reform, not to mention the part played by the Republicans in their fierce opposition against it, after the election of Donald Trump in 2016.

"Organisation of social insurance should be treated as one part only of a comprehensive policy of social progress. Social insurance fully developed may provide income security; it is an attack upon Want. But Want is one only of five giants on the road of reconstruction and in some ways the easiest to attack. The others are Disease, Ignorance, Squalor and Idleness." William Beveridge

"A bone to the dog is not charity. Charity is the bone shared with the dog, when you are just as hungry as the dog." Jack London

Chapter B
Equality

Vocabulary list

IMMIGRATION	**L'IMMIGRATION**
to immigrate / an immigrant	immigrer / un immigrant
a would-be immigrant	un candidat à l'immigration
to attract, to appeal / attraction	attirer / l'attrait
a pull factor	un facteur d'attractivité
to aspire to / to yearn	aspirer à / désirer ardemment
an opportunity / a future prospect	une chance / une perspective d'avenir
misery / miserable	le malheur / misérable
poverty-stricken, in dire straits	dans le dénuement
to flee a country	s'enfuir d'un pays
a refugee	un réfugié
an asylum seeker / to seek refuge	un demandeur d'asile / chercher refuge
to shelter / a shelter	recueillir / un asile, un refuge
to endure hardships	traverser des épreuves
the lure of a better life	l'attrait d'une vie meilleure
to break with the past	rompre avec le passé
illegal immigration	l'immigration illégale
to tighten border controls	renforcer les contrôles aux frontières
an alien	un ressortissant étranger
a newcomer	un nouvel arrivant
an illegal alien, an illegal	un clandestin
a stowaway	un passager clandestin
the undocumented	les sans-papiers
a smuggler	un passeur
a fake ID, a fake passport	une fausse carte d'identité, des faux papiers / un faux passeport
to integrate	s'intégrer
a work permit	un permis de travail
a residence permit, a Green Card (US)	une carte de séjour
a citizen / citizenship	un citoyen / la citoyenneté
quotas	les quotas
restrictive / selective	restrictif / sélectif
to naturalise / naturalisation	naturaliser / la naturalisation
to assimilate, to acculturate	assimiler, s'acculturer
multicultural, multiracial	multiculturel / multiracial
race	l'ethnie (race : ne convient pas en français)
ethnic / an ethnic group	ethnique / une ethnie, un groupe ethnique
mixed / mixed-race marriage	le mariage mixte
an expatriate, a stateless	un expatrié, un apatride
a flow, an influx / to flock to	un flux, un afflux / affluer
to flood	submerger
exploitation / to be exploited	l'exploitation / être exploité
to be expelled from	être expulsé d'un pays
to be turned away at the border	être refoulé à la frontière
to seal one's borders	fermer ses frontières
an immigration policy	une politique migratoire

RACISM	LE RACISME
anti-immigrant feelings	les sentiments xénophobes
xenophobia / racism	la xénophobie / le racisme
xenophobic / racist	xénophobe / raciste
to let in / to keep out migrants	laisser entrer / empêcher d'entrer les migrants
intolerance / intolerant	l'intolérance / intolérant
biased, prejudiced	plein de préjugés
a stereotype	un stéréotype
a burden	un fardeau
to resent / resentment	mal accepter, ne pas supporter / le ressentiment
to segregate / segregation	discriminer, séparer / la ségrégation
a ghetto	un ghetto
a scapegoat	un bouc émissaire
the color bar (GB) / color line (US)	la discrimination raciale
racial hatred / racial bias	la haine raciale / les préjugés raciaux
racial tensions / attacks / violence	les tensions / attaques / violences raciales ou racistes
to fuel tensions	alimenter, nourrir les tensions
to be discriminated against	être victime de discrimination
to propagate a hate speech	propager les discours de haine
a racist slur, racist taunts	une insulte raciste / des provocations racistes
anti-Semitism / an anti-Semitic remark	l'antisémitisme / une remarque antisémite
a revisionist	un négationniste
a black / an Afro-American	un Noir / un Afro-Américain
a Jew	un Juif
affirmative action	la discrimination positive
the fight for equality	la lutte pour l'égalité
a color-blind society	une société libre de discriminations raciales
a slave	un esclave
slave trade	la traite des esclaves
to abolish apartheid	abolir la ségrégation raciale (Afrique du Sud)
white supremacy	la suprématie des blancs
nativism	la préférence nationale
racial profiling, driving while Black	délit de faciès
a second-class citizen	un citoyen de seconde zone
the NAACP (National Association for the Advancement of Colored People)	une association américaine de défense des droits des Noirs

WOMEN'S RIGHTS	LES DROITS DES FEMMES
the gender gap	l'écart, le fossé entre hommes et femmes
male / female	du sexe masculin / féminin
gender imbalance	le déséquilibre entre sexes
gender inequalities	les inégalités entre hommes et femmes

misogyny / a misogynist	la misogynie / un misogyne
sexism / sexist bias	le sexisme / les préjugés sexistes
women empowerment	la prise d'autonomie des femmes
franchise, suffrage, the right to vote	le droit de vote
feminism / a feminist	le féminisme / un(e) féministe
a contraceptive, a condom	un contraceptif, un préservatif
women's reproductive rights	les droits des femmes en matière de reproduction
to legalise / legalisation	légaliser / la légalisation
birth control	le contrôle des naissances
abortion	l'avortement
teenage pregnancy	les adolescentes enceintes, les grossesses de mineures
a termination of pregnancy	une interruption volontaire de grossesse (IVG)
to perform / to have an abortion	pratiquer une IVG / avorter
maltreatment	la maltraitance
domestic violence, domestic abuse	la violence conjugale
a sex worker	une prostituée
to ill-treat / to abuse	maltraiter
to batter / to rape	battre / violer
a sham / a forced marriage	un mariage blanc / forcé
female genital mutilation / circumcision	l'excision
to be on maternity leave	être en congé maternité
to look after one's children	s'occuper de ses enfants
to bring up / to raise a child	élever un enfant
a housewife	une femme au foyer, une ménagère
childrearing	l'éducation des enfants
a day care centre / childcare facilities / a nursery	une crèche / une garderie
household chores	les corvées ménagères
a working mom (US) / mum (GB)	une maman qui travaille
a time-consuming task	une tâche chronophage
the double day of women, women's second shift	les deux journées en une seule
a glass ceiling	un plafond de verre
to juggle / balance family and career	jongler / concilier entre famille et carrière
the pay gap / equal pay	l'écart des salaires / l'égalité des salaires
an equal opportunity policy	une politique d'égalité des chances
to achieve equality	parvenir à l'égalité
to legislate / to implement	légiférer / mettre en œuvre
parity / fairness	la parité / l'équité
the Equal Pay Act	la loi sur l'égalité des salaires
wage disparities	les disparités salariales
a career woman	une carriériste
boardroom barriers	les freins à l'avancement professionnel
to make the grade	être à la hauteur

to be economically independent	être financièrement indépendante
to get ahead in politics	progresser en politique
to require stamina	nécessiter de la ténacité, persévérance

SAME-SEX COUPLES	**L'HOMOSEXUALITÉ**
gay, homosexual	gay, homosexuel
a gay-friendly society	une société ouverte aux gays / favorisant les droits des homosexuel(le)s
to be straight	être hétérosexuel
homosexuality, sexual orientation	l'homosexualité, l'orientation sexuelle
a lesbian	une lesbienne
the LGBT movement (Lesbian, Gay, Bisexual and Transgender)	le mouvement LGBT (lesbien, gay, bisexuel et transgenre)
the gay / the LGBT community	la communauté gay / LGBT
gay rights	les droits des homosexuels
a gay-friendly club	une discothèque où les homosexuels sont les bienvenus
to marry sb, to get married to sb	se marier avec qqn, épouser qqn
a wedding ceremony	une cérémonie de mariage
to tie the knot, to get hitched	se passer la bague au doigt
a civil partnership, a civil union	une union civile, un PACS
a couple / a partner	un couple / un compagnon, une compagne
to move in with	s'installer avec
to set up house with	se mettre en ménage avec
same-sex parents / LGBT parenting	une famille homoparentale / l'homoparentalité
to legalise / to ban gay marriage	légaliser / interdire le mariage gay
to be prejudiced against	avoir des préjugés contre
homophobia / homophobic / a homophobe	l'homophobie / homophobe / un homophobe
a homophobic crime	un crime homophobe

BONUS	**BONUS**
to get something ***straight***	aller droit au but, être parfaitement clair
to go ***straight***	devenir honnête
straight *away*	tout de suite, immédiatement
straight *off*	sans hésiter, d'un coup
straight *up*	honnêtement
to be well ***set****-up*	avoir les moyens financiers
to ***set*** *about doing sth*	commencer à faire qqch
to ***set*** *up on one's own / to* ***set*** *oneself up*	s'établir à son compte
to ***set*** *sb up*	tendre un piège à, monter un coup contre
to ***set*** *upon sb*	attaquer qqn

Translation: French-to-English exercise

Intégrer les policiers dans la société (adapté de *Eurotopic*)

Après l'assassinat de cinq policiers à Dallas, l'ambiance est chauffée à blanc aux États-Unis. Un sniper a abattu des policiers depuis un parking, pendant une manifestation dénonçant les violences policières à caractère raciste.

Les États-Unis vont-ils connaître une nouvelle vague de troubles ethniques ? Les événements de Dallas, Baton Rouge et Falcon Heights ont montré à quel point les rapports entre les citoyens afro-américains et la police s'étaient dégradés.

Il faudrait que les policiers vivent dans les villes et dans les quartiers dans lesquels ils patrouillent. Ainsi, leur présence ne serait pas ressentie comme étrangère, mais ils seraient des voisins qui font leurs courses au même magasin et dont les enfants vont à la même école que ceux du quartier, et ils nourriraient les mêmes aspirations pour la communauté.

Il fut un temps où les parents parlaient à leurs enfants d'abeilles venant butiner des fleurs ; aujourd'hui dans les familles noires, les parents expliquent à leurs enfants comment se comporter quand ils sont arrêtés par la police pour survivre à cette rencontre. Tant que la police n'éradiquera pas ces lacunes et ces injustices, elles iront s'envenimant.

Adapted press excerpts (about 400 words)

Excerpt 1 – Miss America 1968: When civil rights and feminist activists converged on Atlantic City (adapted from *TheConversation.com*)

At this year's Miss America pageant, the first openly **lesbian** contestant, Erin O'Flaherty, will compete for the crown in Atlantic City. Flaherty's participation will represent yet another step toward a more **inclusive** and **diverse** pageant. [...] During the 1930s – the pageant's early years – **regulations** explicitly stipulated that contestants must be of "the **white race**." But by 1968, the Atlantic City chapter of the **National Association for the Advancement of Colored People** was determined to break the beauty queen color line. In a meeting with pageant officials, chapter leaders pushed for **integration**. [...] Thanks to **civil rights** and **feminist activists**, 1968 was perhaps the most exciting year in the Miss America pageant's history. Newspapers and magazines delighted in the drama of the events and broadcast the **activists**' messages to a mass audience.

Excerpt 2 – Leaders pledge more help for refugees; critics say pledges are not enough (adapted from *L.A.Times*)

Global leaders have promised to better **protect the rights** of **refugees** and **migrants**, and undertake a more coordinated **response** to the world's deepening **crisis** of **displaced** people. But **human rights** and **humanitarian** groups criticized the **agreement** for failing to address the magnitude of the problem. How to deal with the world's more than 65 million **displaced people** was the focus of the U.N. high-level **summit** on the largest **movement** of **refugees** and **migrants** in 70 years. The agreement is expected to lead to the development of standardized guidelines on the treatment of migrants in **vulnerable situations**, and herald more **equitable** sharing of **hosting** refugees. But many human rights and **humanitarian** groups slammed the resolution for failing to mandate **concrete action** that obligates countries to do their **fair share**.

Excerpt 3 – Latest Religious Liberty Battle: Church-Affiliated Colleges And LGBT Students (adapted from *NPR*)

A California lawmaker's push to reduce **discrimination** against **LGBT** people at **religious** colleges and universities sparks new **debate** over the separation of church and state. As a child, Anthony Villarreal knew he was different. "I was conflicted. I was Christian. And I had an idea that I might be gay. But I was in denial." But in his final college semester, a loud argument with his boyfriend over whether he should **come out** led his neighbors to call the cops, and he was arrested for **domestic violence**. Soon after, the university dismissed him. Villarreal is convinced he was **kicked out** because he's **gay**. Villarreal was never charged with domestic violence, and there's no proof the university dismissed him for being gay. In fact, the university says it never **discriminates** against students based on **sexual orientation**. But Villarreal says many **LGBT** students at **faith-based schools** feel pressured to be someone they're not.

Excerpt 4 – Bus driver says Brexit racism rise "alarming" (adapted from *Sky News*)

An Asian bus driver has told the TUC conference how **racist attacks** have increased dramatically since the Brexit vote. Abdul Rashid, from Middlesbrough, said the speed at which **racism** had risen since the EU referendum was alarming. "After the **toxic language** used during the EU referendum **campaign**, as a result **racist attacks** on **black communities**, **refugees** and those perceived to be of **migrant backgrounds** rose dramatically across the UK," he said. "I work as a bus driver and soon after the result I was told by someone getting on my bus to enjoy my job while it lasted. Soon I would be 'going home'". Even though **racism** existed before, the speed it has risen since the EU referendum is alarming. In London police received 599 **allegations** of **racist abuse** over the 24 hours following the EU referendum.

Food for Thought and Quotations (about 500 words)

Asylum seeker, refugee and migrant

Broadly speaking, refugees are forced to flee for their lives, while immigrants choose to move to another country. A *refugee* is a person who is forced to flee from persecution and who is located outside of their home country. There are different categories, such as political, economic or environmental refugee. An *asylum seeker* has fled his or her country and is asking for protection in another country: he or she is a claimant *seeking* refuge and will therefore be termed a refugee only when his or her case has been decided. A *migrant* is a person who is outside their country of origin, currently on the move or with temporary status or no status at all in the country where they live. An *economic migrant* moves countries for a job or a better economic future, however *migrants*' motivations are complex and therefore labeling a migrant as "economic" can be simplistic.

The American Civil War Amendments

The 13th Amendment abolished slavery in the US in 1865: "*Neither slavery nor involuntary servitude, except as a punishment for crime whereof the party shall have been duly convicted, shall exist within the United States, or any place subject to their jurisdiction.*" The 14th Amendment addresses citizenship rights and equal protection of the laws: "*no State shall make or enforce any law which shall abridge the privileges or immunities of citizens of the United States; nor shall any State deprive any person of life, liberty, or property, without due process of law; nor deny to any person within its jurisdiction the equal protection of the laws*". The 15th Amendment prohibits governments from denying U.S. citizens the right to vote based on race, color, or past servitude: "*the right of citizens of the United States to vote shall not be denied or abridged by the United States or by any state on account of race, color, or previous condition of servitude.*"

The glass ceiling

The expression is a metaphor defining "*an unofficially acknowledged barrier to advancement in a profession, especially affecting women and members of minorities*". It was first coined in 1979 by American feminists to protest against barriers in the careers of women in the corporate ladder, regardless of their achievements or qualifications. Today it also refers to sex and racial inequalities and differences. More recently, new notions have appeared, such as the glass escalator (more men access functions in sectors previously occupied in majority by women, and reach higher responsibilities faster than them) and the sticky floor (to describe the limitations applied on women to climb up the social ladder and wage differences). In the Western world today, the average pay of a woman, for the same job and qualifications as a man, is about 25 percent lower.

Same-sex marriage

In 2016, same-sex marriage is legal in Argentina Belgium, Brazil, Canada, Colombia, Denmark, Finland, France, Iceland, Ireland, Luxembourg, Mexico, the Netherlands, New Zealand, Norway, Portugal, South Africa, Spain, Sweden, the United Kingdom, the United States, and Uruguay. Polls show a relatively high support in the Western world, but in many countries opposition remains strong and sometimes violent protests have occurred. In linguistic terms, most English dictionaries have included in their definition of the term *marriage* gender-neutral or explicit mentions of same-sex unions. Even if some minor religious communities today support gay marriage, major religions oppose it. Other types of arrangements have been made possible since the 2000s, such as the French PACS (Civil Solidarity Pact) or civil unions / civil partnerships. They are generally considered as a first step towards marriage for same-sex couples.

"During my lifetime I have dedicated myself to this struggle of the African people. I have fought against white domination, and I have fought against black domination. I have cherished the ideal of a democratic and free society in which all persons live together in harmony and with equal opportunities. It is an ideal which I hope to live for and to achieve. But if needs be, it is an ideal for which I am prepared to die." Nelson Mandela, 1964

"Achievement has no color." Abraham Lincoln

"Pit race against race, religion against religion, prejudice against prejudice. Divide and conquer! We must not let that happen here." Eleanor Roosevelt

"Who would be free themselves must strike the blow. Better even to die free than to live slaves." Frederick Douglass

Chapter C

Crime and justice

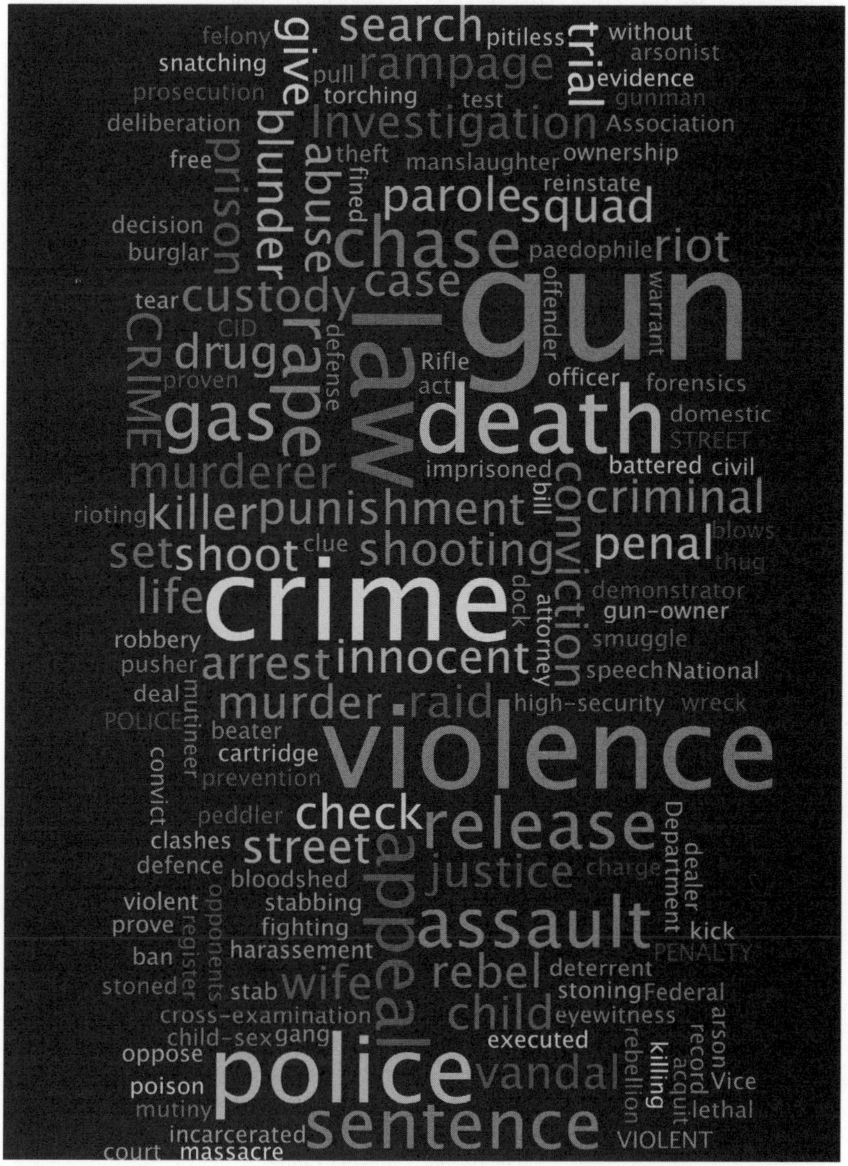

Vocabulary list

PETTY AND STREET CRIME	**LA PETITE CRIMINALITÉ**
crime	la criminalité
an offence / an offender	un délit / un délinquant
a crime / a criminal	un délit, un crime / un criminel
a felony / a felon	un crime / un criminel
the crime rate	le taux de criminalité
violence	la violence
street violence	la violence urbaine
organized crime	le crime organisé
juvenile delinquency	la délinquance juvénile
a criminal record	un casier judiciaire
fraud	la fraude, l'escroquerie
to counterfeit, to smuggle / counterfeiting	contrefaire / la contrefaçon
to embezzle / embezzling	détourner / le détournement de fonds
petty crime	la petite délinquance
prevention	la prévention
a security guard / a bodyguard	un vigile / un garde du corps
to set off an alarm	déclencher une alarme
to reinforce / reinforced	renforcer / blindé, renforcé
a thief / theft / to steal	un voleur / un vol / voler
a shoplifter / shoplifting	un voleur à l'étalage / le vol à l'étalage
snatching	le vol à l'arrachée
a burglary / a burglar	un cambriolage / un cambrioleur
a hold-up, a robbery	un braquage, un vol
an arson / an arsonist	un incendie criminel / un pyromane
a blackmail / a blackmailer	un chantage / un maître chanteur
drug trafficking / a trafficker	le trafic de drogue / un trafiquant de drogue
a drug dealer, a pusher, a peddler	un dealer, un revendeur de drogue
a vandal / vandalism	un vandale / le vandalisme
a thug	un voyou
a looter / looting	un pilleur / le pillage
to mug / mugging / a mugger	agresser / une agression / un agresseur
a mugshot	un cliché pris pendant une garde à vue
to fight / fighting	se battre / des échauffourées, des incidents
to burn out / a car torching	incendier / un incendie de voiture
to wreck, to vandalise / a vandal	saccager, vandaliser / un vandale
to rampage around	tout saccager
a rioting demonstrator	un casseur
a rebel / rebellion / to rebel	un rebelle / une rébellion / se rebeller
violent clashes	des affrontements violents
an insurgent / insurgency	un insurgé / l'insurrection
to repress street violence	réprimer la violence urbaine
the riot police / a riot shield	la police anti-émeutes / un bouclier anti-émeutes
a bludgeon	une matraque

handcuffs	des menottes
to impose a curfew	instaurer, décréter un couvre-feu
a clamp-down on	une répression sévère
tear gas, pepper gas / a smoke grenade	le gaz lacrymogène, une grenade fumigène

VIOLENT CRIME	**LES CRIMES VIOLENTS**
a manslaughter	un homicide involontaire
a homicide	un homicide volontaire
a murder / a murderer	un meurtre / un meurtrier
a first / second degree murder (US)	un meurtre au premier / deuxième degré
a killer / a serial killer	un tueur / un tueur en série
bloodshed	un bain de sang
to kick / to punch / to deal blows	frapper (coups de pied / de poing) / donner des coups
to strangle	étrangler
to poison	empoisonner
to shoot / to shoot at / a shooting	abattre / tirer sur / une fusillade
a mass murderer / a massacre	un tueur de masse / un massacre
to assault / an assault	agresser / une agression violente
stabbing / a wound / a stab	l'agression au couteau / une blessure (causée) / un coup de couteau
indecent assault / an exhibitionist	l'attentat à la pudeur / un exhibitionniste
cold-blooded, pitiless	de sang-froid, sans pitié
to rape / rape / a rapist	violer / le viol / un violeur
a gang rape	un viol collectif
domestic violence	la violence domestique
ill-treatment	les mauvais traitements
a battered wife / a wife beater	une femme battue / un mari violent
child abuse	la violente infligée aux enfants
harassment	le harcèlement
a child-sex abuse	un abus sexuel sur enfant
a paedophile (GB) / pedophile (US), a child molester / abuser	un pédophile
incest	l'inceste

GUN VIOLENCE	**LA VIOLENCE ARMÉE**
firearms	les armes à feu
a handgun / a shotgun	une arme de poing / un fusil de chasse
ammunition	les munitions
a bullet / a cartridge	une balle / une cartouche
a gun-owner / gun ownership	un propriétaire d'arme à feu / la possession d'armes à feu
gun control	la réglementation des armes à feu
a gun licence, a gun permit	un permis de port d'arme
gun sales	la vente d'armes à feu
gun culture	la culture des armes à feu

a shooting range	un stand de tir
at gunpoint	à bout portant
the NRA (National Rifle Association)	la NRA (association des détenteurs d'armes à feu)
to be trigger-happy	avoir la gâchette facile
self-defense (US), legitimate defence (GB)	l'autodéfense, la légitime défense
a vigilante / vigilantism	un membre de groupe d'autodéfense / les milices privées
a gunman	un homme armé
the death toll	le nombre de victimes
to pull the trigger	appuyer sur la gâchette
a killing / shooting spree	un accès de folie meurtrière
a shooting rampage	un carnage
the gun lobby	le lobby des armes à feu
a gun-rights activist	un défenseur du port d'arme
a background check	une enquête / vérification sur les antécédents
to register a weapon	déclarer une arme
to restrict	restreindre, limiter
to ban / to outlaw guns	interdire les armes à feu
a bill	un projet de loi
a law	une loi
law enforcement	le respect de la loi
teenage violence	la violence chez les jeunes

POLICE ACTION	**L'ACTION DES FORCES DE L'ORDRE**
the police (pluriel)	la police / les forces de police
a constable / a policeman	un agent de police en ville (GB) / un agent de police (en France un gendarme hors des villes)
to be on the beat	faire une ronde de police
law and order	l'ordre public
to break the law	enfreindre la loi
a police officer / an inspector	un policier / un inspecteur
a private detective	un détective privé
the Crime / Narcotics / Vice squad	la brigade criminelle / des stupéfiants / des mœurs
to investigate / an investigation	enquêter / une enquête
to set up / carry out an inquiry	ouvrir / mener une enquête
to be under suspicion / a suspect	être suspecté / un suspect
to chase, to give chase / a chase	poursuivre / une poursuite
a police roadblock	un barrage de police
an identity check	un contrôle d'identité
a raid / to raid a place	une descente de police / faire une descente
to search / a search warrant	une fouille / un mandat de perquisition
to shadow / a shadowing	suivre, filer / une filature

a clue / evidence, proof	un indice / des preuves
forensics / a forensic scientist	la médecine légale / un médecin légiste
to arrest / an arrest	arrêter / une arrestation
to give oneself up	se rendre
custody	la garde à vue
to be remanded in custody	rester en détention provisoire
to question / an interrogation	soumettre à... / un interrogatoire
a fingerprint	une empreinte digitale
to confess / a confession	avouer / des aveux
to make a statement	faire une déposition, une déclaration
to charge sb with	inculper qqn de
a blunder / to blunder	une bavure / commettre une bavure
to release / a release	relâcher / une remise en liberté
the FBI (Federal Bureau of Investigation	le Bureau fédéral d'investigation américain
NSY (New Scotland Yard)	les services d'enquête de la police judiciaire britannique
the CID (the Criminal Investigation Department)	la police judiciaire britannique

JUSTICE	**LA JUSTICE**
punishment / to punish	le châtiment / punir
the civil / penal code	le code civil / pénal
the law	la justice
a lawsuit	une action en justice
the court of justice / the courtroom	le tribunal / la salle d'audience
a Justice of the Peace	un juge de paix
a barrister (GB) / an attorney (US)	un avocat
to prosecute / the prosecution	poursuivre / l'accusation (la partie plaignante)
a lawyer (US), a solicitor (GB)	un notaire
a judge, a magistrate	un juge, un magistrat
a defendant	un accusé, un prévenu
the dock	le banc des accusés
an eyewitness	un témoin oculaire
a case	une affaire
a test case	une affaire qui fait jurisprudence
in the eye of the law	au regard de la loi
a trial / to be tried, to stand trial	un procès / être jugé
innocent until proven guilty	la présomption d'innocence
the speech for the defense / to plead	la plaidoirie / plaider
the cross-examination	le contre-interrogatoire
to deliberate / the deliberation	délibérer / la délibération
to acquit sb / an acquittal	acquitter qqn / un acquittement
an appeal against a decision	un appel contre une décision
a conviction / to convict sb of sth	une condamnation / reconnaître qqn coupable de...

the verdict	le verdict
to be sentenced to	être condamné à
to be fined for sth	être condamné à une amende pour
a custodial sentence	une peine ferme, sans sursis
a suspended sentence	une condamnation avec sursis
damages	des dommages et intérêts
to appeal / an appeal	faire appel / un appel
the bail / to bail out	la caution / libérer sous caution
to be incarcerated, to be imprisoned	être incarcéré
a cell	une cellule
a high-security prison	une prison de haute sécurité
prison overcrowding	la surpopulation carcérale
a mutiny / a mutineer	une mutinerie / un mutin
the visiting room	le parloir
solitary confinement	l'isolement
to free, to release a prisoner	libérer un prisonnier
an electronic tag	un bracelet électronique
to be on parole	être en liberté conditionnelle
hard labour	les travaux forcés
a penal colony	un bagne

DEATH PENALTY	**LA PEINE DE MORT**
capital punishment	la peine capitale
a death sentence	une condamnation à mort
a death row inmate	un condamné à mort
to be executed	être exécuté
stoning / to be stoned to death	la lapidation / être lapidé
hanging / gas chamber / electric chair / firing squad / lethal injection	la pendaison / la chambre à gaz / la chaise électrique / le peloton d'exécution / l'injection létale
to abolish / the abolition	abolir / l'abolition
an abolitionist	un partisan de l'abolition
to restore, reinstate / the restoration	rétablir / le rétablissement
proponents, advocates / to support	les partisans / militer pour
opponents, critics / to oppose	les opposants / s'opposer à
a reprieve	un sursis
to prove sb innocent, to exonerate	innocenter qqn
innocence / guilt	l'innocence / la culpabilité
a wrongful conviction	une condamnation à tort
a miscarriage of justice	une erreur judiciaire
to pardon	gracier
to be jailed for life	prendre / être condamné à perpétuité
life imprisonment without parole	perpétuité incompressible / sans possibilité de remise de peine
to act as a deterrent	avoir un effet dissuasif

Translation: English-to-French exercise

Disadvantaged and outraged youths rebel (adapté de *The Independent*)

A lack of prospects and social discrimination are behind the riots in several British cities. These youths live in the heart of wealthy British cities, but they do not feel part of them.

The warning signs have been flashing for many years, particularly in London, in the reports of mobs of youths "steaming" commuters on London trains and buses to relieve them of their valuables. It has been visible in the resurgence of knife assaults and gang shootings.

The state departments of education, welfare, health and housing have failed these groups. Far too little has been done by successive generations of politicians and public servants to integrate these individuals into normal society. The fuse for this explosion has been burning down for years, perhaps even decades.

Adapted press excerpts (about 400 words)

Excerpt 1 – 27 words: Deconstructing the Second Amendment (adapted from CNN)

It's only a **sentence** long; 27 words that barely take up a full line on the **Bill of Rights**.

A well regulated ***Militia****, being necessary to the* ***security*** *of a free State, the right of the people to* ***keep*** *and* ***bear Arms****, shall not be infringed.*

And yet, for years, those 27 brief words have been the source of contentious **debate** – seen by some as an **inalienable protection** against **tyranny**; by others as a dangerous anachronism. What is a militia? At the time of the American Revolutionary War, militias were groups of **able-bodied men** who protected their towns, colonies, and eventually states. One of the biggest challenges in interpreting a centuries-old document is that the meanings of words change or diverge. In other words, it didn't mean the state was controlling the militia in a certain way, but rather that the militia was prepared to do its duty.

Excerpt 2 – Walking while black – Baltimore promises police reforms after blistering federal report (adapted from *The Economist*)

For John Locke, the problem with **anarchy** is the "want of a common judge". In the pre-political "state of nature", simple **conflicts** between **individuals** can quickly turn **bloody** – or even **deadly**. But in political society, Locke wrote, **legislators, judges** and **police** mediate and calmly resolve tussles before they escalate. Society is supposed to work on this principle, though in reality, **officials** are known to occasionally veer from their role as **honest, impartial defenders** of the **public good**. In Baltimore, the crime of "driving while black" is joined by similar **offences** that might be called "walking while black" or "standing while black". **Officers** repeatedly **arrest suspects** whose only **infraction** is "standing in front" of a house "and looking around". They undertake "**unlawful arrests** for **conduct** that is not **criminal**" and often **haul suspects** to the **station** without **cause** or **evidence**.

Excerpt 3 – How Science Is Putting a New Face on Crime Solving (adapted from *National Geographic*)

Here the **investigation** took an unexpected turn. Based on the available **evidence**, the **detectives** still believed her **killer** was perhaps a member of the Mexican crew who had fled the area soon after **committing** the **crime**. But the person in the **DNA-generated** portrait had pale skin and freckles. His hair was brown, and his eyes were probably green or blue. His ancestry, the **analysis** said, was northern European. "We kind of had to take a step back and say all this time, we're not even in the right direction," Mancuso says. But armed with this new **evidence**, he is optimistic. "I think at some point we can **solve this case**, because we have such a good DNA **sample** and this **profile**," he says. DNA phenotyping is a relatively recent arrival in forensic science, and some critics question how useful it will be. The facial composites it produces are predictions from genetics, not photographs.

Excerpt 4 – Making a Murderer: Brendan Dassey has conviction overturned (adapted from *Sydney Morning Herald*)

Brendan Dassey, one of the men who were the focus of the critically acclaimed Netflix documentary Making a Murderer, has had his **conviction overturned**. Dassey, 26, had been **convicted** of **first-degree intentional homicide, second-degree sexual assault**, and mutilation of a corpse. He was serving a **sentence** of 41 years **jail** in Columbia **Correctional Institution** in the US state of Wisconsin. He was not **due for parole** until 2048. Dassey's **case** was resurrected in **court** because his **confession** was **forced**, and that he was "fed" details of the case by his police **interrogators**. During the original **investigation** Dassey was **questioned** three times with no **legal representation** or adult present. Dassey initially **confessed** but then later **recanted** his confession.

Food for Thought and Quotations (about 500 words)

Crime in the UK

Between 1970 and 2000, the number of crimes soared in Britain, which led most politicians to use it as an argument to attract votes. Prevention programmes were put in place to fight criminality, which led to a gradual surveillance society: CCTV cameras in most cities, neighbourhood watch, and increased means for police forces. The CCTV scheme has proved efficient in public areas, neighbourhoods and car parks. Since 2000, the successive governments have also implemented measures to fight against petty crime, burglary and nuisances that wear out communities. Today, a convicted offender can choose the house arrest alternative, by wearing an electronic device which will monitor movements, thus allowing not to remain in a prison cell. In 2000 and 2006, there were riots in Britain that forced the government to impose a curfew on youngsters, which led to a fall in crimes. Unfortunately, antisocial behaviour has not declined since then, and Brexit has recently caused another type of incivilities and acts of violence to develop on the streets of Britain, in the form of racist provocations and attacks on minorities.

Crime in the US

The question of crime divides citizens torn between tolerance policies and rigour laws. Destitute families live in areas fled by the others classes, hence public authorities have designed housing projects. And in the 90s rose the welfare, services and security to fight against urban segregation. For instance, New York has become one of the safest cities after decades of urban violence. The "zero tolerance" policy and the"*broken window*" theory have improved the police performance by developing precincts to guarantee a local quality of life, more efficient education services and improved security. In consequence, the punishments have become more severe and a "no-weapons" policy has been initiated. Later, other cities have also raised teenagers' awareness and promised them jobs if they abide by the law. Nevertheless punishments are extremely severe even for petty crime. Also, the police forces also fight against criminal organizations: since 1993 violent crimes have declined while the number of inmates increased to almost seven million.

Gun control in the US

The expression "gun control" refers to the control of firearms in terms of politics, legislation, and enforcement of measures, in order to restrict access to, the possession or the use of firearms. It is today a highly controversial issue, as the debate on an individual's right to bear arms can be felt as a restriction on liberty. Proponents of gun-control legislation assert that the strict enforcement of gun-control laws saves lives and reduces crime. Opponents claim that restrictions on guns guarantee that citizens can use firearms for self-defense purposes and for safer communities. Today, the Second Amendment has been subject to intense debate but what remains clear is that 1.5 million Americans have been killed by a firearm since 1968, in other words about 85 fatalities each day.

Death Penalty in the World (Source: Amnesty International)

At least 1,634 people were executed in 25 countries in 2015. This represents a stark increase in the number of executions recorded: in 2014 there had been 1,061 executions in 22 countries worldwide. This is the highest number of executions in more than 25 years. Most executions took place in China, Iran, Pakistan, Saudi Arabia and the USA – in that order. China remained the world's top executioner – but the true extent of the use of the death penalty in China is unknown as this data is considered a state secret; therefore the total excludes the thousands of executions believed to have been carried out in China. At least 20,292 people were on death row at the end of 2015. The following methods of execution are used across the world: beheading, hanging, lethal injection and shooting.

"Many that live deserve death. And some that die deserve life. Can you give it to them? Then do not be too eager to deal out death in judgement." J.R.R. Tolkien, *The Fellowship of the Ring*

"The end of law is not to abolish or restrain, but to preserve and enlarge freedom. For in all the states of created beings capable of law, where there is no law, there is no freedom." John Locke

Chapter D

Politics and power

Vocabulary list

REGIMES AND IDEOLOGIES	LES RÉGIMES, LES IDÉOLOGIES
a political regime	un régime politique
self-determination	l'autodétermination
a citizen / citizenship	un citoyen / citoyenneté
to govern / government	gouverner / le gouvernement
self-government	l'autonomie
a nation / national	une nation / national
nationalism / a nationalist	le nationalisme / un nationaliste
a republic / republican	une république / républicain
a democracy / democratic	une démocratie / démocratique
constitution / constitutional	une constitution / constitutionnel
a monarchy / a monarch	une monarchie / un monarque
a kingdom / a king, a queen	un royaume / un roi, une reine
a regent	un régent
a principality / a prince, a princess	une principauté / un prince, une princesse
a dynasty	une dynastie
to succeed by / a successor	succéder à / un successeur
abdication / to abdicate	l'abdication / abdiquer
the Head of State	le chef d'État
to run, to rule, to lead / a ruler, a leader	diriger, un dirigeant
the ruling party	le parti au pouvoir
a president / presidency	un président / la présidence
an ideology	une idéologie
party membership	l'adhésion à un parti
left-wing / a left-winger	la gauche / une personne de gauche
right-wing / a right-winger	la droite / une personne de droite
progressivism / progressive	le progressisme / progressiste
socialism / a socialist	le socialisme / un socialiste
communism / a communist	le communisme / un communiste
anarchy / an anarchist	l'anarchie, un anarchiste
a demagogue	un démagogue
a populist	un populiste
corrupt	corrompu
jingoism	le chauvinisme
revolution / a revolutionary	la révolution / un révolutionnaire
a utopia	une utopie
vote-catching	le clientélisme
a one-party system	un système à parti unique
the center / a centrist	le centre / un centriste
liberal / liberalism	aux idées progressistes OU partisan du libre-échange / le libéralisme
conservative / a conservative	le conservatisme / un conservateur
imperialism / an imperialist	l'impérialisme / un impérialiste
authority / authoritarianism	l'autorité / l'autoritarisme
extremism / an extremist	l'extrémisme / un extrémiste

totalitarianism / totalitarian	le totalitarisme / un totalitarisme
to oppress / an oppressor	opprimer / un oppresseur
a despot / despotism	un despote / le despotisme
a tyrant / tyranny	un tyran / la tyrannie
a dictator / dictatorship	un dictateur / une dictature
neo-nazism / a neo-nazi	le néonazisme / un néonazi
fascism / a fascist	le fascisme / un fasciste
a puppet regime	un régime fantoche
to overthrow / a coup	renverser / un coup d'État

POLITICS AND ELECTIONS	**LA POLITIQUE, LES ÉLECTIONS**
the separation of powers / the three branches	la séparation des pouvoirs / les trois pouvoirs
the legislative / executive / judicial power	le pouvoir législatif / exécutif / judiciaire
politics / a policy	la politique (en général) / une politique (mise en application)
bipartism	le bipartisme
the common good	le bien commun
a political party	un parti politique
a politician	un homme / une femme politique
to state / a statement	déclarer / une déclaration
to pledge oneself to / a pledge	promettre de / une promesse
to propose / a proposal	proposer / une proposition
a proponent / an opponent	un partisan / un opposant
to advocate / an advocate	soutenir / un défenseur
to debate / a debate	débattre / un débat
to question / questionable	mettre en doute / discutable
to challenge, to dispute / a dispute	remettre en question / un conflit
to found / to fund	fonder / financer
fund-raising	la collecte de fonds
to run for office	être candidat aux élections
franchise	le droit de vote
to register / registration	s'inscrire sur les listes électorales / l'inscription
a candidate	un candidat
the run-up to the elections	la dernière ligne droite avant les élections
an adviser / to advise / advice	un conseiller / conseiller / des conseils
an election campaign	une campagne électorale
a slogan / a poster	un slogan / une affiche
the presidential / general election	les élections présidentielles / législatives
a would-be candidate	un candidat potentiel
a challenger	le challengeur
the local elections	les élections municipales
to vote / voting	voter / le scrutin
to go to the polls	aller voter
a population sample	un échantillon représentatif

polling day	le jour du scrutin
an exit poll	un sondage à la sortie des urnes
to turn out / the turnout	participer / la participation
a high / a low turnout	une participation forte / faible
a polling booth / a ballot box	un isoloir / une urne
to stuff the ballot boxes	faire du bourrage d'urne
an electoral landslide	un raz-de-marée électoral
a sudden shift	un brusque retournement
a stronghold	un bastion
to abstain / abstention	s'abstenir / l'abstention
an absentee voter	un abstentionniste
to vote by proxy	voter par procuration
electoral rigging	la fraude électorale
the outcome	les résultats
to secure a parliamentary majority	s'assurer une majorité au Parlement
a swing to the left / right	un virage à gauche / à droite
a crushing defeat / an overwhelming victory	une défaite cuisante / une victoire écrasante
the voting system	le système électoral
a by-election	une élection partielle
a constituency / a constituent	une circonscription / un électeur
the first-past-the-post system (UK)	le scrutin uninominal à un tour

THE UNITED KINGDOM	**LE ROYAUME-UNI**
Parliament	le Parlement
the (House of) Commons	la Chambre des communes
The (House of) Lords	la Chambre des lords
a MP (Member of Parliament)	un député
a hereditary / life peer	un pair héréditaire / à vie
a frontbencher / a backbencher / a cross-bencher	un membre du gouvernement / un député au Parlement / un député non-inscrit
to applaud / applause	applaudir / des applaudissements
the ayes / the noes	ceux qui votent pour / contre
an Act of Parliament	une loi votée par le Parlement
filibustering	l'obstruction parlementaire
a motion / an amendment	une motion / un amendement
a bill	un projet de loi
the Labour Party, the Labour	le parti travailliste, les travaillistes
the Conservative Party, the Tories	le parti conservateur, les conservateurs
the Lib-dems	les libéraux-démocrates
the Speaker / the Lord Speaker	le président (Communes / Lords)
No.10, 10 Downing Street	la résidence du Premier ministre, le Premier ministre
The Cabinet	l'organe de décision du gouvernement de Sa Majesté
Whitehall	le gouvernement

The Shadow Cabinet	le cabinet fantôme (membres de l'opposition)
the PM (Prime Minister)	le Premier ministre
the Deputy Prime Minister	le vice Premier ministre
The Welsh Office, the Scottish Office / The Northern Ireland Office	le ministère chargé du Pays de Galles / de l'Écosse / de l'Irlande du Nord
The Foreign Office / Secretary	le ministère / ministre des Affaires étrangères
The Department of Health / The Health Secretary	le ministère / ministre de la Santé
The Department of Education / The secretary for Education	le ministère / ministre de l'Éducation
public schooling	l'enseignement public
The Lord Chancellor / 's office	Le ministre / ministère de la Justice
the Home Office / Secretary	le ministère / ministre de l'Intérieur
the Treasury / the Chancellor of the Exchequer	le Trésor / le ministre des Finances
The Queen's Speech	le discours de la Reine, le programme annuel législatif écrit par le gouvernement
PAYE (pay as you earn)	le prélèvement à la source
taxation / the taxpayer / the taxman	la fiscalité / le contribuable / le fisc
a tax return	une feuille d'impôt
public expenditure	les dépenses publiques
the National Audit Office (GB)	la Cour des comptes
devolution / devolved matters	la décentralisation / les questions déléguées
local authorities	les autorités locales
the civil service / a civil servant	la fonction publique / un fonctionnaire
THE UNITED STATES	**LES ÉTATS-UNIS**
the Founding Fathers	les Pères fondateurs
Congress	le Congrès (les deux assemblées législatives)
the Senate	le Sénat
the House of Representatives	la Chambre des représentants
the Speaker of the Senate / of the House of Representatives	le Président du Sénat / de la Chambre des représentants
a Senator / a Representative	un sénateur / un représentant
a Democrat / the Democratic Party	un démocrate, membre du Parti démocrate / le Parti démocrate
a Republican / the Grand Ole Party (GOP)	un républicain, membre du Parti républicain / le Parti républicain
the White House	la Maison Blanche, la Présidence
the Oval Office	le bureau du Président des États-Unis à la Maison Blanche
to administer / administration	administrer / l'administration
the incumbent president	le président en exercice, sortant
the president-elect	le président élu
a term of office	un mandat

to pledge allegiance	prêter serment
an oath	un serment
the Inaugural Address	le discours d'investiture
checks and balances	l'équilibre des pouvoirs
a county	un comté
a sheriff	un shérif
a caucus	un rassemblement électoral
misdemeanour	un écart de conduite
to impeach / impeachment	la procédure de destitution du président
the Pentagon / the Department of Defense	le Pentagone / le ministère de la Défense
the State of the Union address	le discours annuel sur l'état de l'Union
The Cabinet	le gouvernement
the Supreme Court	la Cour suprême
a Justice	un juge de la Cour suprême
judicial review	le Conseil constitutionnel
the Federal Courts	les cours fédérales de justice
the State Department / the Secretary of State	le ministère des affaires étrangères : le Département d'État / le ministre des affaires étrangères
Foreign policy	la politique étrangère
The Secretary of the Treasury	le ministère des finances
a public utility	une entreprise du service public
public debt	la dette publique
the Attorney General / the Justice Department	le ministre / ministère de la Justice
Law and Order	l'ordre public
The Secretary / Department of Education	le ministre / ministère de l'Éducation
Social Care	la couverture sociale
Public Health	la santé publique
the Secretary of Labor / the Labor Department	le ministre / ministère du Travail
a federation of states	une fédération d'États
a State Governor	un gouverneur d'État
a government official	un fonctionnaire
red tape	la tracasserie administrative

Translation: French-to-English exercise

Après le Brexit, l'UE doit se recentrer sur l'essentiel (adapté de *Ouest France*)

Après le Brexit, l'Europe doit se réinventer en se débarrassant de ce qui l'entrave inutilement. Ce départ n'est peut-être pas une si mauvaise nouvelle. Ce serait même une chance pour que l'Europe se réinvente sur des bases solides et cohérentes.

Les Britanniques doivent encore concrétiser un projet de mise en place des négociations officielles de sortie. Des pays ont rejoint le noyau dur et n'ont pas su le consolider ni l'enrichir. D'autres se sont vite alignés sur la politique américaine. D'autres ont fermé leurs frontières face à la détresse des migrants, contribuant ainsi à malmener l'âme de l'Europe, ses valeurs, ses principes.

La famille Europe devrait suivre un régime d'amaigrissement. Revenir à l'essentiel, bannir la bureaucratie, en finir avec le gaspillage, la langue de bois et les promesses non tenues. L'Europe est une nécessité, surtout si elle se refait une beauté dans le miroir de l'exigence et de la réalité tout en restant modeste et concrète.

Adapted press excerpts (about 400 words)

Excerpt 1 – Politics and the New Machine (adapted from *The New Yorker*)

Every **election** is a morality play. The **Candidate** tries to speak to the **People** but is thwarted by Negative **Campaigning**, vilified by a **Biased** Media, and haunted by a War Record. I am who I am, the Candidate says, and my **Opponents** are flunkies. The modern **public-opinion poll** has been around since the Great Depression. **Election pollsters** sample only a minuscule portion of the **electorate**. The promise of this work is that the sample is exquisitely **representative**. But the lower the response rate the harder and more expensive it becomes to realize that promise, which requires both calling many more people and trying to correct for "**non-response bias**" by giving greater weight to the answers of people from **demographic groups** that are less likely to respond.

Excerpt 2 – The Long Road to Brexit (adapted from *The Wall Street Journal*)

One of the ironies of Brexit is the unforgettable photograph of Margaret Thatcher campaigning to "Keep Britain in Europe" shortly before a 1975 **referendum**. The architecture of "Continental Drift" neatly fits strong-willed **political leaders** into the decade-by-decade decisions on Europe in an era of diminishing British influence. Churchill is essential for understanding the beginning of the European movement. Throughout his life, he believed in free trade. He encouraged the development of a European movement that would lead to economic recovery and even, in his own phrase, "a United States of Europe." But Churchill never saw Britain as part of such a European union. He spoke of Britain as being "with" Europe but not "of" it. There was never any doubt that he valued the "**special relationship**" with America above all. Late 2019, uncertainties remain under the leadership of Boris Johnson in a divided United-Kingdom.

Excerpt 3 – Democracy in America (adapted from Alexis de Tocqueville)

There is a **country** in the world where the great **revolution** which I am speaking of seems nearly to have reached its natural limits; it has been effected with ease and simplicity, say rather that this country has attained the consequences of the **democratic revolution** which we are undergoing without having experienced the revolution itself. The emigrants who fixed themselves on the shores of America in the beginning of the seventeenth century severed the **democratic principle** from all the principles which repressed it in the old **communities** of Europe, and transplanted it unalloyed to the New World. It has there been allowed to spread in **perfect freedom**, and to put forth its consequences in the **laws** by influencing the manners of the country. It appears to me beyond a doubt that sooner or later we shall arrive, like the Americans, at an almost complete **equality of conditions**. But I do not conclude from this that we shall ever be necessarily led to draw the same **political consequences** which the Americans have derived from a similar **social organization**.

Excerpt 4 – "Before the Law," a parable from Kafka's novel *The Trial*, read by Orson Welles

Before the **law**, there stands a guard. A man comes from the country, begging admittance to the **law**. But the guard cannot admit him. May he hope to enter at a later time? That is possible, said the guard. The man tries to peer through the entrance. He'd been taught that the law was to be accessible to every man. "Do not attempt to enter without my permission," says the guard. I am very powerful. Yet I am the least of all the guards. From hall to hall, door after door, each guard is more **powerful** than the last. By the guard's permission, the man sits by the side of the door, and there he waits. The man waits for years, staring at the guard and lavishing him with **bribes**. He grows old and enfeebled. Finally, he asks why, despite the fact that "every man strives to attain the law," nobody else but him has ever come to attempt passage through its doors. "Nobody else but you could ever have obtained admittance," the guard replies. "This door was intended only for you! And now, I'm going to close it." Welles then comments that "the logic of this story is the logic of a dream... a nightmare."

Food for Thought and Quotations (about 500 words)

Main political parties in the UK

The idea of political parties first took form in Britain. During the English civil wars of the 1640s and 1650s, the Whigs wanted to curtail the power of the monarch while the Tories – today the Conservatives – were seen as the patriotic party.

Today there are three major political parties in the British system of politics: The Labour Party (often called New Labour), the Conservative Party (frequently called the Tories) and The Liberal Democrat Party (known as the Lib Dems). UKIP, the UK Independence Party gained influence after the vote in favour of Brexit. There are also a handful of regional parties (the SNP for Scotland, Plaid Cymru in Wales, Sinn Fein in Ulster). Since 2010, the Conservatives have been leading the UK government, under the responsibility of Theresa May after the resignation of David Cameron in June 2016. In 2019, Boris Johnson became Prime minister.

Main political parties in the US

The American political system is a two-party system. Throughout history, power has alternated between two major parties, the Democratic Party and the Republican Party, even if minor parties have always existed on the sidelines. They were born out of the *dissent* between Federalists and Antifederalists (partisans of a strong federal government v. strong local governments). Today they are termed the Democratic Party (Franklin D. Roosevelt, J. F. Kennedy, Barack Obama for example) and The Republican Party (referred to as the GOP, Grand Old Party, including Abraham Lincoln, Ronald Reagan, George Bush). Both are based on a compromise between conservatism and liberalism (i.e. the right and the left of European politics), and are equally attached to democratic principles and individual liberties. However the means differ: the Democratic Party is more attached to *active federal intervention* in all areas of public life, whereas the Republican Party favours more autonomy and limited central control.

Brexit

The UK has been drifting away from the European Union since it joined in 1973. It has long been questioning EU agricultural policy, quarrelling over the EU budget, cherishing its budget rebate, and calling for a vast free-trade zone. Amid growing Euroskepticism, David Cameron made matters worse by refusing to sign a treaty meant to save the euro, revising Britain's European commitments, and pledging to organize a referendum on Britain's EU membership in 2016, for which polls predicted a victory of the "outers". It has happened, Britain is exiting the EU. Yet leaving the Union might not be in Britain's or Europe's interest. Britain's crucial role in finance or defense necessarily has to be under close European scrutiny. Free trade and a single market (supported by Britain) should not drive countries further apart, and imply that Britain will have to fund cohesion aid to the poorest countries, even out of the EU. After several reports, Brexit should occur early 2020.

About the role of the State in the USA

In a 2015 speech, Barack Obama aimed to define the role of the State. He quoted Abraham Lincoln, a Republican, to point out that the purpose of his policy is not to create an irresponsible nanny state, which would be diametrically opposed to the notion of free enterprise, a core American concept. According to him, all Americans should benefit from equal opportunities, such as free education or health for instance, but should not rely on the State to be assisted and nurtured. The role of the State is to streamline the job-seeking process, immigration, and discuss on *culture war* issues serenely. It aims to reassure those who feared that the country was running deeper into debt and that there would be no end to government spending. Nonetheless, Obama's political vision also placates those who defend Reaganomics, that is as little governmental intervention in the economy as possible. According to him, a balance must necessarily be found between state intervention and *laissez-faire*.

*"My fellow Americans, ask not what your country can do for you, ask what you can do for your country."*John Fitzgerald Kennedy

"My policies are based not on some economics theory, but on things I and millions like me were brought up with: an honest day's work for an honest day's pay; live within your means; put by a nest egg for a rainy day; pay your bills on time; support the police. Margaret Thatcher

Section 8

The economy

Chapter A

Working life

Vocabulary list

EMPLOYMENT	**L'EMPLOI**
work / a worker	le travail / un travailleur
employment	l'emploi
an employee / an employer	un employé / un employeur
a job / a position	un emploi / un poste
an occupation, a trade	un métier, une profession
a part-time / full-time job	un emploi à temps partiel / complet
the civil service	la fonction publique
the public / private sector	le secteur public / privé
a fixed-term contract / a permanent contract	un CDD / un CDI (contrat à durée déterminée / indéterminée)
a temp / to temp	un intérimaire / faire de l'intérim
the workforce, the labour force, the manpower	la main-d'œuvre
working conditions	les conditions de travail
a working day (GB) / a workday (US)	une journée de travail, un jour ouvrable
self-employed	indépendant / auto-entrepreneur
the 35-hour working week	la semaine des 35 heures
a day off	un jour de congé
to work overtime	faire des heures supplémentaires
an unskilled / skilled worker	un ouvrier qualifié / spécialisé
a blue-collar / white-collar worker	un travailleur manuel / un employé de bureau (un col bleu / col blanc)
a civil servant	un fonctionnaire, agent de l'État
a senior civil servant	un haut fonctionnaire
job security	la sécurité de l'emploi
a calling, a vocation	une vocation
a breadwinner	le soutien de famille
a low-paid / highly-paid job	un emploi peu / bien rémunéré
wage, wages	le salaire
a monthly pay	un salaire mensuel
gross / net pay	le salaire brut / net
career prospects	les perspectives de carrière
a career as a journalist	une carrière de journaliste

SEEKING A JOB	**RECHERCHE D'EMPLOI**
to join the labour force	rejoindre le marché de l'emploi
a job opportunity / a job title	une opportunité d'emploi / un intitulé
to offer a job	proposer une offre d'emploi
a vacancy	un poste vacant
a job hunt	une recherche d'emploi
a job seeker	un demandeur d'emploi
to apply for a job	postuler
to fill in a form	remplir un formulaire
an application	une candidature
an application form	un formulaire

a CV (GB), a résumé (US)	un curriculum vitæ, un CV
skills	les compétences, les qualifications
credentials	les références
work experience	les expériences professionnelles
an asset	un atout
a headhunter	un chasseur de têtes
a human resources department	un département de ressources humaines
an appointment	un rendez-vous (professionnel)
to recruit / to hire	recruter / embaucher
to appoint sb to a post	nommer qqn à un poste
to sign a contract	signer un contrat
a probationary period / a trial period	une période d'essai
a training period / session	un stage de formation
a trainee, an intern	un stagiaire
to train	former
to specialize in	se spécialiser dans
an assignment as / to get tenure	une affectation / obtenir sa titularisation
promotion by merit	la promotion / l'avancement au mérite
to be reassigned / transferred	être muté
to climb the ladder	monter dans la hiérarchie
a training programme (GB) / program (US)	un programme de formation

PROFESSIONAL INVOLVEMENT	**L'ENGAGEMENT PROFESSIONNEL**
a workaholic	un bourreau de travail
involvement	l'investissement, la participation, l'engagement
to earn / to make a living	gagner sa vie
to be in charge of	être responsable de
to clock in / to clock out	pointer à l'arrivée / au départ
job satisfaction	la satisfaction professionnelle
competence, expertise	la compétence
to show / to lack expertise	faire preuve de / manquer de compétence
to be industrious, hardworking	travailleur
conscientious	consciencieux
diligent	appliqué
reliable	fiable
lazy, idle	paresseux
lackadaisical	nonchalant, apathique
careless	négligent
unreliable	indigne de confiance
to botch up one's work	bâcler son travail
to moonlight	travailler au noir
to be busy	être occupé
a team / teamwork	une équipe / le travail d'équipe
a nine-to-five job	un emploi de bureau
to do shift-work	faire les trois-huit, travailler par roulement

a day shift / night shift	l'équipe de jour / de nuit
to be on sick leave	être en congé maladie
holidays with pay / paid leave	les congés payés
an expense account	les notes de frais
a disablement pension	une pension d'invalidité
health and safety regulations	les règles de sécurité
a labour inspector	un inspecteur du travail

UNEMPLOYMENT	**LE CHÔMAGE**
to give one's notice	donner son préavis à qqn
to dismiss / to sack	licencier / mettre à la porte
to lay off sb / a layoff	licencier / un licenciement
a redundancy	un licenciement
mass redundancy	un licenciement collectif
to be made redundant	être licencié
to resign / resignation	démissionner / une démission
to quit	quitter un emploi
the jobless, the unemployed	les sans-emploi, les chômeurs
the unemployment figures	les chiffres du chômage
the long-term unemployed	les chômeurs de longue durée
to lose one's job	perdre son emploi
to downsize, to streamline	dégraisser les effectifs
a tenuous job, a precarious job, a casual job	un emploi précaire
early retirement	la retraite anticipée / la préretraite
unemployment	le chômage
severance pay	une prime de licenciement
a golden handshake / parachute	un parachute doré
social contributions	les contributions sociales
unemployment benefits	les indemnités chômage
unemployment allowances	les allocations chômage
to be on the dole (GB, colloq.)	toucher des allocations chômage
to be on welfare (US)	toucher les allocations chômage
to check in at the job centre	pointer à l'agence pour l'emploi
the unemployment rate	le taux de chômage
to switch to / to retrain	se reconvertir dans
to resume work	reprendre le travail

UNIONS AND TENSIONS	**SYNDICATS ET TENSIONS**
a trade union	un syndicat
a spokesperson	un porte-parole syndical
a union member / a trade unionist	un travailleur syndiqué / un syndicaliste
a union representative	un représentant syndical
a shop steward, a union representative	un délégué syndical
a joint committee	une commission paritaire
to join a union	s'affilier à un syndicat, prendre sa carte
labour strife	les conflits du travail

labour unrest	l'agitation sociale
to back up a claim	soutenir une revendication
social discontent	les tensions / le mécontentement social
a grievance / a demand	une doléance / une exigence
better working conditions	des meilleures conditions de travail
a wage increase, a pay rise	une augmentation de salaire
to meet demands	satisfaire les revendications
the bargaining power	le poids dans les négociations
to break off negotiation	quitter la table des négociations
to go on strike	faire grève
the right to strike	le droit de grève
a striker / a strike call	un gréviste / un appel à la grève
a picket	un piquet de grève
a staggered strike	une grève tournante
work-to rule	la grève du zèle
to be strikebound	être paralysé par la grève
a rejection / to reject	un rejet / rejeter
to lead a strike / a leader	mener une grève / un meneur
a draft agreement / to agree (on)	un protocole d'accord / être d'accord (sur)
a settlement / to settle for	un accord, une entente / s'entendre sur
a collective agreement	une convention collective
an incentive	une incitation, un encouragement
to yield	céder
to end a strike	mettre fin à une grève

WORK TRENDS	**LES TENDANCES DE L'EMPLOI**
a trend	une tendance
the rural exodus	l'exode rural
the drift to towns	la migration vers les villes
a reassignment / to be reassigned	une mutation / être muté
to relocalise / relocation	délocaliser / les délocalisations
to run a business	diriger une entreprise
flexibility	la souplesse, la flexibilité
a sabbatical	un congé sabbatique
time off, spare time	du temps libre
to be released from	être libéré de
a work-free society	une société libérée du travail
commuting / to commute	les déplacements professionnels réguliers / faire la navette
teleworking	le télétravail
to work from home	travailler à domicile
telecommuting	le télétravail, le travail à domicile / à distance
convenient, time-saving	pratique, qui permet des gains de temps
the leisured classes	les nantis
a billionaire	un milliardaire
a spendthrift	une personne dépensière

the rich / riches	les riches / les richesses
the wealthy, the affluent	les riches
to launch a start-up	lancer une start-up
an entrepreneur	un entrepreneur
a freelance	un travailleur indépendant

A SELECTION OF JOBS	**QUELQUES MÉTIERS**
accountant	comptable
actor / actress	acteur / actrice
air hostess	hôtesse de l´air
architect	architecte
baker	boulanger
bank clerk	employé de banque
bookseller	libraire
builder, mason	maçon
butcher	boucher
caretaker	concierge
chemist	pharmacien
consultant	conseiller
cook	cuisinier
customs officer	douanier
dentist	dentiste
dustman	éboueur
electrician	électricien
engineer	ingénieur
farmer	agriculteur
fireman	pompier
fisherman	pêcheur
gardener	jardinier
hairdresser	coiffeur
jeweller	bijoutier
journalist	journaliste
judge	juge
labourer	ouvrier du bâtiment
lawyer (GB), barrister (US)	avocat
lorry driver	chauffeur de camion
mechanic	mécanicien
miner	mineur
model	mannequin
nanny	nounou
nurse	infirmier
office worker	employé de bureau
painter	peintre
plumber	plombier
policeman, constable	policier, agent de police
postman	facteur
priest	curé

psychiatrist	psychiatre
psychologist	psychologue
receptionist	réceptionniste
sailor	marin
salesman	vendeur
secretary	secrétaire
servant	domestique
shepherd	berger
shoemaker	cordonnier
shop assistant	vendeur / vendeuse
student	étudiant
surgeon	chirurgien
tailor	tailleur (vestimentaire)
taxi driver	chauffeur de taxi
technician	technicien
translator	traducteur
waiter / waitress	serveur
watchmaker	horloger
writer	écrivain

Translation: French-to-English exercise

Mais où sont passés les 10 millions d'Américains qui ne travaillent pas? (adapté de *Slate*)

Souvent érigé en modèle de quasi-plein emploi, le marché du travail américain a toutefois un vilain petit secret qui contribue à expliquer son taux de chômage si enviable, d'un peu moins de 5 %: des millions d'hommes en âge d'être actifs sont tout simplement sortis du jeu. Ils n'apparaissent pas dans les statistiques du chômage puisque ces dernières prennent en compte les gens qui poursuivent une démarche de recherche d'emploi.

Un rapport récent d'un conseil d'économistes a mesuré que 11,7 % des hommes âgés de 25 à 54 ans ne travaillaient pas et que, parmi ces derniers, l'immense majorité (cinq sur six) n'avait pas travaillé l'année précédente. Ils sont donc totalement exclus du marché du travail, et n'ont à peu près aucune chance de le réintégrer un jour.

Plusieurs caractéristiques augmentent la probabilité de faire partie de cette armée invisible: les hommes noirs, les célibataires et ceux qui n'ont pas de diplôme sont les plus touchés. Leur éloignement du travail est lié au remplacement des métiers manuels qui exigent de la force physique par des machines, et au déplacement des emplois vers les métiers tertiaires qui exigent des qualifications élevées. Le fait qu'un homme sur huit aux États-Unis ait été condamné pour un crime expliquerait aussi les difficultés de cette partie de la population à trouver un travail.

Adapted press excerpts (about 400 words)

Excerpt 1 – There's No Place Like Home / Office (adapted from *Good Magazine*)

Are **work spaces** like PodShare the future of **creative collaboration** – or too close for comfort? Elvina Beck, the 31-year-old **co-founder** of PodShare, has an **entrepreneur**'s knack for **tech-savvy** euphemisms. Beck has visions for pods around the globe. This kind of **mobility** is designed for a generation increasingly turning to **freelance work** for **flexibility** or supplemental cash. 34 percent of the American **workforce** is composed of **freelancers**. Among millennials, that figure rises to 38 percent. These people are working from coffee shops and libraries, **co-working spaces** and their own apartments. They're largely unmoored from the trappings of traditional **office** life and can work remotely from whatever Wi-Fi-enabled corner of the earth they can afford.

Excerpt 2 – Future Works (adapted from *The Economist*)

The **global economy** is in the midst of the Fourth Industrial Revolution. Technological innovation and **globalization** are starting to transform every aspect of how **economies** and the **businesses** within them work. Nowhere is this change likely to be experienced more acutely than in the **workplace**. New skills will be needed, and some existing **skills** will become **redundant**. Robots will replace workers in some places, and become valuable **colleagues** in others. Some **workers** will earn more than ever, and enjoy higher benefits and greater **autonomy**. Many more face the **prospect** of trying to eke out enough money to live on from **work** that may be **temporary**, **unsatisfying** and poorly paid. It will address a range of **challenges** including how to **recruit**, **motivate** and **retain workers** with scarce, valuable **talents**, who may enjoy unprecedented **choices**.

Excerpt 3 – Where today's jobs are most likely to vanish tomorrow (adapted from *Washington Post*)

Nationwide, about 10 percent of **workers** are currently in professions that will shrink from 2014-2024. That's a set of jobs that encompasses much more than **blue-collar manufacturing**. The group also includes **air traffic controllers**, **accountants**, **mailmen**, some kinds of **computer programmers**, as well as professions in **farming** and **fishing**. Workers in these fields have a reason to worry about their future economic **prospects**, even if they have **jobs** right now. Jobs in **service** and **tourism professions** will be hard to **automate** or **outsource** but don't necessarily **pay well**; safe jobs in a changing economy aren't by definition good jobs. But a hotel worker scraping **to get by** has a different kind of anxiety from a middle-aged **coal miner** who can't expect to find work at all next year.

Excerpt 4 – The Jobs Perplex (adapted from *Forbes*)

With U.S. unemployment low, why is job dissatisfaction and anxiety so high? Employment **dissatisfaction** and **anxiety** is the norm. Added to this in recent years has been the growing contingent, **part-time** and **project-based** nature of employment – not reflected in the main **official** job **numbers**, but what Americans see every day. And we're likely to see it continue for the following four reasons. 1. No matter how low the overall unemployment **rate** is, it is never low enough for a segment of the political spectrum. 2. The rapid rise of **joblessness** during the recent **Great Recession** continues to haunt us. 3. We recognize that employment has become more **contingent**, project-based and **insecure.** 4. We see the growth of **lower-wage jobs**, particularly as **replacement** jobs for **laid off** workers.

Food for Thought and Quotations (about 500 words)

Adam Smith's division of work

In *The Wealth of Nations* (1776), political economist Adam Smith defines economic growth, the core of which lies in the notion of division of labour as the society's motivation and capacity to produce efficiently. The Wealth of Nations opens with a famous passage describing a pin factory in which 10 persons, by specializing in various tasks, turn out 48,000 pins a day, compared with the few pins that each could have produced alone. Investment and prior organisation are paramount in this success story. This virtuous circle (further growth implies further creation of skills and jobs) could be assimilated to an almost Newtonian "machine" for growth, except that Smith's growth machine did depend not on the laws of nature, but rather on human nature, a far more complex force. Thus, the wealth of nations would grow only if individuals, through their governments, did not inhibit this growth by catering to the pleas for special privilege that would prevent the competitive system from exerting its benign effect. This goes in sharp contrast with a Marxian conception of work.

David Ricardo's wage theory

Adam Smith thought that the wages had to be sufficient to allow workers to live and to support their families. David Ricardo, an economist of the early 19th century, wrote that the "natural price" of labour was simply *the price necessary to enable the labourers to subsist and to perpetuate the race,* which was consistent with the Malthusian theory of population. According to him, if wages rose above subsistence, the number of workers would therefore increase, which would consequently lower the wages. A similar process would regulate upward the wages considered below the subsistence level. By 1850, most British workers were approaching the subsistence level, and population already aimed to catch up with the bare necessities of subsistence, through unions of workers or various means of pressure.

Karl Marx and Frederich Engels: on the working conditions in England in the mid-19th century

Karl Marx accepted Ricardo's theory stating that the value of a product is based on the quantity of labour used to produce it. However, he considered that it was the high proportion of unemployed workers that led to wages regulation, not the means of pressure on the part of the population. In a study conducted with German philosopher Frederich Engels in the 1840s in Manchester, Marx argued that the industrial workers had lower incomes and worse living conditions than their pre-industrial peers. Their critique of industrialisation led to further Marxist interpretations of history and to the *Communist Manifesto*, a political pamphlet published in 1848.

John Maynard Keynes' theory of purchasing power

After the Great Depression of the early 1930s, the Keynesian purchasing power theory of wages identifies the relation between wages and employment and the business cycle, by studying the influence of consumption and investment on economic activity. According to him, variations of wages have a significant impact on consumption since they represent most of the national income. If people consume less, demand for goods and services falls, and so does job creation. Such a theory has to take into consideration many factors (political, economic and social, as well as less objective factors), and it has since then led other economists to study more factors to explain the evolution of wages. One particularly worthy of mention is the 1960s theory of human capital, coined by the American economist Theodore W.Schultz to refer to a reserve of stock of productive knowledge and skills of workers.

"A man must always live by his work, and his wages must at least be sufficient to maintain him. They must even upon most occasions be somewhat more; otherwise it would be impossible for him to bring up a family, and the race of such workmen could not last beyond the first generation." Adam Smith, *The Wealth of Nations*

"How long will it be necessary to pay City men so entirely out of proportion to what other servants of society commonly receive for performing social services not less useful or difficult?" John Maynard Keynes

Chapter B

Business, finance and trade

Vocabulary list

ECONOMIC SYSTEMS	**LES SYSTÈMES ÉCONOMIQUES**
capitalism	le capitalisme
capital	le capital
liberalism	le libéralisme
liberal	libéral : 1 / partisan du libéralisme économique 2 / progressiste
laissez-faire	le laissez-faire économique
protectionism	le protectionnisme
to nationalise	nationaliser
a tax / taxation	une taxe, un impôt / l'imposition
to develop / development	développer / le développement
to rise, to increase, to go up	augmenter, croître
growth	la croissance
a fast-growing economy	une économie en pleine expansion
to thrive	prospérer
to fall, to decrease, to go down	diminuer, baisser
recession	la récession
a boom / to thrive	un plein essor / prospérer
a slump / to collapse	une forte baisse / dégringoler, s'effondrer
an economic crisis	une crise économique
an economic downturn / the recovery	une récession / la reprise économique
a downswing	une décroissance, un ralentissement
gloomy prospects	des perspectives sombres
steady	régulier, constant
an economic policy	une politique économique
to boost the economy	soutenir l'économie
the economic stagnation	la stagnation économique
inflation / deflation	l'inflation / la déflation
the inflation rate	le taux d'inflation
stagflation	la stagflation (inflation et stagnation économique)
austerity measures	des mesures d'austérité
a wage freeze	un gel des salaires
the Chancellor of the Exchequer	le ministre des Finances britanniques
the Secretary of the Treasury	le Secrétaire du Trésor américain

FINANCE	**LA FINANCE**
the Stock exchange	la Bourse
a stock, a share	une action (terme général / d'une entreprise)
a stockholder, a shareholder	un actionnaire
a broker	un courtier
a trader	un opérateur en bourse, un trader
insider trading	le délit d'initié
to speculate / speculation	spéculer / la spéculation

to fluctuate	fluctuer
to appreciate / depreciate	prendre de la valeur / se déprécier
to soar / to drop	monter en flèche / chuter
the bull market	le marché haussier
the bear market	le marché baissier
to be in the doldrums	être en plein marasme, stagner
return on investment	le retour sur investissement
to insure / an insurer	assurer / un assureur
a life insurance policy	une police d'assurance-vie
a financial transaction	une transaction financière
a commercial bank	une banque d'affaires
a bailout plan	un plan de renflouement, de subvention
debt / the debt crisis	la dette / la crise de la dette
the foreign exchange market (the Forex)	le marché des devises
the exchange rate	le taux de change
a currency	une monnaie, une devise
the single currency	la monnaie unique
to owe	devoir
a loan / to borrow	un prêt, un emprunt / emprunter
a mortgage	un prêt, une hypothèque
the principal / the interest	le capital / les intérêts
to pay back / a repayment	rembourser / un remboursement
to default	ne pas honorer une dette
default	le défaut de paiement

MONEY	**L'ARGENT**
a coin	une pièce
change, spare change	de la petite monnaie
a banknote, a bill	un billet
a cheque (GB) / a check (US)	un chèque
a bank / a banker	une banque / un banquier
a branch	une agence bancaire
a bank account	un compte bancaire
to open / to close a savings account	ouvrir / fermer un compte d'épargne
a credit card	une carte de paiement
an ATM (automatic teller machine), a cash point	un distributeur automatique de billets (DAB)
to cash / to withdraw	encaisser / retirer (de l'argent)
to be thrifty	être économe
to be spendthrift	être dépensier
to be stingy	être radin, avare
to save up / savings	économiser / des économies
a monthly payment	une mensualité
a deposit	une caution, un acompte, un dépôt
an overdraft	un découvert
a dud cheque, a rubber cheque	un chèque en bois, sans provision

to be in the red	être dans le rouge
to be in the black	avoir un solde créditeur
a (credit) balance	un solde (créditeur)
to change money	changer de l'argent
to buy foreign currency	acheter des devises
the pound sterling	la livre sterling
a dollar, a euro, a yen	un dollar, un euro, un yen
a quarter	25 cents de dollar US
a dime	10 cents US
a fiver	un billet de £5
to pay cash	payer comptant

BUSINESS AND TRADE	**LES AFFAIRES ET LE COMMERCE**
business	les affaires
a trade surplus	une balance commerciale excédentaire
a trade deficit	une balance commerciale déficitaire
a businessman / -woman	un homme / une femme d'affaires
a business centre / a trade centre	un quartier d'affaires
a business	une entreprise, une affaire
to lead a busy life	mener une vie très occupée
a medium-sized business	une PME (petites et moyennes entreprises)
a family business	une affaire / entreprise familiale
profit	le profit, le bénéfice
deficit	le déficit
the turnover	le chiffre d'affaires
to benefit	profiter à, être utile à
profitable	rentable
profitability	la rentabilité
the yield / the output	le rendement
losses	les pertes
to do / lose business	faire des affaires / perdre de la clientèle
a deal	un accord, une affaire
to strike a deal	conclure un accord
a corporation	une société, une entreprise
a firm, a company	une entreprise, une compagnie
a limited-liability company	une SARL (société à responsabilité limitée)
a multinational	une multinationale
a group / a branch	un groupe / une succursale
a subsidiary	une filiale
a merger / to merge	une fusion / fusionner
a department	un service (dans l'entreprise)
the board of directors	le conseil d'administration
a managing director, a CEO (chief executive officer)	un directeur général, un PDG
a sales manager	un directeur des ventes
a personnel resources manager / director	un directeur des ressources humaines (DRH)

the management	la direction
a head of department	un chef de personnel
to downsize / to upsize	réduire / augmenter les effectifs
the corporate culture	l'esprit / la culture d'entreprise
the corporate identity	l'image de marque d'une société
economic / economical	ayant trait à l'économie / peu coûteux

THE MARKET	**LE MARCHÉ**
a supplier / to supply	un fournisseur / fournir
a retailer / to retail	un détaillant / vendre au détail
a shopkeeper	un commerçant, un marchand
a wholesaler / wholesale	un grossiste / la vente en gros
domestic / home trade	le commerce intérieur
international trade	le commerce international
stock management	la gestion des stocks
storage / a warehouse	le stockage / un entrepôt
an order / to order	une commande / commander
an invoice / to invoice sb for sth	une facture / facturer qch à qqn
VAT(value-added tax)	la TVA (taxe sur la valeur ajoutée)
to cut / to slash prices	baisser / casser les prix
the leader	le numéro 1
a challenger, a competitor	un rival, un concurrent
to grab a market	prendre un marché
competition / to compete with	la concurrence / concurrencer
to target	cibler
a breakthrough	une percée, une victoire
a monopoly	un monopole
a market share	une part de marché
a bid, a tender	un appel d'offre
the cost / purchase price	le prix de revient / le prix d'achat
aggressive	agressif
a customs tariff	un tarif douanier
customs duties	les droits de douane
the customs (services)	les douanes
the balance of trade	la balance commerciale
a trade war	une guerre commerciale
supply and demand	l'offre et la demande
imports / to import	les importations / importer
exports / to export	les exportations / exporter
to shelter	protéger
a sheltered market	un marché protégé
quotas	les quotas
an economic blockade	un blocus économique
to enforce sanctions	appliquer des sanctions
trustbusting	les lois anti-trust
a free-market economy	l'économie libérale

to set up	fonder, monter
a product / to produce	un produit / produire
a brand, a make	une marque

BONUS	**BONUS**
*mind your own **business***	mêle-toi de tes affaires
***business** is business*	les affaires sont les affaires
*the **customer** is always right*	le client a toujours raison
*time is **money***	le temps c'est de l'argent
***money** talks*	avec l'argent on obtient tout
*to spend **money** like water*	l'argent (lui) file entre les doigts
***Money** does not grow on trees*	l'argent ne pousse pas sur les arbres
*to get one's **money** worth*	en avoir pour son argent
*a **miser** will father a **spendthrift** son*	à père avare fils prodigue
*a **cheap** shot*	un coup bas
*on the **cheap***	au rabais
*life is **cheap***	la vie est sans importance
*to cut **costs** / to cut corners*	rogner sur les dépenses
*to **brand** sb as sth*	désigner qqn comme qch
***branded** in the memory*	inscrit, gravé dans la mémoire
*to give somebody a **free** hand*	donner carte blanche à qqn
***free** as a bird*	libre comme l'air
*she's really **coin**ing it*	elle sait faire des affaires
*two sides of the same **coin***	les deux facettes d'un même problème
*to pay sb back in the same **coin***	rendre à qqn la monnaie de sa pièce
*a **position** of **trust***	un poste de confiance
***tried** and **trusted** methods*	des méthodes fiables, prouvées
*in **company***	en société
*to keep bad **company***	avoir de mauvaises fréquentations

Translation: French-to-English exercise

Extraits adaptés de : *Le capital au XXIe siècle*, Thomas Piketty

La répartition des richesses est l'une des questions les plus vives et les plus débattues aujourd'hui. Des moyens existent pour que la démocratie et l'intérêt général parviennent à reprendre le contrôle du capitalisme et des intérêts privés tout en repoussant les replis protectionnistes et nationalistes.

Depuis les années 1970, les inégalités sont fortement reparties à la hausse dans les pays riches notamment aux États-Unis. L'histoire de la répartition des richesses est toujours une histoire profondément politique et ne saurait se résumer à des mécanismes purement économiques.

L'histoire des inégalités dépend des représentations que se font les acteurs économiques, politiques, sociaux, de ce qui est juste et de ce qui ne l'est pas, des rapports de force entre ces acteurs, et des choix collectifs qui en découlent.

Adapted press excerpts (about 400 words)

Excerpt 1 – What is the Nash equilibrium? (adapted from *Washington Post*)

Economists can usually explain the past and sometimes **predict** the future – but not without help. One of the most important tools at their disposal is the Nash equilibrium. This simple **concept** helps economists work out how **competing companies set** their **prices.** One of the best-known illustrations is the prisoner's dilemma: two criminals in separate prison cells face the same offer from the public prosecutor. If they both confess to a bloody murder, they each face ten years in jail. If one stays quiet while the other confesses, then the snitch will get to go free, while the other will face a lifetime in jail. And if both hold their tongue, then they each face a minor charge, and only a year in the clink. Collectively, it would be best for both to keep quiet. But given the set-up, an **economist** armed with the concept of the Nash equilibrium would predict the opposite: the only stable outcome is for both to confess.

Excerpt 2 – Against happiness (adapted from Schumpeter, *The Economist*)

A weird assortment of gurus and **consultancies** is pushing the cult of happiness, to make it a **competitive advantage**. The idea of "happiness hygiene" says that, just as we brush our teeth every day, we should think positive thoughts and write positive e-mails.The **trend** is not confined to the **private sector**. Several governments (America, Britain, France and Australia) now publish for the **benefit** of their citizens regular reports on levels of national **well-being**. Businesspeople have long known there is **money** to be made in the **field. Firms** are keen to extract happiness from their **employees** as the service sector plays an ever greater role in the **economy**. As **customers**, most people prefer run-of-the-mill companies' service with a smile rather than a snarl.

Excerpt 3 – Deflation ugly step-sister of inflation (adapted from *Otago Daily Times*)

Deflation is the ugly step-sister of **inflation**. When deflation emerges and **prices** are **falling**, firms seek to cut **costs** and **unemployment rises**. Consumers postpone **spending** in anticipation of further price falls. **Cash** becomes king. As prices fall and unemployment rises, **wage** rates tend to fall. People find it harder to pay their **debts** such as **mortgages**. They sell their houses causing house prices to fall. Yet the debts remain. We are currently in very strange **economic** terrain. Our economy appears to be **booming** with headline annual **growth** of almost 4% in New Zealand. **Asset prices** such as **housing** and **shares** have **rocketed** in recent years. Many people are feeling a lot **wealthier** on paper. But many others aren't. Their **incomes** have **stagnated** in recent years. Those who don't own **property** or **shares** are excluded from our economic success story.

Excerpt 4 – An Introduction to the Financial Markets (adapted from *The Balance*)

What are the **financial markets**? First, they go by many terms, including **capital markets**, Wall Street, even simply "the markets". Whatever you call them, financial markets are where **traders buy** and **sell** stocks, **bonds**, **derivatives**, **foreign exchange** and **commodities**. These markets are where **businesses** go to raise **cash** to grow, companies reduce **risks**, and **investors** make **money**. Financial markets create an open and regulated **system** for **companies** to obtain large amounts of **financial capital** to grow their **businesses**. Markets allow these businesses to **offset risk**. Since the markets are public, they provide an open and transparent way to set prices on everything traded. These prices rightly or wrongly assume that all available knowledge about everything traded is taken into consideration.

Food for Thought and Quotations (about 500 words)

The Great Depression of the 1930s

The worst and most emblematic economic crisis in modern history was the Great Depression, further to the Wall Street stock market crash of 1929 (Black Tuesday). The consequences of the slump in the price of shares caused many banks to go bankrupt, after years of rampant speculation and a disconnection between prices and the actual value of stocks. In the following months, the industrial production declined and the unemployment rate soared to 25 percent of the working population. After a slight improvement in 1931, another crisis occured, that contaminated most European economies, which decided to devalue their currencies. The fallout was dramatic and the effects on trade were devastating. The election of Franklin D.Roosevelt in 1932 was the opportunity to take radical action and start a recovery process, termed the New Deal. On Inaugural Day, he declared that "*the only thing we have to fear is fear itself.*" The crisis did not come to an end until war broke out in Europe in 1939.

Capital and capitalism

The word comes from Latin from *capitalis*, from *caput* "head." As explained in Wikipedia, the term "stock" is derived from the Old English word for stump or tree trunk. It has been used to refer to all the moveable property of a farm since at least 1510. In Middle Ages France, contracted loans interest specified payment in heads of cattle as a unit of capital. Adam Smith defines capital as *"that part of a man's stock which he expects to afford him revenue"*. Karl Marx defines it rather as wealth that originates in the process of circulation itself. Capitalism, also termed free market economy is the major economic system in the Western countries. It is defined mainly by the privately-owned means of production (trade and industry) and the distribution of income through financial markets. Broadly speaking, there are different forms of capitalism, the varying factors being state intervention, competition in markets, definitions of private property and importance of social policies.

Economic v. economical

According to the Oxford English Dictionary, *economic* is an adjective related to economics (the science) or the economy (the resource). *Economical*, on the other hand, means giving good value or return in relation to the resources used or money spent; sparing in the use of resources or money. In other words, *economic* refers to the economy, finances, or wealth, while *economical* describes something that saves money or resources or is not wasteful of money or resources. Both adjectives have the same adverb, *economically.*

"Price is what you pay. Value is what you get." [...] *"Rule No. 1: Never lose money. Rule No. 2: Never forget Rule No. 1."* Warren Buffett

"You can't tax business. Business doesn't pay taxes. It collects taxes." Ronald Reagan

"Entrepreneurial capitalism takes more people out of poverty than aid." Bono

"When the rate of return on capital exceeds the rate of growth of output and income, as it did in the nineteenth century and seems quite likely to do again in the twenty-first, capitalism automatically generates arbitrary and unsustainable inequalities that radically undermine the meritocratic values on which democratic societies are based." Thomas Piketty

Chapter C

Consumption

Vocabulary list

CONSUMER SOCIETY	**LA SOCIÉTÉ DE CONSOMMATION**
a customer, a client / to consume	un client / consommer
a consumer	un consommateur
a purchaser / to purchase	un acquéreur / acquérir, acheter
purchasing power	le pouvoir d'achat
to shop / to do one's shopping	faire les magasins / les courses
to go on a shopping spree	faire des folies
compulsive buying	l'achat compulsif
a whim	un caprice
the affluent society	la société d'abondance
to waste / squander money	gaspiller de l'argent
to be broke, squint	être fauché
customer service	le service clients
consumerism	le consumérisme
consumers' rights	les droits des consommateurs
a consumer group	une association de consommateurs
a class action	une action de groupe (en justice)
a guarantee	une garantie
a boycott	un boycott
to claim damages	demander des dommages et intérêts
a lawsuit	un procès
to receive compensation	se faire indemniser
to be refunded, to get a refund	être remboursé
to exchange sth for	faire un échange de qch contre

CONSUMPTION	**LA CONSOMMATION**
a shop / sales assistant	un vendeur / une vendeuse
a salesman / saleswoman	un vendeur / une vendeuse
customer satisfaction	le service consommateurs
a complaint	une plainte
customer dissatisfaction	le mécontentement des clients
customer feedback	les réactions des consommateurs
poor service	la mauvaise qualité de service
the quality standards	la qualité
deception	la tromperie
to return an item	retourner un article
out of order	en panne
faulty, defective	en panne, défectueux
available, in stock	disponible, en stock
unavailable / availability	non disponible / la disponibilité
the after-sales service	le SAV (service après vente)
to buy cash / a payment	acheter en liquide / le paiement
a discount / a rebate	une réduction / un rabais
a bargain	une bonne affaire

credit	le crédit
the down payments	l'apport initial
the instalments	les mensualités
online shopping	le shopping en ligne / l'achat sur Internet
a mail order	la vente par correspondance
to order from a catalogue	acheter par correspondance
to hire / to rent	louer, prendre en location
to bargain for sth	marchander
to be able to afford sth	avoir les moyens de
cheap / expensive	bon marché / cher
affordable / costly	abordable / coûteux
free / exorbitant	gratuit / prohibitif, exorbitant

SHOPS	**LES MAGASINS**
a boutique	une boutique de mode
an outlet	un point de vente
a shop / a store	une boutique / un magasin
the lay-out	l'agencement
a shelf (pl.shelves)	une étagère / une gondole
a stall	un étal, un stand, un kiosque
a section / a department	un rayon
a shopwindow	une vitrine
a basket	un panier
a trolley	un chariot
a barcode	un code-barre
a range of products	une gamme de produits
a security guard	un vigile
the checkout	la caisse (supermarché)
a cash register, a till	une caisse (appareil)
a cashier	un caissier / une hôtesse de caisse
a discount store	un magasin discount (à marge réduite)
a corner store	un magasin de proximité
a baker / a baker's shop	un boulanger / une boulangerie
a butcher's shop	une boucherie
a grocer's shop	une épicerie
a deli(catessen)	un traiteur
a caterer / to cater for	un traiteur / préparer des repas pour
a tobacconist	un marchand de tabac
a launderette	une laverie automatique
a dry cleaner's	une teinturerie / un pressing
an antique shop	un magasin d'antiquités
a pet shop	une animalerie
a factory outlet	un magasin d'usine
a cheese counter	le rayon fromages
a specialty store	un magasin spécialisé
a shopping precinct	une zone commerçante piétonnière

a franchised store	un magasin franchisé
a chain store	un magasin appartenant à une chaîne
a store chain	une chaîne de magasins
a general store, a variety store	un bazar
a service company	une société de services
a delivery man	un livreur

MARKETING	**LE MARKETING**
a (business) dpartner	un partenaire commercial
a market study / research	une étude de marché
research / to do research	des recherches / faire des recherches
the consumer profile	le profil de consommateur
a case study	une étude de cas
to launch / a launch	lancer / un lancement
a target / to target	une cible / cibler
to analyse	analyser
an analysis	une analyse
a sample	un échantillon
a cross-section	un échantillon représentatif
a poll / to poll	un sondage / sonder
a market	un marché
to market	commercialiser
a product	un produit
a consumer good	un bien de consommation
consumer durables	des biens de consommation durables
an item	un article
goods	la marchandise
to offer	proposer
offer and demand	l'offre et la demande
upscale / downscale	haut de gamme / bas de gamme
a loss-leader	un produit d'appel, un article promotionnel
branded goods	les produits de marque
brand image	l'image de marque
to build consumer loyalty	fidéliser les clients
a sales drive	une campagne promotionnelle

ADVERTISING	**LA PUBLICITÉ**
an advertisement, an advert (GB) / an ad	une publicité, un spot publicitaire
an advertising campaign	une campagne de publicité
to advertise a product	faire la publicité d'un produit
a commercial	un spot publicitaire (TV, radio)
advertising in print	la publicité dans les journaux
outdoor advertising	l'affichage public
advertising on air	la publicité sur les ondes
online advertising	la publicité sur Internet
soft-sell advertising	la publicité non invasive

invasive advertising	la publicité invasive
comparative advertising	la publicité comparative
targeted advertising	la publicité ciblée
misleading advertising, deceptive advertising	la publicité mensongère
an advertising agency	une agence de pub
a publicist	un publicitaire
to convey a message	faire passer, transmettre un message
a slogan, a motto	un slogan, une devise
a caption, a catch phrase	une légende, expression-clé (phrase choc)
a banner	une bannière publicitaire
a pop-up window	une fenêtre contextuelle
to sponsor / sponsoring	parrainer / un parrainage commercial
to influence / to induce	influencer / persuader, inciter
to appeal to	cibler pour plaire à
to draw attention	attirer l'attention
to arouse the interest	susciter l'intérêt
to cat the eye / eye-catching	attirer l'œil / accrocheur
to convey an impression	donner une impression
to entertain / entertaining	divertir / divertissant
witty / hilarious	spirituel / hilarant
dull / boring	terne / ennuyeux
a hype / to hype	un battage publicitaire / organiser un battage
an ad-free website	un site internet sans publicité
brainwashing	le lavage de cerveau
to brainwash customers into buying	conditionner les consommateurs à acheter
an advertising space	un espace publicitaire
a leaflet / a folder	un prospectus / un dépliant
a brochure	une brochure
a free sample	un échantillon gratuit
a special offer	une offre spéciale
a demo item	un article de démonstration
a neon sign	une enseigne lumineuse
a banner, a pop-up window	une bannière, une fenêtre pop-up
a poster / a bill	un poster / une affiche
a hoarding (GB) / a billboard	un panneau d'affichage
a mailing list	une liste d'adresses
a jingle	un jingle publicitaire
a slot	un créneau horaire
the audience rating	le taux d'écoute, l'audimat

BONUS	**BONUS**
*to talk **shop***	parler boutique
*you've come to the wrong **shop***	vous vous trompez d'adresse
*to **shop** around*	chercher (pour comparer)
*in-**store** promotion*	publicité sur le lieu de vente

to be on special ***offer***	être en promotion
to set great ***store*** *by something*	accorder beaucoup d'importance à qch
to ***market*** *oneself*	se vendre
money ***laundering***	le blanchiment d'argent
attention, interest, desire, action (AIDA)	4 objectifs d'une publicité (attention, intérêt, désir, action)
to be ***consumed*** *by*	être rongé par / être dévoré par
to pay ***attention*** *to*	écouter
to strike the ***imagination***	frapper l'imagination
monkey ***business***	des manigances
to get down to ***business***	en venir au fait, se mettre au travail
to be left behind	être largué, être à la traîne
a one-of-a-kind ***product***	un produit unique
ignorance is bliss	le bonheur est dans l'ignorance
at any ***rate***	en tout cas
*overrated / to over****rate***	surfait / surestimer
to ***slot*** *into*	bien s'insérer, s'adapter (dans un groupe)
to be in great ***demand*** *as*	être très populaire / demandé en tant que
to cut off sb's ***supplies***	couper les vivres à qqn

Translation: French-to-English exercise

Snapchat suit les pas de Facebook sur la publicité ciblée (adapté du *Figaro*)

Snapchat proposera bientôt aux marques de diffuser leur publicité grâce à l'observation plus fine des comportements de ses utilisateurs. Sans s'aligner sur les stratégies publicitaires de concurrents comme Facebook ou Google, l'application franchit un nouveau pas vers les annonceurs.

En 2014, le jeune entrepreneur revendiquait le souci de ne pas faire de Snapchat une application « louche », qui surveille ses habitués pour vendre leurs données. « Nous voulons voir si nous sommes capables de délivrer une expérience qui soit amusante et informative, comme les publicités l'étaient autrefois, avant qu'elles ne deviennent désinvoltes et ciblées » expliquait-il dans un billet de blog, aux débuts de leur effort de monétisation.

Depuis, le réseau social n'a eu de cesse de développer de nouveaux outils publicitaires à destination des annonceurs ou des médias. Le nouveau ciblage comportemental de Snapchat reste pourtant encore loin du niveau de précision de Facebook, qui utilise aujourd'hui près de cent critères pour définir une audience, dont l'âge, le genre, la localisation, le type de mobile, l'opérateur mobile, le système d'exploitation et l'historique de navigation.

Adapted press excerpts (about 400 words)

Excerpt 1 – Understanding consumer society is critical to addressing sustainability (adapted from *The Guardian*)

We need to shift our thinking from a blind **faith** in technology to a deeper **understanding** of the links between our **lifestyles** and the environment. "**Sustainability** doesn't come naturally" to the human species, the evolutionary biologist Richard Dawkins once remarked. His implication was that somehow it's our collective **patterns of behaviour** that are leading us astray, our natural aspirations for the good life that divert us inevitably from **success** in addressing ecological **challenges**. Faith in technology is probably our single most obvious "backstop" belief. If all else fails, we are a clever species, right? We have extraordinary powers of **creativity** and **innovation**. So when it comes to saving our vision of social progress in the face of declining environmental **qualities**, it's our own **technological capability** that we reach for.

Excerpt 2 – The Dogma of Advertising and Consumerism (adapted from *The Huff Post*)

It's not clear how many **advertisements** we are exposed to every day. Taking into account the **average** hours of **TV viewing**, **radio listening**, **newspapers / magazine reading**, **internet surfing**, public street and transport use; common estimates range from around 250 to 3000 daily. Regardless of which is more accurate, there's no doubt that being **exposed** to **adverts** is an extremely significantly common and almost necessary part of human experience in the modern world. As well as showing us products, adverts also present us with **values**, **ideals** and **social standards**. They draw upon major personal **themes** such as **beauty**, **happiness**, **love**, **companionship**, **sex**, and **self-image**, in a positive but **unrealistic** light to **promote** their **product**. As a consequence, these adverts are potentially shaping us towards mental states, which are in fact, quite inhibiting, insecure, and unhealthy.

Excerpt 3 – Adblock Plus, Created to Protect Users From Ads, Instead Opens the Door (*The International New York Times*)

Adblock Plus, an **ad blocker** now used on more than 100 million **devices**, started out as an almost utopian idea a decade ago. It was an **open-source project** and quickly built it up with the help of volunteers who also wanted to make the internet faster, less cluttered and safer from **malware**. Its motto: "We want to make the internet better for everyone. Purging bad ads is a good start." But shortly after that, in 2011, Adblock Plus was altered and became a tool that, instead of **blocking** bad ads, **allowed** ads it deemed "acceptable" to be seen, often for a price – a controversial move that has positioned it as a **gatekeeper** between **advertisers** and its huge user base.

Excerpt 4 – How marketers will win (*Future of Marketing*)

Marketing is on the ascent. It has frequently led at big **consumer products** companies. Now its **influence** is growing everywhere: at B2B companies, **professional services firms**, companies dominated by **engineering** or **logistics**. You can see marketing's rise on **business** bestseller lists, on YouTube playlists, in the new **brands** that have broken away and differentiated themselves, and in the explosion of **marketing start-ups** (and what **investors** are paying for them). **Marketing** is becoming a more powerful and resource-rich function of **business**. In today's **digital world,** marketing is the **function** responsible for **creating** and **sustaining** a long-lasting relationship with the most important **asset** of any **business** – the **customer**. In an always-on world, **consumer expectations** are changing.

Food for Thought and Quotations (about 500 words)

The contradictory meanings of consumerism

The term "*consumerism*" has several definitions, that can easily be confused and lead to major misunderstandings. First, it can refer to the consumers' interests and their protection (fair treatment, information and consideration for the consumer). Secondly, it can mean a high level of consumption, which has to do with economic growth (economic materialism and senseless consumption frenzy). This meaning gave birth to the identification of a market-linked force that leads to a dehumanisation of consumers linked to the excesses of globalisation. Today, in economics and politics, the term has gained a rather negative connotation, linked to waste, excessive materialism and illusion of affluence. But it remains clear that wealthy consumers are both the ideal targets and sources of inspiration for marketing agencies, since their lifestyles are a standard for all consumers, particularly the poor ones that will be given an impression of affluence if they purchase a product that is desired by wealthy people.

Biodynamic or organic

Biodynamic products are considered rather similar to organic ones but they have additional requirements that make them not as healthful. Biodynamic farms are mostly self-sufficient; fertilizer and animal feed, for example, are grown there instead of being brought in. Different certifications and different philosophies imply that biodynamics finally depend on the coherence of an ecosystem, since all the living species live in osmosis. In the long term, plants grown with biodynamics might better adapt to their environment and finally not need to be helped by man anymore, which makes a difference with organic products which do not take into account all the environmental criteria. In the long term, biodynamic products may be actually even more healthy for our planet than organic ones, since the production process is more coherent with the natural resources and environment.

What makes an efficient ad?

The question boils down to asking whether it is the product or just the ad itself that counts. First, an ad must include the product name and its specific characteristic. It also needs to catch people's attention, given the high proportion of ads one may encounter in just one day. An effective headline, a catchy illustration can easily do so. Offering the customer a bargain, or stating the benefits are simple strategies that have worked for centuries! A more recent strategy is to create an *advertorial,* that is to say an advertisement that looks like a news article in a paper, on TV or in your newsfeed on Flipboard or Facebook. However, consumers tend to prefer ads that contain self-derision, humour and simple everyday features rather than special effects or elaborate technical or commercial artefacts, probably because simplicity makes the difference. 2015's most shared ad, Friends Furever, is a very simple, low-budget found footage composition featuring couples of different animals, mixed with Walt Disney's Robin Hood soundtrack. The message conveyed is "together, but not the same". The name of the product was easy to be remembered, since it was Google's Android.

"Advertising is legalized lying." H.G. Wells

"It is important to bear in mind that political campaigns are designed by the same people who sell toothpaste and cars." Noam Chomsky

"What's great about this country is America started the tradition where the richest consumers buy essentially the same things as the poorest. You can be watching TV and see Coca-Cola, and you can know that the President drinks Coke, Liz Taylor drinks Coke, and just think, you can drink Coke, too. A Coke is a Coke and no amount of money can get you a better Coke than the one the bum on the corner is drinking." Andy Warhol

"What the mass media offers is not popular art, but entertainment which is intended to be consumed like food, forgotten, and replaced by a new dish." W.H. Auden

Chapter D
Globalisation and Language

Vocabulary list

GLOBALISATION	LA MONDIALISATION, LA GLOBALISATION
to go global	se mondialiser
a pro-globaliser	un mondialiste
the modern times	les temps modernes
Americanization (US)	l'américanisation
Westernisation (GB)	l'occidentalisation
a superpower	une superpuissance
the culture, the idea	la culture, l'idée
world views	les visions du monde
a market economy	l'économie de marché
a borderless world	un monde sans frontières
a flat world	un monde sans frontières, un monde nivelé
the global village	le village mondial
interchange / exchange	les échanges
the connectivity / to connect	la connectivité / relier, connecter
interconnectedness	l'interconnectivité
interdependence	l'interdépendance
interrelated	indissociables
unique	unique, particulier, exceptionnel
liberalisation (GB)	la libéralisation
the liberalization (US) of trade	la libéralisation des échanges
the free flow of goods	la libre circulation des biens
to shape	former, donner forme à, façonner
a policy / politics	une politique / la (science) politique
a current trend	une tendance récente
the pros and cons	les avantages et les inconvénients
the benefits and pitfalls	les bienfaits et les dangers
the case for / the case against	les arguments pour / contre
poverty alleviation	la lutte contre la pauvreté
a global alternative, alter-globalisation	l'altermondialisme
global cooperation	la coopération au niveau mondial
a label	une étiquette

THE GLOBAL ECONOMY	L'ÉCONOMIE MONDIALE
to extend, to intensify	s'étendre, s'intensifier
a movement / a move	un mouvement / un déplacement, un coup
a movement of people, a migratory movement	un mouvement migratoire
capital movement	les mouvements de capitaux
capital flow	les flux de capitaux
dissemination of knowledge	la diffusion des savoirs
cross-boundary waters	les eaux limitrophes
an institution	une institution
economic / cultural / political globalisation	la mondialisation de l'économie / culturelle / politique
a free trade area	une zone de libre-échange

a network	un réseau
to link	lier, relier
a corporate giant	un géant industriel
to break into a market	pénétrer un marché
to capture a market	s'emparer d'un marché
to widen / widening	s'élargir / grandissant
to deepen / the deepening	s'approfondir, se renforcer / l'intensification
social relations	les relations sociales
shorter distances	la réduction des distances
global integration	l'intégration au niveau mondial
fierce competition	la compétition effrénée
to deregulate / deregulation	déréglementer / la déréglementation
to deregulate prices	libérer les prix
flight of capital	la fuite des capitaux
economies of scale	les économies d'échelle
outsourcing	la sous-traitance, l'externalisation
to set up a factory	installer une usine
a call centre	un centre d'appels
supply-chaining	la gestion de la chaîne logistique
a commodity	produit, marchandise, ressource
to embody / disembodied	incarner, représenter / désincarné
influence / influent, influential	l'influence / influent
proximity	la proximité
to be close to	être à proximité de / être sur le point de
the GDP (gross domestic product)	le PIB (produit intérieur brut)
the ITO (International Trade Organisation)	l'OMC (l'organisation mondiale du commerce)

CULTURE AND SOCIETY	**LA CULTURE ET LA SOCIÉTÉ**
standardisation	l'uniformisation
local / national / domestic	local / national / intérieur, national
universal	universel
ubiquitous	omniprésent
to partake in / to partake of	participer à / tenir de (qualité)
to cross	traverser, aller au delà de
an evolution / to evolve	une évolution / évoluer
a revolution / to revolutionise	une révolution / révolutionner
hybridisation	l'hybridation
homogenisation	l'homogénéisation
conflict intensification	l'intensification des conflits
to spread / the spread	se propager, s'étendre / la propagation, la diffusion
social dumping	le dumping social
sale below cost	la vente à perte
competitiveness	la compétitivité

to keep up with / to catch up with	se maintenir au niveau de / rattraper un retard
to lag behind	être à la traîne
the cultural exception	l'exception culturelle
the odd one out	l'exception, l'intrus
fair trade	le commerce équitable
a fair trade product	un produit issu du commerce équitable
guilt-free foods	des aliments à consommer sans honte
fair trade clothes	des vêtements du commerce équitable
handicrafts	des produits artisanaux
fair competition	la concurrence loyale
unfair trade rules	des règles commerciales déloyales
small producers	les petits producteurs
to bypass the middleman	court-circuiter les intermédiaires
to go mainstream	se populariser
a guaranteed price	un prix minimum garanti
consumer awareness	la prise de conscience des consommateurs

COMMUNICATION AND LANGUAGE	**LA COMMUNICATION ET LA LANGUE**
the global language	la langue mondiale
a mother tongue	une langue maternelle
a native speaker	un locuteur natif
the English language / English	l'anglais, la langue anglaise
an English-speaking country	un pays anglophone
fluency / to speak fluent English	l'aisance / parler couramment l'anglais
to communicate / communication	communiquer / la communication
a declaration, a statement	une déclaration, une affirmation
a question / an answer	une question, une réponse
to utter / an utterance	formuler, prononcer / une formulation, une parole
to highlight	mettre en valeur
to lay stress on	souligner l'importance de
affirmative / negative	(phrase) affirmative / négative
interrogative / exclamatory	interrogative / exclamative
an exchange	un échange, un débat
a talk	une conversation, une discussion
small talk	des banalités
a conversation / to converse	une conversation / converser
to debate sth	débattre de qqch
a debating point	un argument
an argument	une dispute
to question	remettre en question, contester
a sentence	une phrase
a phrase, an expression	une proposition (un syntagme), une expression
a set phrase	une expression figée

a catch phrase	une formule, un slogan
a buzzword	un mot à la mode
to coin a word	inventer un mot
to look up in the dictionary	rechercher un mot dans le dictionnaire
a cliché	un cliché
a commonplace	un lieu commun, une platitude
a critic / a criticism	un critique (d'art…) / une critique
a polemic / polemical	une polémique / polémique
colloquial, informal	familier
foul language	langage grossier
derogatory	désobligeant, péjoratif
a controversy / controversial	une controverse / débattu
biased, one-sided	partial, partisan, subjectif
derision / derisive	la dérision / moqueur
to qualify a statement	nuancer ses propos
to distort sb's views	déformer les pensées de qqn
a figure of speech	une figure de style
an understatement, a euphemism	une litote, un euphémisme

USING THE LANGUAGE	**UTILISATION DE LA LANGUE**
translation / to translate	traduire / la traduction
to express oneself	s'exprimer
to make oneself understood	se faire comprendre
an accent	un accent (oral)
a proficiency test	un test de compétence
to follow an English course	suivre des cours d'anglais
to be good / bad / hopeless at languages	être bon / mauvais / nul en langues
to speak poor / broken English	parler mal l'anglais
mumbo jumbo, gibberish, gobbledygook	du charabia
slang	l'argot
a dialect	un dialecte
a lingua franca	une lingua franca
globish	l'anglais international / mondial simplifié
to mean / the meaning	signifier, vouloir dire / le sens
meaningless	dénué de sens
to rephrase	reformuler
in other words	en d'autres termes
a plain style	un style clair
correctness	la correction
grammar	la grammaire
vocabulary	les mots, le vocabulaire
a keyword	un mot-clé
a colon, a semi-colon	deux points, un point-virgule
period, full stop	point
quotation marks, inverted commas	les guillemets
quote / unquote	ouvrez / fermez les guillemets

dash / hyphen	tiret / trait d'union
brackets	les parenthèses
a saying, a proverb	un dicton, un proverbe
stress	l'accentuation
pronunciation / to pronounce	la prononciation / prononcer
rhythm, intonation	le rythme, l'intonation

BONUS	**BONUS**
to lose / to find one's ***tongue***	perdre, avaler / retrouver sa langue
on the tip of one's ***tongue***	sur le bout de la langue
has the cat got your ***tongue?***	tu as avalé ta langue ?
tongue*-lashing*	des remarques cinglantes
a slip of the ***tongue***	un lapsus
a revealing ***phrase***	une phrase qui veut tout dire
hold your ***tongue!***	tiens ta langue
a ***tongue****-twisting sentence*	une phrase difficile à prononcer
to trip off the ***tongue***	venir tout seul
to bite one's ***tongue***	se mordre la langue
to keep a civil ***tongue***	rester poli
tongue*-in-cheek*	une remarque au second degré
tongue*-tied*	muet (qui n'arrive pas à parler)
tongues *will wag*	cela va faire jaser !
mind your ***language / Language!***	Sois poli !
a set ***expression****, a stock* ***phrase***	une phrase toute faite
to use flowery ***words***	faire de grandes phrases
a highflown ***phrase***	une phrase ampoulée
to put in a good ***word*** *for sb*	glisser un mot en faveur de qqn
upon my ***word!***	ma parole ! / parole d'honneur !

EXTRA BONUS: some expressions coined by William Shakespeare	**EXTRA BONUS**
It's Greek to me	C'est du chinois !
To have a sense of fair play	jouer franc jeu
All that glitters isn't gold	tout ce qui brille n'est pas or
Wear one's heart on one's sleeve	laisser voir ses sentiments
Break the ice	briser la glace
The lady doth protest too much	Elle en fait trop pour être honnête
Clothes make the man	L'habit (ne) fait (pas) le moine
A laughing stock	être la risée
Too much of a good thing	Il ne faut pas abuser des bonnes choses
In a pickle	être dans le pétrin

Translation: French-to-English exercise

L'aurore (adapté d'un article éponyme du *Monde diplomatique* et d'un extrait de Jean Giraudoux, *Électre*, 1937)

– Comment cela s'appelle-t-il, quand le jour se lève, comme aujourd'hui, et que tout est gâché, que tout est saccagé, et que l'air pourtant se respire, et que tout est perdu, que la ville brûle, que les innocents s'entretuent, mais que les coupables agonisent, dans un coin du jour qui se lève ?

– Cela a un très beau nom. Cela s'appelle l'aurore.

Une lueur d'espoir s'est levée à Seattle, alors que s'éteignait le siècle. Trop longtemps dépossédés de leur parole, des citoyens y ont dit avec force : « Assez ! » Assez d'accepter la mondialisation comme une fatalité. Assez de voir le marché décider à la place des élus. Assez de voir le monde transformé en marchandise. Assez de subir, de se résigner, de se soumettre.

La mondialisation – et le laxisme des dirigeants politiques – a favorisé, au cours de la dernière décennie, la mise en place discrète d'une sorte d'exécutif planétaire dont les quatre acteurs principaux sont le Fonds monétaire international, la Banque mondiale, l'Organisation de coopération et de développement économiques et l'OMC.

Adapted press excerpts (about 400 words)

Excerpt 1 – The Environmental Cost Of Growing Food (adapted from NPR)

Let's say you're an **environmentally** motivated eater. You want your diet to do as little damage as possible to our **planet's forests** and **grasslands** and **wildlife**. But how do you decide which food is **greener**? Take one example: sugar. About half of America's sugar comes from sugar cane, and half from sugar beets. They grow in completely different **climates**. Sugar cane is a tropical crop, and sugar beets grow where it's colder and dryer. Each one has an **impact** on the **environment** – sometimes a dramatic impact – but in very different ways. The Florida soil is fertile, but once exposed to air, it starts to decompose. It turns into **carbon dioxide** and vanishes. In 50 or 100 years, so little soil will be left, it may not be possible to farm here anymore.

Excerpt 2 – Inventing the future (adapted from *Le Monde diplomatique*, English edition)

What sort of **world** do we want? It doesn't take a seer to conclude that "if things go on like this, they're going to have to stop" (a slogan from May '68). The real question is how. That's the role of futurologists, and there's no shortage of **predictions**. The experts in **thinktanks** and **credit rating agencies** are today's oracles: their task is to identify which factors in the current data will play a determining role in the future, mainly on an **international scale**, using contemporary indicators and criteria that are just as opaque as the auguries of the past. The major thinktanks are preoccupied with **global security**, **peace**, **defence**, **terrorism** and **technology**, and particularly their significance for the US.

Excerpt 3 – English is de facto global language (adapted from BBC)

Should English be the major **global language** of communication? **English** does seem to be the *de facto* "global" language of the the 21st century. It has followed on from French which was the **lingua franca** of the 19th and early 20th century. Having your own **language** as the one which everybody else has to learn gives you a real **advantage**. What is nice about Esperanto is that it respects **majority** and **minority languages** alike. It belongs to no country or government, it is not identified with the powerful. It doesn't replace one's **mother tongue**. It was always intended as a **second language** for everybody whenever they're reduced to pointing and smiling.

Excerpt 4 – Globalisation backlash 2.0 (adapted from *The Economist*)

The first great era of **globalisation** in the 19th century saw the share of **trade** rise eightfold between 1820 and 1913. The emergence of the railway and steamship allowed products to be sent speedily across **borders**. The war brought an abrupt end to the **trend**. Both Germany and Russia saw the war as a way of enhancing **patriotism** and countering the rising power of **socialism**. In short, **globalisation** can mean rapid change in **industries** and across **economies**; change that many people find it difficult to adjust to. The war hastened the arrival of **democracy**; if the workers had to fight for their **country**, why couldn't they vote? Perhaps **globalisation** can only go so far before it provokes a political reaction. "*We cannot simultaneously pursue democracy, **national determination** and **economic globalisation**. If we want to push globalisation further, we have to give up either the nation state or democratic politics*", ***Dani Rodrik*** writes in The Globalisation Paradox.

Food for Thought and Quotations (about 500 words)

Globalisation (GB) / Globalization (US)

The term refers to the process of increasing international integration consequent to the exchange of products, people, ideas, and other aspects of culture. Even though it originates in the development of transportation means and the rise of the telegraph technology in the early 19th century, the term is a very recent one (it appeared in its modern meaning in the late 1970s). Internet and mobile phone networks have been a major factor of the global development of ideas, trade and economic activities, to a point that has generated interdependence between the cultural and economic sectors. According to the International Monetary Fund, four basic aspects of globalisation can be identified: trade, capital, migration, and knowledge. According to Wikipedia, academic literature today commonly subdivides globalisation into three major areas: economic, cultural and political globalisation.

Economic globalisation

It is the economic integration of a global marketplace that encourages an easier movement of goods, services, technology, and capital. Whereas the globalisation of business is centered around the diminution of international taxes and tariffs, economic globalisation encourages international economic reforms and fosters international investments, which is just profitable for business. Of course there are social consequences to such processes, for example an increased race for profit that will compel businesses to seek a cheaper workforce (a process called outsourcing), with negative consequences on employment and more generally on wages. Economic globalization therefore refers to the globalisation of production, competition, technology and business, but also the globalisation of the social ills that it implies.

Cultural globalisation

It is the gradual standardisation of cultural diversity around the world. Caused mainly by the development of wireless communications, electronic commerce, popular culture, and international travel, it has become a trend toward homogeneity that would theoretically tend to erase the cultural diversity, even though in reality the phenomenon is not that clear-cut. Sectors that seem to confirm this homogenisation concern the human experience as a whole, such as travel, entertainment, music and cinema, food or clothing. However, Pierre Bourdieu claimed that *the perception of consumption could be seen as self-identification and the formation of identity: likes and tastes were greatly influenced by culture. The concept of one's own culture is now in a period of change due to globalization*. However, an illustration of globalisation as a whole could be the spread of international forms of communication, such as Globish, a simplified global means of communication in numerous dialects derived from English, and also the movement towards an international standard for the language.

Political globalisation

It is generally considered that another goal of globalisation is to imply a political reduction of the importance of the notion of nation states, even though this idea remains an ideal concept that is not verified in today's international context, far from it. But supranational institutions such as the European Union, the WTO or even the G8 have the capacity to extend national functions to facilitate international agreements. Furthermore, the increasing influence of non-governmental organisations has helped spread philanthropic projects around the world. As for cultural and economic globalisation, this idea remains theoretical, which can be illustrated by the growing isolationist strategies of some countries that refuse this evolution.

"And the owners not only did not work the farms any more, many of them had never seen the farms they owned." John Steinbeck

"Globalization, as defined by rich people like us, is a very nice thing... you are talking about the Internet, you are talking about cell phones, you are talking about computers. This doesn't affect two-thirds of the people of the world." Jimmy Carter

Section 9

International context

Chapter A

The world

Vocabulary list

THE WORLD	**LE MONDE**
the north / northern	le nord / au nord / septentrional
the south / southernmost	le sud / le plus au sud / méridional
the east / easterly	l'est, l'orient / venant de l'est / de l'orient
the west / western	l'ouest, l'occident / de l'ouest / occidental
the continents	les continents
Asia	l'Asie
Europe	l'Europe
Africa	l'Afrique
the Americas	les Amériques
Oceania	l'Océanie
the Arab states	les États arabes
the Near East	le Proche-Orient
the Middle East	le Moyen-Orient
the Far East	l'Extrême-Orient
South-East Asia	le sud-est asiatique
Western Europe	l'Europe occidentale
the developed countries	les pays développés
the developing countries	les pays en développement
the emerging countries	les pays émergents
the industrialised countries	les pays industrialisés

SOME COUNTRIES	**SÉLECTION DE PAYS**
England / Wales / Scotland / Ulster	L'Angleterre / le pays de Galles / l'Écosse / l'Irlande du Nord
Great-Britain / the United-Kingdom	La Grande-Bretagne / le Royaume-Uni
The United States of America	les États-Unis d'Amérique
the European Union (the EU)	l'Union européenne
Ireland	L'Irlande
France	La France
Germany	L'Allemagne
the Netherlands	Les Pays-Bas
Belgium	La Belgique
Spain	L'Espagne
Portugal	Le Portugal
Italy	L'Italie
Greece	La Grèce
Switzerland	La Suisse
Austria	L'Autriche
Poland	La Pologne
Russia	La Russie
Finland	La Finlande
Sweden	La Suède
Norway	La Norvège
Denmark	Le Danemark

Iceland	L'Islande
Canada	Le Canada
Quebec	Le Québec
Brazil	le Brésil
the West Indies	les Antilles
Australia	L'Australie
New Zealand	La Nouvelle-Zélande
Japan	Le Japon
China	La Chine
India	L'Inde
Burma	la Birmanie
Morocco	le Maroc
Egypt	L'Égypte
Turkey	La Turquie

LANGUAGES / ADJECTIVES	**LANGUES / ADJECTIFS**
English	anglais / anglaise
Welsh	gallois / galloise
Scottish	écossais / écossaise
Irish	irlandais / irlandaise
French	français / française
German	allemand / allemande
Dutch	néerlandais / néerlandaise
Spanish	espagnol / espagnole
Portuguese	portugais / portugaise
Italian	italien / italienne
Greek	grec / grecque
Swiss	suisse
Austrian	autrichien / autrichienne
Belgian	belge
Polish	polonais / polonaise
Russian	russe
Finnish	finlandais / finlandaise
Swedish	suédois / suédoise
Norwegian	norvégien / norvégienne
Danish	danois / danoise
Icelandic	islandais / islandaise
American	américain / américaine
Canadian	canadien / canadienne
Brazilian	brésilien / brésilienne
West Indian	antillais / antillaise
Australian	australien / australienne
a New Zealander	néo-zélandais / néo-zélandaise
Japanese	japonais / japonaise
Chinese	chinois / chinoise
Indian	indien / indienne

Burmese	birman / birmane
Moroccan	marocain / marocaine
Egyptian	égyptien / égyptienne
Turkish	turc / turque

EXCEPTIONS	**EXCEPTIONS**
a Briton	un Britannique
a Northern Irishman / woman	un Irlandais du Nord
a Welshman / woman	un Gallois
a Scotsman / woman	un Écossais
a Dane	un Danois
a Finn	un Finlandais
a Frenchman / woman	un Français / une Française
an Irishman	un Irlandais
a Dutchman	un Néerlandais
a Pole	un Polonais
a Spaniard	un Espagnol
a Turk	un Turc
a Quebecker	un Québécois
a Swiss	un Suisse
a Swede	un Suédois

DEMOGRAPHY	**LA DÉMOGRAPHIE**
a state, a State	un État
a territory	un territoire
a region	une région
a border, a boundary	une frontière
the frontier	la frontière sauvage
a people / to people	un peuple / peupler
a capital city	une capitale
a national anthem	un hymne national
the population density	la densité démographique
overpopulation	la surpopulation
the population growth	la croissance démographique
a baby boom / bust	une explosion / un effondrement démographique
heavily populated, populous	fortement peuplé
scarcely populated	faiblement peuplé
overcrowded	surpeuplé
mass migration	les mouvements migratoires massifs
a inhabitant / to inhabit	un habitant / habiter
uninhabited	désert, inhabité
the birth rate / the death rate	le taux de natalité / de mortalité
the fertility rate	le taux de fécondité
an age pyramid	une pyramide des âges
an age group	une classe d'âge

the gender imbalance	le déséquilibre hommes-femmes
the sex ratio	le ratio garçons-filles
an ageing population	une population vieillissante
a census	un recensement
the distribution	la répartition
a community	une communauté
per capita income	le revenu par habitant
an estimate	une estimation
to forecast / forecast	prévoir / des prévisions
to project / projections	projeter / des projections
to rise, to increase	augmenter
to level off	se stabiliser
to decrease, to fall, to lower	baisser, chuter, décroître
to improve / to worsen	s'améliorer, progresser / empirer
to decline	chuter
to peak	culminer
to collapse	s'effondrer
to boost	donner une impulsion à
a trend, a tendency	une tendance
to take action	prendre des mesures

DECOLONISATION, REFUGEES	**LA DÉCOLONISATION, LES RÉFUGIÉS**
a native (of)	un autochtone (de)
an ID card, an identity card	une carte d'identité
a colon	un colon
a coloniser	un colonisateur
an empire / imperialist	un empire / impérialiste
the slave trade	la traite des esclaves
a slave ship	un navire négrier
emancipation	l'émancipation
to enfranchise	affranchir, libérer
autonomy	l'autonomie
independence	l'indépendance
devolution	la décentralisation
a commonwealth	une communauté
freedom	la liberté (de faire)
liberty	la liberté (politique)
the Third World	le tiers-monde
foodstuffs	des denrées alimentaires
a burden	un fardeau
underfed	sous-alimenté
to airdrop food supplies	larguer des vivres
emergency food aid	l'aide alimentaire d'urgence
a refugee	un réfugié
a refugee camp	un camp de réfugiés
an asylum	un asile

to seek asylum	demander l'asile
humanitarianism	l'humanitarianisme
a charity	une association caritative
a NGO (non-governmental Organisation)	une ONG (organisation non gouvernementale)
a volunteer	un bénévole
an ethnic group / minority	un groupe / une minorité ethnique
ethnic cleansing	le nettoyage ethnique
debt relief	l'allégement de la dette
debt cancellation	l'effacement de la dette
to raise funds for	lever des fonds pour

ORGANISATIONS, ABBREVIATIONS AND ACRONYMS	**LES ORGANISATIONS, ABRÉVIATIONS ET ACRONYMES**
the League of Nations	la Société des Nations
the European Union (the EU)	l'Union européenne
the Council of Europe	le Conseil de l'Europe
the International Monetary Fund (IMF)	le FMI (Fonds monétaire international)
NATO (North Atlantic Treaty Organisation)	l'OTAN (l'Organisation du Traité de l'Atlantique Nord)
the UNO (United Nations Organisation)	les Nations Unies (l'ONU)
the WHO (World Health Organisation)	l'OMS (l'Organisation mondiale pour la Santé)
the Security Council	le Conseil de Sécurité
the World Bank	la Banque mondiale
UNESCO (the United Nations Educational Scientific and Cultural Organisation)	l'UNESCO
UNICEF (the United Nations International Children's Emergency Fund	l'UNICEF
the BRICS	le Brésil, la Russie, l'Inde, la Chine et l'Afrique du Sud
the Red Cross	la Croix rouge
Doctors Without Borders	Médecins sans Frontières
the Geneva Convention	la Convention de Genève
ASEAN (the Association of Southern Asian Nations)	l'ANASE
the Group of Eight, the G8	le G8 (Canada, France, Allemagne, Italie, Royaume-Uni, États-Unis, Russie, Japon)
the WTO (World Trade Organisation)	l'OMC (Organisation mondiale du commerce)
the OECD (Organisation for Economic Cooperation and Development)	l'OCDE

Translation: French-to-English exercise

Des Européens unis dans la diversité (adapté de la traduction officielle du site europa.eu)

L'Union européenne est une famille de pays démocratiques européens décidés à œuvrer ensemble à la paix et à la prospérité. Il ne s'agit pas d'un État destiné à se substituer aux États existants, mais l'Union européenne va plus loin que toute autre organisation internationale. En fait, c'est une organisation unique en son genre. Les États qui la composent ont mis en place des institutions communes auxquelles ils délèguent une partie de leur souveraineté, afin que les décisions sur des questions spécifiques d'intérêt commun puissent se prendre démocratiquement au niveau européen.

L'Europe est un continent caractérisé par de nombreuses traditions et langues différentes, mais aussi par des valeurs communes. Ce sont ces valeurs que défend l'Union européenne en instaurant une coopération toujours plus étroite entre ses peuples, en renforçant l'unité tout en préservant la diversité et en faisant en sorte que les décisions soient prises le plus près possible du citoyen.

Dans le monde de plus en plus interdépendant qui sera celui du XXIe siècle, le citoyen européen devra plus que jamais coopérer avec des peuples d'autres pays, dans un esprit de curiosité, de tolérance et de solidarité.

Adapted press excerpts (about 400 words)

Excerpt 1 – The amazing benefits of being bilingual (adapted from BBC)

Most people in the **world** speak more than one **language**, suggesting the human brain evolved to work in multiple **tongues**. If so, asks Gaia Vince, are those of us who speak only one language missing out? Many **countries** have more than one **official national language** – South Africa has 11. People are increasingly expected to speak, read and write at least one of a handful of "super" languages, such as **English, Chinese, Hindi, Spanish or Arabic**, as well. So to be monolingual, as many **native** English speakers are, is to be in the minority, and perhaps to be missing out. **Multilingualism** has been shown to have many social, psychological and lifestyle advantages. Moreover, researchers are finding a swathe of health benefits from speaking more than one language, including faster stroke recovery and delayed onset of dementia.

Excerpt 2 – The empire strikes back (adapted from *The Economist*)

The big achievement of the **Commonwealth**, a 54-member club sprung from the **British empire**, is its existence. Its current guise dates from 1949, when an **alliance** of Britain and a clutch of former **colonies** was rejigged to allow India to remain a **member** despite its plan to become a **republic**. Since then almost every former British **colony** has signed up to a club that retains the British **monarch** as its head. In a recent poll, half of Britons and Canadians could not name any Commonwealth activity. A quarter of Jamaicans thought Barack Obama was its head. As Britain inches towards the EU exit, many Conservatives wonder whether the Commonwealth might provide the template for an **alternative trade regime**.

Excerpt 3 – United by a Catchy Acronym (adapted from *The New York Times*)

BRICs, the now familiar term for **Brazil, Russia, India, China** and the growth of their economies and influence, have formalized their club and extended their reach by inviting **South Africa** to join. But do their meetings and joint statements really allow them to punch above their individual weight? What do these countries share beyond a common interest in bolstering their **global** clout? The most durable thing about the BRICs is the acronym itself. They cannot be ignored – emerging markets accounted for two-thirds of global economic growth over the past five years. But combining individual countries into classes based on catchy acronyms adds neither influence to their groupings nor insight into their futures.

Excerpt 4 – Age, kids and jobs affect where Americans live (adapted from *USA Today*)

The core of large **metropolitan areas** – cities of at least 1 million – drew a net 2.7 million young **adults** in the decade that ended in 2010. But they lost a net 1.4 million **children** and **family-age adults** (aged 30-49). Their suburbs gained a net 3.9 million people in the same age groups. Suburbs attracted people in every age group except 20-to-24-year-olds. Whether the **Millennials** – the generation of people born beginning around 1982 – make a U-turn to **suburbia** when they have kids is still in question [...] Certainly, the historical pattern has been for people to leave... There could be something different about the Millennial generation. So far, the needle hasn't moved.

Food for Thought and Quotations (about 500 words)

Population growth 2000-2100

According to the UN, the current world population (7.3 billion) is expected to reach 9.7 billion in 2050 and 11.2 billion in 2100. Until 2050, half of the world's population growth is expected to be concentrated in nine countries: India, Nigeria, Pakistan, DRC (Congo), Ethiopia, Tanzania, the USA, Indonesia and Uganda. China and India will remain the two largest countries in the world, each with more than 1 billion people, and India overtaking China by 2022. Meanwhile, the global number of persons aged 60 or above is expected to more than double by 2050 and more than triple by 2100: in Europe or in the USA a third of the population will be over 60 years of age by 2050. Life expectancy has increased significantly in the least developed countries in recent years, and is expected to carry on improving over the century. The young population of some regions of the world (South America, Africa...) will represent an opportunity to balance the ageing population of other areas. However, the predicted increase of population will complicate efforts to stamp out poverty, inequality and hunger. It might place further strain on health and education systems all around the world.

The English-speaking world today

Today, English is the second most popular mother tongue in the world, with an estimated half billion native speakers. English is the native mother-tongue of Britain, Ireland, USA, Canada, Australia, New Zealand and some Caribbean countries. But in about sixty more countries (Nigeria, Uganda, South Africa, India, Pakistan, Singapore, Philippines, Fiji, etc.), English is either the "official language" or spoken as a first language on a daily basis. Most of them are former colonies which have thoroughly integrated English into their institutions. It is also the common language for many non-English speakers worldwide, and almost a third of the globe's population – about 2.5 billion people – have basic competence in its use, whether written or spoken.

The European Union

The European Union is an economic and political union between 28 European countries (or 27, if one excludes the UK after the Brexit vote in 2016) that together cover much of the continent. The European Economic Community (EEC) was created in 1957 after the Treaty of Rome, and defined cooperation between six countries: Belgium, Germany, France, Italy, Luxembourg and the Netherlands. Since then, a single market and currency have been put in place and today the EU continues to develop towards its full potential, not only economic but also social. Thanks to the abolition of border controls between EU countries in 1993

(Treaty of Maastricht), people can today travel anywhere on the continent. An other purpose is to promote human rights both internally and around the world. Human dignity, freedom, democracy, equality and the rule of law are the core values of the EU. Multilingualism is central to the EU's cultural diversity: today the EU has 24 official languages.

The USA

The United States of America is the world's third largest country in size and nearly the third largest in terms of population. Its area is 9,826,630 square kilometres and its population over 300 million people. More than twice the size of the European Union, the United States has high mountains in the West and a vast central plain and it is bordered by two oceans and two countries (Canada and Mexico). Throughout its history, it has been a nation of immigration. In the early 17th century, settlers moved from Europe to the New World, established colonies, and displaced the native peoples. The settlers fought for their independence from Britain in the late 18th century and formed a union of thirteen states based on a new constitution in 1776. The nation continued to expand westward during the 19th century and even though it can be considered relatively young, it has become a global power, if not the leading economic power. Today, it is a federation of fifty states, plus the District of Columbia (Washington D.C). The biggest cities are New York, Los Angeles, Chicago and Houston.

"Population, when unchecked, increases in a geometrical ratio. Subsistence, increases only in an arithmetical ratio." Thomas Malthus

"After all the fertile land in the immediate neighbourhood of the first settlers were cultivated, if capital and population increased, more food would be required, and it could only be procured from land not so advantageously situated." David Ricardo

Chapter B

Soft and hard power

Vocabulary list

HUMAN RIGHTS	**LES DROITS HUMAINS**
individual liberties	les libertés individuelles
basic rights	les droits fondamentaux
civil liberties	les droits civiques
freedom of speech / opinion / thought / assembly / worship	liberté d'expression / d'opinion / de pensée / de réunion / de culte
protection	la protection
assistance	l'assistance
security / safety	la sécurité / l'absence de danger
national unity	l'unité nationale
legality, lawfulness	la légalité
liberty, equality, fraternity	liberté, égalité, fraternité
to promote human rights	défendre les droits de l'homme / droits humains
to guarantee	garantir
to abide by the law	respecter la loi
to enforce the law	faire respecter la loi
legitimate / legitimacy	légitime / la légitimité
a fundamental / inalienable right	un droit fondamental / inaliénable
the violation of human rights	la violation des droits humains / de l'homme
to push for change	militer pour le changement
to defend the weak	défendre les faibles
to uphold a principle	faire respecter un principe
censorship	la censure
to censor	censurer
to erode, to infringe on	éroder / empiéter sur
to restrict free speech	limiter la liberté d'expression
to be detained without charge	être détenu non inculpé
to remand sb into custody	placer qqn en détention provisoire
arbitrary power	l'arbitraire
an encroachment of the State	un empiétement de l'État
human rights abuses	les violations des droits de l'homme

HUMAN RIGHTS ABUSES	**VIOLATIONS DES DROITS DE LA PERSONNE**
a regime	un régime
totalitarian / totalitarianism	totalitaire / un totalitarisme
a dictatorship	une dictature
oppressive / repressive	oppressif / répressif
a dictator / a tyrant	un dictateur / un tyran
intimidation	l'intimidation
oppression / the oppressed	l'oppression / les opprimés
to crackdown on	réprimer
a death squad	un escadron de la mort
torture / a torturer	la torture / un bourreau
an execution / an executioner	une exécution / un bourreau

cruel / cruelty	cruel / la cruauté
inhumane	insensible, cruel
inhuman	inhumain
to exterminate / extermination	exterminer / l'extermination
to cleanse	nettoyer, purifier
to intern	interner, déporter
a concentration camp	un camp de concentration
a death camp	un camp d'extermination
to wipe out	exterminer
transportation	la déportation
rootlessness / to uproot	le déracinement / déraciner
exile	l'exil
an exile	un exilé
reduced to slavery	réduit à l'esclavage
enslaved	asservi

DIPLOMACY	**LA DIPLOMATIE**
the Foreign Office	le ministère des affaires étrangères (GB)
the Foreign secretary (GB)	le ministre des affaires étrangères (GB)
the Department of State (US)	le ministère des affaires étrangères (US)
the Secretary of State (in charge of the Department of State)	le Secrétaire d'état aux affaires étrangères (US)
foreign affairs	les affaires étrangères
the international stage, the world stage	la scène internationale
international law	le droit international
a diplomat / diplomatic	un diplomate / diplomatique
diplomacy	la diplomatie
a consulate	un consulat
a consul	un consul
an embassy	une ambassade
an ambassador	un ambassadeur
an envoy, an emissary	un émissaire
an attaché	un attaché
to be appointed	être nommé
a peacemaker	un conciliateur, pacificateur
a spokesman / spokeswoman	un porte-parole
a counterpart	un homologue
diplospeak	le langage diplomatique
to negotiate (GB) / to negociate (US)	négocier
negotiation, negociation	des négociations
talks	des pourparlers
peace talks	des pourparlers de paix
a summit	un sommet
a round table	une table ronde
the negotiating table	la table des négociations
the international community	la communauté internationale

international relations	les relations internationales
a consensus, a compromise	un consensus, un compromis
an agreement	un accord
a pact	un pacte
a treaty	un traité
to sign an agreement	signer un accord
to ratify a treaty	ratifier un traité
to foster a relationship with	entretenir des relations avec
to strike an alliance	former une alliance
a diplomatic breakthrough	une victoire diplomatique
a humanitarian mission	une mission humanitaire
to break off diplomatic relations	rompre les relations diplomatiques
to resume diplomatic relations	reprendre les relations diplomatiques
a thaw / a chill	un réchauffement / un refroidissement
to normalize relations	normaliser les relations
to make a concession	faire une concession
the mediator	le médiateur
to pledge to do	promettre de faire
to reach a settlement	conclure un accord
to recall an ambassador	rappeler son ambassadeur

POWER	**LE POUVOIR, LA PUISSANCE**
hegemony	l'hégémonie
a superpower	une superpuissance
expansionism	l'expansionnisme
unilateral / bilateral / multilateral	unilatéral / bilatéral / multilatéral
a bloc	un bloc
isolationism	l'isolationnisme
bipolar / multipolar	bipolaire / multipolaire
the balance of powers	l'équilibre des forces
a design	une intention, un projet
a member state	un État-membre
a founding member	un membre fondateur
to retaliate / retaliation	appliquer des mesures de représailles / des mesures de représailles
to enforce a resolution	appliquer une résolution
to maintain peace	maintenir la paix
the duty to interfere	le devoir d'ingérence
a peace process	un processus de paix
a blue helmet	un casque bleu
military intervention	une intervention militaire
a peacekeeper	un soldat de la paix
to authorize the use of force	autoriser le recours à la force
a stalemate, a deadlock	une impasse
an ultimatum	un ultimatum
to veto a decision	mettre son véto à une décision

THE MILITARY	**LES MILITAIRES**
the Army	l'armée
the troops / a trooper	les soldats / un homme de troupe
a soldier	un soldat
a private	un simple soldat
a serviceman	un militaire
a conscript / conscription (GB)	un appelé / le service militaire
a draftee / the draft (US)	un appelé / le service militaire
to be declared fit / unfit	apte / inapte, réformé
a conscientious objector	un objecteur de conscience
the rank and file	la troupe
a commanding officer	un commandant
to command	commander
a non-commissioned officer	un sous-officier
the hierarchy	la hiérarchie
stars / stripes / chevrons	étoiles / galons / chevrons
a uniform	un uniforme
to serve / be in the forces	servir / être dans l'armée
to enrol / to enlist	enrôler / s'engager dans l'armée
Join the Army	Engagez-vous !
the barracks	la caserne
the garrison	la garnison
a salute	un salut
fatigue / fatigues	les corvées / un treillis
night-vision goggles	des lunettes de vision nocturne
a gas mask	un masque à gaz
a flak jacket / a bulletproof jacket	un gilet pare-balles
drill, training	les exercices, l'entraînement
a drill instructor	un sergent instructeur
to march (past, on)	marcher au pas, défiler
attention / at ease	garde à vous / repos
a deserter / to desert	un déserteur / déserter
a mutineer / a mutiny	un mutin / une mutinerie
a traitor / treason	un traître / la trahison
the MP (Military Police)	la police militaire
a court martial	une cour martiale
a firing squad	un peloton d'exécution
to have someone shot	faire fusiller qqn

ARMED FORCES	**LES FORCES ARMÉES**
the Army corps	les corps d'armée
the Defence Minister	le ministre britannique de la défense
the Defense Secretary	Le secrétaire d'État à la défense américain
the Land forces	l'armée de terre
a unit	une unité
a division / a brigade	une division / une brigade

a regiment	un régiment
a battalion	un bataillon
a squad / a squadron	un escouade / un escadron
a platoon	une section
the infantry / the cavalry	l'infanterie / la cavalerie
a tank	un char
the signals	les transmissions
the artillery	l'artillerie
the Navy	la marine de guerre
the Royal Navy (GB)	la marine de guerre britannique
the US Navy	la marine de guerre américaine
an admiral	un amiral
a naval officer	un officier de marine
a lieutenant	un lieutenant
the fleet	la flotte
a warship	un navire de guerre
a battleship	un cuirassé
a submarine	un sous-marin
an aircraft carrier	un porte-avions
the Air Force	l'armée de l'air
the Royal Air Force (GB)	l'armée de l'air britannique
the US Air Force (USAF)	l'armée de l'air américaine
a pilot	un pilote
a war plane / a bomber	un avion de guerre / un bombardier
a helicopter	un hélicoptère
a fighter (plane)	un avion de combat
a scouting plane	un avion de reconnaissance
to scout	aller en éclaireur / en reconnaissance

Translation: French-to-English exercise

Soft power, hard power et smart power : le pouvoir selon Joseph Nye (adapté de *Slate*)

Avec son nouvel ouvrage, l'internationaliste américain poursuit sa réflexion sur la notion du pouvoir étatique au XXIe siècle. Après avoir défini le soft et le hard power, comment Nye voit-il le futur du pouvoir ?

Le soft power s'oppose au hard power, la force coercitive, militaire mais aussi économique, qui comprend la détention de ressources naturelles. Le soft, lui, ne se mesure ni en « carottes » ni en « bâtons », pour reprendre une image chère à l'auteur. Stricto sensu, le soft power est la capacité d'un État à obtenir ce qu'il souhaite de la part d'un autre État sans que celui-ci n'en soit même conscient.

La puissance étatique ne peut être que soft ou que hard. Théoriquement, un État au soft power développé sans capacité de se défendre militairement au besoin est tout au plus influent, et encore dans des limites évidentes.

À l'inverse, un État au hard power important pourra réussir des opérations militaires, éviter certains conflits ou imposer ses vues sur la scène internationale pour un temps, mais aura du mal à capitaliser politiquement sur ces « victoires ». L'idéal selon Nye ? Assez logiquement, un savant mélange de soft et de hard. Du pouvoir « intelligent » : le smart power.

Adapted press excerpts (about 400 words)

Excerpt 1 – Making up (adapted from *The Economist*)

From the earliest days America sought to **stand apart** from the vanities and machinations that had **corrupted monarchies** in Europe. Long before anyone had heard of an "**ethical foreign policy**", before the **revolution** even, America saw itself as a **model** for a better world. Over the course of a century or two, the **monarchies** and **dictatorships** gradually caught up. **Influence** abroad increasingly stemmed not just from **hard power** but also from **legitimacy**. Thanks to symbols ranging from Hollywood to NASA, America can draw on a rich store of **soft power**. Its **statesmen** generally do set out to make the world a better place. But the message can get scrambled. After the devastating attacks of September 11th 2001, American **foreign policy** lost its compass.

Excerpt 2 – The Return of the Utopians (adapted from *The New Yorker*)

What can today's **movements** for social and economic reform learn from the intentional communities of the nineteenth century? Contradiction and hypocrisy have always hovered over the utopian project, shadowing its promise of a better world with the sordid realities of human nature."There is a **tyranny** in the womb of every utopia," the French economist and futurist Bertrand de Jouvenel wrote. Indeed, utopia's name has become so tarnished that it has recently been used almost interchangeably with its evil twin, **dystopia** – a word coined by John Stuart Mill, three and a half centuries after the publication of More's Utopia, to describe a society that was "too bad to be practicable."

Excerpt 3 – Why Is the American Military So Bad at Teaching Others How to Fight? (adapted from *Slate*)

The task goes far beyond what U.S. **soldiers** are trained to teach. **Military training** is more complicated than many realize. Training is not just a matter of teaching soldiers how to **shoot** straight and **maneuver** on a **battlefield** (which American trainers do well). If the goal is to turn the fighting completely over to the local **armed forces**, then training must also involve teaching them how to conduct and call in **air strikes**, gather **intelligence** and apply it to **tactical operations**, **logistics**, and plan **operations** on a **strategic** or **theater-wide** level. To do all these things goes well beyond the abilities of American **infantry** or **special-operations forces** assigned to a **training mission**. In other words, the way we currently train, it may never be possible to make our client-armies completely **self-reliant**.

Excerpt 4 – Progress, regress and human rights (adapted from *Le Monde diplomatique*, English edition)

What or who is the referent of the statement "all humans are **born free**"? It is easy to realize that on the empirical level the sentence is undetermined, meaningless, empty. We are absolutely dependent on the care of others at the time of birth. We can refer to "**natural rights**", yet natural rights are **social constructs**. It implies a **commitment**, a **value**, a **norm**. If we accept the foundational sentence of modernity as valid, then we are in duty bound to treat all **humans** as our **equal** in the sense that they like us, are equally **freeborn**. The American founding fathers described **freedom** as the foundation in the most precise and philosophical way. They wrote: "we take these truths to be **self-evident**". The sentence expresses **commitment**, **responsibility**.

Food for Thought and Quotations (about 500 words)

Diplomacy

Diplomacy is the established method of influencing the decisions of foreign governments and peoples through dialogue and / or negotiation to prevent war or violence. It originates from ancient Greek, meaning an object folded in two. This folded document conferred a privilege, in particular a permit to travel. By extension, it came to refer to favours granted by rulers for an official mission. By 1900, the European diplomatic practices, inherited from the Renaissance idea of bilateral relations between sovereign states, expanded all through the world. Today it concerns summits, conferences, parliamentary diplomacy, but also non-official diplomacy and the work of civil servants for international affairs. A diplomat refers to an official representative allowed to carry out negotiations on behalf of a state.

Army and armed forces

Generally speaking, the term "*army*" refers to an organized military force equipped for fighting on land. "*Armed forces*" refers to a country's differed armed corps: army, navy, and air force. In the Encyclopaedia Britannica, *Army* is defined as a large organized force armed and trained for war, especially on land. The term may be applied to a large unit organized for independent action, or it may be applied to a nation's or ruler's complete military organization for land warfare. Throughout history, the character and organization of armies, political variations or weapons themselves have altered the definition and role of armies. Throughout history, they have been made up of professionals or amateurs (army or militia), of mercenaries fighting for money or of patriots fighting for a cause.

The Universal Declaration of Human Rights (1948) – Articles 1 to 5

Article 1. All human beings are born free and equal in dignity and rights. They are endowed with reason and conscience and should act towards one another in a spirit of brotherhood.

Article 2. Everyone is entitled to all the rights and freedoms set forth in this Declaration, without distinction of any kind, such as race, colour, sex, language, religion, political or other opinion, national or social origin, property, birth or other status. Furthermore, no distinction shall be made on the basis of the political, jurisdictional or international status of the country or territory to which a person belongs, whether it be independent, trust, non-self-governing or under any other limitation of sovereignty.

Article 3. Everyone has the right to life, liberty and security of person.

Article 4. No one shall be held in slavery or servitude; slavery and the slave trade shall be prohibited in all their forms.

Article 5. No one shall be subjected to torture or to cruel, inhuman or degrading treatment or punishment.

"*I hope that our wisdom will grow with our power, and teach us, that the less we use our power the greater it will be.*" Thomas Jefferson

"*If all mankind minus one, were of one opinion, and only one person were of the contrary opinion, mankind would be no more justified in silencing that one person, than he, if he had the power, would be justified in silencing mankind.*" John Stuart Mill, On Liberty

"*That's the whole point of good propaganda. You want to create a slogan that nobody's going to be against, and everybody's going to be for. Nobody knows what it means, because it doesn't mean anything.*" Noam Chomsky

Chapter C

Terrorism and warfare

Vocabulary list

TERRORISM	**LE TERRORISME**
terror	la terreur
a terrorist	un terroriste
a spate of terrorism	une vague d'attentats
a bomb scare	une alerte à la bombe
a terrorist attack	un attentat terroriste
a terrorist group	un groupe terroriste
to mount a terrorist attack	organiser un attentat
to carry out an attack	perpétrer un attentat
a suicide attack	un attentat suicide
a plastic explosive	un engin au plastic
random bombings	des attentats à la bombe aveugles
a time bomb	une bombe à retardement
a civilian target	une cible civile
to execute / an execution	exécuter / une exécution
to slaughter	massacrer
a massacre / a slaughter	un massacre
a mass killing	une tuerie
a genocide	un génocide
to terrorize	terroriser
to hit a target	frapper une cible
to gun down	abattre
to blow up	faire sauter
an abduction / an abductee	un enlèvement / un otage (retenu prisonnier)
to take sb hostage	prendre qqn en otage
to detain / a detainee	retenir en captivité / un détenu
a hostage	un otage
hostage taking	la prise d'otages
a hostage taker	un preneur d'otages
to imprison	emprisonner
to swap hostages	échanger des otages
to rescue	sauver, libérer
to release, to free	libérer
to issue an ultimatum	fixer un ultimatum
to tighten security	renforcer la sécurité
border controls	les contrôles aux frontières
to X-ray luggage	passer les bagages aux rayons X
drastic measures	des mesures radicales / draconiennes

WAR	**LA GUERRE**
World War 1 (US), WWI	la Première Guerre mondiale
The Second World War (GB), WWII	la Seconde Guerre mondiale
to break out	éclater
to initiate a conflict	amorcer un conflit

the escalation of violence	l'escalade de la violence
to be doomed	être condamné
a ceasefire	un cessez-le-feu
a truce	une trêve
a peace agreement / a peace treaty	un accord de paix / un traité de paix
disarmament	le désarmement
to defuse a crisis	désamorcer une crise
to trigger off a conflict	déclencher un conflit
to be drawn into war	être entraîné dans la guerre
to go to / to be at war	aller / être en guerre
to wage war	faire la guerre
hostility	l'hostilité
a pact of neutrality	un pacte de neutralité
a coalition	une coalition
to side with	prendre le parti de
a conflict zone	une zone de conflit
a battle / the battlefield	une bataille / le champ de bataille
the enemy lines	les lignes ennemies
to aggress / an aggressor	agresser / un agresseur
the front / the rear	le front / l'arrière
a campaign / an attack	une campagne / une attaque
an ambush	une embuscade
to loom / looming	menacer / menaçant
to harass	harceler
a war of attrition	une guerre d'usure
a war of nerves	une guerre des nerfs
a trench warfare	une guerre de tranchées
guerilla warfare / a guerilla	la guérilla / un guérillero
full-scale war	la guerre totale
a blitzkrieg (GB)	une guerre éclair
an attack, an onset / an action	une attaque / un combat
a surgical strike	une attaque chirurgicale
collateral damage	les dégâts collatéraux
a landing	un débarquement
an air raid	un raid aérien
backup	les renforts

WARFARE	**LES HOSTILITÉS**
to conquer / to invade	conquérir / envahir
a conquest / an invasion	une conquête / une invasion
to occupy / to retreat	occuper / battre en retraite
an occupation / a retreat	une occupation / une retraite
to stampede away / a stampede	partir à la hâte / la débâcle
warlike	belliqueux
to overcome	battre, vaincre
to outnumber	submerger en nombre

to crush	écraser
to launch an offensive	lancer une offensive
an onslaught	un assaut
a manoeuvre, a move	une manœuvre, une action
a strategy	une stratégie
a landmark	un point de repère
a target / to target	une cible / cibler
to snipe / a sniper	tirer (caché) / un tireur d'élite
anti-aircraft defense fire	un tir de DCA (défense contre-aérienne)
an artillery barrage	un tir de barrage d'artillerie
a sham attack	une attaque simulée
a diversion	une diversion
to encircle	encercler
a freedom fighter / to resist	un résistant / résister
sabotage	le sabotage
reprisal, retaliation	des représailles
war crimes	les crimes de guerre
pitiless, relentless	impitoyable, implacable
a crime against humanity	un crime contre l'humanité
a round up, a roundup	une rafle
to ensnare	prendre au piège
a mass execution	une exécution de masse
a breach of convention	une violation de convention
to surrender to	se rendre, capituler devant
to extradite	extrader
an international court	une cour pénale internationale
war reparation	les réparations de guerre
a prisoner of war (a POW)	un prisonnier de guerre
the release of prisoners	la libération de prisonniers
damage	les dégâts
rubble	les décombres
ruins	les ruines
cannon fodder	la chair à canon
the Allies	les Alliés
a war memorial	un mémorial de guerre
a ceremony	une cérémonie
a veteran	un vétéran, ancien combattant
to commemorate	commémorer
a tribute	un hommage
to award a medal to	remettre une médaille à

WEAPONS	**LES ARMES**
a weapon / weaponry	une arme / l'armement
a blade	une lame
a sword	une épée
a dagger	une dague

a spear	une lance
a slingshot	un lance-pierres
an arrow / a bow	une flèche / un arc
an archer	un archer
a cannon / cannonball	un canon / un boulet de canon
gunpowder	la poudre à canon
ammunition, ammo	les munitions
a pistol	un pistolet
a rifle	un fusil
a gun	une arme à feu, un fusil / un canon
a machine-gun	une mitrailleuse
a bullet	une balle
a handgrenade	une grenade
anti-personnel landmines	des mines antipersonnel
a mortar	un mortier
a cluster-bomb	une bombe à fragmentation
a shell	un obus
a warhead	une ogive
a missile	un missile
a cruise missile	un missile de croisière
a homing missile	un missile à tête chercheuse / téléguidé
a rocket / a rocket-launcher	une roquette / un lance-roquettes
mustard gas	le gaz moutarde
napalm	le napalm
nerve gas	le gaz paralysant
weapons of mass destruction (WMDs)	les armes de destruction massive
chemical warfare	la guerre chimique
bacteriological warfare	la guerre bactériologique
nuclear warfare	la guerre nucléaire
an arms dealer	un marchand d'armes
an arms manufacturer	un fabricant d'armes
the arms race	la course à l'armement
arms exports	les exportations d'armes

NUCLEAR PROLIFERATION	**LA PROLIFÉRATION NUCLÉAIRE**
a nuclear weapon	une arme nucléaire
a nuke	une tête nucléaire / une bombe nucléaire
to deploy nukes	déployer des bombes nucléaires
A-bomb / H-bomb	la bombe atomique / bombe à hydrogène
a nuclear test	un essai nucléaire
nuclear fallout	les retombées radioactives
to detonate	faire exploser
a nuclear warhead	une ogive nucléaire
an anti-missile shield	un bouclier anti-missile
intercontinental	intercontinental
a short- / long-range missile	un missile à courte / longue portée

the launchpad	l'aire de lancement
fissile materials	les matériaux fissiles
to enrich uranium	enrichir l'uranium
a nuclear weapons facility	une installation de production d'armes nucléaires
a uranium-processing facility	une usine d'enrichissement d'uranium
the Nuclear weapons Non-Proliferation Treaty (the NNPT)	le traité de non-prolifération nucléaire
a deterrent	un moyen de dissuasion
the nuclear deterrent power	la force de dissuasion nucléaire
to retaliate	riposter, user de mesures de représailles
the strike force	la force de frappe
to pose a threat	représenter une menace
a rogue state	un État-voyou
nuclear disarmament	le désarmement nucléaire
a moratorium	un moratoire
an onsite inspection	une inspection sur site
to call for sanctions	demander des sanctions
to demand	exiger
to ban nuclear testing	interdire les essais nucléaires
to dismantle facilities	démanteler les installations
a nuclear-free zone	une zone dénucléarisée
cyberwar	la guerre informatique

Translation: French-to-English exercise

Les sociétés modernes vulnérables au fanatisme (adapté de *Libération* et *La Croix*)

L'espérance spontanée des Français encourageant les responsables politiques à trouver ensemble les réponses à ces agressions a été déçue : les petits calculs ont engendré un profond scepticisme sur leur capacité collective à écarter la menace. Tout le monde aurait beaucoup à perdre face à une montée des extrêmes. Excepté ceux qui veulent en finir avec le respect du droit et ajouter ainsi des tensions sur le territoire national.

Nos sociétés ne savent plus produire de l'espérance, elles sont désormais incapables de donner à leurs valeurs rationnelles, tolérantes, humanistes, ce caractère de grandeur et de noblesse sans lequel elles ne sont que des coquilles creuses. Un vide qui ouvre la porte au retour de Dieu sous son visage humainement le plus mortifère.

Adapted press excerpts (about 400 words)

Excerpt 1 – Counter-terrorism – Driving away the shadows (adapted from *The Economist*)

Early intervention to prevent **terrorism** is tough to get right. Britain does not do a bad job. Like other countries, Britain puts as much, if not more effort into **dissuading** vulnerable people from following the **extremists**' proclamations. Much of this work comes under the **Prevent strategy**. Prevent is one of four strands of **counter-terror** efforts, alongside **Pursue** (to stop **attacks**), **Protect** (to reduce **vulnerability**) and **Prepare** (to minimise the impact of **attacks**). It includes Channel, a programme in which those identified as being at risk of **radicalisation** are offered a tailored package of education, counselling and support.

Excerpt 2 – Criminals are the law in Syria (adapted from *Le Monde diplomatique*, English edition)

Late last year, a report by **Human Rights Watch** titled To Stem the Flow of Syrian **Refugees**, Stop the Barrel Bombs (a **barrel bomb** is a large metal canister packed with **shrapnel** and **explosives**, hurled from an aircraft) evoked the lesson of Hama: "What makes the Syrian war so ugly is that the Assad government is also **attacking civilians** who live in areas seized by the **armed opposition**. The aim of this **war-crime strategy** is to depopulate these regions and send a lesson to other Syrians that they will be attacked if the opposition takes their neighbourhood."

Excerpt 3 – From Hiroshima to a Nuke-Free World (adapted from *The International New York Times*)

As the highest-ranking official in an American administration ever to visit Hiroshima, Secretary of State John Kerry paid respects to the victims of one of the most devastating **acts** of World War II and reflected on how Japan and the United States have forged a strong **alliance** over the past 70 years. He also emphasized that "**war** must never be the first **resort**" and urged a continued push for a world free from **nuclear weapons**. President Obama has achieved some important measures, most notably the 2015 Iran **nuclear deal**, which has significantly curbed Iran's ability to develop a **nuclear weapon**, and the 2010 New START treaty mandating cuts in the number of **strategic nuclear warheads** deployed by the United States and Russia to 1,550 **warheads** each.

Excerpt 4 – Is Cyberwar Turning Out to Be Very Different From What We Thought? (adapted from *Politico*)

In a 2012 speech, then-**Secretary of Defense** Leon Panetta warned Americans they could face a "cyber Pearl Harbor" someday at the hands of a **terrorist group** or **enemy state**. But for the most part, **cyberwar** hasn't yet turned out that way – at least so far. The world has not yet seen nations use computers to **launch surprise attacks** on factories or refineries, **set tanks on fire**, **bring down aircraft**, or shut down an adversary's **military**. Nor have we seen terrorists use computers to **wreak** much destruction at all. With rare exceptions like the Stuxnet virus that took out Iran's nuclear centrifuges, what we have seen from nation-states is more the sort of behavior one would expect from **spies** than **soldiers**, establishing cyberspace as a clear realm for **espionage** and less so for **war**.

Food for Thought and Quotations (about 500 words)

The UN (United Nations Organisation)

The United Nations is an international organization founded in 1945, at the end of the Second World War. It is currently made up of 193 Member states, which together promote international co-operation. Today, the United Nations can take action on the issues confronting humanity in the 21st century, such as peace and security, climate change, sustainable development, human rights, disarmament, terrorism, humanitarian and health emergencies, gender equality, governance, food production, and more. The organization won the Nobel Peace Prize in 2001. However, evaluations of the UN's effectiveness have been mixed. Some commentators claim that the organization is an important force for peace and human development, while others have blamed its inefficiency and corruption. There is no denying that the UN has taken on major military and peacekeeping missions across the world with varying degrees of success.

A History of Warfare, by John Keegan

This reference book gives a comprehensive historical overview of *warfare* (engagement in or the activities involved in war or conflict) around the world, from primitive ages to the 20th century. The subject is studied through five main themes: war in human history, fortifications, flesh, iron, and fire. The author insists that the most noble persons in society are not the philosopher-kings but the warrior caste, which makes a difference with previous analyses of warfare. Keegan also argues that the Western society has created a dichotomy in which politicians seek peace and commerce while the military guarantee the use of force if necessary. This opposition is termed **soft** / **hard** power (power of conviction / use of force). Peacekeepers, he finally suggests, would benefit from studying primitive warmaking, in order to understand the risks posed by the war against terrorism, an invisible enemy that can strike globally.

The START treaty on nuclear proliferation

The U.S.-Soviet Strategic Arms Reduction Treaty, known as START 1, was signed in 1991 by U.S. President George H.W. Bush and Soviet President Mikhail Gorbachev. START 1 was the first international treaty to provide for consistent reductions of U.S. and Russian strategic nuclear weapons. It guaranteed the stability of the strategic balance and served as a framework for further agreements. "*The New START Treaty responsibly reduces the number of nuclear weapons and launchers that the United States and Russia deploy, while fully maintaining America's nuclear deterrent*", declared President Barack Obama while signing the 2010 agreement. In other words, this updated treaty aims to divide by two the number of strategic nuclear missile launchers, while ensuring new inspection and verification processes that will make it more transparent.

The future of warfare

Robotic weapons, whether autonomous or remote controlled, have generated widespread controversy in recent years. Robots play a prominent role in our collective vision of future combat, through science-fiction movies and their anthropomorphic cyborgs. In reality, robots must be defined precisely: they are programmable machines that can sense and interact with their environment. Therefore, most advanced weapons systems are robotic, including cruise missiles, drones, and air and missile defense systems. These already exist and spread fast through the various countries involved in a conflict. The goal is to deploy unmanned forces on the battlefield, thus limiting the number of casualties. Another possibility is to offer soldiers combined equipment, in order to improve reaction times, precision, and strength. The ultimate goal is to develop super-soldiers, but these designs inevitably raise ethical and tactical concerns, particularly as regards the place of such cyborgs in a democratic society, and the necessity to define their responsibility in the military decision loop. Clearly there is still a long way to go to master the implications of these technological improvements.

"*We shall defend our island, whatever the cost may be, we shall fight on the beaches, we shall fight on the landing grounds, we shall fight in the fields and in the streets, we shall fight in the hills; we shall never surrender.*" Winston Churchill

Chapter D
Intelligence

Vocabulary list

INTELLIGENCE SERVICES	**SERVICES DE RENSEIGNEMENT**
espionage, intelligence	l'espionnage, les renseignements
counter-espionage	le contre-espionnage
an agent	un agent de renseignements
to inform / an informer	informer / un informateur
information	des informations, renseignements
a secret mission	une mission secrète
secrecy / a secret	le secret / un secret
a spy / to spy	un espion / espionner
security	la sécurité (intérieure)
industrial espionage	l'espionnage industriel
a double agent	un agent double
to go on a mission	partir en mission
to defect to the enemy	passer du côté de l'ennemi
a defector	un transfuge
the MI5, MI6 (Military Intelligence 5, 6)	la direction de la sécurité intérieure / extérieure britannique
SIS (Secret Intelligence Service)	le service britannique de renseignements et espionnage
the NSA (National Security Agency)	la NSA (sécurité intérieure US)
the CIA (Central Intelligence Agency)	la CIA (sécurité extérieure US)
the Intelligence service	les services secrets
a global surveillance program	un programme de surveillance mondiale
to violate the Espionage Act	enfreindre la loi sur l'Espionnage
mass surveillance	la surveillance de masse / massive
government secrecy	le secret d'État

SURVEILLANCE STRATEGIES	**LES STRATÉGIES DE SURVEILLANCE**
a surveillance society	une société surveillée
privacy	le droit à la vie privée / l'intimité
to intrude on / to breach sb's privacy	porter atteinte à la vie privée de qqn
to arrest	arrêter
to search	fouiller
CCTV (closed circuit television)	la surveillance caméra en circuit fermé
to record	enregistrer
video surveillance	la vidéosurveillance
a monitor	un moniteur
to monitor	surveiller
to keep a watch on someone	mettre qqn sous surveillance
to spy on sb	espionner qqn
to track sb	suivre la trace de qqn
a bug / to bug	un micro caché / placer qqn sur écoute
to tap sb's phone	placer qqn sur écoute téléphonique
to eavesdrop / eavesdropping	écouter / les écoutes illicites
to put sb on file	ficher qqn

police footage	des séquences vidéo filmées par la police
a police state	un État policier
the promotion of privacy	la défense de la vie privée
data / personal data	des informations, des données personnelles
a database	une base de données
to retrieve data	rechercher des données
to gather data, to collect data	rassembler des données
to mine / utilize data	exploiter des données
to store data	enregistrer, conserver des données
a bank statement	un relevé bancaire
a telephone bill	une facture de téléphone
a medical record	un dossier médical
measure / countermeasure	mesures / contre-mesures
intelligence gathering	la collecte de renseignements
tradecraft	les (techniques de) renseignements
clandestine	clandestin
codebreaking	le décodage
cryptanalysis	la cryptanalyse
a spy satellite	un satellite espion
satellite photography	la photographie satellite
furtive watch	la surveillance furtive
a dead-letter box	une boîte aux lettres secrète
a cut-out	un intermédiaire fiable (un coupe-circuit)
a spy ship	un navire espion / collecteur de renseignements
disinformation	la désinformation
identity theft	l'usurpation d'identité
an infiltration technique	une technique d'infiltration
an agent provocateur / an inciting agent	un agent provocateur
forgery	la contrefaçon
device concealment	le fait de cacher un appareil pour espionner
mobile phone tracking	la localisation de téléphone portable
a tracking system	un système de repérage

ACTIVISM	**L'ACTIVISME**
a leak	une fuite
the disclosure	la divulgation, dénonciation, publication
a revelation	une révélation
classified	secret
transparency	la transparence, la clarté
activism	l'activisme, le militantisme
the right to information privacy	le droit au respect de la vie privée
the civil society	la société civile
a whistleblower	un lanceur d'alerte
a dissident	un dissident
a subterfuge	un subterfuge

a contractor	un indépendant, un contractuel
a tally	une liste, un recensement
a cascade / torrent of disclosures	une cascade de révélations
to divulge / to leak information	divulguer des informations
a prior authorization	une autorisation préalable
to bolster	soutenir, renforcer
evidence	des preuves
to restraint	contraindre, retenir
to root out	démanteler, éradiquer
a subpoena	une assignation / citation à comparaître
an operative	un opérateur, un agent
to collect information	recueillir des informations
implicit / explicit	implicite / explicite
anonymity	l'anonymat
to underscore	souligner
to grant asylum	accorder l'asile

LEAKS	**LES FUITES**
an anonymous source	une source anonyme
a non-profit organisation	une organisation à but non lucratif
a volunteer	un bénévole
to launch a website	lancer un site web
to publish	publier
to encrypt / the encryption	crypter, chiffrer / le cryptage, le chiffrement
a password / a passphrase	un mot de passe / une phrase de chiffrement
a full cache	une mémoire cache pleine
to access documents	accéder à des documents
a trove	un trésor
reportedly	selon certaines sources
an estimate	une estimation
theft of government property	vol de propriétés d'État
a domestic spying program	un programme d'espionnage intérieur
an investigation	une enquête
an investigation report	un rapport d'enquête
to claim a database	prétendre détenir une base de données
an expenditure	une dépense
a compilation of documents	une compilation de documents
a diplomatic cable	un câble diplomatique
graphic footage	des images choquantes
to shed heat / to shed light	mettre de l'huile sur le feu / mettre au jour
a war-related secret	un secret ayant trait à la guerre
to map	cartographier
corruption	la corruption
an insurgent	un insurgé

a source	un indicateur
a primary source	une source primaire, directe
a data breach	violation, fuite de données
sensitive data	des données sensibles
the headquarters, the HQ	le quartier général, le QG
the flow of information	la diffusion des informations
to regulate	réguler, réglementer
indictment / to indict	la mise en accusation / inculper
a defense line	une ligne de défense
the freedom of speech	la liberté de parole
to bring information to the public	informer le public
uncensorable	non censurable
the bulletproof hosting	un hébergement internet à l'épreuve des balles
to endanger lives	mettre des vies en danger
to abridge freedom	restreindre la liberté

PRIVACY	**LA VIE PRIVÉE**
to have nothing to hide	n'avoir rien à cacher
to erode individual liberties	rogner les libertés individuelles
to protect one's privacy	protéger son intimité
data protection legislation	la loi sur l'informatique et les libertés
commercial abuse	les abus commerciaux
a safeguard	un garde-fou
to safeguard	protéger
special powers	des pouvoirs spéciaux
to monitor sb's e-mail	surveiller la correspondance électronique
to observe sb	observer qqn
a cookie	un mouchard informatique, un cookie
a computer hacker	un pirate informatique
to poke one's nose into	fourrer son nez dans
to pry into private lives	fouiller dans la vie intime
a snooper	un fouineur
to snoop on	espionner qqn
an intrusion / intrusive	une intrusion / intrusif
to be wired	être branché
to impersonate sb	usurper l'identité de qqn
the global village	le village planétaire / « global » (anglicisme)

BONUS	**BONUS**
professional confidentiality	le **secret** professionnel
*to keep a **secret***	garder un secret
*to let sb in on a **secret***	mettre qqn dans la confidence
*to **leak** out / in*	être divulgué / s'infiltrer
*counsel for the **defence***	avocat de la défense

witness for the ***prosecution***	témoin de l'accusation / à charge
to come to sb's ***defence***	prendre la défense de qqn
a ***control*** *freak*	qqn qui veut out contrôler
damage ***control***	le contrôle des dégâts
to ***control*** *over someone*	prendre le contrôle sur qqn
under control / out of ***control***	sous contrôle / hors de contrôle
spin ***control***	la manipulation des médias
to out a ***spy***	révéler l'identité d'un espion
a spook ***network***	un réseau de barbouzes
protect *one's resources*	protéger ses informateurs
a sleeper ***agent****, a deep cover agent*	un agent dormant
a false flag ***operation***	une opération sous faux pavillon
sigint (signals intelligence)	le renseignement à partir de signaux électromagnétiques
hackint (hacking intelligence)	le renseignement par piratage
comint (communication intelligence)	l'écoute des communications radio
geoint (geospatial intelligence)	le renseignement géospatial
humint (human intelligence)	le renseignement à partir d'informations humaines

Translation: French-to-English exercise

La confiance en Obama ébranlée (adapté du *Figaro*)

La NSA aurait espionné trois présidents français entre 2006 et 2012. Les relations franco-américaines pâtiront de ce scandale. La confiance de la France est durablement entamée. Les protagonistes de cette lamentable affaire sont censés œuvrer en alliés face aux ambitions nucléaires de l'Iran, aux manœuvres de la Russie ou à la barbarie conquérante de l'État islamique.

On entend déjà les sarcasmes d'Ali Khamenei, de Vladimir Poutine et du « calife » Al-Baghdadi. Les présidents américains se méfient donc des présidents français, qui leur ont pourtant maintes fois démontré leur franchise ! Malgré les discours, Barack Obama n'a rien changé aux méthodes de Bush et Cheney. C'est une erreur stratégique qui affecte le standing de l'Amérique, et un échec de plus pour ce président américain que les Français avaient plébiscité.

Adapted press excerpts (about 400 words)

Excerpt 1 – Hackers create "Eye of Sauron" – inspired malware to spy on international agencies and has already hit 30 organizations, experts say (adapted from *The Daily Mail*)

A **hacker** group known as "Strider" has been in stealth for five years, as it carried out **cyber-espionage attacks** against select **targets** across the globe. In the hidden **malware**, experts found references to "Sauron" the all-seeing title character in The Lord of the Rings, which earn them the name "ProjectSauron". Using Remsec, an advanced piece of hidden malware, these online **pirates** have been **spying** on organizations in Russia, China, Belgium, Iran and Sweden since 2011. Remsec shares certain unusual **coding** similarities with another older piece of nation state-grade **malware** known as Flamer, or Flame. The malware used in these secretive attacks focuses on **intelligence-gathering**, which functions as a framework allowing Project Sauron to infect and **control computers**, move across **networks** and **exfiltrate data**.

Excerpt 2 – "Shadow Brokers" Leak: Was the N.S.A. Hacked? (adapted from *The New York Times*)

The release on websites of what appears to be **top-secret** computer code that the National Security Agency has used to **break into** the **networks** of foreign governments and other **espionage targets** has caused deep concern inside American **intelligence agencies**, raising the question of whether America's own elite operatives have been **hacked** and their methods revealed. They contained genuine samples of the code – though somewhat outdated – used in the production of the N.S.A.'s custom-built **malware**. Most of the code was designed to **break through** network **firewalls** and get inside the computer systems of competitors like Russia, China and Iran. That, in turn, allows the N.S.A. to place "implants" in the system, which can lurk unseen for years and be used to **monitor network traffic** or enable a debilitating computer attack.

Excerpt 3 – What Snowden and Manning Don't Understand About Secrecy (adapted from *The Atlantic*)

Government often finds bad reasons to keep **information hidden**, but the recent indiscriminate **leaks** are foolish. There are many **legitimate reasons** for governments to keep secrets, among them the need to preserve the **element of surprise** in military operations or criminal investigations, to permit leaders and diplomats to bargain candidly, and to **protect the identities** of those we ask to perform dangerous and difficult missions. The most famous **leakers** in American history were motivated not by a general opposition to **secrecy** but by a desire to **expose** specific wrongdoing.

Excerpt 4 – Green light to powers for UK spy agencies to collect bulk data (adapted from *The Independent*)

Powers that allow **spy agencies** to harvest **bulk data** were today given the go-ahead by the UK's terror-law watchdog. Prime Minister Theresa May welcomed the findings claiming it showed how the powers, which she is currently trying to cement in legislation, are of "crucial importance" to **MI5, MI6 and GCHQ**. [...] Bulk powers "play an important part in **identifying, understanding** and **averting threats** in Great Britain, Northern Ireland and further afield". The techniques are used across a range of agency activity, from **cyber-defence**, **counter-espionage** and **counter-terrorism** to child sexual abuse and **organised crime**.

Food for Thought and Quotations (about 500 words)

Deep Throat: The Watergate (1972)

Watergate was a major political scandal that occurred in the United States in the 1970s, following a break-in at the Democratic National Committee (DNC) headquarters in Washington, D.C. and President Richard Nixon's administration's attempted cover-up of its involvement. The origins of the Watergate hotel break-in lay in the hostile politics of the 1960s, mainly the Vietnam War that divided the US population. In such a harsh political climate, a forceful presidential campaign seemed essential to the president's key advisers. Mark Felt, the "Deep Throat" was an informant for *Washington Post* journalists Bob Woodward and Carl Bernstein. He revealed that the Nixon Administration was energetically abusing the powers of the presidency by covering up the wrongdoings. Nixon was compelled to resign two years after. Since then, the suffix *-gate* has been used many times to allude to political scandals.

Whistleblowers: Edward Snowden and PRISM

A whistleblower is a person who informs on a person or organization regarded as engaging in an unlawful, unethical or immoral activity. They can reach out to the media, government, law enforcement but also face severe retaliation from those who are alleged of wrongdoing. The ethical implications of whistleblowing revolve around debates about whether and when one has an obligation to blow the whistle. One famous whistleblower is Edward Snowden, a former National Security Agency contractor, who disclosed classified material on top-secret NSA programs including the PRISM surveillance program to *The Guardian* and *The Washington Post* in June 2013. PRISM was a clandestine monitoring program that aimed to collect internet communications from major US internet companies (Microsoft, Apple, Yahoo!, AOL, Facebook, YouTube, Google, Skype, Twitter and so on), and thus create the number one source of gathered raw intelligence in the US.

After the NSA hacking, the NSA hacked!

It seems that the National Security Agency has recently been hacked, several years after the Snowden revelations. A collective of hackers known as the Shadow Brokers is selling off cyber-spying tools, which allegedly belong to the U.S. government, in an online auction. Analysis of software made freely available to prove its legitimacy suggests that it is genuine, and belongs to the National Security Agency. The Shadow Brokers claimed that their initial public release of the software included tools that could be used to break into firewall systems from companies. They urgently patched vulnerabilities in their firewall systems, which may have been exploited since as early as 2013. Such an event does not come without a sense of irony, since the NSA was itself at the core of a hacking scandal a few years ago, when Edward Snowden revealed that NSA agents had been successfully developing global surveillance programs for decades.

Wikileaks

WikiLeaks is an international not-for-profit media organisation that publishes secret information, news leaks, and classified media from anonymous sources. Julian Assange, an Australian Internet activist, is generally considered as its founder. The broad principles on which their work is based are the defence of freedom of speech and media publishing. In ten years, WikiLeaks has sustained and triumphed against legal and political attacks designed to silence their anonymous sources. Some of the stories Wikileaks has broken concern abuses of human rights, government transparency, spying and (counter-)intelligence, ecology, corruption, internet filtering, finance and censorship. For example, they released confidential information on the war in Afghanistan, in Iraq, on the Guantanamo Bay detention camp. They involuntarily made available the diplomatic cables of the US Department of State in 2011. In 2013, Bradley Manning, a United States Army soldier, disclosed to WikiLeaks nearly three-quarters of a million classified or unclassified but sensitive military and diplomatic documents. He was convicted by court-martial of espionage.

"*Under observation, we act less free, which means we effectively are less free.*" Edward Snowden

"*In a time of universal deceit – telling the truth is a revolutionary act.*" George Orwell, *1984*

Appendices

Appendix 1

Review cards about language

Review card 1

All irregular verbs in English

Infinitif	Prétérit	Participe passé	Traduction
abide	abided / abode	abided / abode	se conformer à
arise	arose	arisen	survenir
awake	awaked / awoke	awaked / awoken	s'éveiller
be	**was / were**	**been**	**être**
bear	bore	borne	porter
beat	**beat**	**beaten**	**battre**
become	**became**	**become**	**devenir**
befall	befell	befallen	advenir
beget	begot	begotten	engendrer
begin	**began**	**begun**	**commencer**
behold	beheld	beheld	contempler
bend	bent	bent	courber
bereave	bereaved / bereft	bereaved / bereft	priver
beseech	besought	besought	implorer
beset	beset	beset	assaillir
bestride	bestrode	bestridden	enfourcher
bet	bet / betted	bet / betted	parier
bid	bade / bid	bid / bidden	offrir / ordonner
bind	**bound**	**bound**	**lier**
bite	**bit**	**bitten**	**mordre**
bleed	**bled**	**bled**	**saigner**
blow	**blew**	**blown**	**souffler**
break	**broke**	**broken**	**casser**
breed	bred	bred	élever
bring	**brought**	**brought**	**apporter**
broadcast	broadcast	broadcast	diffuser
build	**built**	**built**	**construire**
burn	**burnt**	**burnt**	**brûler**

Infinitif	Prétérit	Participe passé	Traduction
burst	burst	burst	éclater
buy	**bought**	**bought**	**acheter**
cast	cast	cast	jeter
catch	**caught**	**caught**	**attraper**
chide	chid	chid / chidden	réprimander
choose	**chose**	**chosen**	**choisir**
cleave	cleft / clove	cleft / cloven	fendre
cling	clung	clung	s'accrocher
come	**came**	**come**	**venir**
cost	**cost**	**cost**	**coûter**
creep	crept	crept	ramper
cut	**cut**	**cut**	**couper**
deal	dealt	dealt	distribuer / traiter de
dig	dug	dug	creuser
dive	dived / dove	dived	plonger
do	**did**	**done**	**faire**
draw	**drew**	**drawn**	**dessiner / tirer**
dream	**dreamt**	**dreamt**	**rêver**
drink	**drank**	**drunk**	**boire**
drive	**drove**	**driven**	**conduire**
dwell	dwelled / dwelt	dwelled / dwelt	résider
eat	**ate**	**eaten**	**manger**
fall	**fell**	**fallen**	**tomber**
feed	**fed**	**fed**	**nourrir**
feel	**felt**	**felt**	**sentir**
fight	**fought**	**fought**	**combattre**
find	**found**	**found**	**trouver**
flee	fled	fled	fuir
fly	**flew**	**flown**	**voler**
forbear	forbore	forborne	s'abstenir
forbid	forbade	forbidden	interdire
forecast	forecast	forecast	prévoir
forget	**forgot**	**forgotten**	**oublier**
forsake	forsook	forsaken	abandonner
freeze	froze	frozen	geler
get	**got**	**got**	**obtenir**

Infinitif	Prétérit	Participe passé	Traduction
gild	gilded	gilded / gilt	dorer
give	**gave**	**given**	**donner**
go	**went**	**gone**	**aller**
grind	ground	ground	moudre
grow	grew	grown	augmenter / grandir
hang	hung	hung	pendre
have	**had**	**had**	**avoir**
hear	**heard**	**heard**	**entendre**
hew	hewed	hewed / hewn	tailler
hide	**hid**	**hidden**	**cacher**
hit	**hit**	**hit**	**frapper**
hold	**held**	**held**	**tenir**
hurt	**hurt**	**hurt**	**blesser**
keep	**kept**	**kept**	**garder**
kneel	kneeled / knelt	kneeled / knelt	s'agenouiller
knit	knit / knitted	knit / knitted	tricoter
know	**knew**	**known**	**connaître / savoir**
lade	laded	laded / laden	charger
lay	**laid**	**laid**	**étendre / poser**
lead	**led**	**led**	**mener**
lean	**leaned / leant**	**leaned / leant**	**appuyer**
leap	leaped / leapt	leaped / leapt	sauter
learn	**learned / learnt**	**learned / learnt**	**apprendre**
leave	**left**	**left**	**quitter**
lend	lent	lent	prêter
let	**let**	**let**	**laisser / louer**
lie	**lay**	**lain**	**être allongé / être couché**
light	lighted / lit	lighted / lit	allumer
lose	**lost**	**lost**	**perdre**
make	**made**	**made**	**faire**
mean	**meant**	**meant**	**signifier / vouloir dire**
meet	**met**	**met**	**rencontrer**
mislead	misled	misled	induire en erreur
mistake	**mistook**	**mistaken**	**se tromper**
mow	mowed	mowed / mown	tondre
overhang	overhung	overhung	surplomber

Infinitif	Prétérit	Participe passé	Traduction
pay	**paid**	**paid**	**payer**
put	**put**	**put**	**mettre / poser**
quit	**quit / quitted**	**quit / quitted**	**quitter**
read	**read**	**read**	**lire**
rend	rent	rent	déchirer
rid	rid	rid	débarrasser
ride	**rode**	**ridden**	**aller à cheval / aller à vélo**
ring	**rang**	**rung**	**sonner**
rise	**rose**	**risen**	**se lever / s'élever**
run	**ran**	**run**	**courir**
saw	sawed	sawn	scier
say	**said**	**said**	**dire**
see	**saw**	**seen**	**voir**
seek	sought	sought	chercher
sell	**sold**	**sold**	**vendre**
send	**sent**	**sent**	**envoyer**
set	**set**	**set**	**fixer / placer**
sew	sewed	sewed / sewn	coudre
shake	shook	shaken	secouer
shave	shaved	shaved / shaven	raser
shear	sheared	sheared / shorn	cisailler / tondre
shed	shed	shed	perdre / verser
shine	shone	shone	briller
shoe	shod	shod	chausser
shoot	shot	shot	tirer
show	**showed**	**showed / shown**	**montrer**
shrink	shrank	shrunk	rétrécir
shut	**shut**	**shut**	**fermer**
sing	**sang**	**sung**	**chanter**
sink	sank	sunk	sombrer
sit	**sat**	**sat**	**être assis**
slay	slew	slain	massacrer
sleep	**slept**	**slept**	**dormir**
slide	slid	slid	glisser
sling	slung	slung	lancer
slit	slit	slit	fendre

Infinitif	Prétérit	Participe passé	Traduction
smell	**smelled / smelt**	**smelled / smelt**	**sentir**
smite	smote	smitten	frapper
sow	sowed	sowed / sown	semer
speak	**spoke**	**spoken**	**parler**
speed	sped / speeded	sped / speeded	aller vite
spell	**spelled / spelt**	**spelled / spelt**	**épeler**
spend	**spent**	**spent**	**dépenser / passer (son temps)**
spill	spilled / spilt	spilled / spilt	renverser
spin	spun	spun	essorer / tourner
spit	spat	spat	cracher
split	split	split	fendre / séparer
spoil	spoiled / spoilt	spoiled / spoilt	gâcher
spread	**spread**	**spread**	**étaler / se répandre**
spring	sprang	sprung	bondir
stand	**stood**	**stood**	**être debout**
steal	**stole**	**stolen**	**dérober**
stick	stuck	stuck	coller
sting	stung	stung	piquer
stink	stank	stunk	sentir mauvais
strew	strewed	strewed / strewn	éparpiller
strike	**struck**	**struck**	**frapper**
string	strung	strung	enfiler
strive	strived / strove	strived / striven	s'efforcer
swear	swore	sworn	jurer
sweep	swept	swept	balayer
swell	swelled	swelled / swollen	enfler
swim	**swam**	**swum**	**nager**
swing	swung	swung	balancer
take	**took**	**taken**	**prendre**
teach	**taught**	**taught**	**enseigner**
tear	tore	torn	déchirer
tell	**told**	**told**	**dire / raconter**
think	**thought**	**thought**	**penser**
thrive	thrived / throve	thrived / thriven	prospérer
throw	**threw**	**thrown**	**lancer**

Infinitif	Prétérit	Participe passé	Traduction
thrust	thrust	thrust	pousser
understand	**understood**	**understood**	**comprendre**
undertake	undertook	undertook	entreprendre
unwind	unwound	unwound	dérouler
uphold	upheld	upheld	soutenir
upset	upset	upset	bouleverser
wake	**woke**	**woken**	**réveiller / se réveiller**
wear	**wore**	**worn**	**porter**
weave	wove	woven	tisser
weep	wept	wept	pleurer
wet	wet	wet	mouiller
win	**won**	**won**	**gagner**
wind	wound	wound	enrouler
withdraw	**withdrew**	**withdrawn**	**retirer**
withstand	withstood	withstood	résister à
wring	wrung	wrung	tordre
write	**wrote**	**written**	**écrire**

Review card 2

A selection of 100 essential irregular verbs

Infinitif	**Prétérit**	**Participe passé**	***Traduction***
be	was / were	been	*être*
beat	beat	beaten	*battre*
become	became	become	*devenir*
begin	began	begun	*commencer*
bind	bound	bound	*lier*
bite	bit	bitten	*mordre*
bleed	bled	bled	*saigner*
blow	blew	blown	*souffler*
break	broke	broken	*casser*
bring	brought	brought	*apporter*
build	built	built	*construire*
burn	burnt	burnt	*brûler*
buy	bought	bought	*acheter*
catch	caught	caught	*attraper*
choose	chose	chosen	*choisir*
come	came	come	*venir*
cost	cost	cost	*coûter*
cut	cut	cut	*couper*
do	did	done	*faire*
draw	drew	drawn	*dessiner / tirer*
dream	dreamt	dreamt	*rêver*
drink	drank	drunk	*boire*
drive	drove	driven	*conduire*
eat	ate	eaten	*manger*
fall	fell	fallen	*tomber*
feed	fed	fed	*nourrir*

Infinitif	Prétérit	Participe passé	*Traduction*
feel	felt	felt	*sentir*
fight	fought	fought	*combattre*
find	found	found	*trouver*
fly	flew	flown	*voler*
forget	forgot	forgotten	*oublier*
get	got	got	*obtenir*
give	gave	given	*donner*
go	went	gone	*aller*
have	had	had	*avoir*
hear	heard	heard	*entendre*
hide	hid	hidden	*cacher*
hit	hit	hit	*frapper*
hold	held	held	*tenir*
hurt	hurt	hurt	*blesser*
keep	kept	kept	*garder*
know	knew	known	*connaître / savoir*
lay	laid	laid	*étendre / poser*
lead	led	led	*mener*
lean	leaned / leant	leaned / leant	*appuyer*
learn	learned / learnt	learned / learnt	*apprendre*
leave	left	left	*quitter*
let	let	let	*laisser / louer*
lie	lay	lain	*être allongé / être couché*
lose	lost	lost	*perdre*
make	made	made	*faire*
mean	meant	meant	*signifier / vouloir dire*
meet	met	met	*rencontrer*
mistake	mistook	mistaken	*se tromper*
pay	paid	paid	*payer*
put	put	put	*mettre / poser*
quit	quit / quitted	quit / quitted	*quitter*
read	read	read	*lire*
ride	rode	ridden	*aller à cheval / aller à vélo*
ring	rang	rung	*sonner*
rise	rose	risen	*se lever / s'élever*
run	ran	run	*courir*

Infinitif	Prétérit	Participe passé	*Traduction*
say	said	said	*dire*
see	saw	seen	*voir*
sell	sold	sold	*vendre*
send	sent	sent	*envoyer*
set	set	set	*fixer / placer*
show	showed	showed / shown	*montrer*
shut	shut	shut	*fermer*
sing	sang	sung	*chanter*
sit	sat	sat	*être assis*
sleep	slept	slept	*dormir*
smell	smelled / smelt	smelled / smelt	*sentir*
speak	spoke	spoken	*parler*
spell	spelled / spelt	spelled / spelt	*épeler*
spend	spent	spent	*dépenser / passer (son temps)*
spread	spread	spread	*étaler / se répandre*
stand	stood	stood	*être debout*
steal	stole	stolen	*dérober*
strike	struck	struck	*frapper*
swim	swam	swum	*nager*
take	took	taken	*prendre*
teach	taught	taught	*enseigner*
tell	told	told	*dire / raconter*
think	thought	thought	*penser*
throw	threw	thrown	*lancer*
understand	understood	understood	*comprendre*
wake	woke	woken	*réveiller / se réveiller*
wear	wore	worn	*porter*
win	won	won	*gagner*
withdraw	withdrew	withdrawn	*retirer*
write	wrote	written	*écrire*

Review card 3

False friends, deceptive cognates

Words are very rascals since bonds disgraced them. [...] Words are grown so false, I am loath to prove reason with them. W. Shakespeare, Twelfth Night, III, I

Deceptive cognates are words in one language which look the same as words in another.

Many thanks to Laure BOURDET, Jérôme QUINTANA and Guillaume ODIN for their help

This word...	**... means...**	**... but does NOT mean...**	***... which is translated by:***
abuse [s]	des insultes, un mauvais traitement	abus	*misuse, excessive use, overuse*
to abuse [z]	insulter	abuser (de)	*to take advantage of, to overuse, to misuse*
to accommodate	loger, recevoir	accommoder	*to prepare, combine, adapt*
to achieve [tch]	accomplir, mener à bien, réaliser	achever	*to complete, finish*
an achievement [tch]	une réussite, un exploit, une réalisation	l'achèvement	*the completion*
actual	réel, concret, vrai	actuel	*current [= cup], present*
actually	en fait, en réalité	actuellement	*currently, nowadays*
adequate	suffisant	adéquat	*proper, suitable*
to advance	faire avancer	avancer	*to move forward*
to advertise (sth)	faire de la publicité (pour qqch)	avertir	*to warn, alert*
Ø advice (U)	un ou des conseils	un avis	*an opinion [= sit]*
affair	une liaison, une relation amoureuse	une affaire	*a case, a bargain, a business*
affluence	la richesse, la prospérité	l'affluence	*rush, crowds*
agenda	ordre du jour	agenda	*diary*
to aggravate (sb)	agacer, exaspérer (qqn)	aggraver qqch	*to make sth worse*
annoying	agaçant, contrariant	ennuyeux	*boring*
application	candidature	application	*implementation*
axe	hache	un axe	*axis*

This word...	**... means...**	**... but does NOT mean...**	***... which is translated by:***
a benefit	un bienfait, une prestation sociale	un bénéfice	*profit*
a cave	une grotte	une cave	*a cellar*
chance	le hasard ; une occasion, probabilité	la chance	*luck*
to charge	faire payer	charger	*to load*
chips	frites	chips	*crisps*
a college [= sit]	une université	un collège	*a junior high school, middle school (US) a (lower) secondary school (GB)*
a commodity [= wash]	bien, marchandise	commodité	*convenience*
to complete sth	achever qqch	compléter qqch	*to supplement sth*
complimentary	gratuit	complémentaire	*complementary*
confidence	la confiance self-confidence : la confiance en soi	une confidence	*a secret ; faire une confidence à qqn : to confide sth in sb*
crude	non-raffiné	cru	*raw*
current [= cup]	actuel(le)	courant(e)	*common, widespread*
a delay	un retard	un délai	*a time limit, a deadline*
to dispose of sth	se débarrasser de qqch	disposer de qqch	*to have sth (at one's disposal)*
to deliver [= sit]	livrer, distribuer ; accoucher	délivrer qqn	*to set sb free, release sb*
deceive [= see] sb	tromper qqn	décevoir qqn	*to disappoint sb*
deception	leurre, tromperie	la déception	*disappointment, disillusionment*
to demand sth	exiger qqch	demander qqch	*to ask for sth, to request sth*
to devise	imaginer	deviser	*to converse*
dramatic	spectaculaire	dramatique	*tragic, disastrous*
engine	moteur	engin (rare)	*machine*
entreprise	une aventure	une entreprise	*a company, a firm*
to evade sth	esquiver, frauder, contourner qqch	évader (s')	*to escape*
eventually	finalement, au bout du compte	éventuellement	*possibly, maybe*
Ø evidence	preuve(s), élément(s), signe(s)	une évidence	*an obvious fact*
extravagant	dépensier	extravagant	*wild, off-the-wall (familier)*
the fabric	le tissu, l'étoffe	une fabrique	*a factory, a mill, a manufacture*

This word...	**... means...**	**... but does NOT mean...**	***... which is translated by:***
the fa<u>ci</u>lities	les équipements, les installations	la facilité	*ease (aisance), easiness; aptitude, ability*
figure	la silhouette, un chiffre	la figure	*face*
to forge sth	contrefaire qqch	forger qqch	*to form, to coin (a new word)*
the <u>fur</u>niture	les meubles, le mobilier	une fourniture	*supp<u>ly</u>*
a <u>ha</u>bit	une habitude	un habit	*a garment, a piece of clothing*
a <u>ha</u>zard	un risque, un danger	un hasard	*ø chance, a coincidence*
in<u>ha</u>bited	habité	inhabité	*unin<u>ha</u>bited*
to injure sb	blesser qqn	une injure	*an insult, an abuse [s]*
the inner city	les quartiers pauvres, défavorisés, souvent centraux (villes US surtout)	le centre-ville	*the city centre (GB), Ø downtown (US)*
a <u>jour</u>nal [= burn]	revue spécialisée (scientifique, etc.)	un journal	*a newspaper*
a <u>jour</u>ney [= burn]	un voyage, un trajet	une journée	*a day*
large	grand, vaste, énorme	large	*wide, broad [= ball]*
a lecture	une conférence, un sermon	la lecture	*reading*
a <u>li</u>brary [= guy]	une bibliothèque	une librairie	*a bookstore (US), bookshop (GB)*
luxury	le luxe	la luxure	*lust, debauchery*
a novel	un roman	une nouvelle	*a short-story*
an oppor<u>tu</u>nity	une occasion, possibilité, chance	l'opportunité	*timeliness, appropriateness*
pa<u>ro</u>le [= road]	la liberté conditionnelle	la parole ; une parole	*speech; a word*
to pass an exam	réussir un examen	passer un examen	*to have an exam*
a <u>pa</u>tron [= rain]	un client, un habitué ; un mécène	un patron	*a boss, an employer*
<u>pe</u>trol	l'essence (GB) (US : gas)	le pétrole	*oil, pe<u>tro</u>leum*
a phrase [= rain]	une expression	une phrase	*a <u>sen</u>tence*
a phy<u>si</u>cian	un médecin	un physicien	*a <u>phy</u>sicist*
a prejudice	un préjugé	un préjudice	*ø <u>da</u>mage [= sit], harm [= car]*
to pre<u>vent</u> sb	empêcher qqch	prévenir qqn	*to tell, to warn sb*
raisins	les raisins secs	les raisins	*grapes*

This word...	**... means...**	**... but does NOT mean...**	***... which is translated by:***
to realize (/ -ise)	se rendre compte, prendre conscience	réaliser qqch	*to achieve, conduct, carry out*
Ø refuse [s]	les déchets, les ordures	le refus	*refusal*
a regime	un régime politique	un régime	*a diet*
to remark (sth)	faire remarquer (qqch)	remarquer qqch	*to notice [= road] sth*
to resume	reprendre	résumer	*to sum up, to summarise*
rude	impoli, grossier	rude	*harsh, rough [= cup] + [f]*
sensible	sensé, raisonnable	sensible	*sensitive*
to sort	trier	le sort	*fate*
spectacles	les lunettes	un spectacle	*a show [= road]*
to support sb	aider, soutenir qqch	supporter qqn	*to bear, tolerate, put up with sb*
sympathetic	compatissant	sympathique, sympa	*nice, friendly*
a utility	un service public	l'utilité	*the usefulness*
versatile	aux talents variés, polyvalent	versatile	*changeable, fickle*

Note de M. Quintana : D'une façon générale, méfiez-vous de la tentation de traduire littéralement tous les mots apparemment transparents, car les « faux-amis partiels » abondent. Par exemple, « excitement » peut parfois se traduire par « excitation », mais plus souvent par « ferveur, passion, engouement ». « Glamour » est un anglicisme possible en français, mais à éviter : préférer « prestige, fascination » selon le contexte. « Special » peut parfois se traduire par « spécial », mais « she's very special to me » veut dire qu'elle m'est « très chère » et non pas qu'elle est très... spéciale ! Donc, redoublez de vigilance !

Review card 4

Differences between British English and American English

British English	American English
aeroplane	airplane
aluminium	aluminum
annexe	annex
anticlockwise	counterclockwise
apologise	apologize
arbour	arbor
aubergine	eggplant
autumn	fall
barrister	attorney
behaviour	behavior
bin	trash can
biscuit	cookie
block of flats	apartment building
bonnet	hood
boot	trunk
braces	suspenders
candy floss	cotton candy
cab	taxi
car park	parking lot
caravan	trailer
chemist's	drugstore
cheque	check
chest of drawers	dresser
chips	french fries
clothes peg	clothespin
colour	color

British English	American English
cosy	cozy
courgette	zucchini
crisps	potato chips
diversion	detour
draught	draft
draw	tie
driving licence	driver's license
dummy	pacifier
enamoured	enamored
estate car	station wagon
favourite	favorite
first floor	second floor
flat	apartment
flyover	overpass
football	soccer
full stop	period
gearbox	transmission
grey	gray
ground floor	first floor
harbour	harbor
high street	main street
holiday	vacation
humour	humor
ice lolly	popsicle
jacket potato	baked potato
jumper, pullover	sweater
kerb	curb
kit	uniform
lift	elevator
liquorice	licorice
loo, toilet	restroom
lorry	truck
mad	crazy, insane
manoeuvre	maneuver
mobile phone	cell phone
motorway	highway

British English	American English
mould	mold
moustache	mustache
mummy	mommy
nappy	diaper
neighbour	neighbor
nought / zero	zero
noughts and crosses	tic-tac-toe
odour	odor
pants	underwear
parlour	parlor
pavement	sidewalk
peckish	hungry
petrol	gas
phone box	phone booth
pitch	field
plough	plow
pocket money	allowance
post	mail
postal code	zip code
programme	program
pyjamas	pajamas
queue	line
railway	railroad
road surface	pavement
rubber	eraser
rubbish	garbage
rumour	rumor
runner bean, string bean	green bean
smoulder	smolder
speciality	specialty
sweets	candy
takeaway	takeout
tea towel, tea cloth	dish towel
telly	TV
the cinema	the movies
the Plough	the Big Dipper

British English	American English
theatre	theater
timetable	schedule
torch	flashlight
trainers	sneakers
trousers	pants
treacle	molasses
tyre	tire
underground	subway
vest	undershirt
waistcoat	vest
wellington boots	rubber boots, rain boots
windscreen	windshield
zebra crossing	crosswalk

Additional notes

Here are the main spelling differences between American and British spelling of English words.

-er / re ending

- **British English**: centre, fibre, litre, theatre
- **American English**: center, fiber, liter, theater

-ize / ise suffix

- **British English**: apologise, organise, recognise
- **American English**: apologize, organize, recognize

-or / -our suffix

- **American English**: behavior, color, humor, labor, neighbor, flavor
- **British English:** behaviour, colour, humour, labour, neighbour, flavour

Double vowels "ae" and "oe"

- **American English:** leukemia, maneuver, estrogen, pediatric, pedophile
- **British English**: leukaemia, manœuvre, oestrogen, paediatric, paedophile

-nse / nce

- **American English**: defense, license, offense, pretense
- **British English**: defence, licence, offence, pretence

Words with / out gemination of the -l

- **American English**: traveling, traveled, traveler, fueled, fueling
- **British English**: travelling, travelled, traveller, fuelled, fuelling

Review card 5

A list of the most common mistakes read in students'papers

DON'TS	DO'S
How ***the*** America went insane.	How **Ø** America went insane.
In ***Ø*** UK, the number of unplanned pregnancies has rocketed.	In **the** UK, the number of unplanned pregnancies has rocketed.
In a speech which was ***write*** by Theresa May herself, the new Prime Minister called for a new "industrial revolution"	In a speech which was **written** by Theresa May herself, the new Prime Minister called for a new "industrial revolution"
After he had ***took / take*** the potion, Harry fell peacefully asleep.	After he had **taken** the potion, Harry fell peacefully asleep.
An animal which ***tend*** to hunt is more likely to survive.	An animal which **tends** to hunt is more likely to survive.
For some, the ***medias are*** becoming less reliable, for others **the *informations*** available on the Internet ***are*** more accurate.	For some, the **media is** becoming less reliable, for others **Ø information** available on the Internet **is** more accurate.
Stonewall Jackson commanded the battlefield without ***open*** his mouth.	Stonewall Jackson commanded the battlefield without **opening** the mouth.
To do a thorough visual presentation is essential to earn a full credit for this course.	**Doing** a thorough visual presentation is essential to earn a full credit for this course. (selon le point de vue à adopter)
Barack Obama ***is*** the American president since 2008.	Barack Obama **has been** the American president since 2008.
In the future, we will have ***too*** smart coffeemakers with sensors.	In the future, we will **also** have smart coffeemakers with sensors.
When he studied why wine goes "sour", Pasteur leapt to the hypothesis that microbes make us "sour" ***also***.	When he studied why wine goes "sour", Pasteur leapt to the hypothesis that microbes make us "sour" **too.**
The ten ***first*** minutes of Wall-E feature no dialogue at all.	The **first** ten minutes of Wall-E feature no dialogue at all.
The text reproduces the form of a diary. ***He*** is extremely well-written.	The text reproduces the form of a diary. **It** is extremely well-written.
To what extent this passage ***is*** a purple patch?	To what extent **is** this passage a purple patch?

DON'TS	DO'S
How this excerpt ***creates*** a sense of horror?	How **does** this excerpt **create** a sense of horror?
More Mexicans have left the US ***that*** entered it since 2009.	More Mexicans have left the US **than** entered it since 2009.
If your home can ***to*** have a digital assistant that ***can controls*** your appliances, you could ***saved*** money.	If your home can **Ø** have a digital assistant that can **control** your appliances, you could **save** money.
The both solution to solve the migrant crisis do not work.	**Ø** Both solution to solve the migrant crisis do not work.
Can we ask ***us*** why so many kids fail to acquire basic reading skills?	Can we ask **ourselves** why so many kids fail to acquire basic reading skills?
This scientifics have long known that hallucinations can result when infection ***inflame*** the brain.	**These scientists** have long known that hallucinations can result when infection **inflames** the brain.
He had ***not*** political debts or party membership in short he was the perfect candidate for the job.	He had **no** political debts or party membership in short he was the perfect candidate for the job.
The ***Democrats*** base ***not*** want to see president Obama fail.	The **Democratic** base **does not** want to see president Obama fail.
A such amazing electoral period deserves an amazing cable network.	Such **an** amazing electoral period deserves an amazing cable network.
At the beginning of ***the*** page 57 of ***Bible***, one can read the following maxim	At the beginning of **Ø** page 57 of **the *Bible***, one can read the following maxim
The boss of Miss Kenton is hard to understand.	Miss Kenton**'s** boss is hard to understand.
One of the ***topic*** I want to study is ***the*** global warming.	One of the **topics** I want to study is **Ø global warming**.
The Mr Stevens' revelation is shocking.	**Ø** Mr Stevens' revelation is shocking.
The main values of this movie are ***the*** dignity, ***the*** courage and ***the*** honor.	The main values of this movie are **Ø** dignity, **Ø** courage and **Ø** honor.
This quote is relevant ***for understanding*** the whole story.	This quote is relevant **to understand** the whole story. (selon le point de vue à adopter)
I want to know what ***is love.*** / / In order to comprehend what ***is saying the journalist*** we will start with a metaphor.	I want to know what **love is.** / / In order to comprehend what **the journalist is saying**, we will start with a metaphor.
He asks her ***to not address*** his father as Bruce but as Caytlin.	He asks her **not to address** his father as Bruce but as Caytlin.
At line 5 and on the ***five first*** pages, we can see...	**On line 5 / Line 5** and on the **first five** pages, there is / are...
He ***is may be*** burning into a elf.	He **may be burning** into **an** elf.
I will come when you ***will talk to me.***	I will come when you **talk** to me.
John ***could not to do*** this on his own.	John **could not do** this on his own.

DON'TS	DO'S
The way ***how*** it is told ***remembers me of*** Anita Desai.	The way **in which** it is told **reminds me of** Anita Desai.
It is ***extracted from*** an article entitled...	It is an **excerpt taken from** an article...
Others people estimate that she ***belongs to*** the White House.	**Other people** estimate that she **belongs in** the White House.
It is a ***situation very strange.***	It is a **very strange** situation.

Review card 6

A list of barbarisms found in papers or heard in class

Barbarism heard or read in class or during oral sessions	Correct word in English
evenement	event
etonnant	surprising
evolvement	evolution
increasment	increase
changement	change
affrontement	confrontation
collapsement	collapse
financement	financing
interessant	interesting
rayonnement	ray
rendement	yield
dirigeants	leaders
cancelment	cancellation
enrichissement	enrichment
resignment	resignation
representant	representative
reglementation	regulation
consomation	consumption
importation	imports
exportation	exports
alternance	alternation
mondialisation	globalisation
to explorate	to explore
to degradate	to degrade
to definate	to define
to filtrate	to filter

Barbarism heard or read in class or during oral sessions	Correct word in English
to inspirate	to inspire
to evocate	to evoke
to invocate	to invoke
to publicate	to publish
to realisate	to direct
to exprimate	to express
to preparate	to prepare
privated of	deprived of
to denunciate	to denounce
to accusate	to accuse
to contribuate	to contribute
to sensibilisate	to sensitize
preoccupated	preoccupied
to examinate	to examine
to extrate	to extract (arracher une dent), to take from
to massacrate	to massacre, slaughter
to provocate	to provoke
to polluate	to pollute
to occupate	to occupy
to significate	to signify, to mean
to commentate	to comment
to developt / developpated	to develop / developed
to applicate	to apply
to communique	to communicate
to disparate	to disappear
to manufacturate	to manufacture
to ressucite	to resuscitate
to expulse	to expel, to deport
to consacred / to consacrate	to be devoted to / to devote
to controlate	to control
to suggerate	to suggest
to participe	to participate
a constat	acknowledgement, observation
to constat	to observe
to deplace	to displace

Barbarism heard or read in class or during oral sessions	Correct word in English
to promove	to promote
to evolute	evolve
intitute	entitled
educal	educational
rentable	profitable
creativeness	creativity
epidemy	epidemic
sovereignity	sovereignty
favourize	to favour
fragilize	to weaken
defavourized	poor – destitute
volunty	willingness
rivality	rivalry
legitimity	legitimacy
penality	penalty
egality, inegality	equality, inequality
threeth	third
fiveth	fifth
fiveteen	fifteen
the 21th (oneth) century	The 21st (first) century
the scientifics	scientists
numeric	digital
Sovietic, Asiatic	Soviet, Asian
communistic	Communist
informatic	computers
approximatively	approximately
ourself, themselves	ourselves, themselves
detress	distress
disincreasing	decrease
gratifiant	gratifying
nocive, nefast	noxious
mens, womens	men, women
to influe	to influence
to demask	to unmask
to enlight	to highlight or to enlighten

Barbarism heard or read in class or during oral sessions	Correct word in English
to depass	to overtake
a processus	a process
retablish	re-establish
a politic	a policy, politics
a politic man	a politician
defenser	defender
realisator	director
productor	producer
observator	observer
nowday, nowaday	nowadays
to explose	to explode
paradoxal	paradoxical
phenomen	phenomenon
principe	principle
temptatious, temptating	tempting
traffickant	trafficker
it felled, it falled, it selled	it fell, it sold et autres V.I.
decalage	discrepancy, contrast
themself	themselves
millenar	millenium
necessar	necessary
quotidianelly	daily
to pratique	to practise
to remplace	to replace
to instore	to settle, to install
the youngs	youths, youngsters
youngness	youth
hungriness	hunger
espece	species
complice	accomplice
conspiration	conspiracy
violency	violence
confiant	confident
Italia, Deutschcountry, Polishland, Spagna, Belgica, Varsovia, Ukrainia, URSS, Europa...	Italy, Germany, Poland, Spain, Belgium, Warsaw, Ukraine, USSR, Europe (liste non exhaustive)

Review card 7

Essential linkwords and linking structures

above all	par dessus tout, surtout
accordingly	en conséquence
after all	après tout
again	de plus, en outre, d'ailleurs
alias, AKA (also known as)	alias, ou (de reformulation, d'équivalence), autrement dit
all the same	malgré tout, quand même, tout de même, au demeurant
all things considered	tout bien considéré
also,...	1 / De plus ; 2 / De même
among others	entre autres
and	1 / et – 2 / de plus (et de nombreuses autres valeurs)
anyway	de toute façon, quoi qu'il en soit
as	étant donné que
as a consequence	de ce fait, en conséquence (de quoi)
as a matter of fact	en fait
as a result	de ce fait, en conséquence (de quoi)
as though, as if	comme si
as well as... (conj. de coord.)	ainsi que, de même que
as well,...	de plus, de surcroît
at any rate	en tout cas, de toute façon
at least	1 / au moins ; 2 / du moins
besides	d'ailleurs, du reste
both... and...	et... et..., à la fois... et...
but	1 / mais ; 2 / (suivi de then) en revanche 3 / cependant
by the way	à propos, soit dit en passant
certainly	certainement
conversely	inversement
despite this	malgré cela
e.g. / eg (du latin exempli gratia)	par ex. / p.e. (par exemple)
either... or...	soit... soit..., ou bien... ou bien...
even better	bien mieux, mieux encore
even so	mais cependant, quand même, malgré cela

first and foremost	avant tout
first of all, first,... second,... third,...	premièrement, primo,... secundo,... tertio,...
for (précédé d'une virgule)	car, en effet, « : »
for all I know	pour autant que je sache
for all that,	malgré cela
for example, for instance	par exemple
for one thing	une raison, c'est que..., entre autres raisons
for one thing..., for another...	d'un côté..., de l'autre...
for this purpose	à cet effet, dans ce but
for this reason	pour cette raison
further,...	1 / En outre ; 2 / D'ailleurs, du reste
furthermore	de plus, en outre
hence	d'où, de là, partant de là
however	cependant, toutefois, pourtant, du reste
i.e. / ie (du latin id est)	i.e. / ie (du latin *id est*) : c.-à-d. (c'est-à-dire), à savoir
if not	sinon
in a word	en bref
in addition	en sus, de surcroît, en outre
in any case, at all points	en tout cas
in conclusion	en conclusion
in effect	en fait, en réalité, dans les faits
in fact	en fait
in most cases	dans la plupart des cas
in other words	en d'autres termes, autrement dit
in spite of that	malgré cela
in that case	en ce cas là
in the first place,... in the second place,...	en premier lieu,... en second lieu,...
in the same way	de même
in this case	dans ce cas
in which case	auquel cas, et dans ce cas
in / by comparison	en comparaison
in / by contrast	par opposition
instead	au lieu de cela
last but not least	dernier point mais non le moindre
let alone	sans parler de..., sans compter..., à plus forte raison...
let's turn to...	envisageons...
likewise	également, pareillement
more than that,...	bien plus
moreover	en outre, de plus
namely	à savoir (peut encore se traduire par « : »), c'est-à-dire
neither... nor...	ni... ni...
nevertheless	néanmoins, toutefois, toujours est-il que, il n'empêche que

next	puis, ensuite
no matter what / how	peu importe ce que / comment
nonetheless	néanmoins, toutefois
nor	1 / ni ; 2 / (général. en tête de phrase, + auxiliaire + sujet) ne... pas davantage, ne... pas non plus
not just / not only... but also...	non pas simplement... mais aussi...
not to mention...	sans parler de, sans oublier..., outre...
notwithstanding	nonobstant, néanmoins
now what about...	maintenant, qu'en est-il de... ?
now,...	1 / or ; 2 / il se trouve que
obviously	de toute évidence
on account of	étant donné
on second thoughts	tout bien considéré
on the contrary	au contraire
on the one hand... on the other hand...	d'une part..., d'autre part... ; d'un côté..., de l'autre...
on the other hand (seul)	1 / en revanche ; 2 / d'un autre côté
on the question of...	sur la question de...
on top of that	qui plus est, en plus de cela
or	1 / (reformulation, équivalence) ou, autrement dit ; 2 / (double possibilité) ou, ou bien ; 3 / mais peut-être ; 4 / sinon
or again	ou encore
or else	sinon, ou alors
or otherwise	sinon, ou alors
or rather	ou plutôt, ou mieux, ou plus exactement
otherwise	1 / sinon ; 2 / (précédé de but) mais à part cela, mais par ailleurs
over and above	par dessus le marché
owing to	en raison de
perhaps, possibly, maybe	peut-être
plus,...	de plus
provided / providing that...	étant donné que
rather,...	mieux, plus exactement
say (= let us say)	disons..., mettons..., par exemple...
secondly	deuxièmement
similarly	de la même façon
so (parfois précédé de and)	donc, par conséquent, aussi, c'est pourquoi
still (général. en tête de phrase, + virgule)	cependant, quoi qu'il en soit, pourtant, malgré cela
that is to say	1 / c'est-à-dire ; 2 / du moins
the reason is...	la raison en est que...
the result is (that)...	le résultat, c'est que..., cela fait que...
then	en ce cas, alors, donc
thereby	de ce fait, par là

therefore	donc, par conséquent
this is because…	c'est parce que…, cela vient du fait que…, la raison en est que…
this is why	c'est pourquoi
this means that… / What this means is that…	1 / cela veut dire que…, en d'autres termes ; 2 / il en résulte que…, cela fait que…
though	cependant, pourtant, malgré tout, quand même
thus	ainsi (au sens de donc, par conséquent)
to cut a long story short	pour conclure
to name only a few	pour n'en citer que quelques-uns, entre autres
to sum up	pour résumer
to this end	à cet effet
too, as well, also	aussi
unless	à moins que
up to a point	dans une certaine mesure
what is more	qui plus est, de plus
whatever	quel que soit
whenever	chaque fois que
which is why	et c'est pourquoi, ce qui explique pourquoi
which means that…	1 / ce qui veut dire que… ; 2 / ce qui fait que…
yet	1 / pourtant, cependant, malgré cela, malgré tout ; 2 / (précédé de and ou de but) et pourtant, mais pourtant

Appendix 2

Correction of the translation exercises and excerpts

Topic one
Mankind

Section 1 – The human being

Chapter A – Mankind and family

English-to-French exercise

- Bien qu'il ne pèse qu'un petit kilo et demi, votre cerveau est votre organe le plus puissant.
- En CE1, le directeur de l'école était un homme corpulent, pesant environ 104 kg et mesurant 1,85 mètre. (Rappel: une livre = 450 grammes un pied = 30 cm un pouce = 2,5 cm)
- Pour les enfants, les parents et la famille jouent un rôle primordial dans l'acquisition de connaissances sur les droits de l'homme et l'aide concrète qui peut leur être apportée, car plus de la moitié des élèves sont informés sur les droits de l'homme par leurs parents, et c'est aussi vers eux qu'ils se tournent en cas de violation de leurs droits.
- Elle hérita du teint clair et des yeux bleus de sa mère, et des cheveux noirs de son père, un Italien.
- On utilise généralement l'âge de 65 ans comme référence pour définir la population « âgée », parce que c'est l'âge de l'admissibilité à / l'âge où l'on obtient certaines pensions de retraite et aux prestations d'allocation vieillesse, et aussi en raison de son lien avec la retraite obligatoire.

Chapter B – Health and Medicine

English-to-French exercise

- La consommation d'alcool, même modérée, avant une intervention chirurgicale peut ralentir la convalescence et affaiblir le système immunitaire.

- Un handicap peut exister même sans avoir la preuve d'une limitation physique ou la présence d'une affection quelconque.
- Informez toujours votre médecin, votre infirmière et votre pharmacien des médicaments que vous prenez, qu'il s'agisse de médicaments sous ordonnance ou en vente libre, ou de remèdes à base de plantes et produits de santé naturels.
- Souvent, les traitements médicaux permettent d'augmenter considérablement l'espérance de vie, mais sans pour autant garantir la guérison.
- Dans certains cas, ces services permettent avant tout d'aider une personne à s'adapter à son handicap dans la vie quotidienne.

Chapter C – Personality and Relations

English-to-French exercise

- Notre avenir, nous le construirons avec la force qui nous caractérise.
- Elle a un tempérament sociable et amical, et s'est révélée capable de travailler en équipe et de nouer d'excellentes relations avec les étudiants de l'école ainsi que les autres collègues.
- Sa personnalité enjouée devint morose et la honte l'obligea à garder tête basse.
- La plupart des couples passent plus d'un an à planifier le jour de leur mariage, mais ne préparent pas du tout leur vie de couple / ne consacrent pas du tout de temps à préparer leur vie de couple marié.
- Ils sont honnêtes, dignes de confiance et guidés par le sens de l'éthique.

Chapter D – Successes and Failures

English-to-French exercise

- Il s'agit du droit des gens à communiquer entre eux, à partager des idées et à faire des affaires.
- Durant les années qui suivirent, il rattrapa le temps perdu, parvenant même à certains moments à achever / faire tenir deux années de scolarité en une seule.
- Il a déclaré qu'il ne prendrait pas d'engagement sur les délais à tenir, et qu'il ne fallait pas confondre vitesse et précipitation, au risque / sous peine d'échouer.// que confondre vitesse et précipitation revenait à foncer droit dans le mur.
- Vivez de l'intérieur l'ascension captivante d'un jeune espoir de la chanson qui deviendra une des pop stars les plus influentes au monde !

- Après le lycée, les jeunes deviennent un peu plus enclins à considérer que la diversité culturelle est une richesse pour un individu comme pour un pays.

Section 2 – Basic needs

Chapter A – Eating and Drinking

English-to-French exercise

- Vous pouvez déguster un plat simple au bar ou profiter d'un vaste choix de plats et de suggestions à retrouver sur notre carte au restaurant.
- Les employé(e)s se font généralement du café ou du thé dans le coin cuisine, et apportent leur déjeuner sur leur lieu de travail.
- L'activité Semences Potagères concernent une trentaine d'espèces différentes parmi les plus consommées au monde comme : la tomate, le concombre, l'oignon, le poivron / piment, le melon, la carotte, la pastèque, la laitue, le chou, le haricot ou encore le chou-fleur.
- Le cours de cuisine professionnel, qui se solda par la présentation d'un menu magistral de quatre plats allant du ragoût de gibier à une mousse, comptait parmi les journalistes non seulement des participants enthousiastes mais aussi des connaisseurs raffinés de leur domaine.
- Les productions maraîchères et fruitières, en particulier les bananes, les oranges et les fruits de la passion ont subi des dégâts importants, et les vignobles ont tous été ravagés.

Chapter B – In the household

English-to-French exercise

- L'économie d'énergie et l'utilisation de matériaux recyclables et à faible toxicité constituent un pas dans la bonne direction, mais il est également important d'y ajouter l'éradication de l'obsolescence programmée.
- L'obsolescence programmée est la production délibérée de produits qui sont construits pour ne pas durer et ne pas être réparés.
- Toutefois il convient de regarder la réalité en face : le bricolage est une manière d'occuper son temps libre, non seulement utile socialement mais qui a aussi son intérêt économique pour les familles ; il convient donc de l'encourager.

- Les rez-de-chaussée (ou premier étage) et premier (ou deuxième) étage se composent exactement sur un même plan : un appartement comprenant une entrée, un séjour, une chambre, un bureau et une salle d'eau ; et de l'autre côté deux grandes pièces en enfilade faisant office de séjour et de chambre.
- Grâce à la mécanisation, les travaux ménagers / tâches ménagères se simplifient mais elles se démultiplient également.

Chapter C – City and Country

English-to-French exercise

- Cette entreprise offre également une expertise et un savoir-faire reconnus en termes d'aménagement de nouveaux quartiers qui préfigurent la ville de demain.
- Ces grands centres commerciaux ont tari les sources de revenu des petits commerçants et fournisseurs de services de proximité, dont bon nombre ont été contraints de fermer.
- Le lèche-vitrines n'est pas une pure perte de temps, car c'est en déambulant devant les étalages de la grand-rue que nous nous imprégnons de ce que les commerces proposent.
- Alors que l'expansion urbaine est l'une des raisons principales de cette augmentation massive du transport par véhicule particulier, le moteur de cette augmentation des transports urbains de marchandises reste la croissance économique et la prospérité.
- Ce phénomène d'exode rural s'explique parfois par l'attraction qu'exercent les modes de vie contemporains, habiter un logement neuf et moderne étant considéré comme un signe de réussite sociale.

Chapter D – Sports and leisure activities

English-to-French exercise

- La course sur route est un sport d'équipe et il est important que vous appreniez tôt à courir au sein d'une équipe et à connaître le code de la route.
- Pourquoi un intervenant voudrait-il obtenir le statut d'observateur au sein d'un organisme qui ne peut même pas avoir la certitude que ses propres membres joueront franc jeu ?
- Lors de la finale, l'Inde a battu l'Angleterre d'un seul point sous les huées de la foule locale, un incident dénoncé par une archère anglaise lors de la conférence de presse comme « allant à l'encontre de l'esprit sportif auquel on est en droit de s'attendre au tir à l'arc ».

- De plus, la communauté dispose à présent de programmes complets qui permettent aux municipalités de renoncer aux pratiques antérieures pour adopter des formes plus écologiques de jardinage et de soins des pelouses.
- La Grèce est bien connue pour avoir donné naissance aux célèbres Jeux Olympiques, aujourd'hui véritable fête du sport dans le monde entier.

Section 3 – Discovering and learning

Chapter A – Transport and Tourism

English-to-French exercise

- Il existe à n'en pas douter un lien entre le développement régional et le tourisme.
- L'importance du tourisme paraît dans le pourcentage supérieur d'emplois dans l'hébergement et la restauration. / On voit l'importance du tourisme par la plus grande proportion d'emplois dans les secteurs de l'hébergement et de la restauration.
- Des lignes d'autobus internationales à bas prix font concurrence aux services ferroviaires internationaux et aux compagnies aériennes à bas coût.
- Les jeunes doivent être informés quant aux risques, pour eux et pour les autres / pour leur sécurité et celle des autres, qu'ils rencontreront après l'obtention de leur permis de conduire / une fois leur permis en poche.
- Lorsqu'il s'agit de lutter contre les incendies dans le métro, les tunnels ferroviaires ou routiers, une chose est sûre : en cas d'incendie, les pompiers doivent faire face à des exigences très particulières.

Chapter B – Education

English-to-French exercise

- Les thèmes abordés varient en fonction de l'année et des matières couvertes par le programme scolaire.
- Il est fait référence à la dénomination française pour nommer les classes : la classe de sixième équivaut à la « Year 7 » britannique, la seconde correspond à la « Year 11 », la 1re est équivalente à la « lower sixth form » et la terminale à la « upper sixth form ».

- Sur le plan universitaire, notre responsabilité est de / engagement consiste à former des étudiants de niveau licence, master et doctorat, dans un environnement qui favorise la pratique intensive / exigeante de la recherche.
- Trois établissements de l'Ivy League sont maintenant présidés par une femme / ont maintenant une femme à leur tête. Les huit universités et collèges universitaires privés qui constituent la Ivy League sont considérés comme étant parmi les plus prestigieux de tous les établissements d'enseignement supérieur aux États-Unis.
- Les jeunes qui prennent une année sabbatique, habituellement entre la fin des études secondaire et le début des études supérieures, en profitent souvent pour voyager ou pour travailler.

Chapter C – The media

English-to-French exercise

- Il éclate de rire en se rappelant son premier enregistrement en juin 1999, dans les locaux de la BBC.
- Un public potentiel de 25 millions de personnes a reçu des informations via la télévision, la radio et Internet.
- Des campagnes de presse à la radio et à la télévision ont relayé des informations permettant une meilleure connaissance et une meilleure appréciation des valeurs de la tolérance.
- Les grandes chaînes de télévision, de radio et autres sociétés d'informations en continu du monde entier se tournent fréquemment vers des organismes de mesure d'audimat pour une analyse objective et précises du comportement des consommateurs.
- On utilise couramment des expressions comme « autoroute de l'information », « révolution de l'information » et « économie de l'information » pour illustrer le rôle prépondérant que joue l'information dans les sociétés modernes.

Chapter D – The Internet

English-to-French exercise

- Le téléchargement illégal des œuvres musicales sur Internet semblait en voie d'affaiblir l'industrie à un point tel qu'on commençait à craindre pour sa survie.
- Les enseignants et formateurs ont besoin de formations complémentaires, en lien avec les associations de protection de l'enfance, sur l'utilisation d'Internet

dans le cadre de l'apprentissage scolaire, afin d'entretenir la sensibilisation aux dangers d'Internet, notamment pour ce qui concerne les espaces de discussion et les forums.

- Google dispose de sa propre politique de respect de la vie privée.
- Internet est devenu un vecteur essentiel de communication et de notoriété pour les entreprises et leurs marques.
- Le contenu du fil d'actualités d'un utilisateur de Facebook se compose de billets et de conversations avec d'autres utilisateurs ou groupes qui ont été ajoutés expressément par cet utilisateur.

Topic two
Understanding our world

Section 4 – Arts, culture and analysis techniques

Chapter A – Beliefs

Exercice de version de presse

Une nation sous l'égide de Dieu

Que tout ceci resurgisse après plus d'un demi-siècle a de quoi surprendre. Depuis le discours de Kennedy, l'idée selon laquelle un homme politique américain, quel qu'il soit, pourrait bannir de la sphère publique tous ceux qui ne sont pas athées est devenue grotesque.

S'il y a bien une place que la piété a prise en politique, c'est celle d'une condition préalable. Thomas Jefferson était peut-être en paix avec lui-même / serein sur ces questions mais de nos jours aucun candidat n'oserait admettre publiquement son athéisme ou remettre en cause l'existence du Tout-Puissant.

Barack Obama est pratiquant. Georges Bush a déclaré que son philosophe préféré était le Christ et commençait tous ses conseils des ministres par une prière. Jimmy Carter, quant à lui, priait jusqu'à vingt-cinq fois par jour. Même Bill Clinton, pécheur devant l'Éternel, prenait toujours soin de se repentir.

Chapter B – Writing and text analysis

Exercice de version de presse

Les écrivains qui étaient aussi espions / L'espion qui écrivait / L'écrivain qui espionnait

« Quand on cherche la vérité, le champagne est le meilleur détecteur de mensonges », écrit Graham Greene dans *Les Chemins de l'évasion* en 1980. « Il encourage les gens à devenir expansifs, voire téméraires, tandis que les détecteurs de mensonges ne sont qu'un défi à mentir encore mieux. » Quand il n'écrivait pas (et parfois alors qu'il écrivait), Graham Greene travaillait comme agent pour le MI6, les services de renseignement britanniques.

Greene fut recruté en 1941 alors qu'il était déjà un écrivain reconnu. Son statut d'auteur lui offrait une bonne couverture pour partir à la recherche d'informations et son goût pour les voyages dans certaines régions stratégiques (le Libéria, le Mexique, Haiti, Cuba, le Vietnam) en faisait un informateur précieux. Sans compter que l'espionnage avait l'avantage de lui fournir une source d'inspiration supplémentaire pour écrire.

Chapter C – Music and cinema

Exercice de version de presse

Radiohead dépasse son angoisse existentielle

Les membres de Radiohead, dont le neuvième album studio est intitulé *A Moon Shaped Pool*, ont remarquablement bien compris la facilité avec laquelle la profondeur peut se perdre dans la banalité. Leur musique est obsédée par le moment où les grandes vérités se transforment en platitudes, où le signal pur rencontre le bruit discordant. Par le passé, Thom Yorke a fortement pimenté ses paroles avec des clichés du quotidien pour suggérer un esprit parasité par des données dépourvues de signification, mais sur ce nouvel album, il va bien au-delà du cynisme.

Il envisage maintenant des vérités plus simples dans un registre jusqu'ici inexploré: l'émerveillement et la stupéfaction. « Cela va au-delà de moi, au-delà de vous », chante-t-il dans le titre Daydreaming [...] Thom Yorke a déjà caressé l'idée de reddition / soumission auparavant, et dans ce dernier opus cette soumission semble presque à son comble. Cela ne veut pas pour autant dire que c'est nécessairement un album de « rupture ».

Chapter D – Picture analysis

Exercice de version de presse

Le musée virtuel de l'Internet

Premier de ce type, le Grand musée de l'Internet attire les foules parce qu'il est disponible 24 heures sur 24, sept jours sur sept. Le web est éphémère, et cette initiative temporaire a rencontré un franc succès, en racontant l'histoire d'Internet pour les générations à venir. Les trois jeunes fondateurs se considèrent davantage comme des conservateurs de musée plutôt que des éditeurs d'un catalogue sans fin.

La sélection fait partie du projet, et a parfois fait l'objet de discussions ou négociations participatives au moyen de votes du public regroupant des professionnels comme des amateurs. Le musée virtuel se compose de 62 pièces placées dans 7 ailes consacrées à l'histoire, aux mèmes, aux médias sociaux et ainsi de suite. Des conservateurs intermittents peuvent y organiser des expositions temporaires. Le projet a eu un énorme succès à ce jour. Heureusement qu'il ne s'agit pas d'un véritable musée, sinon les gens y seraient serrés comme des sardines.

Section 5 – Science and technology

Chapter A – Fundamental sciences

Exercice de version littéraire

Les nombres idéaux

En tant que réalités, les nombres se conduisent mal. Cependant, il existe depuis très longtemps une pensée profondément ancrée chez les gens que les nombres sont censés se tenir correctement. La notion abstraite de nombre est entourée d'une aura de pureté, qui a peu à voir avec la trivialité du comptage des perles, des dialectes ou des nuages. Il doit donc y avoir un moyen de discuter des nombres sans que l'inévitable stupidité de la réalité ne s'y insère pour les perturber. Les règles strictes qui régissent les nombres « idéaux » constituent la science arithmétique, et leurs conséquences les plus abouties constituent la théorie des nombres.

Il n'y a qu'une seule question pertinente à poser, lorsqu'on fait la transition des nombres en tant qu'objets pratiques aux nombres en tant qu'objets formels. Une fois qu'a été prise la décision d'encadrer la théorie des nombres toute entière dans un système idéal, est-il vraiment possible d'y parvenir de façon exhaustive ? Les nombres sont-ils vraiment purs, cristallins et réguliers au point de pouvoir en représenter totalement la nature sous les traits d'un système formel ?

Chapter B – Space exploration and movement

Exercice de version de presse

Découverte d'une planète potentiellement similaire à la Terre sur un système solaire voisin

Des astronomes ont récemment déclaré avoir détecté une planète en orbite autour de l'étoile Proxima du Centaure, la plus proche voisine de notre système solaire. Chose curieuse, la planète se trouve dans la zone dite de Boucle d'or, et pourrait être ni trop chaude ni trop froide. Cela signifie que de l'eau liquide peut se trouver à sa surface, rendant ainsi la vie possible.

Hormis sa taille et la distance qui la sépare de son étoile parente, cette planète reste drapée / entourée d'un grand mystère. Les scientifiques travaillent à partir de modèles informatiques qui ne proposent que de maigres / simples suppositions : les conditions pourraient être similaires à la Terre, mais pourraient tout aussi bien être infernales comme sur Vénus, ou froides comme sur Mars.

Une équipe de scientifiques et de géants technologiques financée par le secteur privé sont en train de concevoir un projet pour développer et lancer une flotte de vaisseaux spatiaux de la taille d'un iPhone d'ici vingt à trente ans.

Chapter C – Research

Exercice de version de presse

Que se passe-t-il quand nos ordinateurs deviennent plus intelligents que nous ?

Aujourd'hui, la recherche se concentre réellement sur l'apprentissage automatique. Ainsi, plutôt que travailler manuellement sur les représentations et les caractéristiques de la connaissance, nous créons des algorithmes qui apprennent, souvent à partir des données brutes. C'est fondamentalement la même chose que fait l'enfant en bas âge.

Le résultat est une intelligence artificielle qui ne se limite pas à un domaine ; ce même système peut apprendre à traduire de et vers n'importe quelle langue, ou apprendre à jouer à n'importe quel jeu d'ordinateur sur une console Atari.

Bien entendu / Évidemment, l'I.A. est encore loin d'avoir la capacité d'apprentissage et d'organisation par mise en relation des savoirs / interdisciplinaire d'un cerveau humain. Le cortex dispose encore de quelques astuces algorithmiques que nous ne savons pas encore adapter aux machines.

Chapter D – Genetics and Ethics

Exercice de version de presse

La bioéthique doit interdire les manipulations génétiques

En France, le Conseil d'État a fait connaître ses recommandations concernant l'assistance à la procréation. Sans céder à l'air du temps des pratiques / sans se laisser influencer par ce qui est pratiqué dans les autres pays européens, souvent plus libéraux, il entend se montrer pragmatique et ne pas brider les évolutions et les attentes de la recherche médicale.

En matière de bioéthique, il s'agit d'interdire des manipulations conduisant à une réification, voire à une marchandisation, des embryons. Ainsi, c'est au nom de « l'intérêt de l'enfant » qu'il rejette l'assistance médicale à la procréation aux femmes célibataires et aux homosexuelles.

De même, le Conseil écarte la légalisation de la gestation pour autrui (GPA), jugeant qu'elle n'est pas sans danger pour la mère porteuse et que l'enfant ne saurait être assimilé à « un objet de transaction »... Certains trouveront le Conseil trop timoré. À ce stade du débat qui s'engage, il nous paraît sage.

Section 6 – Our pale blue dot

Chapter A – Wildlife and resources

Exercice de version littéraire

Un point bleu pâle

Regardez encore / de nouveau ce petit point. C'est ici. C'est chez nous. C'est nous. Sur ce point se trouvent tous ceux que vous aimez, tous ceux que vous connaissez, tous ceux dont vous avez entendu parler, tous les êtres humains qui ont existé, et qui ont vécu leur vie.

La Terre est une toute petite / minuscule scène dans / au sein d'une vaste arène cosmique. Songez aux fleuves de sang déversés par tous ces généraux et ces empereurs qui devinrent / afin de se rendre les maîtres éphémères d'une fraction d'un point, drapés dans leur gloire et leur triomphe.

Nos postures, notre (propre) soi-disant importance personnelle / imaginée / fantasmée, l'illusion que notre situation dans l'univers serait privilégiée, sont remises en question par ce pâle point de lumière. Notre planète est une minuscule tache isolée que la grande nuit cosmique enveloppe. Dans notre obscurité, dans toute cette immensité, rien ne semble indiquer / nous n'avons aucun indice nous permettant de penser qu'une aide viendra d'ailleurs pour nous sauver de nous-mêmes.

Jusqu'à présent, la Terre est le seul monde connu à abriter la vie. Il n'y a aucun autre lieu, du moins dans un futur proche, vers où notre espèce pourrait migrer / où notre espèce pourrait se réfugier. Visiter, oui. S'installer, pas encore. Que cela vous plaise ou non, pour le moment c'est la Terre qui est notre repaire / repère.

Chapter B – Energy

Exercice de version de presse

Les investissements mondiaux dans l'énergie baissent sauf pour les renouvelables

Les investissements mondiaux dans le secteur de l'énergie ont chuté de 8 % l'an dernier, reflétant les prix bas du pétrole et du gaz et la baisse des coûts. Presque la moitié de cette baisse est imputable aux États-Unis, où la chute des prix du pétrole et l'essor récent du gaz de schiste, ainsi que la déflation des prix dans le secteur de l'énergie, ont joué un rôle croissant.

La Chine est restée le plus grand investisseur au monde en matière d'énergie, en dépit d'un ralentissement du rythme de sa croissance économique continue. Malgré cette baisse mondiale, les investissements dans les énergies renouvelables sont restés solides en 2015. La transition vers les énergies propres a été menée par les politiques gouvernementales, entamée par / menée par les pays qui encouragent une croissance sobre / peu gourmande en carbone. Les énergies renouvelables se taillent la part du lion des fonds d'investissement disponibles, grâce à une baisse sensible du coût des éoliennes et des panneaux solaires.

Les chiffres de l'investissement traduisent l'ambiance qui a précédé l'accord historique sur le changement climatique obtenu à Paris en décembre dernier. En vertu de cet accord, près de 200 pays ont convenu de maintenir la hausse des températures mondiales à moins de 2 degrés Celsius au-dessus des niveaux pré-industriels. Atteindre cet objectif nécessitera de nouvelles politiques publiques favorisant les énergies peu économes en carbone au détriment des énergies fossiles.

Chapter C – Climate change

Exercice de version de presse

La sécheresse en Californie: une maladie chronique

La Californie a cessé de prendre les choses à la légère / d'être détachée face à la crise de l'eau. Cette semaine, pour la deuxième fois de son histoire, le Golden State a imposé des restrictions d'utilisation de l'eau. Cette mesure fait suite à / est la conséquence de cinq années de sécheresse grave et aux chutes de neige hivernales les plus basses jamais enregistrées.

En Californie, l'utilisation de l'eau en milieu urbain est demeurée relativement stable au cours des vingt dernières années, en dépit d'une augmentation massive de la population. Cette prouesse reflète les incitations tarifaires et les technologies permettant d'économiser l'eau comme les toilettes à faible consommation d'eau. De façon remarquable, la consommation d'eau par habitant a considérablement diminué en Californie, passant de 876 litres par jour en 1996 à 638 en 2016 (soit une baisse de 25 % entre 1996 et 2016).

Les agriculteurs, qui reçoivent l'eau provenant d'autres sources, ne sont que peu soumis au fardeau des nouvelles règles. À moins que les conditions climatiques ne changent radicalement, et rapidement, ils le devront néanmoins.

Chapter D – Ecology

Exercice de version de presse

L'heure de la décroissance : pour sauver la planète, l'économie doit se contracter

La véritable originalité du rapport de l'ONU sur les objectifs du développement durable tient au fait qu'il reconnaît les tensions inhérentes entre le développement économique et l'écologie de notre planète. Du moins en apparence. Son préambule affirme que « la planète Terre et ses écosystèmes sont notre foyer », et souligne la nécessité d'atteindre « l'harmonie avec la nature ». Il appelle à « des modes durables de production et de consommation, grâce à des niveaux plus élevés de productivité économique ».

Ce langage montre une prise de conscience que notre système économique a terriblement mal tourné – que nous ne pouvons pas continuer à grignoter notre planète sans gravement compromettre notre sécurité et notre prospérité, et même la viabilité de notre espèce sur le long terme.

Mais à y regarder de plus près, une contradiction flagrante se fait jour. Le rapport demande à la fois moins et plus, en même temps. Cet appel pour davantage de croissance intervient à un moment étrange, alors que nous réalisons à peine / commençons à peine à réaliser qu'elle est physiquement impossible. Les scientifiques nous expliquent que nous faisons voler en éclats les limites de notre planète à une vitesse vertigineuse et assistons à la plus grande extinction de masse depuis plus de 66 millions d'années.

La dure vérité est que notre surchauffe écologique est presque entièrement due à la surconsommation dans les pays riches, en particulier occidentaux.

Topic three

In our time

Section 7 – Politics and society

Chapter A – Welfare, wealth and solidarity

Exercice de version de presse

Arrêtons de dorloter les super-riches !

Nos dirigeants ont appelé à des « sacrifices partagés », mais ce faisant ils m'ont épargné. J'ai demandé à mes amis richissimes à quelle sauce ils allaient être mangés. Eux aussi avaient été épargnés. Alors que les pauvres et les classes moyennes combattent pour nous en Afghanistan, que la plupart des Américains ont du mal à joindre les deux bouts, nous, les super-riches, nous continuons à bénéficier de nos exceptionnels allégements fiscaux / réductions d'impôts. [...]

Les législateurs de Washington nous comblent de tous ces bienfaits, et de bien d'autres encore, se sentant obligés de nous protéger, comme si nous étions des chouettes tachetées ou d'autres espèces menacées. C'est bon d'avoir des amis haut placés. Si vous gagnez de l'argent avec de l'argent, comme c'est le cas pour la plupart de mes amis super-riches, votre taux d'imposition est peut-être un peu plus faible que le mien. Mais si vous gagnez de l'argent par votre travail, votre taux d'imposition dépassera le mien, et de loin.

Chapter B – Equality

Exercice de thème de presse

Police must be integrated in society

Tensions are running high in the US after the killing of five policemen in Dallas. A sniper shot officers from a parking garage during a demonstration against racist police violence.

Is the US facing a new wave of racial violence? The events in Dallas, Baton Rouge and Falcon Heights show how deteriorated relations are between Afro-Americans and the police.

Policemen should live in the cities and neighbourhoods that they patrol. By doing so, they would not be perceived as strangers, but rather neighbours who go shopping at the grocery store, whose kids go to school with their kids and who have the same hopes for the community.

There was a time when parents taught their children about the birds and the bees; now parents in black homes are teaching their kids how to act if police arrest them so they will survive it. The longer these flaws and injustices in the police remain unaddressed, the longer they will fester away.

Chapter C – Crime and justice

Exercice de version de presse

Les jeunes défavorisés et indignés se révoltent

L'absence de perspectives / projets et la discrimination sociale sont les causes des émeutes en cours / actuelles dans plusieurs villes britanniques. Ces jeunes vivent en plein centre de villes britanniques fortunées / riches, mais n'ont pas le sentiment / l'impression d'en faire partie.

Les signes avant-coureurs étaient perceptibles depuis de nombreuses années déjà, en particulier à Londres, dans les reportages sur les bandes de jeunes qui délestent les voyageurs de leurs objets de valeur dans les trains et les bus londoniens. Ou dans la recrudescence des agressions à l'arme blanche et des fusillades entre bandes.

Les ministères de l'Éducation, de l'Aide sociale, de la Santé et du Logement ont failli à leurs obligations envers ces populations. Les générations successives de politiques et de fonctionnaires ont fait trop peu pour intégrer ces individus dans la société civile. Le détonateur de cette bombe était armé depuis des années, peut-être même des décennies.

Chapter D – Politics and power

Exercice de thème de presse

After Brexit, EU must now focus on essentials

After Brexit, Europe must define itself anew by casting off useless impediments. Britain exiting the EU may well not be such bad news. It could even be an opportunity for Europe to reinvent itself on a solid and coherent basis.

The British have yet to come up with a concrete plan for when to start official exit negotiations. Some countries joined core Europe and failed to strengthen or enrich it. Some others quickly aligned themselves with American policy. Others closed their borders to the distress of the migrants, thus ill-using the very soul of Europe, its values and its principles.

The European family should slim down, focus on the essentials, ban bureaucracy and put an end to wastage, empty talk and unfulfilled promises. Europe is a necessity, particularly if it can freshen itself up in view of the challenges and the realities it faces, all the while remaining modest and concrete.

Section 8 – The economy

Chapter A – Working life

Exercice de thème de presse

Where on Earth have the ten million Americans without a job gone?

Often shown as a model of almost full employment, the US labor market nevertheless has a dirty little secret that helps explain such an enviable unemployment rate, a little less than 5%. Millions of men old enough to be active are simply out of the game. They do not appear in unemployment statistics since these take into account active jobseekers.

In a recent report, a board of economists have quantified that 11.7% of men aged 25 to 54 are unemployed, and among these, the vast majority (five in six) have not worked the previous year. Therefore they are totally excluded from the labor market, and have virtually no chance of returning one day.

Many features increase the likelihood of being part of this invisible army: black men, single men and men without degrees are the most affected. Their exclusion from the workforce is related to a replacement of manual jobs that require physical strength by machines, and the shift of jobs to tertiary occupations that require high qualifications. The fact that one out of every eight adult men has got a felony conviction also accounts for the difficulties encountered by this part of the population in finding work.

Chapter B – Business, finance and trade

Exercice de thème

Capital in the 21st century

The distribution of wealth is one of the most controversial and debated issues today. There are ways for democracy and public interest to manage to regain control of capitalism and private interests while also rejecting protectionist and nationalist attitudes.

Since the 1970s, inequalities have gone on the rise again in rich countries, particularly the United States. The history of the distribution of wealth is still a deeply political one and should not be reduced to purely economic mechanisms.

The history of inequalities depends on the conceptions of right and wrong according to economic, political and social players, the power relationships between these players, and the implied collective choices.

Chapter C – Consumption

Exercice de thème de presse

Snapchat is following in the footsteps of Facebook on targeted advertising

Snapchat will soon offer brands the possibility of broadcasting their advertisements through a subtler behavioural analysis of its users. Without lining up with the advertising strategies of competitors like Facebook or Google, the application takes a further step towards advertisers.

In 2014, the young entrepreneur claimed he did not intend to make Snapchat a "shady" application, which monitors its regular users to sell their data. "We want to see if we can deliver an experience that is fun and informative, like commercials used to be, before they became flippant and targeted" he explained in a blog post, in the early days of their monetization effort.

Since then, the social network has continued to develop new advertising tools for advertisers or media. However Snapchat's new behavioural targeting is still far from Facebook's level of accuracy / the level of accuracy of Facebook, which now uses nearly a hundred criteria to define an audience, including age, gender, tracking, mobile carrier and type, operating system and browsing history.

Chapter D – Globalisation and Language

Exercice de thème de presse

Dawn

– "What is it called / What do you call it, when the day rises, like today, and all is wasted, all is ransacked, and the air however can be breathed / but you can still breathe the air, and everything is lost, and the city burns, and the innocent kill each other, but the culprits are dying, in a corner of the day which rises / of the rising day?"

– It has a very beautiful name. It is called dawn.

As the century faded, from Seattle came a glimmer of hope. For too long deprived of the right to speak, citizens said "Enough!" with force. Enough of accepting globalisation as an inevitable fate. Enough of decisions made by the market rather than by elected politicians. Enough of seeing the world turned into a commodity. Enough of subjection, relinquishment, or submission.

Over the past ten years globalisation combined with the laxity of politicians has favoured the discreet implementation of a kind of planetary executive, consisting of four main actors: the International Monetary Fund, the World Bank, the Organisation for Economic Cooperation and Development and the WTO.

Section 9 – International context

Chapter A – The world

Exercice de thème

Europeans united in diversity

The European Union is a family of democratic European countries, committed to working together for peace and prosperity. It is not a State intended to replace existing states, but it is more than just another international organisation. The EU is, in fact, unique. Its Member States have set up common institutions to which they delegate some of their sovereignty so that decisions on specific matters of joint interest can be made democratically at a European level.

Europe is a continent with many different traditions and languages, but also with shared values. The EU defends these values. It fosters co-operation among the peoples of Europe, promoting unity while preserving diversity and ensuring that decisions are taken as closely as possible to the citizens.

In the increasingly interdependent world of the 21st century, it will be even more necessary for every European citizen to co-operate with people from other countries in a spirit of curiosity, tolerance and solidarity.

Chapter B – Soft and hard power

Exercice de thème de presse

Soft power, hard power and smart power: power according to Joseph Nye

In his new book, the American internationalist continues to reflect on the notion of state power in the 21st century. After having defined soft and hard power, how is Nye considering the future of power?

Soft power is opposed to hard power, the coercive force, military but also economic, that includes the possession of natural resources. As for soft power, it cannot be measured in "carrots" or in "sticks" to use an image dear to his heart. Strictly speaking, soft power is the ability of a State to get what it wants from another State without the latter even being aware.

State power can only be soft or hard. Theoretically, a state with developed soft power without the military capacity to defend itself if required is at best influential, not without obvious limitations.

Conversely, a state with significant hard power can achieve military operations, prevent some conflicts or impose its views on the world stage for a time, but will struggle to capitalize politically on these "victories". What is the ideal, according to Nye? A clever mix of soft and hard power, logically termed smart power.

Chapter C – Terrorism and warfare

Exercice de thème de presse

Modern societies vulnerable to fanaticism

The spontaneous hope of the French, who had encouraged their political decision-makers to find a common response to the attacks, has been disappointed: their tiny calculations have prompted a deep sense of scepticism as regards the leadership's collective ability to ward off the threat. If extremism increased, everyone would have a lot to lose – everyone except those who want to put an end to the respect of the law and thus stir up tensions in the country.

Societies are no longer capable of creating a sense of hope. Nor are they capable any longer of endowing their rational, tolerant and humanist values with the grandness and nobility without which they are merely empty shells. This sense of emptiness opens the door for the return of God in his most deadly guise.

Chapter D – Intelligence

Exercice de thème de presse

Trust in Obama shattered

The NSA allegedly spied on three French presidents from 2006 to 2012. Relations between France and the US will suffer as a result of this scandal. France's trust has been enduringly shaken. The protagonists of this pathetic case are supposed to work as allies in dealing with Iran's nuclear ambitions, Russia's manoeuvres and the barbaric conquests of the Islamic State.

One can already hear the sarcastic remarks of Ali Khamenei, Vladimir Putin and the "caliph" al-Baghdadi. So the American presidents are wary of the French ones, despite their demonstrations of frankness! Despite his speeches, Barack Obama has made no changes to the methods of Bush and Cheney. That is a strategic error which will compromise America's reputation, and an additional failure for this US president to whom the French had given their overwhelming / widespread support.

Appendix 3
Sources

Topic one
Mankind

Section 1 – The human being

Chapter A – Mankind and family

Excerpt 1 – The evolution of family life (*The Telegraph*)

http://www.telegraph.co.uk/sponsored/finance/personal-economy/11121353/
evolution-family-life.html

Excerpt 2 – A Statisical Portrait of the "Typical" American; This Is Your Life, Generally Speaking (*The New York Times*)

http://www.nytimes.com/1992/07/26/weekinreview/statisical-portrait-
typical-american-this-your-life-generally-speaking.html?pagewanted=all

Excerpt 3 – The look of a leader (*The Economist*)

http://www.economist.com/news/business/21620197-getting-top-much-do-
how-
you-look-what-you-achieve-look-leader

Excerpt 4 – Thank viruses for your skin and bone (*The New Scientist*)

https://www.newscientist.com/article/mg22129583-300-origin-of-organs-
thank-
viruses-for-your-skin-and-bone/

Chapter B – Health and Medicine

Excerpt 1 – The problem of pain (*The Economist*)

http://www.economist.com/news/international/21699363-americans-are-increasingly-addicted-opioids-meanwhile-people-poor-countries-die?zid=318&ah=ac379c09c1c3fb67e0e8fd1964d5247f

Excerpt 2 – Researchers develop genetic test that can predict your risk of Alzheimer's disease (*The Los Angeles Times*)

http://www.latimes.com/science/sciencenow/la-sci-sn-alzheimers-genetic-risk-20160706-snap-story.html

Excerpt 3 – Bernie Sanders' Long History With Alternative Medicine (*Time Magazine*)

http://www.economist.com/news/business/21620197-getting-top-much-do-how-
you-look-what-you-achieve-look-leader

Excerpt 4 – Patient's self-rating of health (PsychCentral.com)

http://psychcentral.com/news/2016/07/17/patients-self-rated-health-beats-medical-tests/107216.html

Chapter C – Personality and Relations

Excerpt 1 – The Screening Room – "People are becoming clouds" (*The New Yorker*)

http://www.newyorker.com/culture/culture-desk/the-screening-room-people-are-becoming-clouds

Excerpt 2 – Obituary – Muhammad Ali (*The Economist*)

http://www.economist.com/news/obituary/21700126-he-was-known-both-and-out-ring-simply-greatest-obituary-muhammad-ali-died

Excerpt 3 – The Psychology of Barack Obama (*National Interest*)

http://nationalinterest.org/commentary/the-psychology-barack-obama-9244

Excerpt 4 – The Psychology of Barack Obama (*National Interest*)

http://nationalinterest.org/commentary/the-psychology-barack-obama-9244

Chapter D – Successes and Failures

Excerpt 1 – Sweet smell of success (*The Economist*)

http://www.economist.com/news/business-books-quarterly/21600652-do-you-
have-what-it-takes-sweet-smell-success

Excerpt 2 – Microsoft has zoomed back to relevance after hitting bottom (Wired.com)

http://www.wired.com/2016/07/microsoft-zoomed-back-relevance-hitting-bottom/

Excerpt 3 – The secrets of success (*Forbes*)

http://www.forbes.com/sites/panosmourdoukoutas/2013/10/13/4-secrets-of-success/#2fc8794c7bfe

Excerpt 4 – Faster, better, cheaper: the successes and failures of NASA (BBC)

http://www.bbc.co.uk/programmes/p04128t6

Section 2 – Basic needs

Chapter A – Eating and Drinking

Excerpt 1 – Robochef gets cooking (*The Economist*)

http://www.economist.com/news/science-and-technology/21648474-ultimate-kitchen-
gadget-home-has-everything-robotic

Excerpt 2 – Jamie Oliver Cookery Courses Praised For Improving People's Eating Habits By Scientists (*Huffington Post*)

http://www.huffingtonpost.co.uk/entry/jamie-oliver-cookery-courses-improving-eating-habits-report_uk_578f4c55e4b011978b1315f0?edition=uk

Excerpt 3 – Organic Valley Traces Milk Back From Table to Farm (*The New York Times*)

http://www.nytimes.com/2016/07/18/business/media/organic-valley-traces-milk-back-from-table-to-farm.html

Excerpt 4 – I don't drink. Don't hold it against me. (*Slate*)

http://www.slate.com/articles/double_x/doublex/2013/01/i_don_t_drink_i_know_you_think_that_makes_me_weird.html

Chapter B – In the household

Excerpt 1 – No place like home (*The Guardian*)

https://www.theguardian.com/money/2014/jan/27/renting-london-costs-twice-
elsewhere

Excerpt 2 – The home of the future (*The Economist*)

http://www.economist.com/node/4343242

Excerpt 3 – How to build your own home (CNN)

http://edition.cnn.com/2013/08/01/tech/gallery/how-to-build-your-own-home/index.html

Excerpt 4 – We are makers (TED Talks)

https://www.ted.com/talks/dale_dougherty_we_are_makers/transcript?language=en

Chapter C – City and Country

Excerpt 1 – Redesigning cities – Los Angeles (*The Economist*)

http://www.economist.com/node/10924156

Excerpt 2 – San Francisco is ground zero for an AirBnB freakout (*Wired*)

http://www.wired.com/2015/11/prop-f-san-francisco-is-ground-zero-for-airbnb-freakout/

Excerpt 3 – Gentrification in Harlem (BBC News)

http://www.bbc.co.uk/programmes/b00bz9zd

Excerpt 4 – Is London's High-Rise Boom Destroying the City's Skyline? (*Slate*)

http://www.slate.com/

Chapter D – Sports and leisure activities

Excerpt 1 – Rio 2016: IOC announce first ever refugee team to compete under the Olympic flag (*The Independent*)

http://www.independent.co.uk/sport/olympics/rio-2016-ioc-announce-first-ever-refugee-team-to-compete-under-the-olympic-flag-a7064001.html

Excerpt 2 – Here's why watching sport makes you cry (TheConversation.com)

https://theconversation.com/heres-why-watching-sport-makes-you-cry-58258

Excerpt 3 – Extreme athletes take major risks. Should we pay for them? (*Washington Post*)

https://www.washingtonpost.com/posteverything/wp/2016/05/25/extreme-athletes-take-major-risks-should-we-pay-for-them/

Excerpt 4 – Gardening is the best medicine for the mind (*The Guardian*)

https://www.theguardian.com/lifeandstyle/gardening-blog/2016/jan/22/gardening-is-the-best-medicine-for-the-mind

Section 3 – Discovering and learning

Chapter A – Transport and Tourism

Excerpt 1 – Hybrid cars – At last, the 48 show (*The Economist*)

http://www.economist.com/news/science-and-technology/21704778-upping-volts-will-make-hybrid-cars-much-cheaper-last-48-show

Excerpt 2 – Spread of Zika, and cloud of fear, threatens Florida's tourism way of life (*Washington Post*)

https://www.washingtonpost.com/news/business/wp/2016/08/01/spread-of-zika-and-cloud-of-fear-threatens-floridas-tourism-way-of-life/

Excerpt 3 – Endless highway: How to drive the ultimate American road trip (CNN)

http://edition.cnn.com/2015/05/07/travel/experts-guide-to-great-american-road-trips/index.html

Excerpt 4 – Could this be the first nuclear-powered airliner? (BBC)

http://www.bbc.com/future/story/20160713-could-this-be-the-first-nuclear-powered-airliner

Chapter B – Education

Excerpt 1 – English universities to raise tuition fees for first time since they trebled (*The Guardian*)

https://www.theguardian.com/education/2016/jul/20/english-universities-to-raise-tuition-fees-for-first-time-since-they-trebled

Excerpt 2 – Grit: The power of passion and perseverance (Ted Talks)

http://www.ted.com/talks/angela_lee_duckworth_grit_the_power_of_passion_and_perseverance

Excerpt 3 – Teaching the teachers (*The Economist*)

http://www.economist.com/news/briefing/21700385-great-teaching-has-long-been-seen-innate-skill-reformers-are-showing-best

Excerpt 4 – Why disciplining kids can be so tricky for parents and teachers (TheConversation.com)

https://theconversation.com/why-disciplining-kids-can-be-so-tricky-for-parents-and-teachers-49083

Chapter C – The media

Excerpt 1 – Regional newspapers – Stop press (*The Economist*)

http://www.economist.com/news/britain/21677662-local-newspapers-are-just-about-managing-survive-stop-press

Excerpt 2 – Don't Tell Me What Happens. I'm Recording It. (TheRinger.com)

https://theringer.com/future-of-tv-chuck-klosterman-what-if-were-wrong-46ecb1a5444#.9h5l67vwt

Excerpt 3 – The future is a smarter world of dumber devices (TechCrunch.com)

https://techcrunch.com/2016/07/25/the-future-is-a-smarter-world-of-dumber-devices/

Excerpt 4 – Some Writing About Writing About TV (NPR)

http://www.npr.org/sections/monkeysee/2015/08/28/435516145/television-2015-some-writing-about-writing-about-tv

Chapter D – The Internet

Excerpt 1 – Sky-Fi (*The Economist*)

http://www.economist.com/news/science-and-technology/21647957-number-companies-have-bold-ambitions-use-satellites-drones-and-balloons

Excerpt 2 – Connected Toys Are Raising Complicated New Privacy Questions (*The technology Review*)

https://www.technologyreview.com/s/601942/connected-toys-are-raising-complicated-new-privacy-questions/

Excerpt 3 – Does the Snapchat generation even know what Yahoo is? (*The New Yorker*)

http://www.newyorker.com/business/currency/does-the-snapchat-generation-even-know-what-yahoo-is

Excerpt 4 – The future of Online learning is massive! (*Huffington Post*)

http://www.huffingtonpost.co.uk/anton-dominique/online-learning_b_4170004.html

Topic two
Understanding our world

Section 4 – Arts, culture and analysis techniques

Chapter A – Beliefs

Excerpt 1 – Why science and religion aren't as opposed as you might think

https://theconversation.com/why-science-and-religion-arent-as-opposed-as-you-might-think-56641

Excerpt 2 – Islam and ecology – In almost perfect harmony (*The Economist*)

http://www.economist.com/blogs/erasmus/2015/08/islam-and-ecology

Excerpt 3 – The Philosopher of Feelings (adapted from *The New Yorker*)

http://www.newyorker.com/magazine/2016/07/25/martha-nussbaums-moral-philosophies

Excerpt 4 – Saving churches for their history – not religion (*The Guardian*)

https://www.theguardian.com/commentisfree/2010/jul/03/ian-jack-church-building-conservation

Chapter B – Writing and text analysis

Excerpt 1 – Literature and film help teach students to understand the brain (UCLA)

http://newsroom.ucla.edu/stories/literature-and-film-help-teach-students-to-understand-the-brain

Excerpt 2 – Trump and Clinton: The Victorian Novel (*The New Yorker*)

http://www.newyorker.com/books/page-turner/trump-and-clinton-the-victorian-novel

Excerpt 3 – War of words (*The Economist*)

http://www.economist.com/news/books-and-arts/21701103-why-even-poets-hate-poetry-war-words

Excerpt 4 – Teaching with Graphic Novels (Edudemic.com)

http://www.edudemic.com/teaching-graphic-novels/

Chapter C – Music and cinema

Excerpt 1 – David Bowie (adapted from Pitchfork.com)

http://pitchfork.com/features/afterword/9786-david-bowie/

Excerpt 2 – Brian de Palma's Phantom of the Paradise (adapted from *The Guardian*)

https://www.theguardian.com/film/2014/mar/09/phantom-of-the-paradise-dvd-review-philip-french

Excerpt 3 – Nirvana baby recreates iconic album cover 25 years later (adapted from *The New York Post*)

http://www.ew.com/article/2016/09/22/nirvana-nevermind-album-cover-behind-scenes

Excerpt 4 – A Facebook First for New York Philharmonic (*The International New York Times*)

http://www.nytimes.com/2016/09/20/arts/music/new-york-philharmonic-facebook-opening-night-175th-anniversary-season.html

Chapter D – Picture analysis

Excerpt 1 – Polaroid photography – Instant forever (*The Economist*)

http://www.economist.com/blogs/prospero/2013/04/polaroid-photography

Excerpt 2 – Through the lens – Capturing the Wild Power of the Sea (*National Geographic*)

http://www.nationalgeographic.com/photography/proof/2016/09/paul-nicklen-qa/

Excerpt 3 – How photography evolved from science to art (TheConversation.com)

https://theconversation.com/how-photography-evolved-from-science-to-art-37146

Excerpt 4 – Here's The Story Behind One Of the Most Heartbreaking 9/11 Photo Ever (*Esquire*)

http://www.esquire.com/news-politics/a48031/the-falling-man-tom-junod/

Section 5 – Science and technology

Chapter A – Fundamental sciences

Excerpt 1 – Why science and engineering need to remind students of forgotten lessons from history (TheConversation.com)

https://theconversation.com/why-science-and-engineering-need-to-remind-students-of-forgotten-lessons-from-history-61356

Excerpt 2 – Teaching mathematics – Time for a ceasefire (*The Economist*)

http://www.economist.com/news/international/21595476-technology-and-fresh-ideas-are-replacing-classroom-drilland-helping-pupils-learn-time

Excerpt 3 – Four More Place Settings at the Periodic Table (*Slate*)

http://www.slate.com/blogs/bad_astronomy/2016/06/09/four_new_elements_get_their_names_proposed.html

Excerpt 4 – How far can a Buddhist approach to biology take us? (adapted from *The New Scientist*)

https://www.newscientist.com/article/mg22129511-100-how-far-can-a-buddhist-approach-to-biology-take-us/

Chapter B – Space exploration and movement

Excerpt 1 – Brave New Worlds (*The Economist*)

http://www.economist.com/news/leaders/21705825-new-discoveries-intelligent-devices-and-irrepressible-dreamers-are-once-again-making-space

Excerpt 2 – The hunt for Planet Nine reveals some strange, far-out objects (*L.A.Times*)

http://www.latimes.com/science/sciencenow/la-sci-sn-planet-nine-objects-snap-story.html

Excerpt 3 – Incoming! New Warning System Tracks Potentially Dangerous Asteroids (space.com)

http://www.space.com/34149-asteroid-impact-warning-system-scout.html

Excerpt 4 – Reality guide: Six problems physics can't explain (*The New Scientist*)

https://www.newscientist.com/article/2106324-reality-guide-six-problems-physics-cant-explain/

Chapter C – Research

Excerpt 1 – Blind, Paraplegic, And Quite Possibly The World's Greatest Athlete: Meet The Bionic Man (*Good Magazine*)

https://sports.good.is/features/mark-pollock-bionic-man-exoskeleton-paralyzed

Excerpt 2 – AI's Language Problem (*MIT technological review*)

https://www.technologyreview.com/s/602094/ais-language-problem/?cmp=em-data-na-na-newsltr_ai_20160822&imm_mid=0e6db7

Excerpt 3 – The jobs we'll lose to machines – and the ones we won't (TED Talks)

https://www.ted.com/talks/anthony_goldbloom_the_jobs_we_ll_lose_to_machines_and_the_ones_we_won_t/transcript?language=en

Excerpt 4 – Are we ready for quantum biology? (*New Scientist*)

https://www.newscientist.com/article/mg22429950-700-are-we-ready-for-quantum-biology/

Chapter D – Genetics and Ethics

Excerpt 1 – Cheating death (*The Economist*)

http://www.economist.com/news/leaders/21704791-science-getting-grips-ways-slow-ageing-rejoice-long-side-effects-can-be

Excerpt 2 – This Must-See Documentary Offers a Raw, Unfiltered View of Abortion from All Sides (*Forbes*)

http://www.forbes.com/story/must-see-documentary-offers-raw-unfiltered-view-of-abortion-from-all-sides

Excerpt 3 – The Search for Schizophrenia Genes (*Slate*)

http://www.slate.com/articles/technology/future_tense/2016/02/schizophrenia_genes_found_not_so_fast.html

Excerpt 4 – Colorado will be the next state to vote on doctor-assisted dying (*The Economist*)

http://www.economist.com/news/international/21705271-bill-stands-good-chance-being-passed-colorado-will-be-next-state-vote

Section 6 – Our pale blue dot

Chapter A – Wildlife and resources

Excerpt 1 – The world has lost a tenth of all its wilderness in the past two decades (*Washington Post*)

https://www.washingtonpost.com/news/energy-environment/wp/2016/09/08/the-world-has-lost-a-10th-of-all-its-wilderness-in-the-past-two-decades/?utm_term=.54c81ca5c54b

Excerpt 2 – World Ocean Summit 2017 (*The Economist*)

http://www.economist.com/events-conferences/asia/ocean-summit-2017

Excerpt 3 – Genetically Modified Bugs Are Great, but GMO Food Still Scares Us. Here's Why. (*Slate*)

http://www.slate.com/articles/health_and_science/climate_desk/2016/08/genetically_modified_mosquitoes_don_t_scare_us_as_much_as_genetically_modified.html

Excerpt 4 – Concerns about a seed-and-pesticide food monopoly (*Christian Science Monitor*)

http://www.csmonitor.com/Business/2016/0915/Bayer-Monsanto-merger-Concerns-about-a-seed-and-pesticide-food-monopoly

Chapter B – Energy

Excerpt 1 – Industry and carbon limits – Claws in the dirt (*The Economist*)

http://www.economist.com/blogs/democracyinamerica/2014/06/industry-and-carbon-limits

Excerpt 2 – One year on: Volkswagen emissions scandal (*The Independent*)

http://www.independent.co.uk/news/business/news/number-of-volkswagens-fixed-in-uk-after-emissions-scandal-simply-unacceptable-a7314701.html

Excerpt 3 – California Offshore Wind Farm Will Float (*Seeker*)

http://www.seeker.com/california-wind-farm-would-float-1961713816.html

Excerpt 4 – U.S., Canada Aboriginal Tribes Form Alliance to Stop Oil Pipelines (*New York Times*)

http://www.nytimes.com/reuters/2016/09/22/us/22reuters-canada-pipeline-aboriginal.html

Chapter C – Climate change

Excerpt 1 – Barack Obama shores up his environmental legacy (*The Economist*)

http://www.economist.com/blogs/democracyinamerica/2016/09/green-light

Excerpt 2 – 10 Years After An Inconvenient Truth, Al Gore May Actually Be Winning (*Wired*)

https://www.wired.com/2016/05/wired-al-gore-climate-change/

Excerpt 3 – The Climate Fixers – Is there a technological solution to global warming? (*The New Yorker*)

http://www.newyorker.com/magazine/2012/05/14/the-climate-fixers

Excerpt 4 – Don't waste CO_2, turn it into bottles and glue (*New Scientist*)

https://www.newscientist.com/article/mg22129593-400-dont-waste-co2-turn-it-into-bottles-and-glue/

Chapter D – Ecology

Excerpt 1 – Global trade deal threatens Paris climate goals (*The Guardian*)

https://www.theguardian.com/environment/2016/sep/20/global-trade-deal-threatens-paris-climate-goals-leaked-documents-show

Excerpt 2 – New York City's Plastic Bag Fee (*The New York Times*)

http://www.nytimes.com/2016/06/08/nyregion/new-york-citys-plastic-bag-fee-is-delayed-amid-scrutiny-in-albany.html

Excerpt 3 – Shell in the Arctic (*Slate*)

http://www.slate.com/blogs/the_slatest/2015/09/28/shell_in_the_arctic_shell_abandons_arctic_drilling_citing_regulatory_and.html

Excerpt 4 – Is the "Ecomodernist Manifesto" the Future of Environmentalism? (*The New Yorker*)

http://www.newyorker.com/tech/elements/is-the-ecomodernist-manifesto-the-future-of-environmentalism

Topic three

In our time

Section 7 – Politics and society

Chapter A – Welfare, wealth and solidarity

Excerpt 1 – The contributory myth: what you pay in isn't what you get out (*The Economist*)

http://www.economist.com/blogs/buttonwood/2016/01/welfare-benefits-0

Excerpt 2 – Housing is essential to ending child poverty (Thecourier.co.uk)

https://www.thecourier.co.uk/fp/opinion/readers-letters/269684/housing-is-essential-to-ending-child-poverty/

Excerpt 3 – Is There a Link Between Mental Health and Gun Violence? (*The New Yorker*)

http://www.newyorker.com/science/maria-konnikova/almost-link-mental-health-gun-violence

Excerpt 4 – Should Charity Be Logical? (*Slate*)

http://www.slate.com/articles/news_and_politics/view_from_chicago/2015/03/effective_altruism_critique_few_charities_stand_up_to_rational_evaluation.html

Chapter B – Equality

Excerpt 1 – Miss America 1968: When civil rights and feminist activists converged on Atlantic City (TheConversation.com)

https://theconversation.com/miss-america-1968-when-civil-rights-and-feminist-activists-converged-on-atlantic-city-64850

Excerpt 2 – Leaders pledge more help for refugees; critics say pledges are not enough (*L.A.Times*)

http://www.latimes.com/world/la-fg-un-refugees-20160919-snap-story.html

Excerpt 3 – Latest Religious Liberty Battle: Church-Affiliated Colleges And LGBT Students (NPR)

http://www.npr.org/2016/08/23/491024769/latest-religious-liberty-battle-church-affiliated-colleges-and-lgbt-students

Excerpt 4 – Bus driver says Brexit racism rise "alarming" (Sky News)

http://news.sky.com/story/bus-driver-says-brexit-racism-rise-alarming-10576633

Chapter C – Crime and justice

Excerpt 1 – 27 words: Deconstructing the Second Amendment (CNN)

http://edition.cnn.com/2016/08/10/politics/what-does-the-second-amendment-actually-mean-trnd/index.html

Excerpt 2 – Walking while black – Baltimore promises police reforms after blistering federal report (*The Economist*)

http://www.economist.com/blogs/democracyinamerica/2016/08/walking-while-black

Excerpt 3 – Ten Things I Wish I Knew When I Started "No Man's Sky" (*Forbes*)

http://www.forbes.com/sites/insertcoin/2016/08/11/ten-things-i-wish-i-knew-when-i-started-no-mans-sky/#5ec0d20a2b7f

Excerpt 4 – Making a Murderer: Brendan Dassey has conviction overturned (*Sydney Morning Herald*)

http://www.smh.com.au/entertainment/tv-and-radio/making-a-murderer-brendan-dassey-has-conviction-overturned-20160812-gqro46.html

Chapter D – Politics and power

Excerpt 1 – Politics and the New Machine (*The New Yorker*)

http://www.newyorker.com/magazine/2015/11/16/politics-and-the-new-machine

Excerpt 2 – The Long Road to Brexit (*The Wall Street Journal*)

http://www.wsj.com/articles/the-long-road-to-brexit-1471636486

Excerpt 3 – Democracy in America (adapted from Alexis de Tocqueville)

norton.com/college/history/america.../ATocqueville-Democracy-Vol_I-1835.pdf

Excerpt 4 – "Before the Law," a parable from Kafka's novel The Trial, read by Orson Welles

http://www.openculture.com/2014/09/kafka-illustrated-with-pinscreen-art.html

Section 8 – The economy

Chapter A – Working life

Excerpt 1 – There's No Place Like Home/Office (*Good Magazine*)

https://www.good.is/features/issue-37-theres-no-place-like-home-office

Excerpt 2 – Future Works (*The Economist*)

http://www.economist.com/events-conferences/americas/future-works

Excerpt 3 – Where today's jobs are most likely to vanish tomorrow (adapted from *Washington Post*)

https://www.washingtonpost.com/news/wonk/wp/2016/09/06/where-todays-jobs-are-most-likely-to-vanish-tomorrow/

Excerpt 4 – The Jobs Perplex (*Forbes*)

http://www.forbes.com/sites/michaelbernick/2016/08/30/the-jobs-perplex-labor-day-2016/#4f6b2163f8f3

Chapter B – Business, finance and trade

Excerpt 1 – What is the Nash equilibrium? (adapted from *Washington Post*)

https://www.washingtonpost.com/business/economy/reinhard-selten-economist-who-won-nobel-prize-for-game-theory-work-dies-at-85/2016/09/01/5fc0b452-707b-11e6-8365-b19e428a975e_story.html

Excerpt 2 – Against happiness (adapted from Schumpeter, *The Economist*)

http://www.economist.com/news/business-and-finance/21707502-companies-try-turn-happiness-management-tool-are-overstepping-mark

Excerpt 3 – Deflation ugly step-sister of inflation (adapted from *Otago Daily Times*)

https://www.odt.co.nz/opinion/deflation-ugly-step-sister-inflation

Excerpt 4 – An Introduction to the Financial Markets (adapted from *The Balance*)

https://www.thebalance.com/an-introduction-to-the-financial-markets-3306233

Chapter C – Consumption

Excerpt 1 – Understanding consumer society is critical to addressing sustainability (adapted from *The Guardian*)

https://www.theguardian.com/sustainable-business/blog/understanding-consumer-society-technology-not-enough

Excerpt 2 – The Dogma of Advertising and Consumerism (adapted from *The Huff Post*)

http://www.huffingtonpost.co.uk/ziad-elhady/the-dogma-of-advertising-_b_2540390.html

Excerpt 3 – Adblock Plus, Created to Protect Users From Ads, Instead Opens the Door (*The International New York Times*)

http://www.nytimes.com/2016/09/19/business/media/adblock-plus-created-to-protect-users-from-ads-opens-the-door.html

Excerpt 4 – How marketers will win (*Future of Marketing*)

http://thefutureofmarketing.eiu.com/

Chapter D – Globalisation and Language

Excerpt 1 – The Environmental Cost Of Growing Food (adapted from NPR)

http://www.npr.org/sections/thesalt/2016/05/05/476600965/the-environmental-cost-of-growing-food

Excerpt 2 – Inventing the future (adapted from *Le Monde diplomatique*, English edition)

http://mondediplo.com/2014/12/16future

Excerpt 3 – English is de facto global language (adapted from BBC)

http://www.bbc.co.uk/programmes/p03bh5kz

Excerpt 4 – Globalisation backlash 2.0 (adapted from *The Economist*)

http://www.economist.com/blogs/buttonwood/2016/07/economics-and-politics-0

Section 9 – International context

Chapter A – The world

Excerpt 1 – The amazing benefits of being bilingual (BBC)

http://www.bbc.com/future/story/20160811-the-amazing-benefits-of-being-bilingual?ocid=fbtvl

Excerpt 2 – The empire strikes back (*The Economist*)

http://www.economist.com/news/britain/21567071-some-british-eurosceptics-see-commonwealth-alternative-europe-it-isnt-empire

Excerpt 3 – United by a Catchy Acronym (*The New York Times*)

http://www.nytimes.com/2012/12/01/opinion/united-by-a-catchy-acronym.html

Excerpt 4 – Age, kids and jobs affect where Americans live (*USA Today*)

http://www.usatoday.com/story/news/nation/2013/04/12/migration-of-americans-by-age-groups/2064717/

Chapter B – Soft and hard power

Excerpt 1 – Making up (adapted from *The Economist*)

http://www.economist.com/news/special-report/21590109-bush-years-america-seemed-overmighty-it-now-pulling-back-making-up

Excerpt 2 – The Return of the Utopians (adapted from *The New Yorker*)

http://www.newyorker.com/magazine/2016/10/03/the-return-of-the-utopians

Excerpt 3 – Why Is the American Military So Bad at Teaching Others How to Fight? (adapted from *Slate*)

http://www.slate.com/articles/news_and_politics/war_stories/2015/10/the_american_military_is_bad_at_teaching_others_how_to_fight.html

Excerpt 4 – Progress, regress and human rights (adapted from *Le Monde diplomatique*, English edition)

http://mondediplo.com/2015/10/23supp

Chapter C – Terrorism and warfare

Excerpt 1 – Counter-terrorism – Driving away the shadows (*The Economist*)

http://www.economist.com/news/britain/21705307-early-intervention-prevent-terrorism-tough-get-right-britain-does-not-do-bad

Excerpt 2 – Criminals are the law in Syria (*Le Monde diplomatique*, English edition)

http://mondediplo.com/outsidein/criminals-are-the-law-in-syria

Excerpt 3 – From Hiroshima to a Nuke-Free World (*The International New York Times*)

http://www.nytimes.com/2016/04/13/opinion/from-hiroshima-to-a-nuke-free-world.html

Excerpt 4 – Is Cyberwar Turning Out to Be Very Different From What We Thought? (*Politico*)

http://www.politico.com/magazine/story/2016/08/is-cyberwar-turning-out-to-be-very-different-from-what-we-thought-214136

Chapter D – Intelligence

Excerpt 1 – Hackers create "Eye of Sauron"-inspired malware to spy on international agencies and has already hit 30 organizations, experts say (*The Daily Mail*)

http://www.dailymail.co.uk/sciencetech/article-3729527/New-spyware-detected-targeting-firms-Russia-China-Symantec.html

Excerpt 2 – "Shadow Brokers" Leak Raises Alarming Question: Was the N.S.A. Hacked? (*New York Times*)

http://www.nytimes.com/2016/08/17/us/shadow-brokers-leak-raises-alarming-question-was-the-nsa-hacked.html?hp&action=click&pgtype=Homepage&clickSource=story-heading&module=first-column-region&region=top-news&WT.nav=top-news&_r=0

Excerpt 3 – What Snowden and Manning Don't Understand About Secrecy (*The Atlantic*)

http://www.theatlantic.com/politics/archive/2013/08/what-snowden-and-manning-dont-understand-about-secrecy/278973/

Excerpt 4 – Green light to powers for UK spy agencies to collect bulk data (*The Independent*)

http://www.independent.co.uk/news/uk/politics/snoopers-charter-spy-gchq-mi5-bulk-collection-a7199026.html

Table des matières

Imprimé en Italie par «La Tipografica Varese Srl» Varese